Identity Safe Classrooms, Grades 6–12

Dedicated to Dorothy M. Steele, EdD

who made it possible.

Researcher, Teacher, Friend

Identity Safe Classrooms, Grades 6–12

Pathways to Belonging and Learning

Becki Cohn-Vargas

With

Alexandrea Creer Kahn

Amy Epstein

Foreword by Claude M. Steele

FOR INFORMATION:

Corwin
A SAGE Company
2455 Teller Road
Thousand Oaks, California 91320
(800) 233-9936
www.corwin.com

SAGE Publications Ltd.
1 Oliver's Yard
55 City Road
London EC1Y 1SP
United Kingdom

SAGE Publications India Pvt. Ltd.
B 1/I 1 Mohan Cooperative Industrial Area
Mathura Road, New Delhi 110 044
India

SAGE Publications Asia-Pacific Pte. Ltd.
18 Cross Street #10-10/11/12
China Square Central
Singapore 048423

Program Director and Publisher: Dan Alpert
Senior Content Development Editor: Lucas
    Schleicher
Associate Content Development Editor: Mia
    Rodriguez
Project Editor: Amy Schroller
Copy Editor: Amy Hanquist Harris
Typesetter: Hurix Digital
Proofreader: Lawrence W. Baker
Indexer: Integra
Cover Designer: Gail Buschman
Marketing Manager: Maura Sullivan

Printed in the United States of America

Library of Congress Cataloging-in-Publication Data

Names: Cohn-Vargas, Becki, author. | Creer Kahn, Alexandrea, author. | Epstein, Amy, author.

Title: Identity safe classrooms, grades 6-12 : pathways to belonging and learning / Becki Cohn-Vargas, Alexandrea Creer Kahn, Amy Epstein.

Description: First edition. | Thousand Oaks, California : Corwin, [2020] | Includes bibliographical references.

Identifiers: LCCN 2020017427 | ISBN 9781544350387 (paperback) | ISBN 9781544350370 (epub) | ISBN 9781544350363 (epub) | ISBN 9781544350356 (ebook)

Subjects: LCSH: Educational sociology. | Identity (Psychology) | Student-centered learning–Study and teaching (Middle school). | Student-centered learning–Study and teaching (High school). | Classroom environment.

Classification: LCC LC191.4 .C64 2020 | DDC 370.15–dc23
LC record available at https://lccn.loc.gov/2020017427

This book is printed on acid-free paper.

SUSTAINABLE FORESTRY INITIATIVE
Certified Chain of Custody
Promoting Sustainable Forestry
www.sfiprogram.org
SFI-01268

20 21 22 23 24 10 9 8 7 6 5 4 3 2 1

Contents

Foreword   vii
  Claude M. Steele

Acknowledgments   ix

About the Authors   xi

Part I. Welcome to the Identity Safe Classroom and School   1

Chapter 1. The Introduction   3

Chapter 2. Educator Identity Safety and the Importance of Self-Awareness   25

Big Ideas: Welcome to the Identity Safe Classroom and School   41

Part II. Student-Centered Teaching   43

Chapter 3. Listening for Student Voices   45

Chapter 4. Teaching for Understanding   68

Chapter 5. Focus on Cooperation   89

Chapter 6. Classroom Autonomy   105

Big Ideas: Student-Centered Teaching   119

Part III. Cultivating Diversity as a Resource   121

Chapter 7. Using Diversity as a Resource   124

Chapter 8. High Expectations and Academic Rigor   149

Chapter 9. Challenging Curriculum   160

Big Ideas: Cultivating Diversity as a Resource   179

Part IV. Classroom Relationships   181

Chapter 10. Teacher Warmth and Availability for Learning   183

Chapter 11. Positive Student Relationships   204

Big Ideas: Classroom Relationships   214

Part V. Caring Classroom Environments   217

Chapter 12. Teacher Skill   220

Chapter 13. Emotional and Physical Comfort   238

Chapter 14. Attention to Prosocial Development   252

Big Ideas: Caring Environments   268

Epilogue: Closing Thoughts   **270**

References   **272**

Index   **287**

Visit the companion website at
https://resources.corwin.com/IdentitySafeClass6-12
for downloadable resources and full-page "Try It Out" activities.

Foreword

Not long ago, after having given a talk on research that my colleagues and I had done on stereotype threat and its impact on schooling and institutional functioning, I got a call from one of the sponsors of the talk, a friend of mine. He began with both genuine and polite praise. But I could tell more was coming. He said there had been many teachers in the audience, that they appreciated hearing about the research, and that, by and large, they agreed with its conclusions. They agreed that the threat of being viewed through the lens of negative stereotypes about one's identity—as minority and low-income students might experience, or as girls and women might experience in especially advanced STEM courses—could affect intellectual performance and even the eventual choices people make as to college majors and career paths. He said they appreciated the implication of this work, that addressing this threat could improve student performance. But—and here I could sense him carefully choosing his words—they were disappointed that I hadn't given them more concrete, practical tactics that teachers could use to reduce and manage these identity pressures in real classrooms. On my end of the line, I had to smile. My friend was being careful. But it wasn't the first time I'd heard this critique. My own wife, Dorothy Steele, and her longtime collaborator and colleague Becki Cohn-Vargas had raised this issue with me many times. It was regular, breakfast-table conversation. And, of course, I had to agree.

The good news is that, as education researchers and as educators with considerable classroom experience, Dorothy and Becki eventually took the matter in hand. Dorothy, along with a strong team of researchers, first launched a groundbreaking research program that empirically identified specific tactics used by teachers who had effectively reduced minority student achievement gaps in K–8 schooling—tactics that had proved broadly effective at achieving a climate of identity safety in the classroom. Next, Dorothy and Becki wrote what I regard—my obvious biases notwithstanding—as one of the most important and useful guides in existence on what teachers in these grades can do to create and sustain a climate of identity safety, *Identity Safe Classrooms: Places to Belong and Learn.* It is a triumph of a book. Scholarly in its connection to the most enlightened traditions of American education. Empirical in deriving its wisdoms, insights, and tactics from elegantly designed and implemented research. Organized beautifully. And more than just accessible, it is written with an empowering empathy, understanding, and clarity.

Then, as some readers will know and is commemorated in the Acknowledgments to this book, tragedy struck. Dorothy Steele, my beloved wife of five decades, passed after a long battle with autoimmune liver disease. At this point, for my part, a sense of meaning went out of many things. Our work and careers had evolved essentially as a joint project over our entire adult lives—rooted in decades of those breakfast-table conversations. Time does not heal a loss like that. But it does bring a sense of perspective—in this case, a recognition that for the sake of that shared project, it is important that the work it helped launch continue.

Thus, it is deeply gratifying to learn of the continued interest in and impact of *Identity Safe Classrooms*. And it is especially gratifying to see this fine new book, *Identity Safe Classrooms, Grades 6–12,* continue this project at such a high level and by extending the principles, wisdoms, and practices of the first book into Grades 6–12 schooling. It is another formidable achievement, distinguished by insight as well as concrete, well-organized strategies and tactics for making our classrooms the safe places in which all of our children can learn and grow. I am proud of this new book and grateful to its authors—again, Becki Cohn-Vargas with Alexandrea Creer Kahn and Amy Epstein—for the distinguished job they have done. I am sure Dorothy would feel this way, too. It is a book you can both admire and use. Should I get another call like the one I described earlier—which I surely will—I will be so proud to point the person in the direction of such a strong, useful, and growing body of important work.

—Claude M. Steele

Professor of Psychology at Stanford University

Author of *Whistling Vivaldi and Other Clues to How Stereotypes Affect Us*

Acknowledgments

We begin these acknowledgments by expressing our love and appreciation for Dorothy Steele. This book is dedicated to her. In October 2016, Alex and Amy were able to meet Dorothy, joining me at Dorothy's home for coffee and conversation about identity safety. Less than six months later, in February of 2017, Dorothy died after a long and noble battle with cancer and liver disease. I was so grateful that they could meet her. Dorothy's pioneering work on identity safety is the foundation for the ideas presented here. Her great heart, compassion, and belief in students are reflected on each page of this book.

The second person we need to acknowledge here is Ben Liepman, son of my sister, Barbara, who randomly sent an email to Alex and me with the heading "to two of my favorite educators." Out of the blue, he introduced us, and we were both the type of people who would take the introduction to heart and meet for lunch. This book springs from the moment we first met for lunch.

We greatly appreciate the entire Leadership Public Schools (LPS) community of educators and students who has opened its doors to identity safety and shared from its vast experience supporting urban youth in the East Bay Area in California. The workshops, professional development tools, student interviews, and more are present on the pages of this book, living up to their equity-focused mission of extending their work to the larger educational community. In particular, Dr. Louise Waters, Michael Fauteux, Kate Levitt, Rebecca Vester, and the participants in the Identity Safety Pilot workshops contributed ideas, and the students spoke candidly about their experiences, sharing vignettes, workshop suggestions, and more.

We express a huge appreciation to Kathe Gogolewski, a compassionate, identity safe educator, who edited the entire book. Kathe has a huge heart and a brilliant mind. She not only took on the challenge of being a volunteer editor, but she added vignettes and ideas.

We thank Claude Steele, Carol Dweck, Milton Reynolds, Eduardo Briceño, Zaretta Hammond, Eddie Moore, Mica Pollock, and Mary Murphy who all took time to share important research and groundbreaking ideas with us that are reflected in the examination of stereotype threat, growth mindset, culturally competent teaching, and equity literacy.

We are also grateful to the educators who contributed vignettes and experiences to bring identity safety to life: Jennifer Abrams, Carlee Adamson, Sue Boudreau, Susan Charles, Matt Colley, Don Cox, Chen Kong-Wick, Julie Mann, Patrice O'Neill, Malik Saric, Randi Thomson-Story, Yah Yee Woo, and David Yusem.

We want to express great appreciation for our editorial team at Corwin. Dan Alpert, our editor, has been a champion of identity safety since he edited the first identity safety book and now this one, together with Mia Rodriguez. Lucas Schleicher, Amy Hanquist Harris, and Amy Schroller guided us through the production process, answering all questions. Maura Sullivan had many creative ideas to help spread the word about the book. And of course, all our reviewers took time to give us feedback. They have all made this a smooth and enjoyable process.

We could not have written this book without the love and support of our families. Becki appreciates her husband, Rito; their children, Priscilla, Melania (with baby Anteo on the way) and David, and their spouses; her sisters Ruth and Barbara; her father, Hans; her mother, Eva; her stepmother, Nina; as well as extended family and friends. Amy thanks her wife, Liat, and her parents, Evelyn and Barry, for their ever-present love and support. Alex shares deep gratitude to her husband, Kenny; sons, Theo and Harris; and parents, siblings, mentors, and friends for their love, support, and inspiration.

Publisher's Acknowledgments

Corwin gratefully acknowledges the contributions of the following reviewers:

Jessica Baldwin
Teacher
Claxton High School
Claxton, GA

Daniel Bauer
Founder
Better Leaders Better School
Tavares, FL

Latricia Borner
Manager, Restorative Discipline/Behavior Intervention
Houston Independent School District
Houston, TX

Lorna Fast Buffalo Horse
Principal
Alliance High School
Portland, OR

Catherine Howard
Visiting Instructor
BATTI Cohort, School of Education,
University of the Pacific
Oakland, CA

Harold Miller
Director of School Transformation Initiatives
Boston Public Schools
Boston, MA

Melissa Miller
Science Instructor
Farmington Middle School
Farmington, AR

Michelle Strom
Language Arts Teacher
Lander Public Schools
Lander, WY

About the Authors

Left to right: Amy Epstein, Becki Cohn-Vargas, and Alexandrea Creer Kahn

Becki Cohn-Vargas is the coauthor with Dorothy Steele of *Identity Safe Classrooms: Places to Belong and Learn*, published by Corwin. She designs curriculum, coaches schools, and produces films for Teaching Tolerance, Edutopia, Not In Our Town, and other educational organizations. She presents internationally at conferences and provides professional development in schools and districts.

Becki began her 35-year career in early childhood education in Sonoma County, California. She lived abroad for five years, where she did earthquake relief at a hospital in the Guatemalan Highlands and produced educational films for the Nicaraguan Ministry of Education. She returned to California and worked as a teacher and principal in Oakland, curriculum director in Palo Alto, and superintendent of a small district in San Jose. In each setting, she focused on educational equity and effective strategies for diverse populations.

Becki and her husband, Rito, live in El Sobrante, California, and have three adult children and one grandchild. With her husband, she has brought college students to do environmental research on their private reserve in the Nicaraguan rainforest.

Alexandrea Creer Kahn is the chief academic officer at Leadership Public Schools, a charter district that oversees three urban high schools. Alex started her career focusing on educational equity as a school improvement partner at Partners in School Innovation. At Partners, she coached teachers and leaders on how to use the cycle of inquiry model to provide access and instructional support for underserved students. In 2009, Alex joined Leadership Public Schools in Oakland, California, as an English teacher. She held several leadership roles before assuming the role of principal in 2012 and then the chief academic officer in 2017. In addition to serving in leadership roles in her organization, Alex has worked with the Stanford Teacher Education Program as an instructor for adolescent development.

Alex lives with her husband and two children in the Bay Area in California.

Amy Epstein is the executive director of data and assessment for Leadership Public Schools. Amy has worked as an administrator and consultant with many school districts, schools, foundations, and other nonprofit organizations to advance equity in education, particularly in the areas of stakeholder voice, evidence-based inquiry and dialogue, coordinated services/tiered support systems, data systems and management, and assessment. This publication will be Amy's first since cowriting a chapter ("Girl Power") for *Beyond Heroes and Holidays* (Lee et al., 1998). Amy and her wife, Liat, live in San Francisco.

Welcome to the Identity Safe Classroom and School

This book is a call for educators to come together and realize a vision of schools as transformative places of opportunity and equity for all students. Identity safety is an approach in which educators create conditions for students of all backgrounds to achieve at high academic levels, based on the assumption that each student is competent and capable and will thrive in an atmosphere of acceptance and compassion.

For students facing negative stereotypes or being viewed as different, identity safety is an essential condition for learning. For all students, it builds respect for self and others in ways that are essential for the future of our communities and the world.

Many schools have sought to employ a color-blind approach as educators attempt to not see color, essentially to ignore cultural differences as a tool to eliminate negative discrimination. It made sense to many that to treat all students alike was both fair and just. And yet, when differences in identity, such as race, religion, culture, and other social identity features are ignored, students of color continue to fall far short of their academic potential. These students need to be "seen"—accepted and valued for who and what they are—as do all students. Academic failure, ostracism, and marginalization are a few of the repercussions incurred from ignoring students' diverse identities. This "blindness" channels us into a state where students of color are subjected to unequal access in educational opportunity as a result of prolonged disengagement with their needs. Students of color are more frequently suspended and expelled, and they often fail their classes. This can turn into a path that has been accurately labeled as a *pipeline to prison*. We need to take action, and it is within our grasp to transform these conditions. Research has provided substantial direction for what we need to do. In line with this research, identity safety and equity pedagogy hold great promise to disrupt these damaging patterns of negative stereotyping while promoting classrooms that treat diversity as an asset. This, in turn, will support students of all backgrounds to prosper both socially and academically.

The beauty of an identity safe approach is that it is a holistic one, offering concrete ways to enhance content, pedagogy, and classroom culture in a way that affirms students' identities and encourages their capacity to learn together with their peers. This book is built upon everyday strategies and stances that give us the power to change harmful educational approaches. We have learned a lot about what it means for a student to feel a sense of belonging in a classroom. We have also come to know what happens to one's psyche when a sense of well-being does not exist for all students. Counternarratives offer an alternative perspective on a history of racial oppression—narratives that allow students to challenge and counter negative stereotypes that have likely plagued them all their lives. Identity safe practices provide students with an inviting and active membership in their classrooms and, consequently, a sense of agency in their educational experience.

Part I: Welcome to the Identity Safe Classroom and School begins with Chapter 1: The Introduction, where we present the concept of identity safety. We describe the research study—the Stanford Integrated Schools Project (SISP)—that demonstrated its effectiveness in meeting the needs of students of all backgrounds, particularly those whose identities have been impacted by stereotype threat. We offer a set of principles that serve as a guide for identity safe practices. We situate identity safety in the context of equity pedagogy and culturally responsive teaching and show how identity safe practices are very compatible with the theory of the growth mindset. We also explain how the book is organized and offer suggestions for ways to approach the use of this book. In Chapter 2: Educator Identity Safety and the Importance of Self-Awareness, we explain how educators are better able to create identity safety for students when they examine their own identities and interrogate the impact of our beliefs and assumptions on our teaching. In this chapter, we also share a bit from our own journeys as we "take a field trip into ourselves." Subsequent chapters in this book are organized around the components that emerged in the SISP study.

As you read this book, we hope that you can incorporate identity safe practices into a larger context for changing our system from one that privileges some and creates barriers for others to one that is compassionate, welcoming, and supportive for everyone. This will both support the students who experience it as well as prepare them to go forth and share these values in the world.

The Introduction 1

When people hear the term *identity safety*, they may first think of it as a way to protect themselves from identity theft. When you are subject to identity theft, you lose control over your money and cannot function as you usually do. It is a scary proposition; simply ask anyone who has experienced it. Now, imagine if your actual identity is stolen from you on a psychic/emotional level. Your sense of self—of who you think you are—feels compromised. Your identity is negatively impacted or stereotyped. You are judged as inferior, or you simply feel that you are not allowed to be yourself. Suddenly, *identity safety* takes on a whole new meaning. What we mean by identity safety encompasses the sense that who you are matters. In an identity safe environment, you are not invisible and do not have to leave part of yourself at the door to feel a sense of belonging. You can be yourself, just the way you are, and thrive in the world.

Identity safe teaching is an evidence-based and student-centered approach in which educators create a classroom environment that promotes respect, acceptance, and belonging. "Identity safe" classrooms are those that validate students' experiences, backgrounds, and identities to promote academic and social success for all students. In 2013, Dr. Becki Cohn-Vargas and Dr. Dorothy M. Steele published *Identity Safe Classrooms: Places to Belong and Learn,* which includes ideas that apply to all grade levels, but with strategies aimed primarily at Grades PreK–5. Many secondary educators used the book and resonated with the ideas; however, they requested more examples for older students. This book is a response to that request. We share student-centered practices for Grades 6–12 with vignettes and strategies for creating identity safety in classrooms. We include references to adolescent development to highlight the many aspects of their unfolding identities. This book also contains ideas for educators at all grade levels, expanding on the content of the first identity safety book. Many new examples can be used or adapted for younger students as well. In addition, we explore the identities of ourselves as educators and individuals, examining our own identity safety, first and foremost, so that we may engage fully in ways to support students.

Principles of Identity Safe Classrooms

Identity safe teaching is not a program with a set of step-by-step strategies, nor is it a specific road that brings you to a particular destination. It is an approach, with a continuous process of reflection and a way of teaching that embodies the following principles that serve as guidelines for educators working to create identity safety:

1. Color-blind teaching that ignores differences is a barrier to inclusion in the classroom.

2. To feel a sense of belonging and acceptance requires creating positive relationships between teacher and students and among students with equal status for different social identities.

3. Cultivating diversity as a resource for learning and expressing high expectations for students promotes learning, competence, and achievement.

4. Educators need to examine their own social identities and feel a sense of identity safety to convey that feeling to students and create an identity safe environment for them.

5. Social and emotional safety is created by supporting students in defining their identities, refuting negative stereotypes, and countering stereotype threat, giving them a voice in the classroom while using SEL strategies.

6. Student learning is enhanced in diverse classrooms by teaching for understanding, creating opportunities for shared inquiry and dialogue, and offering a challenging, rigorous curriculum.

Identity safe educators work to create a sense of belonging by valuing diversity and cultivating interdependence across race, gender, religion, and other differences. They employ a constellation of practices that draw from students' lives, cultures, and interests, while promoting prosocial development. They also work to help students learn to manage their own learning. Educators seek to operate from a growth mindset and convey that understanding to classes. Students are taught that mistakes and errors can be their "friends" that provide valuable information on specifically how to improve. Little by little, students gain a sense of competence that leads to academic growth. This will ultimately help them develop confidence in their own capacities and abilities.

The identity safe classroom is intentionally *not* color-blind in practice, nor does it seek to minimize or ignore individual and cultural differences. Rather, educators acknowledge the strength of diversity and look at individual differences as assets that provide richness and value. Educators work on a daily basis to eliminate stereotyping and offer counter-narratives to negative messaging about intelligence, gender, and race. They also examine implicit and explicit biases that serve as barriers to achievement. Identity safe classrooms support students of all backgrounds and social identities in reaching their capacity to achieve at higher levels.

Some diversity professional development models focus primarily on the educator engaging in self-examination of privilege and implicit biases, while others focus on specific strategies for engaging students. In our approach, we seek to both harness and bridge the two. We work on multiple levels simultaneously. We work to examine ourselves, our beliefs, assumptions, and our own identities. We aim to implement strategies that allow students to become competent learners and thinkers, which will lead to a sense of confidence in themselves as they navigate their lives in and out of school. We work to help reverse the feeling some students have internalized that they are not smart and capable. And we seek to understand and take steps to change the policies and practices that perpetuate inequities, often deeply embedded in many of our educational systems.

We suggest that educators practice these research-based principles in a holistic way rather than as a linear or sequential program. The many examples of strategies we offer are not specific "things to do" in a particular order, but rather they are shared to illuminate how educators can develop mindsets and teach in ways that engage their students and lead to identity safety. It affords the opportunity for each educator, along the continuum of experience, to become increasingly centered on transformative ways of thinking and being that make a safe space for all to belong.

Situating Identity Safety in the Context of Culturally Relevant Teaching and Equity Pedagogy

Identity safe teaching works in concert with a variety of approaches described as culturally responsive pedagogy and equity literacy. Asa Hilliard (2002) explains that culture refers to a shared set of beliefs and practices for a group of people who navigate their environment and lives together. Let's take a moment to look at how culture has been approached by educators in the United States over the last five decades.

In the 1970s, *multicultural education* was the term educators employed as they recognized and valued the different cultural backgrounds of their students. I (Becki) am reminded of my first job. In 1973, I was as an assistant preschool teacher at the West Santa Rosa Multicultural Center (2019), which still exists after 50 years in the same facility. At that time, educators were just beginning to incorporate content integration as the definition of multicultural education. Often, the content we used was limited to learning about diverse leaders and multicultural celebrations. Curriculum that only highlights "heroes and holidays" was a good start—necessary, but not sufficient.

In the 1990s, Gloria Ladson-Billings (1994) proposed an expanded view of "cultural relevance" that extended beyond merely integrating aspects of the student cultures. She sought to overcome the negative impacts caused by the policies and practices of the *dominant culture* (defined here as the attitudes and behaviors of the most privileged set of the population; in the United States, this faction consists of White people, males, and heterosexuals). Ladson-Billings stated that one primary aim of culturally relevant teaching, for example, is to provide African American students with the opportunity to work toward academic excellence while maintaining a connection to African and African American culture. She also explains that the purpose of including the students' cultures does not mean drawing information from students to simply form a bridge for them to assimilate into the dominant culture. Later, Dolores Lindsey and colleagues (2007) developed a continuum for educators to become culturally proficient. They claimed that educators need to learn about, esteem, and advocate for the cultures of their students in a process that also includes understanding the impact of the dominant culture on their students. Sonia Nieto (2013) describes the terms *cultural relevance* and *cultural proficiency* as having similar definitions, explaining that she incorporates aspects of both when she uses the term *culturally responsive teaching*. The latter she defines as a stance where teachers learn about their students' backgrounds and lives, teaching in a way that reinforces and affirms student identities.

However, another caveat merits consideration. When seeking to acknowledge student cultures, educators run the risk of stereotyping a student based on a set of descriptors commonly associated with the student's group. To address this issue, Kris Gutierrez and Barbara Rogoff (2003) use the term *repertoires of practice*, meaning that individuals can draw from a range of practices that include their life experiences. They suggest, in turn, that drawing from our students' repertoires of practice, rather than defining their cultural traits, will likewise benefit students by acknowledging and valuing their experiences, while educators may use the information to inform their practice. This will help educators who seek to acknowledge culture avoid the tendency to stereotype an ethnic or other group of people.

Equity Literacy

Professor Paul Gorski (2017), expressing concern that educators might address culture in a cursory manner while ignoring the need to create equitable conditions, introduced the concept of *equity literacy*. Gorski's equity literacy framework provides a focused approach for educators to recognize and observe inequities and seek to redress them. Gorski describes equity literate educators as those who identify and interrupt inequitable interactions, curriculum, and school policies. Equity literate educators strengthen their skills and capacities to facilitate dialogue and take action both in the moment and in the long term. They move to rectify inequities and seek to create bias-free environments.

Identity Safe Educators Incorporate Culturally Relevant Teaching and Equity Literacy

Identity safe teaching practices are anchored in culturally responsive pedagogy. Educators explicitly affirm their students' identity, extending beyond culture and race to all aspects of their multiple social identities as a condition of belonging in the classroom. Identity safe educators seek to become equity literate as part of efforts to ensure students do not feel invisible and devalued while engaging in efforts to generate accepting and equitable environments. Identity safety is not possible in an environment that is not equitable. Conversely, a school environment is not equitable unless all students feel a sense of identity safety and belonging. Educators incorporate equity literacy by breaking down stereotypes and working to remedy discriminatory practices and policies.

Where did the concept of identity safety come from?

Stereotype Threat and the Origins of Identity Safety

The concept of identity safety originated as an antidote to a social-psychological phenomenon known as stereotype threat. In stereotype threat theory, the fear of confirming negative stereotypes about social identity manifests when people worry that they will be judged by a stereotype—and even without realizing, unintentionally confirm it (C. M. Steele et al., 2002). Claude Steele (2019) explains that threat may arise even when a person does not feel that a stereotype about them is personally true:

> Sometimes, this is a worry about behaving in a way that would result in them being perceived that way. But as long as they are identified with school, I believe they resist believing or internalizing the stereotype. That's the struggle. Once they give up on schooling and find another domain of life to identify with, they may or may not believe the stereotype. At that point, though, it is largely irrelevant to them since they no longer care about school. But until then, I believe they are fighting valiantly not to believe the stereotype.

Researcher Dr. Mary Murphy (Mitchell, 2016) describes how stereotype threat can be at play even when it is not overtly expressed. She says it is like having a "snake loose in the house." You do not need to see it to feel frightened. In the same way, a person who fears they will be judged negatively can allow this perception to affect their performance. In her presentation at Harvard, Murphy pointed out that at Harvard's Annenberg Hall, many statues and portraits of predominantly White men are displayed. She says that walking through that hall every day can serve as a signal to women and people of color that they do not belong, even those who have been accepted to Harvard with its rigorous standards. First Lady Michelle Obama wrote this in the introduction to her senior thesis at Princeton University (Robinson, 1985):

> My experiences at Princeton have made me far more aware of my "Blackness" than ever before. I have found that at Princeton, no matter how liberal and open-minded some of my White professors and classmates try to be toward me, I sometimes feel like a visitor on campus; as if I really don't belong. Regardless of the circumstances under which I interact with Whites at Princeton, it often seems as if, to them, I will always be Black first and a student second. (p. 2)

Negative stereotypes, whether believed by the student or not, have been found to lower performance and achievement, particularly affecting students of color (Steele et al., 1995; Steele, 2010). Imagine how these stereotypes can imprint students over time. This phenomenon affects a person's sense of confidence and competence and ultimately can adversely influence their opportunities in life.

STEREOTYPE THREAT EXTENDS TO MANY TYPES OF SOCIETAL STEREOTYPES

Charles, a middle school principal, tells about a time he was called into the superintendent's office. The superintendent stated that a parent had reported that Charles had been seen hugging another man on the school grounds. At first, Charles was confused. He was not public about the fact that he was gay, and to his recollection, he had never hugged any man at school. Later, he realized it was the time his brother had visited the campus. Being called out made Charles feel very uncomfortable. He felt the superintendent was insinuating he had done something inappropriate. An experience such as this exemplifies how stereotype threat can damage a person's sense of belonging. The fear that he was being judged as behaving inappropriately stayed with him and took years to overcome. Charles explains that only at age 47 and 16 years into his career, when he moved to a different district and gained the confidence to feel that he was an effective administrator, did he feel safe to tell his school community that he was gay.

Stereotype threat also is communicated when people feel ignored. A feeling of invisibility can trigger a sense of threat for Native Americans students when their identities are not validated while negative stereotypes surround them in mainstream media. When classrooms are *not* identity safe, students from negatively stereotyped groups can experience a visceral and deep-seated sense that they are not considered smart, concluding that they do not belong in academic settings.

Stereotype Threat Research

To investigate stereotype threat, researchers Claude Steele and Josh Aronson (1995) gave White and African American college students a portion of the Graduate Records Exam (GRE). One group was told that the tests measured intellectual ability. The other group was specifically informed that this was *not* a diagnostic test of intellectual ability. Black students in the first group who thought their intellectual ability was not being tested scored equal to White students (controlling for SAT scores). In the second group, with students who thought their intellectual ability was being measured, Black students underperformed.

Stephen Spencer and his colleagues (1999) had similar results when triggering the negative stereotype that women are less competent than men in mathematics. Two groups of college students were given a math test. Female students who were told the test did not show gender differences performed equally well as male participants. Female students who thought they were being tested for mathematical ability underperformed in relation to men. Multiple research studies (Spencer et al., 2016) have tested the impact of stereotype threat across many arenas (e.g., race, gender, age) with similar results.

THE GOLF STUDY

One of the most illuminating stereotype threat studies involved the game of golf. Researcher Jeff Stone and colleagues (1999) devised an experiment that played on several opposing stereotypes. They gave groups of White and Black Princeton University students several different versions of the golf experiment. One group was told that with the golf test, the researchers were measuring natural athletic ability. The results: Black students (often stereotyped as good athletes) were not negatively affected when they were told the task measured natural athletic ability. White students (who are stereotyped as lesser athletes) performed worse than another group of White students who were not told anything about the task.

Subsequently, they did another version of the study. Groups of Black and White participants were told that the same golf experiment was a task that measured strategic intelligence in sports. In this version, stereotype threat was triggered for the Black students, and they played golf much worse than their White counterparts, who are not subject to the stereotype of being less intelligent. This study shows that even when a specific stereotype is not expressed or stated, the threat is, as Claude Steele (1997) explained, "in the air."

From Reducing Stereotype Threat to Creating Identity Safety

As the extensive research on stereotype threat demonstrated the pernicious and pervasive nature of stereotypes, Claude Steele (2010), along with his wife, Dorothy Steele, and colleagues at Stanford University, wanted to identify requisite educational conditions for positive identity development, conditions strong enough to overshadow negative and racially biased stereotypes. They coined the term *identity safety*, highlighting the fact that people need to feel safe, free from threat, and confident within the context of their social identities. They proceeded to examine qualities that might constitute an identity safe environment where social identities are valued as assets as opposed to liabilities. Their assertion was that such an environment would be strong enough to inoculate students against the pervasive power of negative stereotypes. They posited that if an environment contained enough cues to lead a person to feel identity safe, perhaps it could aim to neutralize the threats. In Chapter 7: Using Diversity as a Resource, we share additional specific strategies for reducing stereotype threat. The Steeles were also cognizant of the fact that due to stereotypes that abound "in the air," the idea of a color-blind environment as an effective means of treating inequity is an illusion in US society and actually detrimental to students of color.

The Dangers of a Color-Blind Classroom

It is likely you have heard someone say, "I don't see color; I don't care if a person is red or blue or green, I treat everyone the same." However, in the world-at-large, differences continue to be significant, whether they are manifested as racial profiling by a police officer or the misidentification of a Latinx keynote speaker as a maid in a hotel. And in the case of education, the differences manifest in the predictability that students of color are ranked at the bottom.

Luvvie Ajayi (2018) explains the effects of the "color-blind" approach:

> It erases our history and the very relevant events of the past that have led to our present situation. It dishonors our ancestors and the work they've done, and it lets people off the hook for centuries of race-based injustice. Saying you don't see race is saying you have nothing to fix. "Colorblindness" and cultural erasure help perpetuate this system of oppression because forced politeness and fear of the "race card" trump actual work and progress. (para. 10)

Ajayi (2018) points out, "Being able to live without having to be defined by your skin color is the hallmark of privilege" (para. 6).

We want to assure readers that we make the assumption that educators who seek to be color-blind are not intentionally trying to stereotype students. We trust that they do not realize that by ignoring differences in identity, students will feel invisible. We believe that once educators become aware of the harm of color-blind practices, they will change their practice.

In a color-blind classroom, differences are ignored or treated as inconsequential. Some educators worry that highlighting racial/ethnic differences and other aspects of identity can be divisive. Yet there is a greater risk when identities are not acknowledged. The interplay of multiple identities within each of us and the complexity of racial and ethnic categories is much deeper than what can be seen on the surface. For example, a student "coded" Black may have a variety of elements that feed into that identity, such as a different ethnic background (Caribbean) or nationality (British). An educator who stereotypes the identities of students might inadvertently negate the identities of Latinx, African, or Asian students through lumping together cultures that are deemed to be alike. An educator who completely ignores differences erases each person's uniqueness.

Across history, societies have continuously withheld recognition of women and people of color. Simone de Beauvoir (Bergoffen, 2018) claimed that most societies constitute a centric view of the male as the primary "self" with the notion of the female as "other." The view of self that portrays women and non-White groups as the "other" has very deep roots and sheds light on why it is so difficult to close the achievement and opportunity gaps and equalize status. The hegemony of White males continues to be prevalent today, resulting in the alienation of women and non-White cultures whose perspectives and contributions have systematically been excluded from history textbooks. Often, when different cultures and ethnicities are highlighted, they are described as the "exotic other," indicating another manifestation of inferiority. The ideas of inferior differences are profoundly rooted in our language, societal structures, and attitudes. Together, these influences contribute to a discourse that is internalized by both dominant and nondominant groups alike. The good news is that research and awareness have brought these issues to light where they are being challenged, disrupted, and redirected.

As culturally responsive educators, we can acknowledge the impact of this biased history both consciously and unconsciously through ways that people interact. To begin, we can acknowledge multiple perspectives on identity and from there teach a critical approach that promotes questioning the status quo (see Chapter 7). The classroom is set in a social context where meaning is created through learning new information, skills, and concepts in conjunction with social interaction as the students grow and develop. In Chapter 2: Educator Identity Safety and the Importance of Self-Awareness, we will talk about ways to reflect on our own attitudes, language, gestures, and behaviors and take a critical approach to help students discover their own social identities.

Counternarratives

We are a bit like fish in a polluted pond who become accustomed to the murky water they swim in and can no longer see it. In our case, we are swimming in toxic water in that we cannot see that the way we view the world is impacted by a series of narratives that set up hierarchies offering advantages based on race and conditions stemming from centuries of White power and privilege. Attitudes still prevail that we live in a meritocracy where personal gains are achieved by merit and people can just pull themselves up by their bootstraps. Negative stereotypes define non-White people and immigrants as lazy, unintelligent, and prone to violence and crime. Unfortunately, this is the water we swim in with our students. The way to begin to change it requires unpacking the racist and biased histories behind this mainstream narrative and seeking out the counternarratives.

Counternarratives are significant for students on two important levels:

1. On the personal level, students need to hear specific counternarratives that contradict internalized fears that their own potential is limited and help them reframe views of their intelligence and their capacities.

2. Learning counternarratives at the community and societal level helps students gain an understanding of oppression and learn to deconstruct the dominant narratives that undermine the value of groups they belong to—dominant narratives that form barriers to their education and other opportunities.

At the personal level, students need to hear counternarratives about their own potential. Mainstream narratives promote the predictability of the "achievement gap" and have contributed to a sense of hopelessness. Zaretta Hammond (2015) speaks of ways that educators can use counternarratives to help students change their internal self-talk and the accompanying negative explanations. She explains that mainstream narratives can cause students to develop insecurities and low expectations that are reinforced by teachers in a negative loop that returns and reinforces the impact to the students. Hammond points out that White supremacy is designed to work in such a way that after students experience years of failure, they learn to internalize their perceived weaknesses, and by the time they reach high school, they are doing it to themselves. By teaching about the growth mindset and offering counternarratives with an alternative perspective on history, expressing genuine belief in their capacity, students come to value their potential and will begin to change their own self-talk and explanatory stories.

Offering counternarratives does not merely serve to debunk negative characterizations or respond to inequities. Counternarratives also include helping students of dominant and nondominant backgrounds discover a wealth of community assets, including the strength, courage, resilience, and tenacity available from people of color (Yosso, 2005). Moving away from a deficit mindset helps students recognize the wide range of contributions by individuals and communities of color.

Counternarratives also benefit students by providing a foundation that serves to equalize status by inviting everyone to join efforts to create an equitable society. This can be accomplished by providing views of history from multiple perspectives and using primary source texts (historical materials written by the people involved, in addition to those by historians of color and others). In addition, counternarratives can be drawn from the voices of local community members, as well as through analysis of current events from a range of sources. Even if you are not an English or history teacher, you can still share information with students to motivate them to seek information beyond the traditional presentation, including everything from the arts to math, the sciences, and the study of languages. We suggest strategies for incorporating counternarratives throughout the book.

Identity Safety as an Antidote to Stereotype Threat: The Research

In 2001, Dorothy Steele, with Claude Steele and a team of social psychologists, initiated a study to examine effective ways to mitigate stereotype threat through a yearlong study of third- and fifth-grade students in 84 integrated elementary school classrooms. The Stanford Integrated School Project (D. M. Steele & Cohn-Vargas, 2013) sought to identify classroom practices that lead to a sense of identity safety. Rather than begin with a set of practices, this study looked at a whole range of teacher practices from the bottom up. Researchers sought to identify practices that helped students feel identity safe and also experience higher levels of achievement.

To do this, a pair of observers, who were not informed about identity safety, visited each of the third- and fifth-grade classrooms three times, completing a 200-item classroom observation form each time. The form was designed to record specific practices that were viewed in the classrooms. The observers rated the presence of what they saw and heard that demonstrated high expectations, classroom relationships, and inclusive and cooperative practices, along with methods of embedding diversity as a resource for learning. In addition, students themselves completed questionnaires that aimed to capture their sense of identity safety, belonging, and autonomy. Standardized test scores were used to examine the impact of identity safe practices on student academic performance.

The data from this study demonstrated the following results: In classrooms with higher levels of identity safety (as observed and reported in student questionnaires), students from every ethnic group demonstrated a more positive feeling about school. These students scored higher on standardized tests and were more motivated to succeed at school than their peers in less identity safe classrooms (classrooms with the presence of fewer observed identity safe practices). This research offered a promising potential for classroom environments that could mitigate the impact of stereotype threat and support achievement and school success for students of color and all students. A constellation of factors emerged that together constitute identity safe practices. These factors we refer to as the components of identity safety and are clustered in four domains to create a framework, which is how this book is organized.

THE FOUR DOMAINS AND 12 COMPONENTS OF IDENTITY SAFE CLASSROOMS

Domain 1: Student-Centered Teaching

1. *Listening for Student Voices*: To ensure that students are heard and can contribute to and shape classroom life

2. *Teaching for Understanding*: To ensure students will learn new knowledge and incorporate it into what they know

3. *Focus on Cooperation*: Rather than focus on competition, to support students in learning from and helping others

4. *Classroom Autonomy*: To support students in responsibility and feelings of belonging

Domain 2: Cultivating Diversity as a Resource

5. *Using Diversity as a Resource*: To include all students' curiosity and knowledge in the classroom

6. *High Expectations and Academic Rigor*: To support all students in high-level learning

7. *Challenging Curriculum*: To motivate each student by providing meaningful, purposeful learning

(Continued)

(Continued)

Domain 3: Classroom Relationships

8. *Teacher Warmth and Availability for Learning*: To build a trusting, encouraging relationship with each student

9. *Positive Student Relationships*: To build interpersonal understanding and caring among students

Domain 4: Caring Classrooms

10. *Teacher Skill*: To establish an orderly, purposeful classroom that facilitates student learning

11. *Emotional and Physical Comfort*: To provide a safe environment so that each student connects to school and to other students

12. *Attention to Prosocial Development*: To teach students how to live with one another, solve problems, and show respect and caring for others

Additional Research on Putting Identity Safety Into Practice

In 2006, with the support of Dorothy Steele, I implemented a dissertation study to begin the process of describing the identity safe components more fully as they appeared in practice. I formed a study group of elementary teachers who worked for one year to define and describe the many ways the components could be approached in classrooms where educators worked to create identity safety in an environment that values the many student identities while countering stereotypes. The book *Identity Safe Classrooms: Places to Belong and Learn* (D. M. Steele & Cohn-Vargas, 2013) brings together Dorothy Steele's SISP (Stanford Integrated Schools Project) research data as well as further work she conducted with a teacher study group and descriptions of the identity safe components from my dissertation research. The research on identity safety continues. Stephanie Fryberg (2016) describes identity safe spaces as culturally congruent places, free of prejudice and stereotypes, where all people feel they can belong and experience success, and where diversity is positively valued. She is currently engaged in research with Mary Murphy, who seeks to link the concepts of the growth mindset with identity safety. Other researchers have also developed identity safety experiments in the laboratory, where positive contact and role models were found to promote identity safety (Davies et al., 2005; McIntyre et al., 2003; Purdie-Vaughns et al., 2008).

The Learning Policy Institute (LPI) has incorporated identity safe teaching as a key component of their *Whole Child Framework for Educational Practice*, based on a synthesis of research (Darling-Hammond & Cook-Harvey, 2018). LPI is currently conducting a case study at the Social Justice Humanitas Academy (SJHA), a school in the Los Angeles Unified School District (LAUSD; Ondrasek & Flook, 2020). According to teacher interviews and observations, researchers observed the use of identity safe practices incorporating trusting relationships and creating a positive climate drawing on diversity as a resource. Humanitas has a high graduation rate that surpasses district averages. In the 2017–2018 LAUSD School Experience Survey, nearly all Humanitas students responded that they "feel safe at school," and 86 percent of Humanitas students said that they "feel like they are part of their school."

The Growth Mindset and Identity Safety

Let us take a moment to explain the connection between identity safety and the growth mindset. These two revolutionary ideas work well together.

Stanford researcher Carol Dweck (2006) found that mindset plays an important role in how people perceive their own abilities. Those who held the belief that their intelligence could be developed with effort and that their brains were malleable, which she called an incremental or growth mindset, progressed better than those who believed that intelligence was innate and unchangeable, which she called a fixed (entity) mindset.

In Dweck's research with children ages four and up, she found that those with a growth mindset continued to apply effort when faced with difficulties, often even enjoying the challenge. On the contrary, those who believed their intelligence was predetermined at birth (described as having fixed mindsets) would give up when they encountered difficulty and stop trying. The good news was that researchers have found they can foster a growth mindset even with students who initially believe otherwise. Students in a range of ages learned about their brains through the metaphor that the brain is like a muscle that can get stronger with use. Students in these studies believed their brains could grow stronger and increased their intellectual abilities and performance.

TWO GROWTH MINDSET EXPERIMENTS

In One Experiment

Four-year-olds were given a choice to work easy puzzles again and again or to try to complete a harder puzzle. Some children believed that intelligence was fixed and chose to repeat the easy puzzles, and others who demonstrated the growth mindset enthusiastically asked for more challenges (Dweck, 2006, p. 17). The researchers found that even at age four, children fell into the same two categories as adults who participated in similar experiments.

(Continued)

(Continued)

In a Hong Kong Study

Adults were asked to agree with one of two statements: (a) You have a certain amount of intelligence, and you cannot do much to change it (that view is called an "entity" or "fixed" mindset); or (b) you can always substantially change how intelligent you are (that is the "incremental" or "growth" mindset; Dweck, 2006, p. 17). All participants were university students studying in English, but they were not fluent. The researchers invited them to take a course to improve their English skills. The majority of those with a fixed or entity mindset (*a* group) were not interested in taking this course. Those with the incremental or growth mindset (*b* group) wanted to take the course.

Dweck's theories have been put into practice by many educators. In a 2015 article, Dweck reflected on a few things they have learned since the publication of her book *Mindset: The New Psychology of Success.* Dweck explained that the growth mindset is not merely about working harder and using more effort. To be effective, effort must incorporate what has been learned along the way, from both previous tries as well as additional input from other sources. Otherwise, a student can get stuck or keep pushing forward, hitting a wall without progressing. She also says that simply acknowledging effort without combining it with higher-level thinking does not help the brain grow.

As in any new theory, obstacles are often revealed in the details or in the complexities of its application. For example, when educators attribute a student's lack of progress as the result of a fixed mindset or equate a student's achievement exclusively to a growth mindset, they are placing all the onus on the student. Rather than using these mindsets as a tool to label students, it is up to us as educators to communicate and teach a growth mindset perspective to students and empower them to apply the theories to and for themselves.

It is also incumbent upon us to ensure that our words match what we truly believe. Dweck (2016) calls it a *false growth mindset* when educators promote a growth mindset without matching their actions to their words. For example, an educator may praise a student's effort so they do not feel left out, even when the student may not be trying and the work is not progressing. Dweck considers one of the worst manifestations of false growth mindset occurs when an educator blames a student's mindset for failures. She describes observing in a school where students were taken to task for not having a growth mindset. She suggests that educators observe, question, and reflect on our own mindsets. When we make mistakes, do we see them as learning opportunities or failures? Do we find ourselves saying, "I am just not good at . . . ?" She also points out that as growth mindset researchers, they came to realize that they created too great a dichotomy between growth and fixed mindsets. She asserts that we all demonstrate a portion of both.

Why is the growth mindset an important element of identity safety? With a growth mindset, stereotypes and stereotype threat do not necessarily become self-fulfilling prophecies. Students do not need to feel limited by external definitions of their intelligence. As we help our students by motivating effort, we can also guide them to discover for themselves and learn to recognize how they are progressing, defying the stereotypes about fixed mindsets and limited capacities that may have dogged them.

Working on developing our growth mindset also helps us as educators to open our perspectives regarding all of our students, watching out for how stereotypes influence our views of them. We can deepen the belief that each of our students has great potential, freeing opportunities for truly promoting identity safety and belonging.

Culturally Inclusive Growth Mindset Culture

Mary Murphy (2018a) describes a *culturally inclusive growth mindset culture* as one that communicates to students the values of a growth mindset in the context of a community of learners. It is the idea that as a classroom community, we are working together as a team to grow our brains and increase our capabilities. Murphy explains that this type of environment highlights interdependence as a way to draw in students from cultures that are traditionally more focused on community and interdependence. This includes an array of cultures (e.g., African American, Native American, Latinx, Asian, and Middle Eastern). This approach transforms a competitive classroom environment to an inclusive space that is more motivating to students from interdependent cultures and may well be transformative for those from more competitive cultures.

An individual's growth mindset is amplified in a classroom culture where no student is left out and students feel that everybody's success is part of their own. Challenges are shared as well. There are many ways to communicate that feeling. For example, students can share strategies they use and describe the different paths they took to solve a problem. The educator can post the different strategies, and when a student is at a loss, the educator can refer the student to the strategy board. This has another metacognitive advantage because it shows how everyone solves problems differently. With a team approach to the idea that we learn from our mistakes, we can help one another tackle challenges together.

Educator Growth Mindset

A significant new research study on educator growth mindset was recently released (2019). Elizabeth Canning, Mary Murphy, and colleagues gathered data from 150 STEM university professors and 15,000 students from across the United States. They collected data from faculty self-reports, including their personal beliefs regarding their own mindsets, and they combined those with student evaluations of their professors and course grades. Researchers analyzed the results and found that for professors with fixed mindset beliefs, the racial achievement gaps were double those of students in courses where the professors endorsed a growth mindset. Also, they found that this was true in spite of the racial background of the professor or the length of time that person was teaching.

The study found that there were four critical points where the growth mindset can be communicated to students for optimal impact:

1. Giving explicit messages about how effort, practice, and learning from mistakes will help their intelligence grow

2. Providing repeated opportunities for practice with specific feedback (see examples in Chapter 10: Teacher Warmth and Availability for Learning)

3. Offering encouraging comments that express high expectations and give direct feedback on how to improve when a student fails or performs poorly (see examples in Chapter 8: High Expectations and Academic Rigor)

4. Ending a semester with final remarks that offer encouragement and hope regarding a student's future potential (see positive presuppositions in Chapter 14: Attention to Prosocial Development)

As educators, it is worth taking time to reflect on our mindsets. We may have fixed mindsets about some things while exercising growth mindsets about others. By educating ourselves and seeking to counter some of our own internalized attitudes and embedded stereotypes and explanatory stories about ourselves and others, we can expand our views of our students' potential. By listening to the words we use with students, we can change the way we communicate. In subsequent chapters in this book, we offer many strategies.

Anchoring Identity Safety in the Context of Adolescent Development

As you consider adolescent development, it is important to examine your operating assumptions, beliefs, or biases when you think about this time period of development. Ask yourself the following questions:

What is adolescence?

What are critical considerations to explore as you engage in your work with adolescents?

What personal experiences will be important to examine, combat, or leverage in the service of your students' needs?

In the United States, stereotypical positive and negative associations abound with respect to adolescence. Among them can be everything from associating it with emotional angst and risk-taking to linking it to a sense of freedom. And while some patterns may exist within adolescence with respect to puberty, the construct of adolescence as we know it is largely a Western construction that gained momentum at the beginning of the 20th century (Fass, 2016). In the United States, the model we use to understand

and interpret adolescence was actually largely driven by American values, beliefs, and economic conditions reflective of the early 1900s. Rising from these attitudes, new at the turn of the century, two critical institutions were formed: high school for all and juvenile court. These institutions created new social structures, laying the foundation and context for what we currently know as adolescence (Fass, 2016).

We know from new advances in brain research that there are biological and cognitive differences between teenagers and adults. Specifically, teenage "brains have both fast-growing synapses and parts that remain unconnected. This leaves teens easily influenced by their environment and more prone to impulsive behavior, even without the impact of souped-up hormones and any genetic or family predispositions" (Ruder, 2008, para. 3). Further, we know from research that the adolescent brain not only processes information differently, but that additional substances dramatically impact the teenage brain much more strongly than the adult brain. Understanding the neurobiology of the teenage brains supports educators in being able to shape practices to better meet the needs of adolescent students.

In sum, it is critical that we challenge some of the socially constructed "truisms" of adolescence so that we may learn and understand the role that we need to hold to best support the unique needs of teenagers. While there are many facets of what constitutes "adolescent development" for the purposes of our book and the connection to identity safety, we stress the use of a developmental approach to understand the various dimensions of what it means to be in this particular period of life.

Holding a developmental stance for adolescents equips practitioners with the skills to employ identity safe practices with the important nuance that it requires. In an interview about their study *Understanding Youth: Adolescent Development for Educators* (Chauncey, 2007), Michael Nakkula and Eric Toshalis suggest that if adults take the time to learn about some of the patterns of adolescent development, we can strengthen our capacity to understand the actions of our students. By doing so, we will find ourselves better prepared to meet their needs. By holding an "applied developmentalist" lens, educators can "resist pathologizing . . . and instead look for opportunities to participate in their growth." Challenging our assumptions and searching for new understanding and awareness create opportunities for connection and a reimagining of possibilities for students during this period of time.

A final and essential consideration for enacting a developmental lens for adolescents is attending to our implicit bias. In a 2018 study (Priest et al.), researchers found that "some of the strongest levels of negative stereotyping reported by White adults working with children were reported toward teenagers. . . . Black and Latinx teens were between one-and-a-half to two times more likely to be considered violence-prone and unintelligent than White adults and White teens." In working to create identity safe environments for students, we must unpack and develop a deep awareness of our cultural biases and how they interact with how we view teens.

Implications for Practice

Throughout the book, we approach identity safety through a developmental lens. The implications for educators can be found in the following chapters:

1. Equalizing student status—Chapter 3: Listening for Student Voices and Chapter 11: Positive Student Relationships

2. Identity development—Chapter 7: Using Diversity as a Resource

3. Implicit bias—Chapter: 3 Listening for Student Voices

4. Expectations—Chapter 8: High Expectations and Academic Rigor

5. Gender identity—Chapter 6: Classroom Autonomy and Chapter 7: Using Diversity as a Resource

6. Relationships—Chapter 10: Teacher Warmth and Availability for Learning and Chapter 11: Positive Student Relationships

7. Trauma-informed practices—Chapter 10: Teacher Warmth and Availability for Learning

8. Self-regulation and executive functioning—Chapter 6: Classroom Autonomy

9. De-escalating conflict—Chapter 12: Teacher Skill

10. Managing emotions and mental health—Chapter 10: Teacher Warmth and Availability for Learning

11. Social pressure and popularity—Chapter 14: Attention to Prosocial Development

What Is in This Book and How You Might Use It

We wrote this book with the goal of providing information drawn from research and organized around descriptions of each of the identity safety domains and components. We include many vignettes to bring the ideas to life and a plethora of practical strategies for implementation. The vignettes, some of which are composites, come from educators from a range of urban, suburban, and rural areas. We use first and last names when they have published either a blog or produced a video. Identity safety is an approach rather than a program, so there is no checklist of strategies or step-by-step implementation procedures. Rather, it is a gestalt, or a constellation of ideas that create a holistic environment.

Part I gives an introduction with an overview of identity safety and includes three chapters. Chapter 1: The Introduction defines identity safety research and a description of the principles and components, along with its origins. We situate identity safety within the field of culturally responsive teaching and equity literacy. Stereotype threat research and the growth mindset are explained and connected to identity safety. Chapter 2 is an exploration of ways educators can explore their own identities and beliefs in the context of belonging and connecting at school. This self-examination is fundamental for allowing educators to create an environment that fosters student identity safety. Each of the authors shares how we view our own social identities and connect it into our roles as educators.

Parts II, III, IV, and V introduce each of the four identity safety domains—one part for each domain—and encompass Chapters 3–14. Each chapter defines the components within that domain. An overview is offered at the beginning of each part.

Chapters begin with "Why It Matters," an explanation of why the component is important and how it links to identity safety. From there, the chapter moves to "Making It Happen," which offers many research-based strategies for implementation. For each component, we seek to identify and describe one or two dilemmas or points of tension that educators may face when they address that area of identity safety. Every chapter ends with a "Chapter Summary," a set of "Check Yourself" questions, and an "End-of-Chapter Activity" or two. At the close of each part, we highlight the big ideas from the part that demonstrate the Identity Safety Principles, and we also provide additional resources.

We close with a brief Epilogue as a call to action and an invitation to stay connected in the journey toward identity safe classrooms and identity safe schools.

Using the Book

This book can be used in a variety of ways and approached from multiple entry points. Educators can read it from start to finish or begin with the first chapter and then move to any other part or chapter as desired. Each part or chapter can stand alone or work in concert with others. Individual educators or partners can read it, reflecting on their practice with the "Check Yourself" questions and the "End-of-Chapter Activities." We highly recommend schoolwide study groups that allow teams to work through the book over many months and perform the activities together. This approach can transform, instill, and empower the school with a safe and accepting culture that feeds prosocial development, promotes academic success, and even eliminates many instances of bullying. Another possibility is to select relevant chapters to share in a jigsaw fashion. Webinars, full-day workshops, and ongoing sessions are available with the authors through our *Identity Safe Classrooms* website, www.identitysafeclassrooms.com. Often, the culture can even spread to the wider community. Feeling good is contagious!

A note: The identity safety approach weaves together mindsets and practices that we continually describe as being intertwined. Yet, to communicate clearly, we have shared it through the lens of the various components. As readers, you may wonder why a particular topic is described as part of one component rather than another. We made intentional choices for where to place the topics. For example, we placed trauma in the part on educator–student relationships because we felt that trauma-informed practice was a fundamental set of skills and mindsets that educators need to develop to create supportive relationships with students who have experienced trauma. Other aspects of behavior management were placed in the part on Chapter 12, a chapter that highlights basic fundamental skills that educators need to be effective.

You will find that the components overlap in some ways and topics emerge from them through different angles in the various chapters. For example, supporting students with diverse gender identities is viewed through the lens of agency in Chapter 6. Then in Chapter 7, we circle back to looking at inclusive practices that enable students with different gender identities to experience the feeling of belonging in the classroom. Later in Chapter 11, gender identity is discussed in the context of relationships. Each time, we refer the reader to the places where the topic has been addressed earlier.

A Word About Terminology

The concept of *social identity*, as defined by social psychologists, refers to how our identities are derived, which often involves the sense of belonging that we get from our membership in different social groups and the emotional value placed on those memberships (Abrams, 1990). We all have multiple affiliations with self-perceptions in regard to each of our social identities. Examples of groups that people can belong to include ethnic, racial, and religious groups, as well as groups that identify with varying gender identities and sexual orientations and those who are differently abled. Social identity can be found in the autism spectrum as well as professions, sports, and other social groups that have relevance in our lives.

As part of creating identity safety, we often use *students of all backgrounds* because in our approach to belonging, we aim to be inclusive of the many diverse social identities in our classrooms. We use the term *Black* to refer to students of African American, African, and Caribbean backgrounds and the term *Latinx* to refer to students with backgrounds from many countries in Latin America. At other times, we refer to *students of color*, which includes Black, Latinx, South Asian, Asian, Middle Eastern, and Native American students. *LGBTQ* is a term that includes lesbian, gay, bisexual, transgender, and questioning identities. The term *intersectionality* refers to people with more than one oppressed identity (e.g., Black and transgender). We examine intersectionality further in Chapter 7.

Throughout the book, we more frequently use the term *educator* (as opposed to *teacher*) to honor our broader audience of teachers, counselors, administrators, and paraprofessionals—in essence, everyone who works with students.

Finally, please note that we use the words *they/them/their* when describing an individual (e.g., "A person can get support if they are willing"). This usage is now accepted in the *Merriam-Webster Collegiate Dictionary* ("They," 2020). We find it to be more inclusive, and it is often used in common parlance.

Meet the Authors and Leadership Public Schools

Becki Cohn-Vargas is the primary author of this book, with Alex Kahn and Amy Epstein writing as contributors. We each have varied skills and experiences, contributing from each of our unique perspectives: Becki is the coauthor of *Identity Safe Classrooms,* written to address elementary classrooms. Formerly, she was an early childhood and elementary teacher, K–8 principal, curriculum director, and superintendent in rural, urban, and suburban public school districts. Now, she is retired from public education and works as an author, presenter, and consultant.

Alex is the chief academic officer at Leadership Public Schools (LPS). She teaches Adolescent Development at Stanford University in STEP, its teacher education program. She has worked as a secondary teacher and principal.

Amy is the executive director of data, assessment, and tiered support at LPS. She is an expert on gathering and using data and has many years of experience in public school districts and nonprofits supporting equity in education. She is leading a major identity safe formative assessment project at LPS and draws from that experience in her writing for this book.

We each share from our own identity safe journeys, as well as stories and vignettes from our experience working with students. As the primary author, I (Becki) use the first person to share vignettes. Amy and Alex also share vignettes and offer numerous examples of equitable practices from LPS. We have also drawn from videos taken of LPS students, describing their perspectives, experiences, and feelings.

Leadership Public Schools (LPS) is a nonprofit, three-high-school charter network in the San Francisco Bay Area in California with schools in Hayward, Oakland, and Richmond. LPS lives up to the mission statement found on its website (n.d.), which states, "Leadership Public Schools is a network of urban charter high schools whose mission is to create educational equity. We empower students for college, career, and community leadership and share our practices on a national scale." The theory of change that guides them includes developing flexible resources with a particular focus on access for students of diverse identities. LPS makes its resources available to the larger educational community through publishing open-source curriculum, lessons, and guides. It cocreates some of these materials as part of various partnerships with national and local educational organizations.

Collaboration on this book was initiated after Becki started working with LPS educators to increase identity safe practices in their system. We also draw from the collective experience of LPS educators working to implement identity safe formative assessment. Throughout this book, they share many innovative LPS strategies and tools that promote identity safety. When we refer to LPS, we are referring to districtwide policies and practices. At other times, we indicate a particular LPS high school to describe a particular practice or share a vignette.

Chapter Summary

In *The Introduction*, we introduced identity safety and presented the identity safe principles. We provided background to help readers understand the theory of identity safety, providing its theoretical antecedents from stereotype threat research. We highlighted a foundational principle that students who feel different in any way do not thrive in a color-blind classroom that ignores differences.

We situated identity safety in the context of a brief history of culturally responsive teaching and equity literacy. We then proposed that students need counternarratives to combat the pervasive influence of deficit thinking and attitudes that devalue and stereotype them. We explained that counternarratives with identity safe practices can enlist all students in an affirming climate that creates access and works to equalize status.

We shared the identity safety research from the Stanford Integrated Schools Project (SISP) and other studies and introduced the domains and components of identity safety that form the basis for the structure of this book. We introduced the growth mindset in this chapter because research has demonstrated a close connection between the theory of the growth mindset and identity safety. We situated identity safety in the context of a developmental approach to adolescent development and pointed out chapters of the book with implications for practice. Finally, we closed with suggestions for ways to use the book, our use of terminology, and an introduction to the authors and to LPS.

TRY IT OUT: END-OF-CHAPTER ACTIVITY

Considering Identity Safety and Your Plans With the Book

Each chapter will conclude with an activity that will allow you to reflect and apply the ideas. For the introductory chapter, we have some questions to help you consider how to approach your use of this book.

1. Reflect on the topics addressed in Chapter 1. Which ones resonate with you, and why?

2. What aspects of identity safety have you already been employing in your role as an educator?

3. What is your experience with counternarratives? Have you used them in your own life? Have you used them with students?

4. Have you read about, studied, or participated in professional development on culturally relevant teaching, diversity, antibias training, and/or equity pedagogy? Share from your own knowledge, experiences, ideas, and opinions as you embark on exploring identity safety.

5. What is your plan for using this book? We recommend finding an accountability partner, study group, faculty team, or several colleagues to work with as you try out the suggested ideas.

 Available for download as a full-page form at **https://resources.corwin .com/IdentitySafeClass6-12**

Educator Identity Safety and the Importance of Self-Awareness

2

Why Educator Identity Safety Matters

As educators, we are more than technicians who mechanically carry out the procedural steps of instruction. We hold the power to transform our students' hearts, minds, and lives through meaningful connections to each other and ourselves. As Parker Palmer (1999) writes, our teaching comes from within our hearts. He suggests we explore how our teaching reflects our deepest internal feelings, beliefs, and identity, bringing forth our integrity. It is highly nuanced and never neutral.

When we speak of educator identity safety, we are speaking of the way that our inner and outer worlds intersect, blend with, and at times collide as we express the many social identities that live within us. We also are speaking of our sense of belonging and connection at the particular school where we work. As with our students, our multiple social identities include these parts of us: our ethnicity, appearance, and gender expression that are visible to others, as well as those parts of ourselves that are hidden below the surface; our hopes and fears; our spirituality; and our political views, to name a few. Whether we are aware of it or not, many aspects of ourselves emerge through our words, our tone of voice, our gestures, and our responses to different situations.

Think about your identity. What parts of yourself do you show when you come to school every day? Do you allow your full self to come out with students and their parents? With colleagues and administrators?

We believe that it is important to take the time to explore our own identities and what gives us a sense of identity safety—not only for ourselves but also to initiate and foster identity safety for our students and others around us. As we take the time to reflect, we gain a deeper understanding of our relationships and what our students might be feeling in our classrooms. We also deepen a sense of compassion, manifesting care in our practice.

Through reflection, we can shine a light on how, in different situations, aspects of our social identities become what social psychologists refer to as *salient*—in other words, they move to the forefront of our minds. Sometimes, parts of ourselves that have remained below the surface may suddenly become salient. And as they do, we often discover whether the newly acknowledged identity feature offers us a sense of belonging and inclusion or not. At one time, I was principal of a school where 90 percent of the students were from Mexican backgrounds, and most were Catholic. As the only Jewish person on campus, I rarely spoke about being Jewish, although I have always been open about it. When it came up in conversation that I do not have a Christmas tree, the school secretary said, "You hate Christmas." Suddenly, my Jewishness became salient, and I felt triggered. A microaggression—a subtle or not-so-subtle biased comment—may suddenly snap us into an awareness of how we may not be fully accepted.

Reflection also allows us to interrogate our own belief systems and our assumptions. We can consider how our core beliefs guide our actions and question whether we need to take a deeper dive into deconstructing the assumptions we make about our students. We consider how we are treating others, our colleagues, our students, and our friends in relation to the many social identities in their lives. Are we taking our privileges for granted and not recognizing barriers others have faced? How can we unearth the subtle and not-so-subtle assumptions we make about others?

Think of how you interact with others at your school site. Do you share your feelings and beliefs? Do you take time to get to know your colleagues and learn about their lives? Do you have people you feel close to and who support you at work? If you teach, do you feel safe inviting colleagues into your classroom?

 ## MAGIC HAT

In identity safety workshops for both adults and students, we often begin with a short, lighthearted journey into understanding and sharing our social identities in the "Magic Hat" activity. Participants design an imaginary magic hat; however, they do not draw it or even write about it. Rather, they take turns verbally describing it to each other so it can defy gravity and be totally fantastic. All participants have a minute or two to describe their hat as they go around the circle.

Here are just a few things to put in your magic hat:

- Imaginary family photos of people you care about: children, parents, siblings, cousins, friends

- Symbols that mean something to you from your ethnicity, religion, profession, and/or nationality

- Things you like to do (hike in the mountains, embroider, sports)

- Acts of community service (organizations, activist or support groups)

- How you express creativity (e.g., paint, play drums, dance, reading)

In 15 minutes, small groups can come to know each other so much better, sharing values and the aspects of their identities that give meaning to their lives.

In this chapter, we will be examining ways to approach reflection on our social identities. Each of us as authors will share a bit about our own journey. As Jennifer Abrams (2019) suggests, there is tremendous benefit when we take a "field trip into our life" and then take a "field trip into our students' lives."

Emotional Resilience and Optimism

In *Onward: Cultivating Emotional Resilience in Educators* (2018), Elena Aguilar, international consultant and expert on coaching educators, highlights a set of mindsets and habits of educators committed to doing the hard work of transforming classrooms and ultimately the world. Aguilar encourages us to focus on the bright moments that help us recharge our batteries and remain positive. She emphasizes knowing deeply who you are as an initial and necessary step toward resiliency, an idea that echoes what we are conveying in this chapter—that first and foremost, we must find our own identity safety. She reminds us to find moments for mindfulness and celebration while seeking to be compassionate and hopeful. She asks educators to consider the context of the dominant culture that normalizes the White people, males, and a heterosexual identity that does not validate many others. By understanding the historical roots, she points out that you can depersonalize your reactions and challenge your assumptions. According to Aguilar, a mindset of emotional resilience helps educators remain strong in the face of the many challenges and dilemmas they face, strengthening their inner courage. We believe that emotional resilience empowers us to connect and feel identity safe. It allows us to be able to adapt to the rapid changes at dizzying speeds, sometimes like a "drop tower" and other times a roller coaster. Finding allies on this path to share the continual learning and offer support in dark moments strengthens our resilience. Continually tending to our own sense of identity safety along the way keeps us vibrant.

Interrogating the Impact of Beliefs and Assumptions on Our Actions: The Ladder of Inference

Throughout this book, we will be posing questions that aim to help educators interrogate their beliefs and assumptions as they seek to support every student. One useful tool for examining our actions and juxtaposing them against our beliefs and assumptions was advanced by organizational development researcher Chris Argyris (1990). The "ladder of inference" serves as a device for questioning ourselves and looking at our actions in relation to the data and facts and how they must pass through a set of beliefs and assumptions in order to arrive at our actions. Using the ladder helps us see how we are very subjective as we extract from what we perceive to be reality, attribute meaning, make assumptions, and finally draw conclusions that drive our actions. If we are willing to examine our own processes, we can ask questions as we move up each rung of the ladder to unpack the ways our biases influence our attitudes and behaviors. We start at the bottom of the ladder and move up the rungs.

LADDER OF INFERENCES

- Actions

- Beliefs

- Conclusions

- Assumptions

- Interpreted reality

- Selected reality

- Observable data and experiences

Here is an example:

Samantha is a six-year-old girl.

Observable data and experiences: On the bottom rung, Samantha, a first grader, is in her classroom observing an English learner struggling to read. She yells across the room, "You are dumb! Why do you read so slowly?"

Selected data: The educator might focus on the fact that they have noticed that Samantha has a pattern of rude comments and insensitive remarks.

Added meaning: Rude and insensitive people care only about themselves.

Assumptions: Children who behave rudely have parents who have not taught them manners.

Interpreted reality: Samantha is a rude and insensitive person with parents who do not care about her behavior.

Conclusions: Samantha cares only about herself and has no manners.

Beliefs: Selfish children need a firm hand and to be punished for their rude behavior.

Actions: Scold her for her behavior and then take action to not allow Samantha to go out to recess.

By examining the process of arriving at the decision to prevent Samantha from going to recess, an educator can stop before reacting and ask if there might be another way to consider Samantha's actions. Luckily, in this case, a counselor approached the school administrator and said, "Perhaps, Samantha is autistic, and therefore, scolding and punishing her will not address her needs." The counselor turned out to be correct. Another approach was taken.

In another example, Roberto was not so lucky. Before people knew much about autism, as a high school student Roberto was having many social problems at school. He was sent to a psychologist who identified him as "narcissistic" and labeled him a sociopath. It took several more years before Roberto was identified as autistic and given the support he needed.

The "ladder of inference" can be a valuable tool to examine our underlying assumptions and beliefs about our students that help us guide our behaviors and educational decisions. This is a useful process for uncovering many kinds of biases. One of the hallmarks of identity safe teaching is the way we shine a light on our own belief systems in order to recognize them for what they are—how they came to be and are coloring our perceptions—and adjust, realign, or reject them appropriately in order to better serve our students and their circumstances.

A Word About White Fragility

In the 2018 book *White Fragility: Why It's So Hard for White People to Talk About Racism*, author Robin DiAngelo describes how White people, in many instances when they are confronted with societal inequities and privilege, find the information to be jarring and upsetting. DiAngelo defines *White fragility* as a form of privilege where a White person claims entitlement to the luxury of feeling comfortable at all times while not recognizing the discomfort or dissonance that is often felt by persons of color. DiAngelo conceptualized White fragility when she was leading professional development for educators, frequently finding that even when there was the tiniest amount of racial stress in the room, White participants demonstrated a range of defensive responses from fear to anger to guilt and an array of reactions from argumentation to awkward silences.

However, as DiAngelo (2018) deconstructed these patterns, she began to view it as resistance to discussing race or even listening to the experiences of people of color. DiAngelo also defines White fragility as a manifestation of advantage and power felt by Whites in the United States. These attitudes are significant because they directly impact how students are treated. The fact that many White educators consistently have low expectations for Black students is evident in the data by Papageorge, Gershenson, and Kang (2018).

LONGITUDINAL RESEARCH SHOWS WHITE TEACHERS HAVE LOWER EXPECTATIONS FOR BLACK STUDENTS

Nicholas Papageorge and colleagues (2018) analyzed data collected by the US Department of Education for a nationally representative group of 6,000 students from the *Education Longitudinal Study of 2002*. The data included student surveys, teacher surveys, and achievement scores. They found that, when asked, teachers thought 68 percent of White students were likely to finish college as opposed to only 37 percent of Black students. In addition, when considering expectations for student success, the expectations of White teachers were 9 percent lower than Black teachers for the same student. The situation becomes even more concerning when we recognize that across the United States, 87 percent of the teaching force is White (Moore et al., 2017). Many of these White educators work in schools located in predominantly communities of color.

DiAngelo (2018) points out that unless educators listen and become aware of the obstacles faced by people of color, they will not recognize or be motivated to make the needed changes to eliminate barriers. She also warns of a zero-sum game in which White people might not be moved to make changes that they fear will lower their sense of entitlement.

For many Whites, DiAngelo (2018) explains, the definition of a racist act is an overt and obvious action taken by racist people. That definition does not take into account that a group of people in power (in this case, Whites, males, etc.) often holds onto the narrative that everything they have gotten in life is because they deserve it. They believe that wealth and prosperity are a direct result of their hard work and higher intelligence. In an extension of this attitude, they might make the assumption that those who have less power and status do not try hard enough. DiAngelo points out that some of the greatest damage to people of color is caused by people who consider themselves to be liberal and progressive, claiming not to be at all racist. With these attitudes, people can exempt themselves from accountability for participating in a system where Whiteness continually privileges them in ways they take for granted. DiAngelo suggests we stop only viewing racism as a series of unfair acts taken by individuals. A more honest appraisal is to recognize how structural racism is intentionally designed to privilege Whites and limit opportunities for people of color. By working to move past defensive attitudes, we can commit to lifetime efforts to dismantle racism and other forms of bias.

How Does White Fragility Relate to Identity Safety?

When we speak of creating identity safety in non-color-blind classrooms, we have to consider what it might feel like from the point of view of our students to have their intelligence questioned or to wonder, *Just where do I stand?* The premise of identity safety is that it operates in the service of creating a sense of belonging for all students. For White educators, it is important to consider the role of privilege in their lives—a privilege that allows them to safely ignore thinking about race—and consider how that in turn might make them insensitive to barriers faced by students of color.

 SOMETIMES UNDERSTANDING PRIVILEGE TAKES TIME TO SINK IN

Peter described having a defensive reaction in a diversity workshop at his university when he was asked to consider White privilege. At the time, he felt angry that he was being confronted with that reality. Yet a few months later while on campus, he had to get to a meeting and found himself taking a shortcut through the campus police department. Suddenly, he realized that—as a White man—nobody looked at him twice. As he passed through, he found himself wondering how different it would be if he was an African American walking through there. Suddenly, what he learned at the workshop made complete sense, and his attitude shifted.

We are speaking not only to White but to educators of all backgrounds. Taking the time to consider ways in which the educational playing field is not level and how assumptions we hold may serve to exacerbate the situation helps all educators take an active role to change it. There is value in exploring different facets of privilege (e.g., White skin privilege, class privilege, and privilege as US citizens). We can also deepen our stance for social justice by addressing other forms of oppression (e.g., anti-immigrant sentiment, Islamophobia, sexism) that emerge in our exchanges with our students.

As identity safe educators of all backgrounds, we should not shy away from these difficult issues. We need to talk about racism and oppression, even if colleagues or students claim that they prefer not to talk about these sensitive topics. We can open dialogue among staff, taking into account the historical roots of racism and other forms of oppression. Part of our responsibility as educators involves navigating these conversations and working through moments of discomfort on the path to creating a collective sense of belonging. In Chapter 7: Using Diversity as a Resource, we offer suggestions for facilitating difficult conversations. We can also commit to ongoing reflection and interrogation of our beliefs in the service of creating equitable conditions for our students.

Inclusive Conditions for Staff Identity Safety: Implications for School Leaders and Staff

It is important to take into account the conditions of identity safety for everyone at a school. Consider the staff at your place of work with many different roles as a whole group. Are all staff members valued and given equal recognition in their roles as contributors to the school or workplace environment? Is there a spirit of camaraderie with moments of celebration? Are any members of the staff excluded? Are staff members comfortable sharing in their personal lives? Does everyone come into the staff room, or do some feel unwelcome there? Do you offer structured opportunities for staff to get to know each other better?

By implementing staff surveys, you can learn how adults feel on campus. You can ask about their sense of belonging, how they are treated, and where they can go for support to resolve problems. At one private school in Virginia, there was only one African American teacher. She was continually asked for advice on how to work with the Black students. Finally, she spoke up and told the administrator that she resented being treated like the "resident expert on Black students." Do you treat any of your staff as the resident "expert" who is always asked to deal with racial questions or concerns about any social identity group?

When we speak of identity safety for staff, we acknowledge the important role of school administrators to create conditions for a positive staff climate. However, we do not place all the responsibility at the administrators' feet. Each member of the staff plays an important role in working for an identity safe school at both the interpersonal and collective level.

At LPS (Leadership Public Schools), district leaders recognized that their focus on rigorous instruction and academic achievement needed to extend to social interactions and a sense of belonging as a prerequisite for engagement. They set a goal to increase the level of belonging, determining that it should not only be for students but for staff as well. They decided to begin with a focus on their professional learning community. Every adult learning event is intentionally designed to begin with a community "connector." They use the term *resource circles* as opposed to "affinity groups" because groupings are flexible or fluid, based on the subject content or the composition of people. Resource circles shift; often, they are heterogeneous, but at times, they are based on subject area, gender, or racial group. Faculty are given opportunities to meet each other in intentional pairs, trios, or small groups to discuss different topics. To ensure a strong feedback loop, sessions end with an open-ended survey. Leaders gather data from the surveys to continue to strengthen the content and ensure the adult learning environment fosters belonging and inclusion.

CREATING A WELCOMING ENVIRONMENT FOR STAFF

Here are a few examples of ways to foster belonging and staff identity safety:

- Hire diverse staff for all roles, reflecting the demographics of the student body.
- Initiate activities for staff to get to know each other and share information and interests both formally and informally.
- Develop and live by inclusive norms and community agreements.
- Turn the staff lounge into a comfortable and inviting place to relax.
- Incorporate wellness programs that focus on staff health and exercise.
- Get staff input on ways to reduce their stress.
- Create opportunities for storytelling and sharing among staff members.
- Recognize and appreciate staff accomplishments and make time for celebrations.
- Take care not to overload staff with multiple demands, deadlines, and too many professional development goals at once.
- Cut meeting time to a minimum while giving opportunities for faculty to plan and collaborate in small groups.

Solicit feedback on a regular basis, giving staff an opportunity to share perspectives and experiences regarding the school environment and culture. Reflect on feedback and make needed changes. Share what was heard in the feedback, even when it is negative, and explain how the leadership will work to make changes.

All schools are continually forced to make new demands, face big challenges, and add new curricular materials to an increasing educator workload. Everyone feels better at school when efforts to create identity safety are situated in the context of positive strategies to improve the lives and well-being of staff along with those of their students.

Taking the Field Trip Into Ourselves

Taking time to reflect and dive deeper into what matters in our identities helps us consider the parts of us that, like an iceberg, protrude above the surface in plain view, as well as those that are hidden below. We also can consider which parts of ourselves we bring to school and which parts we only share with friends and others who are close to us. In the activity at the end of the chapter, we share a process for a personal field trip of this nature. Our many social identities engender different feelings and meanings for us. For some, our religion has been significant in defining who we are. For others, activism for a cause, a hobby, or a particular sport is a big part of our identities. Our identities constantly shift and are in flux as different aspects of it become suddenly salient: We give birth to a child, experience a transition to a new profession, or undergo a surgery that makes it less possible to run in a marathon. Recognizing these shifts, we also gain awareness that our identity is less about what we do than who we are as people. We often define ourselves by what we do, but in reality, our identities are more fluid. The "who" of us is not the same as the "what" of us. And yet, each of these aspects of our social identity has an impact on how we see ourselves and how we see others. We make choices within the context of these salient aspects as well as the deeper levels of our identity, choices that influence the well-being of others and ourselves.

Considering the way our own identities are braided together to form a conception of self helps us understand how to nurture and safeguard diverse identities in our classrooms and help everyone feel visible and counted. Students can also greatly benefit from opportunities to take a field trip into themselves, getting in touch with those aspects that provide meaning in their lives.

Our Journeys

As authors, we each have written a few brief paragraphs about our identities and our personal journeys as an abridged example of our experience, taking a "field trip into our inner lives." As we examine our own vulnerabilities, we can model how reflection allows us to sharpen our lenses and better create identity safety for our students.

Becki's Journey

I was born in the shadow of the Holocaust. Both my parents fled the Nazis, who killed and scattered many of our relatives. I grew up with generational trauma from my parents' experiences that occurred less than seven years before I was born.

I always felt a strange feeling of guilt that my life was so much easier than my parents' lives. Although I was called a "dirty Jew" by my classmates a few times in middle school, I grew up with privilege, and my family tried to shelter me from suffering. But I needed to experience life for myself. My parents could not understand why I took so many risks and did not simply pursue the "good" life they were trying to make for me. From deep inside, I had a passion to work for a world where people were equal and nobody suffered from bias and injustice. In the 1980s, I traveled to Nicaragua and spent three years there, working at the Ministry of Education. There, I learned so much as they were working to create an equitable society. Even though the ideal of an equitable society in Nicaragua was not achieved, I came to believe that education was the path to both work for social justice and prepare tomorrow's leaders to continue the struggle for an equitable world. I returned to the United States and worked as a teacher and later a school administrator with a desire to transform education. That path has also been complicated, as public education has been under attack for many years now.

When I learned about identity safety, it resonated with my beliefs about the need for belonging and creating equal status among students. My journey has been one of continually learning from my own mistakes, being aware of White skin privilege, and always seeking to acknowledge and transform my implicit biases. I constantly check and question myself. Am I really understanding my students' experiences? What traumas have they experienced? How can I be sure I am not trying to be a "savior"? How I can create a sense of belonging for my students? I also need to work to change some of my own oversensitivities. I have learned to mitigate my worries about being judged, but I have never completely outgrown them. In the last two years, anti-Semitic hate crimes have greatly increased, triggering some of those old fears from my childhood. Taking my own field trip into myself, I cannot help but feel the powerful need for identity safety and compassion as we are all navigating the complexities of being human and alive together on our one planet.

Alex's Journey

I grew up in the Bay Area in a complex and unique family. It was there I learned what it felt like to belong. I am the product of a White mother and Black father and have two stepparents (one White and one Mexican American). I have nine siblings spanning the ages of 18 to 40 and whose ethnicities range from White to mixed-race Black and Mexican to mixed-race Black and White. Irrespective of our differences, we all prioritize a commitment to support and love one another. I spent most of my childhood in the Bay Area but also spent four formative years in a small, rural town in Washington State. It was there where I first experienced othering and racism. In spite of this, I grew up learning and knowing that feeling accepted and valued simply for who we are creates the opportunities and environment to tackle the unbelievable. The experience of navigating multiple intersecting identities at a time when being of mixed race was still new has helped to define who I am. These experiences afforded me with the opportunity to value the role of belonging in creating opportunity for others.

My passion for education started at an early age. While neither of my parents attended college, I felt early on that it was a hope they had for me. Growing up in the 1980s and 1990s in the Bay Area, I was surrounded by an incredibly diverse community. And while there was such richness in the fabric of our community, access to resources was frequently stratified along racial lines. My local high school exemplified these inequalities in many ways but primarily through the use of a tracked system to sort students by ability or "college readiness." Students in the "higher" track were most frequently identified as White or Asian. Through middle school test scores and what felt like sheer luck, I was placed during my freshman year on the "accelerated" track at my high school. I moved through my high school experience with reasonable success and ease, but when a close friend of mine struggled to get out of her tracked math and English courses (even with advocacy and tutorial support), I learned firsthand how the systems and structures within education can not only enact harm but also deeply undermine students' self-efficacy and confidence beyond the high school years.

The experience of watching my friend struggle to get basic access to courses inspired my work in education. I have spent all of my career working in communities similar to that in which I grew up. I have worked in many roles (education consultant, teacher, principal) and now currently as the chief academic officer at Leadership Public Schools. While I have felt fortunate to work in education in a myriad of roles, being a teacher has been the most fulfilling and impactful. My hope for our book is that it will support educators in doing the critical, life-changing work that they do every day in the classroom.

Amy's Journey

My great-grandparents and grandparents fled to the United States from anti-Semitic hardship and terror in Eastern Europe. I grew up in a family with a strong New York Jewish cultural identity and sturdy egalitarian values. My parents called out racial and gender injustices and taught us to stand up and speak out. They helped me notice and want to disrupt inequity, whether at home, school, or in the bigger world. Coming out as a lesbian deepened my understanding of othering and the harm it creates, as well as the power and solidarity of claiming one's full identity in the world.

I grew up with unfettered access to opportunities to explore my interests and develop my skills because of my Whiteness, my parents' ascending income, and the value my family placed on learning and education. In college, I found people who felt like home, many of whom are still my closest friends and collaborators. I found support and kinship to unpack and face up to White-skin and economic privilege and to commit to racial and economic justice work. As a White person working predominantly in communities of color, my anchors for respectful collaboration are listening, humility, self-reflection, and authenticity. I have been helped tremendously by mindfulness practices and by cultivating intention-setting, gratitude, and compassion practices in my daily life. I have at times in my life experienced denigration, isolation, or risk as a Jewish person, woman, and lesbian. These experiences further my resolve to contribute to the eradication of bigotry and deepen my empathy and desire to stand up for all humans facing marginalization or injustice.

Chapter Summary

We began *Educator Identity Safety and the Importance of Self-Awareness* by sharing the importance of educators examining our own sense of identity safety in the world and at the school. We presented ways to address and open the process. It is rarely smooth and risk-free, but sometimes, the path to safety for everyone may mean uncomfortable realizations for some. Still, the lifting of these obstacles is well worth the internal work when we become free to experience the safety, compassion, and understanding that arrive in its place. A wonderful aspect about this experience is that it tends to spill over into all areas of our lives, both personal and professional.

We introduced the concept of White fragility, a hypersensitive reaction by White people who have not yet deeply examined history with all the implications introduced in the context of racial tension. This stance often turns conversations about oppression into uncomfortable and defensive moments. We must not allow White fragility to impede efforts to listen and address painful realities. The process of acknowledging privilege and implicit biases is part of what is required to gain the courage to change structural racism and other biases. At the end of the day, our unintentional blindness and implicit biases can cause us to engage in behaviors and actions that hamper a sense of belonging for students and fellow staff. We also discussed the importance of taking steps to create identity safety for a staff as a whole.

We showed that as we take the field trip into ourselves, we can consider our values, what matters to us, what has influenced our lives, and what has changed along the way. As authors, we each shared a brief example of self-exploration; we modeled how we can examine aspects of ourselves that contribute to our roles as educators, reminding ourselves why we are in education. Whether in writing or in a group, we always have the choice to decide what we feel safe to share.

We suggest that students can engage in a similar process, taking a field trip into their lives with a goal to more deeply understand their life experiences, motivations, values, fears, and gifts. The compassion we feel for them is the juice for this process. It will extend to them as well as our colleagues. Additionally, self-discovery will ultimately assist in this learning process, and indeed, our success with our students depends on it.

TRY IT OUT: END-OF-CHAPTER ACTIVITIES

What follow are two self-reflection activities Alex and Amy designed and presented to the LPS Identity Safety Study Group. One activity addresses race, and the second involves gender. Complete the reflections individually and then share with others in small groups. The goal of the following reflection questions is to provide an opportunity to engage in various aspects of your identity. Note any other memories or ideas that seem relevant to you.

Racial and Ethnic Identity Autobiography

Family Background

Where did your parents grow up? What are/were their racial and ethnic backgrounds?

Are there different races and ethnic groups in your family (e.g., parents, siblings, extended family)?

What ideas did you grow up with regarding race relations? Do you know? Have you ever talked with your family about this? Why or why not?

Do you think of yourself as White? Black? Asian? Latinx? Native American? Mixed? Or simply as "human?" Do you think of yourself as a member of an ethnic group? What is its importance to you?

Neighborhood

What was the racial makeup of the neighborhood you grew up in?

What was your first awareness of race—that there are different "races" and that you are a member of a racial group?

- What was your first encounter with another race? Describe the situation.
- When and where did you first hear the N-word or other similar racial slurs?
- What messages do you recall getting from your parents about race? From others when you were little?

School

What was the racial makeup of your school? Of its teachers?

Think about the curriculum: What ethnic and racial groups were represented in the curriculum? How were they described? How did the school celebrate the achievements and celebrations of different ethnic and racial groups?

What cultural influences impacted your life (e.g., TV, advertisements, novels, music, movies, etc.)? What color God was presented to you? Angels? Santa Claus? The tooth fairy? Dolls?

What was the racial makeup of organizations you were in (e.g., Girl Scouts, soccer team, church, etc.)?

Was there interracial dating? Racial slurs? Do you recall any conflict with members of another race?

Have you ever felt or been stigmatized because of your race or ethnic group membership?

Present and Future

What's the most important image or encounter that you've experienced regarding race? Have you felt threatened? In the minority? Have you felt privileged? Are you at a loss to think of even one single experience?

What is the racial makeup of the school/organization you currently work in? Of your circle(s) of friends? Your neighborhood? Does it meet your needs? Do you want to change anything?

What goals do you have for the future with regard to race and ethnicity?

Source: Adapted from a Pacific Educational Group Workshop (n.d.).

Gender Identity Autobiography Prompts

This activity supports autobiographical consideration of your own gender identity (Trevor Project, 2019):

Biological sex	What the doctor declares about you at birth
Gender identity	How you feel on the inside
Gender expression	How you present yourself to others
Gender presentation	How the world sees you
Sexual orientation	Who you are attracted to romantically

Early Childhood

What was your first awareness of your gender identity in any one or more areas of the spectrum—that there are different "genders" and that you are a member of a group?

Describe an early recollection of the following moments. Try to remember details about the circumstances, reactions of others if others were involved, and your feelings and thoughts at the time.

- Yourself as a gendered being

- Someone else noticing and/or calling out an aspect of your gender identity

- Enjoying or appreciating an aspect of your gender identity

- Hiding an aspect of your gender identity

- Being confused by an aspect of gender identity

- Something about the gender identities of your family members or other people

Family Background

What gender identities are represented in your family?

What ideas and beliefs about gender identity did your parents grow up with?

What messages do you recall getting from your parents about gender or from others when you were growing up? Was gender identity discussed, and if so, which aspects of the spectrum were discussed?

To what degree was and is your family comfortable with your gender identity?

What do you wish your family better understood about your gender identity?

What was the impact of any family-held religious beliefs or norms related to gender identity?

Neighborhood/School/Community

To what extent was diversity of gender identity visible in the neighborhood you grew up in?

What messages and expectations about gender identity were prevalent in your neighborhood, and how did this impact you?

What was your first encounter with a gender identity you found very different from your own? Describe the situation.

When and where did you first hear the phrase "That's so gay" or other similar homophobic slurs?

What kinds of models of gender identity did you encounter in school?

To what degree did you have access to learn in school about people across the gender identity spectrum?

What ideas and messages about gender identity were prevalent in school? What ideas and messages did you receive in other settings, such as sports teams, Girl/Boy Scouts, school clubs, places of worship, and the like?

Did you ever feel stigmatized or threatened by your gender identity? Describe.

To what extent did school help you develop a positive gender identity?

Think about an experience of how you learned about an "expected" social behavior or attitude attributed to your gender.

Present and Future

What are the prevalent ideas and messages about gender identity in your workplace, circle of friends, and geographic community? What people and/or conditions support you in developing and holding a positive gender identity?

To what degree do you think about gender identity on a daily/weekly basis, and what are some examples of these thoughts and the situations in which they arise?

What do you encounter (internally or externally) as obstacles to a positive gender identity?

What is a meaningful recent experience you've had as an adult regarding gender identity? You may have felt affirmed, confused, threatened, attacked, or been impacted in some other way.

What are your goals regarding gender for the future?

 Available for download as a full-page form at **https://resources.corwin .com/IdentitySafeClass6-12**

Big Ideas: Welcome to the Identity Safe Classroom and School

This part was guided by the following Identity Safety Principles:

1. Color-blind teaching that ignores differences is a barrier to inclusion in the classroom.

2. To feel a sense of belonging and acceptance requires creating positive relationships between teacher and students and among students with equal status for different social identities.

3. Cultivating diversity as a resource for learning and expressing high expectations for students promotes learning, competence, and achievement.

4. Educators need to examine their own social identities and feel a sense of identity safety to convey that feeling to students and create an identity safe environment for them.

5. Social and emotional safety is created by supporting students in defining their identities, refuting negative stereotypes, and countering stereotype threat, giving them a voice in the classroom while using SEL strategies.

6. Student learning is enhanced in diverse classrooms by teaching for understanding, creating opportunities for shared inquiry and dialogue, and offering a challenging, rigorous curriculum.

These principles, as shared through the first two chapters, include the following big ideas:

- The theory of identity safety grew out of the desire to mitigate the impact of stereotype threat.

- Color-blind classrooms that seek to ignore and minimize differences create a barrier to inclusion for students who are different and stigmatized either visibly or below the surface. By validating and appreciating diversity as a resource for a classroom community, students come to feel identity safety and belonging.

- Counternarratives offer an alternative view to those dominant mainstream narratives that draw from a history of discrimination and inequality. Using counternarratives, students deconstruct some of the negative stereotypes and myths that have served to hold them back.

- Asking ourselves hard questions about our assumptions and beliefs will help uncover biases and hidden attitudes that inhibit our ability to support our students and rectify actions that are less than supportive.

- Identity safety is an approach that synchronizes well with the theory of the growth mindset as well as a range of equity-focused and culturally relevant teaching models and equity literacy.

- Viewing youth through a developmental lens offers educators the opportunity to reimagine possibilities for reaching and supporting adolescents.

- To better serve the needs of students, educators can examine their own sense of identity safety in their lives and at school. Taking a "field trip" into ourselves and later involving the students in a "field trip" into themselves will strengthen understanding and compassion for ourselves and others.

For Further Study

- Article: "Carol Dweck Revisits the Growth Mindset" (2015) from *Education Week*, www.edweek.org

- Book: *Identity Safe Classrooms: Places to Belong and Learn* (2013) by Dorothy M. Steele and Becki Cohn-Vargas

- Book: *Whistling Vivaldi and Other Clues to How Stereotypes Affect Us* (2010) by Claude M. Steele

- Handout: *A Handbook for LGBTQ Young People* (2019), free and downloadable from The Trevor Project, www.thetrevorproject.org/wp-content/uploads/2019/10/Coming-Out-Handbook.pdf

- PowerPoint Presentation: *Creating Growth Mindset Cultures to Mitigate Inequalities in Higher Education* by Mary Murphy, Indiana University Education, https://s3-us-west-2.amazonaws.com/csafiles2017/2018+Items/Mindset+Panel+Final.pdf

- Website: *Equity Literacy Institute*, www.equityliteracy.org

Student-Centered Teaching

Student-centered teaching is a way of teaching that places the student at the heart of learning experiences, curricular decisions, and many features of classroom life. By ensuring that students are front and center for all their considerations, secondary educators can combine their love of the subject with the essential purpose of education, which is to provide an interactive pathway between teaching and learning through meaningful engagement.

We begin by examining these student-centered identity safety components because unless student interests and concerns are paramount, a classroom cannot be identity safe. If aspects of the students' identities are ignored and if they feel that they do not belong or their thinking is not valued, it is difficult, if not impossible, for them to participate in their classrooms. When students are heard and believe that their ideas matter, participation and learning will flow.

The following are short definitions of the four components that make up the domain of student-centered teaching in identity safe classrooms. Each will be fully explored in subsequent chapters.

1. *Listening for Student Voices* means educators are listening and responding, taking into account student ideas, feelings, and beliefs. Each student can become fully present and contribute to and shape life in the classroom. Students feel their voices matter when they collaborate in developing classroom norms and are included in important decisions. In writing, *voice* is the expression of a person's personality and identity. We refer

to "listening for student voices" because we are looking to the educator to create a space where every student develops their unique voice in all aspects of the classroom. In identity safe classrooms, educators are listening and paying attention to the subtleties of student expression.

2. *Teaching for Understanding* means educators work to ensure students gain new knowledge and incorporate it into what they already know. This is done through synthesizing new knowledge into prior learning and making the content comprehensible and interesting so the students will retain it. Across all content areas, students can learn to recognize, critique, and analyze multiple perspectives and solve problems in creative ways, using their imaginations. For example, knowing how to determine an average by taking three numbers, adding them, and dividing by three is not the same as knowing what an average means and understanding the difference between the mean, median, and mode. By making the learning opportunities meaningful, students can feel that their contributions matter. Student will engage and deepen understanding when they experience a *growth mindset culture*, where the goal is to grow their minds individually and in concert with others.

3. *Focus on Cooperation* means that each student learns from and helps others. In identity safety, the focus on learning to cooperate goes beyond traditional collaborative lessons and small-group activities. Identity safe teaching has an emphasis on creating a spirit of cooperation. A sense of interdependence that "we are in this together" permeates their experience, extending from how students treat one another to all forms of large- and small-group instruction. Many students come from backgrounds that are focused on interacting together as a community. Providing opportunities to draw from that spirit of community creates familiarity and safety for students from community-oriented backgrounds. For others who come from more individualistic backgrounds, learning to cooperate gives them a valuable skill. Cooperative groups, designed to equalize and raise student status, will help them develop agency in academic interactions.

4. *Classroom Autonomy* means to promote a sense of agency in each student and help them feel they can forge their own opinions and actions while taking responsibility for their lives. Autonomy is a need that is deeply wired into our biological makeup, a trait that is visible in all species of animals. Children are like birds who are born helpless yet will, however, one day flap their wings and flutter out of the nest. In adolescence, young people are testing their wings with many false starts, yet with practice, they are getting better and better on their own. In an identity safe classroom, educators work to support students as they strive toward autonomous action and equal status with their peers.

In these four chapters, the components of student-centered teaching form a foundation for structuring classroom life and learning. Taken together, they provide a map for ways that student ideas and thinking can be seen and heard. We show how students can take responsibility for their learning and collaborate with one another while drawing from their own and each other's identities.

Listening for Student Voices 3

Why Listening for Student Voices Matters

It is fitting to start our journey toward identity safety for secondary students by exploring ways to create space for recognizing and amplifying their voices in their classroom. As educators, we need to listen, listen, listen. As students develop their social identities and come to understand the multiple aspects of themselves, they also need the opportunity to express themselves and discover their uniqueness, both verbally and nonverbally. Educators can play an important role in enhancing this process.

Many pressures can impede student voice in the classroom. Required high school curriculum and the push toward meeting college entrance requirements put tremendous burdens on educators to "cover" content and can inadvertently influence them to suppress student voice. This pressure can interfere with taking the time for creating a safe space to hear, share, and draw from students' ideas. In actuality, preparing students for college would logically involve helping them learn to express themselves, as this is a meaningful competency for navigating the complexities of college life on their own. In this chapter, we will explore ways to open up opportunities for students to find and express their voice, along with ways to assure them that we are listening deeply.

Listening for Student Voices is an *equitable practice* that asks educators to truly listen to every student. Educators have the role of monitoring classroom activity—what is said and not said—and drawing student voices out. Students develop confidence through opportunities to formulate and express feelings, beliefs, ideas, questions, theories, and arguments.

Listening for student voices is also important for another reason. We introduced Paul Gorski's (2017) model for "equity literacy" in Chapter 1: The Introduction. Educators can detect bias when it manifests in classroom interactions and in curricular materials. For example, they notice who dominates and who is left out of conversations. They use these observations to reach out to students whose voices are not being heard and find ways to include them. They work to notice and dismantle biases or blind spots in curriculum, instruction, and classroom norms and routines that could be privileging some student voices over others.

In this chapter, we offer many examples and participation strategies that promote listening for student voices as educators get to know their students, affirm them, and help them find their own voices. As educators learn about microaggressions, implicit bias, and code-switching, they can better support students of all backgrounds.

A final benefit of listening for student voices involves what educators do with what they have heard. While gaining familiarity with students' minds, a listening educator will have a mirror for reflecting on the effectiveness of their lessons. Did the students gain the intended knowledge through this lesson? If so, what is our next step? If not, what can we do differently?

In an identity safe classroom, educators see and disarm inequity and provide learning opportunities that support students to develop voice and identity along with mastering subject area knowledge and skills.

Listening for Student Voices: Making It Happen

Equalizing Status by Making Space for All to Participate

Making room for all students to be heard opens doors for educators to work toward equalizing status among peers. Large classes of students usually have a few who speak up at every juncture. Yet others are more shy and reticent. Some English learners feel awkward speaking and never open their mouths. Finding equitable ways for everyone to participate can be a daily battle.

An important beginning is to discuss with students why an equitable exchange of ideas matters. The teaching of listening as a skill supports adolescents in strengthening their emotional intelligence while cultivating content and linguistic mastery. From there, you can work together to establish specific routines and agreements for sharing the airwaves. Regularly changing the size of the groups—from partners to small groups to large groups—shifts the dynamics, enabling every student to speak. With students in groups, you can circulate, noticing patterns of participation and hearing what is being said.

Large-Group Strategies

In whole-group activities, varying the means of calling on students from the standard hand raising can create more equitable participation. The use of whiteboards, hand signals, and sticky notes requires each student to respond simultaneously, and you can quickly scan the room to see the responses. You can collect the sticky notes and read some of them aloud to the class.

Small-Group Strategies

A range of listening and sharing protocols offers structured ways to teach listening and support students in developing their thoughts by giving specific times and actions for each member of the group.

TALKING STICK

The talking stick (Indigenous Corporate Training, 2015) has been used by various Native American cultures. The stick is passed around the group, and only the person holding it speaks. The talking stick was used to teach patience, self-discipline, and respectful listening. Educators can explain how historically some Native American groups used a talking stick or eagle feather in council circles, potlatches, and other cultural events. As in all strategies, the effective way to use the talking stick needs to be modeled and taught.

- All students listen respectfully to the speaker without talking and with body language that expresses compassion and support to your peers.

- When one student stops speaking, the stick is handed to the next person in the circle.

- When it is your turn, introduce yourself.

- If the receiver does not wish to speak, it is passed to the next person.

- Listen without interrupting.

- Make an effort not to repeat previous comments.

You can always use a symbolic item as a "talking piece," including a beautiful shell, feather, or an item that means something to the group.

Think/Pair/Share

Partnering has become a commonly used strategy for encouraging participation. As such, it is worth taking the time to analyze it and ensure that its full potential for identity safety is realized. "Think/pair/share" involves asking students to think independently, then discuss with a partner, and finally share with the class. It can be used in a variety of ways by allowing students to explain a process or concept in their own words, explore their opinions on a topic, and respond to higher-level thinking questions. It can be part of a quick reflective experience or a longer activity that incorporates accountability strategies, such as asking each partnership to write down three main points that will be collected. While partners are working, educators can circulate. When the group-share time arrives, educators can refer to ideas that were heard or ask partners to share with the whole group. When using this strategy, it is important to teach, model, and practice to establish and sustain contributions that are robust and stimulating without being superficial.

When teaching the steps and expectations of partner sharing, explain the objectives, including the time frame allotted to speak and how to demonstrate respectful listening. Students can model the process, followed by a whole-group conversation to reflect on how well they met the objectives. This involves addressing content as well as their successes for working together, which include participating equally and listening to each other.

When educators pay attention to who is partnered together, they ensure that (1) one student is not doing all the thinking or working, (2) students are not turning work time into social time, and (3) all students are participating and coping well. Sometimes, pairing advanced students with those in a middle range is more effective than pairing an advanced student with one who is operating at a much less advanced level. The advanced student may become impatient and do all or most of the work while the other student may quit trying from a sense of inferior capability. Rather, pairing a midlevel student with a student who is less advanced increases opportunities for both to participate. In some classes, sticking with pairings for up to a semester brings deeper levels of connection and collaboration. For other classes, rotating pairs more frequently is useful as a way of gaining more experience through shorter pairings with various personalities and energy levels.

Think/pair/share and partnering activities are a valuable leading-edge method of formative assessment.

Jigsaw

The "jigsaw" method (Jigsaw Classroom, 2019) allows students to gain expertise on a topic and teach the new information to their classmates. Students first work in expert groups where together they learn a particular segment of content. Then, they go into a second group where each one is an expert in a part of the content and shares it with their other peers. This model gives each student the opportunity to be the "expert." Social psychology professor Elliot Aronson (Aronson & Patnoe, 1997) attributed

USING THINK/PAIR/SHARE TO CULTIVATE A GROWTH MINDSET CULTURE

An additional benefit of think/pair/share is to create a sense of classroom community where students are learning from each other.

- Think or write: Ask students to reflect on three aspects—what they did well, what aspects need growth, and what they will do differently in the future.

- Share three ideas with a partner.

- Students share their partner's three ideas with the class.

In this way, students can learn from each other. Often, time does not permit everyone to share. If this is the case, they can write their partner's ideas on a sticky note and post it. The educator can then select several sticky notes to share with the group.

the creation of the jigsaw method to his University of Texas (UT) graduate students. After some racially charged incidents that created tension among students in a high school, the graduate students developed the jigsaw method to offer a safe way for each student to make a significant and equitable contribution to the learning of the whole group.

Structured Listening Protocols

Structured listening protocols are carefully timed activities in which each student speaks on a particular topic while peers listen. The listeners then ask clarifying questions and

JIGSAW STEPS

The *Jigsaw Classroom* website (www.jigsaw.org) offers the following steps for this process:

1. Divide students into small groups of five or six students, referred to as Jigsaw Groups.

2. Assign a group leader.

3. Divide lesson content into five or six discrete content areas.

4. Assign each student in the Jigsaw Group to a different content segment.

5. Allow students to read their content segment once or twice without memorizing it.

6. Form Temporary Expert Groups. One student from each of the Jigsaw Groups comes together with the others who studied the same content segment.

7. Have Temporary Expert Groups discuss the segment they read and identify main points.

8. Return students to their Jigsaw Groups.

9. Ask each student to present and teach their segment to the rest of their Jigsaw Group.

10. Circulate to listen to groups working together and to clarify any points of confusion. Also, ensure that there are no problematic group dynamics.

11. Give a quiz or a simple writing activity at the end to ensure content has been learned.

Adjust the steps to meet your classroom's needs. This method equalizes status and offers each student a chance to learn independently, be scaffolded with members of their Temporary Expert group, and finally become the expert in their Jigsaw Group.

give feedback, and finally the initial speaker reflects on what they heard. A wide range of structured listening protocols can be used to develop the following specific skills:

- Listening without interrupting
- Asking for clarification
- Responding to high-level analysis and synthesis questions
- Hearing and responding to valuable feedback from peers

Careful preparation and monitoring ensures students understand the objectives of a structure that asks them to listen without interrupting, as the idea may be foreign to them. Carefully timed steps provide each participant with an equal time to speak. Using these strategies offers students a rare opportunity to be fully heard without the typical interjections. They learn that a crucial part of listening is honoring the speaker without cutting in or responding prematurely, although they might be tempted to do so.

What follow are two examples of structured listening protocols. Writing prompts and directions can focus on virtually any topic and can be aligned with learning standards and goals.

Method One: Storytelling Protocol

1. *Introduction* (2 min.): Define the purpose and explain the process to the entire class. Provide a fair method to determine the speaking order (e.g., their birthdays). Instruct them to select a timekeeper.

2. *Individual quick-write* (10 min.): Give time for individual reflection and writing. Provide questions on prompt sheets to elicit ideas and/or a personal story.

3. *Individual speaker time* (5 min.): Ask each speaker to choose how to describe the answers to the questions on the prompt sheet. Have speakers share at least two ideas with no interruptions.

4. *Group members respond to the speaker* (2 min.): They paraphrase what they heard, make suggestions, or express appreciation to the speaker. Speaker is to remain silent and listen.

5. *Speaker responds* (1 min.): Speaker responds to what was heard.

6. *Repeat* (8 min. per speaker): Do steps 3–5 for each member of the group.

7. *Small-group reflection* (2 min.): Small group reflects on the process of working together.

8. *Whole-class reflection* (5–10 min.): Students reflect on what they learned and share insights.

Method Two: Dilemma or Problem-Solving Protocol

1. *Introduction* (2 min.): Define the purpose and explain the process. Explain how the class will work with the information that results from solving this problem or dilemma. In some cases, students select one of the solutions to try. Provide a fair method to determine the speaking order. Instruct them to select a timekeeper.

2. *Individual quick-write* (10 min.): Give time for individual reflection, thinking, and writing. Provide questions on prompt sheets that describe a dilemma or problem. Ask students to pose solutions.

3. *Individual speaker time* (5 min.): Speaker shares about the problem and proposes solutions with no interruptions.

4. *Group members respond to the speaker* (2 min.): They paraphrase what they heard and ask clarifying and probing questions to go deeper into the problem and proposed solutions. Speaker is to remain silent and listen.

5. *Speaker responds* (1 min.): Speaker makes clarifications and answers probing questions.

6. *Group members offer suggestions* (3 min.): The group proposes additional solutions.

7. *Speaker responds* (2 min.): Speaker draws conclusions, summarizing learnings from the process of both thinking about the problem and hearing suggestions.

8. *Repeat* (13 min. per speaker): Do steps 3–7 for each member of the group.

9. *Small-group reflection* (2 min.): Small group reflects on the process of working together. In some cases, they select a solution and continue working to implement it.

10. *Whole-group reflection* (5–10 min.): Whole group reflects on the different problems and dilemmas, sharing the solutions. Sometimes, they come to consensus on a solution and work together on next steps.

Note: Determine the size of the groups by the time available.

Incorporating Active Participation, Anticipatory Set, and Closure as Part of Identity Safety

A beginning social studies teacher in a North Carolina high school said to his coach, Janet, "I'm sorry, but I prefer to not interrupt the flow of my lectures to have the students express their ideas."

Janet, a bit surprised, replied, "Then how can you know what the students are really learning? How do you know they really are listening, even when the class is quiet?"

Janet explains that beginning teachers often ask her how can they design lessons to ensure that their students' minds are continuously engaged. She shares *active participation* with them, an approach in which students are actively engaged for a minimum of once every 10 minutes. Active participation is a way to promote listening for student voices because when students participate, the process to encourage them to express and be heard becomes both obvious and natural. It also validates their thinking as an asset. For students who have experienced adverse learning experiences, ascribing value to their thinking is critical to reshaping their relationship to learning.

Active participation is a strategy drawn from the work of Madeline Hunter, a UCLA professor, who is known for developing mastery teaching strategies. Two kinds of active participation are characterized: *overt active participation*, in which the students outwardly express their thinking verbally or in writing, and *covert active participation*, where students are asked to be engaged within their minds through questions, visualizations, or problem-solving exercises.

Hunter (1982) promoted the use of active participation continually throughout a lesson. It is used during the *anticipatory set*, while initiating a lesson by accessing what each student already knows about a topic. A simple question given to students can spark their interest. Jamal, a math teacher, wanted his students to understand number components, so he gave his students a question: Which would you rather have: a penny doubled each day for a month or $1,000,000? (Answer: In 30 days of doubling a penny, you accumulate over $5,000,000). The students were totally captivated.

Lessons continue with a variety of strategies inserted every 10 minutes, including prompts to elicit covert participation, such as a question or visualization, together with overt participation, including a quick-write, think/pair/share, or asking students to record responses on a whiteboard.

Similarly, Hunter's model of *closure* asks each student to use active participation to individually summarize the key learnings of the lesson. Again, this can be done with partners, quick-writes, or "exit cards" handed in as students leave the class. Short closure activities consolidate learning and assist with retaining content.

Active participation is also used to elicit student opinions or experiences. When I was a school principal, I was called to an eighth-grade classroom after a bullying incident. Initially, the students appeared uncomfortable and were not willing to share. So I handed out sticky notes and asked students to write about their personal experiences with bullying without adding their names. I collected the notes and read some aloud, careful not to "out" any particular student. I now had their rapt attention and learned their true feelings about the situation. Then, they could discuss solutions openly.

With practice, incorporating active participation becomes a regular part of all lessons. Active participation is a powerful engagement strategy that invites students to feel heard and more deeply connected with content and their peers.

Finding Their Voice Through Self-Affirmation

At the beginning of 10th grade, my English teacher asked all students to write the 10 most important things in our lives. The teacher collected the papers and repeated the activity midyear and again at the end of the year on the same sheet of binder paper. The first 10 items I listed included summer vacation and a boyfriend that I did not have. By the end of the year, my final list included peace, having a mind that "thinks real thoughts," and making a difference in the world. These became the values that guided me for the rest of my life. I still have that faded piece of binder paper after 50 years.

The simple experience of students exploring and articulating their values strengthens both their self-confidence and voice. Self-affirmation theory came out of a research study (Sherman & Cohen, 2006) that was replicated many times. Researchers gave a "study group" of students the opportunity to write a short narrative about two or three values that were most important to them, explaining why. In contrast, the "control group" was also asked to write a short narrative about another topic. The difference between the two groups was that members of the study group considered and affirmed the values they believed in while the control group did not.

The researchers developed this intervention because they theorized that students, especially those from groups that have been negatively stereotyped about their ability, might improve their academic performance if they felt their values mattered. Results showed that this simple exercise served to improve grades for all students. However, it made the greatest difference in academic performance for Black students in the study group, especially those who previously had the lowest academic scores. This improvement reduced the racial achievement gap by 40 percent. The higher achievement effect lasted for a minimum of two years.

The researchers acknowledged that the impact of self-affirmation interludes may be relatively brief; however, they point out that over time, with multiple opportunities, the impact can be sustained. They posited that giving students an opportunity to engage with and express what matters to them would enhance their personal integrity and competence. Secondly, this enhanced sense of self could serve to overshadow and diminish the threatening cues and concomitant stress provoked by stereotype threat.

This simple activity made a difference in an experimental research context, just as the values assignment described earlier impacted my life. At LPS Oakland, before taking the annual state test in English language arts a few years ago, students were asked to do a quick-write about their values. That year, the school's Academic Performance Index (API) improved 97 points. This activity has become institutionalized at testing time and may contribute to their continuously improved achievement scores.

Educators can offer multiple opportunities for students to express their uniqueness and find their voice in a variety of ways on a consistent basis. This can be done in all subject areas as a way to affirm integrity and help students develop a positive academic identity.

In language arts, students find their voice through reading meaningful literature, analyzing it, explaining their thinking, and writing poems, narratives, and essays. There are so many opportunities to assign prompts to help students learn about themselves through reading and reflecting on the literature, as well as writing to express ideas and feelings, all of which can help students clarify their personal values.

Through visual and performing arts, students can express inner feelings and creativity, discovering the inside world of the self. In the sharing of their projects—through discussions about their creations—trust builds and shows students that their ideas are valued and worthy of respect.

Students can also discover their voices in both math and science, often considered topics that are less inclined toward natural expression. Self-expression is available when students learn to explain their thinking and discover new approaches and solutions. They gain confidence when they can describe how they solved a particular problem or corrected a mistaken notion.

In all subject areas, students need opportunities to reflect on how they work together and treat each other during classroom activities. These experiences, especially when exercised in all curricular areas, can be a tremendous benefit for students in finding and expressing their voice.

Engaging English Learners

A group of administrators wanted to better understand the experience of English learners at the high schools in their district. They spent an entire day shadowing individual English learners by observing them in each of their classes. To their surprise, many English learners—even some who had been in the country for over a year—sat silently in all classes, barely uttering a word, and appeared not to be engaged in any capacity. Researcher Stephen Krashen (1981) determined that most English learners spend a few days to six months in a *preproduction* period while they absorb the new language before they attempt to speak. Yet for some English learners, the silence lasts much longer than the preproduction stage necessitates. Educators need to monitor students to ensure they are not sitting quietly without learning and support them in active engagement and inclusion in classroom life.

Julie Mann teaches English learners who recently arrived in the United States at Newcomer High School in Queens. "Model, model, model" is her best advice. She regularly writes a sample assignment on a chart while verbally explaining her thinking as she writes. She also creates templates with graphic organizers to help students organize their ideas. Over time, she removes the scaffolds so they do not become dependent on them.

Julie also transforms given resources designed for fluent English speakers, breaking lessons into segment pieces, scaffolding each step. First, she pulls out vocabulary. Then, she creates journal questions related to the topics so students can formulate their ideas and write responses. She assures students that the journal writing need not be grammatically correct at first. She uses think/pair/share to allow students to express their ideas with a single other student. With this careful scaffolding, students feel more confident to participate in whole-group discussions.

For English language fluency in classrooms with diverse English levels, it is indeed a dance to achieve the right pacing and appropriate scope for everyone to experience full inclusion. The educator must balance the needs of English learners as they engage in curriculum alongside fluent students. It is important to find activities so even those new to the country can participate in meaningful ways. Here are a few identity safe strategies that bolster the inclusion of the English learners while not slowing the pace for fluent speakers:

- Teach them gestures to express comprehension or confusion.

- Use whiteboards to spark visual understanding.

- Use listening comprehension activities to grow receptive vocabulary.

- Encourage them to write down their ideas, and the educator or a fellow student can read them to the class.

- Change partners. At times, buddy them with a fluent student who does not speak their language to encourage both to make efforts to communicate clearly. At other times, partner two students together who speak the same language to have a deeper conversation in their primary language.

- Use scaffolds such as discussion prompts and cloze sentences (sentences with room to fill in the blanks).

- Engage students with visual aids and realia (items from real life).

- Use formative and summative assessments to deepen understanding. Also, ensure assessments are aligned to their current level of proficiency.

Having a bilingual buddy who speaks their language can strengthen their sense of belonging. However, take care not to allow them to interact exclusively in their own language or only with peers who share their background. Pairing them with a buddy who doesn't speak their language is a growing experience for both. When I was in high school, my biology teacher partnered me with two hearing-impaired students from Guam. I was tasked with teaching them about DNA and recall their blank looks with my first attempt. I hardly knew what I was talking about. So I started by scrutinizing the diagrams and words in our science textbook. Eventually, I figured it out. It became an unforgettable experience, both in learning to clearly explain scientific concepts and in a much deeper understanding of DNA for the two boys—and for me, too! The opportunity for English speakers to strengthen their comprehension can be an added bonus.

Creating Value and Expression for Home Language and Home Cultures

How can home languages and cultures be valued in identity safe classrooms? One great way is to embed many opportunities for sharing into everyday lessons and routines. For example, asking simple questions such as, "How would you say that word in your language?" or "What formula for multiplication did you use when you were taught math?" can offer a sense of community and inclusiveness.

The process of learning English can be very difficult, especially for older students who may remain silent in the fear that they will make fools of themselves. In identity safe classrooms, the space to make errors and the spirit of cooperation can offer lifesaving relief for those students. Julie Mann (2012), the teacher described in the previous section, wanted her English learners to feel a sense of belonging while still valuing their home cultures. Over the years, she developed a curriculum to help them express their feelings about their home culture and language, as well as how they've felt since arriving in the United States. They joined with another school where the immigrant students were partnered with a US-born peer and shared their stories. Julie's English learners became highly respected once the others learned of the trials and tribulations of their peers in leaving their homeland and coming to their new country. The US-born peers also were able to experience empathy for their English learner classmates in the process.

A few years later, Julie created a new project in which she asked her immigrant students to share about someone who welcomed them into their new lives in the United States. Then, she asked them to "pay it forward" by welcoming another newcomer. Julie videotaped student stories and shared them in an exhibition on Ellis Island called *First Person American*. The projects created a sense of pride and empathy and empowered her students.

Listening and Watching Through the Cacophony

Within a typical school day and across the rotations of many classes, commingled student voices may sound like cacophony—a loud and jarring roar. Just as the photographer develops a discriminating eye that can focus upon the most essential and meaningful elements, an educator can sharpen listening skills. An astute educator attends to both what a student says and doesn't say, while also noticing who speaks more often and who says practically nothing. By using structured listening activities such as those described earlier, educators can monitor how students initiate and elaborate on both their ideas and peers' ideas while forming theories about life.

Listening for student voices also includes *watching* or observing students carefully because up to 90 percent of communication may be nonverbal. Educators can watch for the congruence or lack thereof between spoken words and nonverbal cues, such as facial expression and tone of voice. Several studies produced a formula that considers 55 percent of communication stemming from body language, 38 percent referring to the tone of voice, and only 7 percent coming from the actual words spoken aloud. Context is always important to consider. Mehrabian (1972), an expert on nonverbal communication, warns that when speech does not match tone and body language, a person should pay *more* attention to nonverbal cues.

An educator can hone the skills of listening for student voices and watching into an art form. While you are deeply observing students, they can in turn notice that you are listening and watching them by paying attention to their verbal and nonverbal messages. Over time, this noticing turns into a kind of superpower, demonstrating to students that you "have their backs."

Listening for, Paying Attention to, and Addressing Implicit Bias and Microaggressions

Implicit Bias

No matter what background we come from, implicit bias is a feature of how our brains work. We included implicit bias in the part about listening for student voices because we need to listen for bias that lurks beneath the surface in ourselves and others, recognizing that it causes great harm.

Implicit bias has these qualities:

- It manifests through unconscious attitudes, emotions, or feelings.
- The person expressing the biased attitude is sometimes unaware of it.
- It can include negative or positive stereotypes about a person or group.
- It will result in automatic reactions, often without conscious intent.

Our brains are designed to operate quickly for survival. Throughout human history, we have always used stereotypes for protection. We fear people and events that are unfamiliar to us or surprise us. Our brains are wired to react, sometimes before we have a chance to think about what we are saying.

Since many of our stereotypes are based on old prejudices and incorrect assumptions about people who are different from ourselves, distorted perceptions creep into our sensitivities. These unconscious attitudes, or implicit biases, are absorbed across our lifetimes. They stem from living in a world teeming with negative stereotypes based on race, religion, ethnicity, gender, intelligence, and disability—the list goes on. In

IMPLICIT BIAS: WHAT IT LOOKS LIKE

Susan was the dean of students in a suburban high school. She tells the story of her youngest daughter, Vignetta. On the first day in ninth grade, Vignetta was nervous and forgot the room number for her math honors class. She entered class a few minutes late, apologizing as she walked in. The teacher, who was White, took one look at Vignetta, who was Black, and immediately said, "You are in the wrong class."

The students, who knew Vignetta from middle school, called out, "No, she is not in the wrong class!"

Susan questioned, "Why did the teacher think she was in the wrong class?" She surmised that it happened because Vignetta was a Black kid—and the teacher assumed a Black student could not be in honors math, adding, "The teacher probably did not even know she was making that assumption."

a system that grants privilege for some and negatively stereotypes others, biases can reside deep within a person. Othering can transfer unconsciously from mother to child, such as when a White mother may squeeze her child's hand as they pass a Black man on the street. We can find ourselves saying and doing things for which our conscious minds will not give credence.

RESEARCH ON IMPLICIT BIAS

Many research studies have shined a light on the way our implicit biases operate. By placing research subjects in situations where they must respond quickly, the biases emerge because people do not have time to think, drawing on automatic reactions that elucidate beliefs housed in their subconscious minds. Here are the results from one study:

Procedure:

- Participants were shown words with positive or negative associations (e.g., happy, awful).

- Images of Black and White faces were rapidly flashed on a screen.

- Participants were asked to classify the words as *pleasant* or *unpleasant*.

Results: White participants classified negative words faster after they were shown Black faces, suggesting a negative association with Black people (Woo, 2015).

In other research, the use of names associated with different racial groups triggered biased attitudes. In a study of 204 educators, predominantly White and female, the following tasks were given:

Procedure:

- Teachers were broken into two groups.
  - One group was given a description of misbehavior by a student with a Black-sounding name.
  - The second group was given the exact same description of misbehavior by a student having a more White-sounding name.

- Both groups were asked to rate the following:
  - The extent to which the student's misbehavior suggested a pattern
  - Whether they could imagine suspending the student in the future

Results: Students with Black-sounding names were significantly more likely to be labeled *troublemakers*, and they were punished more harshly. Black teachers in the study also punished Black students disproportionately, similar to the White teachers (Okonofua & Eberhardt, 2015).

There is hopeful news. Our brains are malleable and therefore implicitly biased associations can be gradually unlearned through a variety of intentional actions. Devine, Forscher, Austin, and Cox (2011) developed a "multifaceted prejudice habit-breaking" eight-week intervention. Participants were given a toolkit of strategies and were assigned to practice at least three of them consistently on a weekly basis.

The research results demonstrated that implicit bias could be reduced by intentionally working on the following areas:

- Positive intergroup relations
- Countering and replacing stereotypes and stereotype threat
- Empathy and perspective-taking
- Viewing people as individuals instead of a member of a group

The strategies for implicit bias reduction that were fully researched and vetted by Devine et al. (2011) in the experimental lab will also work well in an identity safe classroom. Educators can raise their awareness of unconscious prejudice and how it works. As part of the process, everyone can take free implicit association tests online through *Project Implicit* at Harvard University (www.implicit.harvard.edu). The tests measure unconscious bias. Beyond that, accepting accountability for our personal behaviors is key.

Strategies that Devine et al. (2011) found to reduce implicit bias are integral to our work as identity safe educators. They include promoting compassion, providing opportunities for relationships with people of different backgrounds, breaking down stereotypes; and understanding each person's unique identity. These actions are practiced on a daily basis as part of creating an identity safe classroom.

STARTING WITH THE SELF AND EXPANDING TO THE WORLD

Matt teaches humanities, including both English and social studies in a diverse San Francisco public school. He incorporates a variety of curricular activities (not just one) to help his students learn to break down stereotypes. He shows the TED Talk *A Call to Men* by Tony Porter (2010), who describes what is called the "Man Box." Porter illustrates how the walls that box men in are actually norms and expectations for tough masculinity, inculcated in boys from an early age. Matt poses questions to his students such as, "What might happen when you try to step out of the box?" and "Do you think there is a woman box or a gender nonconforming box?"

(Continued)

(Continued)

Matt tasks his students to explore the layers of their identities. He models by sharing from his own life. Then, he asks his students to reflect on their identities by writing in journals about themselves (e.g., socioeconomic status, racial, or ethnic identity). He asks them to fill in and then ponder the statements, "I am_____. But I am not_____." Capitalizing on the high level of trust Matt has already built in his classroom, he reminds students to tell peers only what they feel comfortable sharing, thereby increasing the trust.

From a personal, internal exploration, Matt expands the classroom focus to historical and current events that exemplify multiple perspectives. His students explore "master narratives" from mainstream and dominant groups, as well as counternarratives that present other perspectives. He teaches important vocabulary to ensure students understand these concepts.

Matt asks his students to question whose perspectives are most often represented in school texts, while contrasting those with the perspectives of individuals and groups who are consistently ignored. Students come to see for themselves how dominant narratives often distort and only tell part of the story. Viewing the narratives side by side, students identify what might be missing. Matt makes sure to point out that a White male perspective is not necessarily wrong, yet it is important not to treat it as the only point of view. Matt's students come to understand how entertaining a diversity of viewpoints is not only more fair, but it is necessary in order to adopt a balanced view of the world. Matt's lessons are designed to move back and forth between outside texts and "self as text."

As part of listening for student voices, we examine and listen for our own biases, and we listen to those of our students. As equity-literate educators, we also watch for biases embedded in schoolwide practices. From there, we are empowered to take swift action to counter all forms of bias and address them as they emerge. By listening/watching for implicit and explicit biases, we create classroom spaces where students feel safe and accepted. As part of this awareness, educators need to understand how biases show up in microaggressions.

Microaggressions

Microaggressions refer to derogatory comments and messages about membership in a group, be it racial, religious, a person's nationality, or otherwise (Sue et al., 2007). They are comments that reveal both implicit and explicit biases—sometimes as innocent and unaware remarks, yet other times intentionally as hurtful and rude. Students facing negative societal stereotypes can find themselves subject to daily microaggressions from a range of educators and students.

COMMON MICROAGGRESSIONS

Here are some examples of microaggressions that a student of color might hear regularly:

- Mispronunciation, jokes, or disparaging comments about their name

- Comments alluding to terrorism (often made to persons of Middle Eastern background)

- Comments about appearance: "Your hair is ugly," or "Check out that butt."

- Comments about intelligence: "You are stupid."

Additional repeated behaviors that devalue, discourage, and impair equity throughout a person's life also may include the following:

- Exclusion and marginalization

- Misidentification, confusing one person with another of the same ethnicity

- Jokes that target ethnicity or intelligence and the like

One common microaggression is when a White person says, "You are so articulate" to an African American. The person saying it often does not realize their own subtext, which can mean, "You are so articulate for a _____" (as if being articulate is rare for people of your race). Luvvie Ajayi (2018) explains how these types of remarks insinuate that most people of color are unintelligent and inarticulate and that the person exceeded what little is expected of them. Unfortunately, these are not isolated comments but instead are commonly and repeatedly heard by many people of color. Over a student's educational career, they take their toll, like a kind of death by a thousand paper cuts.

An important caveat involves considering the experience of microaggression as it is perceived by the person who hears it rather than the speaker's intent. The person making the comment may think or say out loud, "But that is not what I meant. You are taking it the wrong way." However, if a person feels degraded by the comment, it is important to listen and acknowledge how the comment is experienced in order to elicit compassion for kinder, more effective, and engaging communication.

Nobody is above making a microaggression. We all have the potential to make comments that we might come to regret. I once ordered a cake for a colleague with a decorative message written on it. When we gathered to eat the cake, the cake turned out to have a spelling error; I blurted out, "Must have been a person who did not know English." The minute it was out of my mouth, I felt like a complete fool, but the words were out. It was then up to me to acknowledge it as a microaggression.

Recently, Amy taught a guest lesson focused on reasoning with a rubric ("Using a Rubric to Learn How to Juggle") in a ninth-grade biology class. The class was about 95 percent Latinx and included just a few African American and mixed-race students. Amy called one of three African American young men by the name of another African American young man in the room. The reaction was strong and swift. The two young men were visibly upset, and the class collectively gasped. Amy felt sharp shame and regret for having caused harm. She recognized her action as a microaggression and that it would be neither helpful nor accurate to address it only as a slip of the tongue. Amy's mind focused on these students' skin color in the context of there being so few African American students in the room, and this actually interfered with Amy seeing these young men clearly as individuals.

Amy grounded herself (internally) to her deep commitment for all students to be safe and seen, to a growth mindset for herself, and to restoring this moment of harm. Fortuitously, she was at a point in the lesson that was about *self-talk*. As an example of self-talk, she shared that she was feeling shame and regret for mixing up Anthony and Ben's names, and her internal self-talk was saying things like, *You are disappointing! You are not a good teacher!* Then, she paused the lesson and said, "I need to name and apologize for what I just did in calling Anthony by Ben's name. Anthony and Ben, I am so sorry! I am so happy to get to meet you today and that we get to do this lesson and juggle and use a rubric together. The fact that I mixed you up when there are so few African American students in this class and in our school makes what I did more hurtful. I am so sorry to put you through that. I sincerely apologize and ask that you charge it to my head and not my heart. And I will never forget your names again!"

The class let out a collective release of breath. Anthony and Ben seemed relieved and accepted Amy's apology. Amy checked in with Anthony and Ben later that day individually. Anthony said this had happened before in another class, and it had not been addressed at all. Both students said they appreciated the apology and moved on to fully participate in the rubric/juggling lesson. Ironically, Amy had just that morning been called "Ellen" by the school office assistant. This is a frequent occurrence for Amy and Ellen, two middle-aged, short-haired White lesbians working in the LPS central office. Amy notes how when this kind of thing happens, belonging can be subtly weakened. She often uses self-talk in these moments to name and ameliorate harm: *I felt unseen. I am here to love and care for myself. I see myself. I belong here. I am thankful for the beautiful people in my life who see me.*

If we hear a microaggression addressed to us or someone else, we can call it out in a way that indicates why the comment was both untrue and hurtful. Whether we deliver a microaggression or get called out for one, we can take responsibility for it without becoming defensive. A feeling of safety grows in a space where students feel confident that microaggressions and all forms of bias will not be tolerated. It's essential to build these skills in ourselves and our students in a way that promotes both trust in each other and confidence in the process.

We have shared a range of examples of listening for student voices in an attempt to illustrate that when students feel heard and when their values, identity, and thinking are validated, trust grows, especially in a racially diverse classroom. By listening and showing genuine interest in the students, educators in all subject areas can help students find their authentic voice.

Dilemmas and Points of Tension

It Is OK to Share Our Vulnerabilities When a Lesson Misses the Mark

As mentioned earlier, by listening to our students, we can learn a lot about ourselves and the efficacy of our teaching. In addition, we can ask ourselves, "How is my teaching working to help with learning,—theirs and mine?" And when we miss the mark with a lesson, sharing our vulnerabilities can strengthen our relationships with students. It is both empowering and comforting for students to realize that their teachers are human and can make mistakes or fall short of the goal. When we can articulate our reflections to our students, it can serve to show them the impact of their voice upon us, their educators.

After reviewing exit tickets, Jenny, a teacher in Maryland, realized that many students still were unclear about the biology lesson. On the following day, she said, "Don't feel bad if you did not get it yesterday—you have company. I learned so much from your reflections. I realized that my lesson did not succeed at getting the point across. So today, I am trying a different way."

When the lesson went well, Jenny told her students, "I went through the tickets, and here is what I want to celebrate. . . ," and then she highlighted what they learned. This level of sharing sends a powerful signal to students that they are within a welcoming and safe environment and encourages them to continue offering their voice to each other and their teacher.

Code-Switching as a Survival Tool and Dilemma Within the Context of an Unfair World

Code-switching is a term used to describe the way we change our behavior in different situations, almost like expressing ourselves in different languages depending on the situation. It may involve how we dress differently when we go to school, attend a party, or simply when we are relaxing at home. It may address the casual way we talk—at times, using "unacceptable" language when talking to friends but never doing so at school. However, code-switching can also be a controversial topic when it highlights how people of color are often forced to adopt mainstream behaviors and language to "fit in" and "succeed" in the larger society that is clearly biased toward White supremacy and patriarchy. Often, Black students experience having their English "corrected" rather than having their educators recognize that their African

American Vernacular English (also referred to as Ebonics) is a valid way of speaking and communicating (Rickford & Rickford, 2000).

Teachers face a dilemma when considering how to approach code-switching. If students do not learn to speak "Standard English," they will lack language skills that allow them entry in mainstream higher education and parts of the workforce. Yet when a student's home language and culture are not valued or if students feel they must assimilate and switch their language use entirely, they are being subjected to a world that denies and devalues their home/community language experience. The message this communicates is a dour one that can be interpreted as a full rejection of their authentic selves.

By defining and discussing code-switching, students develop perceptions that allow them to analyze their approach to speaking and make personal choices in the context of the language and culture they want to address. When discussing the complexity of code-switching, our students will realize that we value their home cultures and languages. From there, we can communicate the need for code-switching and the reality that students often feel when torn about maintaining their family ways of interacting and speaking while being pressured to assimilate. We can also teach students to be more accepting of the fact that everyone code-switches and to hold back on judging themselves and their peers.

Take a minute to reflect on your teaching. A good question to ask is this: "Am I acknowledging a range of vernacular patterns in writing and speaking while teaching the difference between the Standard English version and the home language?" By using culturally rich literature that is available at every grade level, we can model the value of each culture's contributions.

Taking a Stand on the N-Word

One of the most controversial moments I experienced while giving a workshop happened in a discussion about the use of the N-word. This occurred in a bullying prevention workshop with people of diverse backgrounds and age groups from across the United States. Many voices and positions were expressed as the room grew tense. A Black woman in her 50s was adamant that the N-word was unacceptable and represented the hate and violence of years of oppression of Blacks in the United States, which matched my personal view. A White high school student from Tennessee explained that all her friends were Black, and since she was accepted by them, they all called one another the N-word freely. A Black police officer from upstate New York was almost in tears, asserting that hearing a White person use the N-Word was ignorant and racist, no matter what the reason. A Black high school student, also from Tennessee, said that among his friends, the word was used as a term of endearment, but if a White person used it, those became "fighting words." This range of positions was in no way unique to the people in that room. Subsequently, educators have shared in other workshops that their students hold a similar range of views.

The N-word carries baggage that cannot be ignored, and we believe that educators must make it clear to students that under no circumstances should the N-word be used. Chiaku Hanson (2016), in her *Huffington Post* blog, writes,

I petition the N-word be banned from the mouths of people of African descent, and especially be banned from the vocabulary of non-Black people. We have to stop justifying the N-word and its meanings [whether the word ends with an "er" or an "a"]. It has the same meaning and its intent is not positive and every time the word is used, it is not used in a positive manner. Just think about it. Almost every time the word is used to describe someone or something, there is a negative connotation behind the usage of the word. If a word cannot be used in court, chances are, it's a bad word.

Dr. Eddie Moore (2017), director and founder of the Privilege Institute and the White Privilege Conference and who has been giving workshops to educators for the last 15 years, suggests that educators go beyond banning the word. He suggests all educators need to reflect on the visceral power of the word in each of our lives and the lives of others. In addition, he feels that every educator needs to study the history of the word both when used verbally and through the unjust treatment of and policies toward Blacks, whether or not they are called the word. This is one arena where identity safe educators should have no grey areas.

Chapter Summary

In this chapter, we launched into the components of identity safety, beginning with the idea of *Listening for Student Voices* from many perspectives. We started by exploring ways to support students in finding their voice. We provided strategies for allowing all voices to be heard, with the aim of equalizing status. We further investigated ways to equalize participation in class through a variety of structures and processes, from using jigsaw activities, where every student becomes an expert in some aspect of the content, to structured listening protocols, where each student is able to share thoughts and feelings and solutions to problems. We described the importance of having students engage in a process of active participation every 10 minutes to maintain engagement throughout lessons. We highlighted the importance of attributing value to students' home languages and suggested strategies for supporting English learners. We also identified activities of self-affirmation, by having students express what matters to them, which can strengthen a student's confidence and help them find their voice.

We then shifted focus to the educator with the idea of developing a "superpower" through noticing our students while attending to both verbal and nonverbal cues. We introduced the need for educators to develop awareness of microaggressions and implicit bias. Negative stereotypes and biases frequently either burst forth in our classrooms or slowly creep in, inducing great harm, especially if they are not addressed. These common occurrences hinder identity safety.

We shared three dilemmas. The first involved admitting when a lesson has missed the mark. While it may be hard to admit, sharing vulnerabilities often strengthens trust and our students' respect for our willingness to be human. The second dilemma concerned ways to approach code-switching. We suggest affirming students' values and validating their dialects and cultures while also teaching them to be fluent in mainstream language use. Presenting the issue to students will help them find their own balance between Standard English and their home dialect. Finally, we took a strong stand on use of the N-word, stating that this was one area where educators must adamantly refuse to allow it.

Listening for student voices is essential in a student-centered, identity safe classroom, and we encourage educators to frequently circle back to this component as we move forward in presenting the rest of the components.

Check Yourself

When considering how you are working on listening for student voices, check yourself with the following questions:

1. How do you create opportunities for students to make authentic choices about their learning? Are the choices motivating for students at different academic levels? How are you helping students learn about and practice making choices?

2. How do you draw English learners into conversation in ways that are comfortable and yet encourage risk-taking?

3. What are ways you can use techniques to promote self-affirmation that align with the research?

4. In what ways can you address code-switching?

5. Has the N-word been said in your classroom? How have you handled it?

TRY IT OUT: END-OF-CHAPTER ACTIVITIES

This activity (D. M. Steele & Cohn-Vargas, 2013) has been used in many study groups. Educators find it illuminating and that it leads to greater student participation.

1. Reflect on your personal experience with speaking in a group, both when you were a student and in the present.
   a. Do you feel free to speak up in groups?
   b. What allows you to feel safe to speak up in one place but not another?

2. Consider your students who come from backgrounds different from yours.
   a. How might their experience be like yours, and how might it be different?
   b. Are any of your students' voices silenced—perhaps not by you, but by past experiences of being marginalized?

3. Observe the speaking patterns in your classroom.
   a. Make a simple tally of who is speaking in the group. Mark the initials of each child who speaks. We suggest you do this more than one time.

4. Analyze your data and determine next steps:

    a. How many students in the class spoke out loud in the discussion?

    b. Which students spoke more than once?

    c. Which students did not speak at all?

    d. What were the social identities of those who spoke and those who did not speak?

5. How can you extend opportunities to ensure everyone gets a chance to speak?

6. Brainstorm three strategies to try to increase participation.

 Available for download as a full-page form at **https://resources.corwin .com/IdentitySafeClass6-12**

4 Teaching for Understanding

Why Teaching for Understanding Matters

When I first became interested in identity safety, I questioned Dorothy Steele, the original researcher, about why a particular style of teaching made a difference in fostering a sense of identity safety. Would it really matter if educators used a more direct instruction model as opposed to constructivist teaching that highlights the importance of meaning-making and understanding?

Dorothy explained that *Teaching for Understanding* emerged as a significant component in the identity safety research because unless students have a basis for deeper understanding, they might not feel fully competent and confident in their knowledge, which would lead to a feeling that they do not belong. Often, course content focuses on memorizing a set of discrete facts and details that can be taught out of context without providing a basis for true understanding. By ensuring that concepts are deeply understood, such as when students learn the link between new knowledge and a larger body of content, they are much more likely to feel competent. This feeling of competence helps them become full participants in the learning experience. The identity safety researchers found a positive correlation between constructivist instruction, a liking for school, and a positive sense of identity safety reported on student surveys—and, ultimately, reflected in higher scores on standardized tests.

Teaching for understanding becomes crucial for academic success as well as an essential ingredient for preparing students for college, career, and community. Students need to understand text well enough to analyze it, synthesize their ideas in their writing, and become adept in higher-level thinking and problem-solving in order to ensure success in college and beyond. Understanding is necessary in forming the building blocks needed to move forward from basic math to meeting college requirements for higher-level math. Learning the formulas for algebraic equations without understanding how they work becomes an activity of memorization and makes it much harder to retain the knowledge as the content grows more complex. This is also true for scientific and other theoretical content.

Without deeper understanding, a student can feel tangled and lost in a forest of seaweed, unable to mark a clear path. Sometimes, students can feign success, memorizing facts that allow them to pass quizzes. However, this does not constitute deeper learning and eventually the information fades from lack of use. In addition, that lost feeling erodes their sense of competence. A series of failures can lead to a sense of *learned helplessness*, a term that researcher Martin Seligman (1975) coined to describe a phenomenon he observed in the laboratory. In a study that is painful to describe, dogs and rats were repeatedly submitted to electric shocks. Eventually, the researchers provided methods to avoid the shocks, but after repeated suffering, the animals did not even bother to try to escape them. The cycle of learned helplessness is found in humans when they feel a lack of control over their personal situations and eventually give up, leading to depression. Research on learned helplessness in education has led to identification of a vicious cycle, where a repeated experience of lack of success decreases motivation. Unmotivated students stop trying, which leads to additional failures (Diener & Dweck, 1978). By teaching in a way that ensures understanding, and with careful scaffolding, students can avoid getting stuck in this cycle. Also, it is important to empower the students with tools to navigate their learning and seek help when they do not understand.

Author Zaretta Hammond (Knight, 2018) speaks of shifting the "cognitive load" from the educator to the student. She explains that many students who have fallen behind become too dependent on adults to help them. Hammond explains that the experience of feeling competent is more effective for building confidence in their capabilities as opposed to the alternative—first attempting to boost confidence alone in order to achieve competence. Teaching for understanding and helping students learn to assess their own progress shifts the cognitive load to students and can thereby lead to a deeper understanding of content. Placing students in the driver's seat and guiding them to experience success can serve to build both competence and confidence.

Across our planet today, people need to be able to navigate multiple perspectives and solve demanding problems. Teaching for understanding helps prepare students for the rapidly changing world of vocations and careers that requires a workforce that is able to understand and express complex ideas in the context of change. We will share specific strategies for teaching for understanding across all content areas, tools that can give students a solid foundation of knowledge and skills that will enable them to function effectively and thrive in our complex world.

Teaching for Understanding: Making It Happen

Finding Relevance and Taking Accountability for One's Learning

One of the biggest disconnects for secondary students is the lack of relevance between their interests and lives and much of what they study in school. They question the value of what they are learning. They hear, "Get good grades and you go to college; then you can make a good salary and your future is secured." The big reward dangled over their heads feels unreal in respect to what they see around them and in the world. For many, the future does not look so rosy. Many students witness family members holding several jobs just to survive. Others have seen siblings go to college and drop out or graduate and then not be able to find a job or afford a home.

In addition to not finding relevance in school, youth are becoming accustomed to more tangible, immediate, and dazzling rewards. Instant gratification is at their fingertips with their cell phones and other devices. How can we, as educators, hope to compete with virtual reality, Snapchat, Instagram, and more? Since we are competing for attention with the array of technological and social distractions, we need to pique our students' curiosity with interesting and challenging material and pedagogy with meaning for them.

I still can recall the time when my physics teacher posed a dilemma to the class. His wife had a fender bender and needed to prove to her insurance company that it was not her fault. Students worked in teams, wrestling with all the details of the accident: her velocity, distance from the other car, and road and weather conditions. We were all getting our licenses at the time, so we scrambled to figure this one out. In every subject area, we can create relevance to motivate and engage our students in understanding. In the following sections, we present strategies that lead to relevance and accountability.

Inquiry Draws in Student Minds and Connects to Their Lives

Inquiry has been broadly defined across the field of education, but most educators consider it a process in which students are introduced to a phenomenon or topic and explore it, generating questions and hypotheses. They then develop investigation plans to test their theories and draw conclusions to make broader meaning from what they learned. Inquiry is learner-focused and learner-driven, requiring students to make predictions, gather evidence, and test their hypotheses. The *Next Generation Science Standards* (NGSS) expect students to engage in authentic investigations linked to core ideas and cross-cutting concepts (big ideas that apply across content areas). Inquiry is highly recommended to help students approach problems using higher-level thinking to synthesize ideas from multiple sources and learn practices that are used in the real world. Often, inquiry sparks genuine curiosity.

Inquiry can be structured as a continuum of learning experiences, negotiated along the way. Instructional coach and author Trevor MacKenzie (2016) describes four kinds of inquiry that incorporate increasing levels of student autonomy:

1. *Structured inquiry:* The educator generates a question and guides students through the steps needed to investigate it.

2. *Controlled inquiry:* The educator identifies essential questions and provides specific resources, and students take it from there, working to investigate and draw conclusions.

YOU DON'T HAVE TO DESIGN ALL INQUIRY-BASED CURRICULUM YOURSELF

You can find many well-designed inquiry-based lessons that meet the Next Generation Science Standards, saving educators the precious time required to create them. Here is one example from a biomedical engineering lesson (RET Program, College of Engineering, 2016):

After investigating the structure of a turkey femur, students make their own prototypes using clay to exactly match bone structure. They are tasked with creating a prosthesis for a turkey and must design a replacement bone to transplant into it. They then develop hand-generated methods to replicate their bone replacement. If a 3D printer is available, the lesson includes an added dimension for replicating the bones. The lesson plan provides all the steps, as well as pre- and postassessments.

This lesson comes from *TeachEngineering* (www.teachengineering.org), a free web-based digital library collection with a series of lessons geared to all grade levels, K–12. The lessons are matched to K–12 engineering standards.

3. *Guided inquiry:* The educator identifies a range of topics. Students select one, identifying the necessary resources to investigate it. Then, they design a product, providing evidence that leads to their conclusions.

4. *Free inquiry:* Students work independently to choose topics, find the needed resources, gather the evidence, and determine the best way to present it.

In some cases, students or small teams are assigned different pieces of a larger topic (e.g., genocide in different nations and historical periods), and then they bring them together to collaboratively understand a particular phenomenon.

While most secondary science, math, and even literacy and social studies curricula resources are designed to be teacher-directed, an educator can compensate for a lack of student-centered activities by inserting inquiry experiences as simple as inviting students to pose questions. This can offer more autonomy to students as they negotiate their responses.

In his blog on inquiry, MacKenzie (2016) advises that the process of adding inquiry can begin with small steps as you choose one of your favorite units and add essential questions. He also suggests you start with one of the types of inquiry described earlier. When introducing inquiry, educators are tasked with addressing the discomfort stemming from uncertainty some students may experience. They can closely monitor these students, encouraging them along the way, helping them over hurdles, and addressing their doubts or ambiguity.

TRUSTING STUDENTS TO FIGURE OUT THINGS THEMSELVES

Christy Alper (2018), a New Jersey high school science teacher, worked with colleagues to incorporate inquiry into their school's biology curriculum. They used a case study to introduce DNA by giving each student a DNA sequence with a corresponding amino acid sequence. They asked students to look for patterns, generate questions, and predict how the proteins were produced. They were guided through the exploratory activities and then worked with peers to interrogate their thinking. For Alper, it proved to be more frustrating than she expected. She found herself wanting to give the right answer rather than trusting the students to use the evidence to examine the phenomenon independently, even when it was a messy process. Alper suggests that for successful inquiry, educators must let go of their controlling tendencies and avoid swooping in to correct students, allowing the process to unfold in a relaxed manner, learning to live with some of the messiness.

Project-Based Learning (PBL)

PBL is a more complex inquiry methodology that engages students in long-term projects where they master key content and skills, gather evidence, and apply what they learned. Through this process, they develop the capacity to reflect on what they have learned and transfer the skills and knowledge to other situations. Edutopia.org has a wealth of information and videos on PBL.

PBL: Preconditions

Before embarking on a PBL project, educators need to give careful consideration to its placement within the arc of the curriculum and ensure that it connects to the learning standards for the course. Educators can identify topics of interest to students that match the course's curricular outcomes. Although the students will be executing the project, the educator needs to be well-versed in the content to ensure that student solutions are based on data rather than random guessing.

Project Selection and Preparation

PBL projects take careful planning. Select open-ended problems that require complex thinking yet contain challenging and attainable solutions. At times, the educator may need to provide some of the critical pieces of information that students have difficulty finding on their own.

PBL often incorporates collaboration, requiring students to obtain some information from their peers to effectively solve the problem. Groups work best with mixed abilities and a blend of personalities with individual accountability built in to the process.

Monitoring and Assessment

Since educators cannot be present in all small groups at once, structured journal prompts help them understand students' rationale, the evidence of data collection, and the methods for revising and repairing mistakes. Students can use rubrics for evaluating their designs and results.

Demonstrating Knowledge

PBL projects offer choices for presenting findings to the class. Posters, role-playing, and PowerPoint presentations allow students to demonstrate learning. Insisting on rigor requires students to provide a full description of the problem, include evidence of their findings, and analyze their results or solutions in order to form the basis for the grade.

All forms of inquiry are excellent strategies for identity safe classrooms because they adopt real-world problems tailored to the interests of the students and serve to teach for understanding. Inquiry activities rely on higher-level thinking skills. Students engage in academic discourse that incorporates and authenticates their identities by drawing from their personal lives and backgrounds.

RESEARCH ON PBL

When researchers investigate PBL, they examine various indicators: test scores, grades, content standards, and thinking skills. Here are the results from one PBL study:

Procedure:

- Eighth-grade history/social studies students researched the time period of the 1800s and created minidocumentaries.

- They were required to use state standards as part of the project and present their documentaries at a community event.

Results: They significantly increased their knowledge of historical research skills (Hernandez-Ramos & De La Paz, 2009).

In a three-year PBL study in the UK, mathematics professor Jo Boaler (1997) also investigated retention of content, an important consideration in math because learning new content builds on a foundation of prior knowledge:

Procedure:

- Boaler compared the use of open-ended projects with a direct instruction approach.

Results: Boaler found that students retain information longer after completing PBL projects. On the UK National Exam, students using PBL scored three times higher than those who did not (Boaler, 1997).

Service Learning: Applying New Understandings

Service learning projects can take knowledge to a new level in a practical and meaningful way that helps the community. There are many types of service learning activities, from beach cleanup campaigns to water-saving projects. The difference between service learning and other volunteering is that students conduct research, plan, and execute activities at various levels of complexity. Educators need to locate service learning projects in the arc of their curriculum and employ rigorous application of the content standards for their particular course. Educators and involved members of the community can collaborate to design and deliver meaningful service learning experiences.

Service learning activities based on the students' interests serve to promote identity safety because students are meaningfully connected to the community in a manner that empowers them to make a positive difference. They learn valuable skills in research and interviewing, as well as in analysis and synthesis of their findings. As part of the experience, they feel valued when taken seriously. Student identities and realities expand as they are authentically participating in the world.

PROJECT TO IMPROVE THEIR SCHOOL

As high school seniors from a private school in the Boston area, Jamilah and Stuart worked on a project to propose ideas for redesigning their school to make it more equitable in status, access, and opportunity for students of all backgrounds. Jamilah chose the project because it had special meaning for her. As one of the few students of color during all her years at the school, she often felt like an outsider.

Stuart, her work partner, also was highly motivated to do this project. He grew up in a small coastal town where most people were White, like himself. Stuart's eyes were opened when he attended a diverse national leadership conference. He wanted to share his developing awareness about diversity with all the students in his school rather than only through a specialized trip offered to only a few students. Through their project, the two hoped to help contribute to a more welcoming environment for future students of color at their school. They started by reading literature about school transformation. Then, they interviewed teachers and administrators from their school, as well as school leaders from around the United States. I met them because they interviewed me about making their school more identity safe.

They synthesized what they learned and led a professional development workshop for their teachers. We stayed in touch, and they told me how it felt to share personal examples of some of the school's inequities with their teachers. They mentioned being surprised when a couple of their teachers were defensive. Overall, Jamilah and Stuart felt they got their message across and were encouraged that their ideas were taken seriously by faculty and administration.

Addressing Identity Safety in STEM Classes

STEM educators sometimes think identity safety is more relevant for the humanities and classes in which the content includes literature and discussion. As we demonstrate in the examples throughout this part, identity safety is an approach to how classrooms function as a whole. The process of creating a sense of belonging and validation of a student's identity encompasses much more than verbal exchanges—it involves the way educators treat students, including how feedback is given and mistakes are handled, and the way that students treat one another.

What's more, negative stereotypes about achievement gaps for students of color in math and science make it imperative for STEM educators to consider how to create identity safety that leads to a strong academic identity. Offering counternarratives and providing models of inventors and mathematicians of color are always beneficial to show students future career options while breaking down the stereotypes. These valuable supports help motivate students to succeed. As a gatekeeper for higher education, advanced math courses are required, and students' grades in those courses influence which college will accept them.

Students who enter community college after failing basic math classes must start with remedial courses that do not factor in as college-level courses. This can turn into a permanent setback. Rosalia was already behind in math when she came to the United States from El Salvador in fourth grade. Her fourth- and fifth-grade teachers were strong in teaching literature but weak in teaching math. By sixth grade, Rosalia had learned English quickly—she won a citywide essay contest—but she struggled with fractions, ratios, and other basic math skills. Through high school, she had good language arts grades, but she had given up on math, which she referred to as her worst subject, repeatedly failing geometry and algebra. After graduating, she attended community college, where she failed math entry exams and was directed to take remedial math. Rosalia tried to remedy this by hiring a tutor, but it was too much to learn in such a short time, and she continued to fail. Eventually, while mastering English Lit with excellent grades, Rosalia dropped out and did not graduate from college. Without passing those crucial math classes, her career options were severely restricted. She eventually was able to start her own business, but she still wants to complete a college degree.

The story of Rosalia is, sadly, not unusual. Here are suggestions for ways to support identity safe achievement for students in all levels of STEM courses:

- Ensure students have a deep understanding of the concepts through a liberal use of supportive scaffolding.

- Create a growth mindset culture where students help one another learn.

- Ensure students feel safe to make and learn from their mistakes.

- Introduce counternarratives to challenge stereotypes that female, Black, and Latinx students are not smart in math and science.

- Consider and reframe intentional and unintentional messages that undermine student competence and confidence.

STEM educators need to watch for the impact of stereotype threat on students, express high expectations that they can become competent in math and science, and identify and fill in the learning gaps that may hamper academic success.

Formative Assessment: Making Meaning to Drive Learning

Identity Safe Formative Assessment Draws From All Domains

In identity safe classrooms, formative assessment (FA) can contribute to the domain of student-centered teaching (Part II), but it also supports many identity safety components. FA facilitates teaching for understanding because both student and educator are monitoring understanding on a regular basis. Classroom autonomy (Chapter 6) is promoted because students learn tools to use independently that they can continue to use across their educational career. FA promotes a focus on cooperation (Chapter 5) and listening to student voices (Chapter 3) because it focuses on listening, learning, and growing together as opposed to competition for the highest grades. For FA to be successful, it is required that students trust both educators and peers, as addressed in the domain of classroom relationships (Part IV). FA promotes cultivating diversity as a resource (Part III) because holding high expectations (Chapter 8) in the context of a challenging curriculum (Chapter 9) requires seeing and valuing the diversity that students bring into the room. Finally, FA takes into consideration the domain of a caring classroom environment (Part V) by paying attention to prosocial development (Chapter 14).

While FA draws from all domains for identity safety, we have placed it in this chapter about teaching for understanding because it is fundamentally about students' agency and opportunity to grow as thinkers and guides of their own learning. With proactive

Graphic of Formative Assessment Feedback Loop

Source: WestEd, Student Agency in Learning Course, 2018.

attention, educators can provide a pathway of growth and success for every student. We can avoid reproducing hierarchies of academic status that can be particularly activated by the evaluative nature of assessment.

Formative assessment is an ongoing feedback loop, organized around three guiding questions: *Where am I going? Where am I now? Where to next?*

This type of robust feedback process stands out as one of the most impactful instructional factors for student learning (Marzano, 2008; Paddington Teaching and Learning, 2013; Visible Learning, 2017). Some cycles will be quick and informal, such as an activity focused on a single standard based on yesterday's exit ticket. Other cycles will be longer and more complex and may involve unpacking and calibrating to a rubric, student goal-setting and monitoring, peer feedback, multiple drafts, and more.

Belief and Counternarrative

The notion of assessment conjures up any number of positive or negative memories for many people. When recalling these memories, feelings of happiness or joy can radiate through one's body with the recollection of an accomplishment. Feelings of heaviness of doubt or shame can also surface if the memory triggers a reminder of a setback or "failure." Historically, the role of assessment in schools has created conditions in which students, particularly students of color and other students who have been marginalized, receive messages that they are less capable at demonstrating the wisdom and knowledge they possess. These messages become stories we tell ourselves which, over time, become beliefs around whether or not we are in fact capable of learning a given subject or task. Enacting equitable learning experiences in schools requires us to disrupt these narratives by communicating to students our belief in them and by designing learning structures and experiences that create stories that are filled with promise and possibility. Formative assessment is a means to practice our deep belief in students' capabilities as thinkers and doers (Zambo & Zambo, 2008). But without identity safety, feedback can be experienced as confirming a stereotype rather than fueling growth.

The Learning Zone

In his TED Talk *How to Get Better at the Things You Care About*, Eduardo Briceño (2017) notes that effective people and teams go through life deliberately alternating between the *learning zone* and the *performance zone*. In the learning zone, we concentrate on what we haven't mastered yet, and we expect to make and learn from mistakes. In the performance zone, we concentrate on what we have already mastered and aim to minimize mistakes. While both zones have an important role, it is a lack of the learning zone that hinders growth for many students. Formative assessment is the enactment of the learning zone. As such, it is crucially important that a growth mindset (see Chapter 1: The Introduction) permeates every step and aspect of the cycle.

Phase One: Where Am I Going?

In this phase, educators and students center on clear learning goals and a view of what the work looks like when done well. *Learning goals* originate from sets of standards, learning targets, daily objectives, or other taxonomies of what students know and are able to do. Students gain the most benefit from formative assessment when they have an opportunity to explore and inform the learning goals so that they are truly understood and valued. When assessment moves forward without this understanding and valuing in place, it may be experienced as a sorting mechanism or a hoop to jump through rather than as a support for learning.

Success/growth criteria represent what the task looks like when done well and as skills progress. Growth criteria are often expressed as rubrics or checklists describing the components and qualities present in the work across a developmental continuum. Review and analysis of "anchor" examples of student work representing different levels of mastery on a task further supports student understanding of quality work. Educators can engage students in calibration to collectively score an anchor piece of work with a rubric and then compare and discuss their ratings to deepen clarity of what the task looks like when accomplished well.

Mary Murphy (2018b) recommends the terminology *growth criteria* to emphasize a focus on growth and cultivate a view of mistakes or current skill gaps as opportunities for growth rather than as markers of failure. In the *Where Am I Going?* phase, we can engage these steps to amplify trust in our growth mindset and in the formative assessment activities:

- Preteach about neuroplasticity: The brain is like a muscle that we grow with effort and practice all through our lives rather than intelligence being fixed from birth.

- Share examples of our own process of using mistakes as learning opportunities.

- Assist students to connect new learning goals to prior understandings and skills.

In this phase, we can personally assure students of their capacity to reach the learning goals we'll be managing together. Student performance may be undermined by the fear of being stereotyped and teacher performance by the fear of being viewed as prejudiced. We can affirm that the feedback they will receive is a reflection of our high standards and our absolute faith that they can reach these standards. *Wise feedback* strategies (see Chapter 10: Teacher Warmth and Availability for Learning) express high expectations and honor students' capacity and progress while providing critical feedback for improvement, thus mitigating trust gaps that can interfere with formative assessment for both students and teachers. We can preadvertise the support that will be available——reflection and planning activities, goal-setting and monitoring, teacher and peer feedback, multiple drafts, retakes, office hours, and so on—so that every student can succeed.

These guiding questions can assist educators to make this phase of the formative assessment cycle identity safe:

- How do we build trust with and among students in the feedback loop?

- To what degree do both educators and students understand and value the knowledge and skills that will be taught?

- How do we express our excitement about the knowledge and skills being taught and their relevance for students' lives?

- How do we express and model a growth mindset and faith in students' capacity to succeed at the task?

- How do we provide opportunities for students to explore, discuss, and give feedback on the learning goals and growth criteria?

- For students seeing less value in the knowledge and skills, how will we hear and respond to their experience and concerns?

- How do we use course syllabi, rubrics, and other formats to communicate learning goals and growth criteria to students?

- Are students clear about instructions, and do they have access to examples of what the task looks like when done well?

Phase Two: Where Am I Now?

In this phase of the feedback loop, students engage with a task or test to produce evidence of learning, and based on this evidence, they receive feedback on their learning in reference to the learning goals and growth criteria. To be identity safe, the task is aligned to rigorous learning goals and is accessible and interesting to students. The connection to learning goals is kept clear by using a rubric or checklist or through a

STUDENT AWARENESS AND VALUING OF LEARNING GOALS

LPS educator Billy Lieberknecht previews learning goals with students at the start of each unit. He and his students work through new vocabulary and clarifying questions, and they connect the learning goals to cross-cutting "big ideas." Billy provides descriptive rubrics and anchor pieces of student work to make clear what the task looks like when done well. Student input continuously shapes the language of the learning goals and rubrics to make it as accessible and relevant as possible; then, those learning goals and rubrics are used throughout the learning. One of his students shared, "It all connects, so there are not just random questions. It all connects to what we are learning, and for me, that is really helpful."

test by demonstrating how items align with specific learning goals. This setup produces very specific evidence of learning that enables educators and students to offer and receive goals-aligned, actionable feedback for growth.

Gathering meaningful evidence is at the heart of formative assessment. It is essential to take into account all the different ways students learn and to avoid placing students on the spot or singling them out in any way. We can boost student agency and comfort working with evidence and feedback by actively teaching and using a set of routines throughout the year. We can create identity safe conditions by continuing to teach and model the growth mindset and enacting the core wise feedback strategies discussed in "Phase One: Where Am I Going?"

Digital technology plays an important role in this phase. Most assessment management platforms now accommodate many task formats and provide reports for both educators and students, including the standard level alongside the overall results. Tools such as the Chromebook add-on Goobric (Bharti, 2015) aid in providing rubric-centered feedback to students. Google apps and platforms such as the website *Sown to Grow* (www.sowntogrow .com) can be used to gather and organize students' goals, reflections, and plans. Some formative assessment is best served through analog means—as verbal academic dialogue or through a paper-based student binder of work, reflections, goals, and plans.

FIVE INSTRUCTIONAL ROUTINES

The following instructional routines support educators to elicit formative evidence of learning during instruction (CASEL, 2019):

1. Elicit evidence through activating prior knowledge.

This is a crucial tool to set a foundation for students to gain new information and additional learning. Prior knowledge can be activated through journals, graphic organizers, anticipatory set activities, and KWL charts (charts made to access prior knowledge—the group works together before a unit of student to identify *K*: what they know and *W*: what they want to learn, and after completing the unit, they summarize *L*: what they have learned). Prior knowledge activation is crucial throughout the learning experience, not just at the start of a unit or lesson.

2. Elicit evidence through academic dialogue.

Academic dialogue is done in ways that assure that all students have equal access to participation. Trios, partner conversations, small groups, and large groups offer differing venues to promote academic dialogue. Each of these structures for dialogues can be modeled and practiced with norms or agreements for how the students can work together. Students also can be taught to express diverse points of view and respectfully listen, even while disagreeing with one another. Educators can use observation tools to document students' progress, and/or students can reflect on their participation and progress toward learning goals.

3. Elicit evidence through questioning.

By planning questions, educators probe for deeper levels of understanding. Students can respond using written, verbal, and graphic modalities. This can be collected as evidence.

4. Elicit evidence through observation and analysis of student work.

Student work offers an insightful lens into student thinking that can be reviewed and analyzed by the educator. The educator can expand the range of student products beyond the traditional written responses to include concept maps, outlines, models, and other ways to demonstrate knowledge.

5. Elicit evidence through peer feedback and self-assessment.

The use of peer feedback and self-assessment is another valuable method for gathering evidence. In identity safe classrooms, not only are the students taught respectful ways of providing feedback, but also care is taken to assure the pairing of students with peers promotes a positive experience and avoids a negative one.

Phase Three: Where to Next?

In this phase, students and teachers reflect on progress, identify growth areas, and plan next steps to improve. FA is sometimes viewed primarily as a process by which teachers get data on student progress. This is certainly one component, but FA's biggest asset is as an opportunity for students to drive their own learning, with our consistent, responsive support. Teachers model a parallel process of reflecting on our progress for supporting student achievement of our high standards. We use our own experience to model the growth mindset and learning process. We can teach and demonstrate a willingness to be vulnerable about "not-yet" areas, while keeping faith that—through sustained effort—we will achieve our goals for student learning. We can model using evidence to identify and improve in priority areas, and show students the sense of competence that arises from taking charge of our learning journey and outcomes.

Phase Three is about where learning and growth go next. Eduardo Briceño (2018) poses four factors critical to ensuring real benefits for learning and establishing a growth mindset:

1. We must *believe* and understand that we can improve.
2. We must *want* to improve—there must be a purpose we care about.
3. We must understand *how* to improve through *deliberate practice*.
4. We must be in a *low-stakes* situation since mistakes are expected and should not merit negative consequences.

We should pause formative assessment if it is feeling like a hoop to jump through or a sorting mechanism rather than tied to a purpose that students value and see as within their reach. The mindsets and practices discussed in Part II: Student-Centered Teaching (Listening to Student Voices, Teaching for Understanding, Focus on Cooperation, and Classroom Autonomy) include many resources for building connection and trust as foundational assets for FA.

Many educators and students grapple with *how* to improve. Research on *deliberate practice* shows the power of identifying and targeting practice toward specific aspects of performance (Briceño, 2018). For example, a musician might work to improve their rhythm for a particular song by listening to a recording of themselves in which the rhythm is weaker and playing just those parts to improve rather than playing the whole song from start to finish. A writer might focus on improving the reliability, relevance, and clarity of the evidence they are using by reading and revising an essay with that goal in mind and while referring to an evidence quality rubric. We need to teach students about deliberate practice and provide routines and protocols that support focused attention to specific growth areas.

Deliberate practice fosters many habits and strategies embedded in identity safety components. Students can do the following:

- Develop a growth mindset to maximize their brain's capacity to learn and retain information (see Chapter 8: High Expectations and Academic Rigor)

- Work with others (see Chapter 5: Focus on Cooperation)

- Self-regulate and manage emotions (see Chapter 6: Classroom Autonomy)

- Give and learn from wise feedback (see Chapter 10: Teacher Warmth and Availability for Learning)

- Build motivation and agency (see Chapter 6: Classroom Autonomy)

In addition, classrooms need the curricular resources for deliberate practice. It can be very helpful for educators of a common subject or course to collaborate to share and strengthen a library of standards-based resources. LPS biology teachers created a common item bank for their genetics unit that allowed them to provide students with multiple practice and retake assessment opportunities.

Grading and Formative Assessment

Grading practices must not inadvertently subvert the formative assessment cycle to a performance zone. If we want to create a rich space for spotlighting and learning from mistakes and gaps as mastery progresses, we cannot have that same performance be equated to a low grade. When a grade is attached, students orient to hiding rather than learning from their weaknesses. When a grade is provided along with feedback, students tend to focus on the grade rather than on the feedback. Illinois English teacher Scott Filkins writes that grading formative assessment "is akin to ranking basketball teams based on how they do in practice" (Heitin, 2015). However, these recommendations can be at odds with school policies about grading or educator ideas about how to ensure students take their work seriously. Options include entering an "as-of" grade that is overwritten (not averaged) as mastery progresses or entering rubric scores that sit in the gradebook but don't count in the grade. When educators grade math or science problems, they can offer partial credit for thinking and problem-solving, taking into account conceptual understanding and what was done well, even when the final answer is incorrect.

GATHERING EVIDENCE OF THE USE OF ACADEMIC DIALOGUE

LPS Spanish teacher Christina Estrada teaches Socratic skills through *Socratic Seminars* and shorter academic dialogue forums integrated throughout her curriculum. Students enjoy Socratic Seminars and view academic dialogue skills as very important for college and beyond, but for many students, performance plateaus somewhere during the first semester.

Christina developed a lesson for students to unpack the Socratic skills rubric, reflect on their strengths and gaps, and identify one or two growth areas to work on through *deliberate practice*. Then each week, students had multiple opportunities for structured academic dialogue and reflection. The reflection asked all students to self-rate on four items the whole class had deemed important: *I was focused and engaged; my body language showed I was focused and engaged; I was listening;* and *I noticed and built on other people's ideas.* Each student then reflected on how they did on their self-selected growth area(s). Students found themselves more tuned in to specific qualities and moves they could make to further strengthen their skills:

> "I would like to make more outside connections next time rather than just focusing on the story."

> "Something that felt hard for me was going against someone's idea because I also want them to know that I respect them! I want to keep trying to go against ideas when that's true for me, even when it's uncomfortable."

Christina worked with the LPS data team to provide students with a monthly report that combined all their reflections. Student growth and confidence accelerated. A student shared this:

> When you're doing the Socratic Seminar, you are thinking about so many things! Taking the time to think through all the different skills involved in academic talk, realizing what I most need to work on, and then having so many chances to do it and reflect has really helped me grow. As a senior, I really appreciate that I feel a lot more confident about being ready for college-level discussion as a result of Ms. Estrada's class.

LPS students were interviewed about the learning in their classes. They too share the power of learning from mistakes and building confidence in their capacities. Ricky (LPS Student Interviews, 2018) spoke about his teacher:

> Honestly, he can say that the retake is optional, but deep inside, he wants us to do the retake. I've known him for just a couple months so far, but I know that he wants us to improve. I would rather take it—he's so nice and kind with us, and he's so supportive when it comes to one of us failing or something. When he says, "Oh, you can do this and this!" I actually do those things because I know that those things are going to support me. And when I do need help, he actually is there.

LPS student Aminesh (LPS Student Interviews, 2018) explained this way:

> For me, I would say confidence is a little bit there, but for me, it's mostly improvement. I keep going back and I'm like, all right, what do I have to improve? OK, I have to improve on this; OK, I got this right; and constantly that question or the same kind of questions pop up, and if I get them constantly right, I'm like, "OK, I understand that, I don't have to improve on that, so I go back to the ones I have to improve on and keep trying to improve. . . . Confidence, yeah, because with improvement for me comes confidence with it.

Dilemmas and Points of Tension

The Power (and Pitfalls) of Peer Feedback

In 2014, a group of LPS English teachers met to discuss how to ramp up the amount and quality of feedback students received about their work. Alongside increased teacher planning time, peer feedback emerged as a leading strategy toward this goal. Building on research out of UCLA (2005), LPS designed and implemented what we then called *crowd-sourced grading* (CSG), a method and web-based tool for peer feedback.

First-year feedback on CSG from students showed both its power and its pitfalls. Many students loved it. Here are some of their comments about how it was beneficial for their learning (Epstein et al., 2017):

> I think that there is an important value in providing this type of feedback to our peers because we get to see where we need to grow but also what we do well. I personally like how when I fill it out I recognize the things that I need to work on myself.

> We know what the expectations are by having a rubric and applying it by grading our peers. I like knowing how I can improve and help others improve on their own work. I like hearing back from my own peers because they are people that I can relate to instead of being judged always by someone who is superior to me, which is usually an adult.

I think that because I gave feedback to my peers based off a rubric I familiarized myself with the rubric and found myself thinking about what I could be doing to better myself as a speaker.

I think these feedback forms are helpful. They help me further understand how the grading is broken down, as well as multiple things that the grader is supposed to look for in your essay or presentation. Also, by giving feedback to my peers, it allows me to give feedback to myself when I practice at home.

However, other student voices (Epstein et al., 2017) illuminated ways that the process might inadvertently reproduce unequal status and further inequity:

I feel like we don't get a lot of context on people so easily. It's very hard to tell, just by looking at someone, if there is a reason behind the way they present and the way they speak. I feel like that can affect the way people grade that person.

I can tell some of the students who get my feedback don't take my ideas seriously because I'm not considered a good student.

It could be that not a lot of people know how to give constructive criticism, and so the way they set their collective feedback could be given in a way that is hurtful or rude toward the person, and I feel like that could be very damaging to a person, although the feedback was not intended to hurt them.

In response to these student voices, LPS paused CSG. We organized a team of educators and an advisory group of students to consider student and teacher experience and outcomes and to suggest ways to improve our model. Our goal was to ensure equal access and opportunity for all students. The team designed key changes to provide an identity safe and academically rigorous and beneficial experience for all students. In 2016, we relaunched the work as *collective feedback*.

Amy and colleagues published an *EdWeek* blog (Epstein et al., 2017), describing six key factors for the work:

1. *Create a culture of respect from day zero.* When ninth graders enter LPS, they come together in a leadership retreat before school starts, where they work on building trust and respect. To quote senior Luis Prado Hurtado, "From the first day, you start to build your mindset. You are constantly reminded that your purpose is to learn and are taught and supported to show respect for your school and community." According to Luis, this paves the way for meaningful peer evaluation.

2. *Teach giving and receiving feedback as skills in their own right.* As a core skill, educators teach and demonstrate how to give feedback by guiding students through sentence starters, personal reflection, and dialogue. Author Jennifer Abrams (2018) suggests providing students with clear examples of what to say and what not to say by teaching sentence stems with language to use:

"One thing you could consider," or "Something you could keep in mind," or "I noticed." Students also need to avoid negative judgments such as, "That's wrong," "That's stupid," or offering discouraging and critical feedback. Rather, they can be taught to give specific, constructive feedback by saying, for example, "I don't see one of the three parts."

3. *Support students to find and use their own voices.* Students learn to give collective feedback in their own voice. In order to avoid generic or impersonal feedback, students can be taught to use some of their "freestyle language" alongside the standards-based rubric language. They also can work with educators on developing assignment-based rubrics. LPS also encourages code-switching, giving space for students to speak and draw from their "home" languages.

4. *Combine digital and face-to-face feedback.* When using online collective feedback tools, LPS students sometimes felt the messaging could be ambiguous and impersonal. Educators responded to students' suggestions and began to complement online tools with face-to-face feedback.

5. *It's all about growth mindset.* Recognizing that the process of offering and receiving feedback can be vulnerable, the growth mindset and the capacity to learn from mistakes and be open to growth enhances the feedback process. To quote 12th-grader Johana Gonzalez (Epstein et al., 2017), "Being able to be vulnerable is hard. But students here know that the whole purpose of feedback is to help you improve and not bring you down."

6. *Keep it in the learning zone!* When LPS first launched crowd-sourced grading, educators discovered that that *peer feedback needs to stay in the learning zone.* Incorporating grading served to diminish the benefits. Even after working to calibrate the scoring, ultimately the student scoring was not sufficiently aligned to the educator's scoring. In addition, when grades are given as part of a feedback process, it is not surprising that students will be focused more on the grade than the feedback. LPS (2019) changed its process and collective feedback was designed to ensure that the peer evaluation was a formative process that did not include a summative grade.

Equitable implementation of collective feedback requires *equity consciousness, habits, and mindsets* that lead to emotional resilience, trust, and belonging. LPS defines equity consciousness as knowledge, language, and skills that enable us to recognize, respond, and redress inequity in our spheres of influence (Gorski, 2018). This includes being able to recognize, respond to, and redress/heal implicit bias, microaggressions, and structural and internalized oppression. It means acknowledging and practicing responsibility in relation to social identity privilege, as well as learning and practicing to be an ally. We draw from the work of Elena Aguilar (2018) to name and teach habits and mindsets such as emotional awareness, self-reflection, and positive self-talk called for by this vulnerable work. For LPS, it has been essential to embed attention to equity consciousness and habits and mindsets in both collective feedback-specific training as well as more broadly in our adult learning communities. The benefits of collective feedback for students—especially those facing negative societal stereotypes—grow as educators advance in these adaptive competencies.

Chapter Summary

In this chapter, we showed how *Teaching for Understanding* is an important ingredient for creating identity safety in students. When their minds are engaged, they gain competence, which leads to confidence in themselves as learners. We also showed that a lack of understanding can undermine students' sense of identity safety due to feeling lost and confused. When feeling confused, it becomes difficult to feel a sense of belonging in the classroom, especially if students around them appear to be grasping the concepts. We gave some specific examples of how to help students gain a deeper understanding through inquiry strategies that can be incorporated into daily activities as well as into longer projects and service learning. We described the importance of teaching for understanding and creating identity safety in STEM courses, especially with regard to preparing them for higher education.

We then addressed formative assessment as a means for students and their educators to investigate whether and how true understanding is occurring and to monitor growth. This iterative process allows students to take accountability for their learning while ensuring they are progressing. It can lead students to connect with their educators and classmates and enable them to develop confidence in themselves as learners, a sense of confidence hardy enough to allow them to skillfully explore and navigate their lessons—even their mistakes, accepting them as viable learning tools. As a point of tension, we described the importance of handling peer assessment carefully to ensure a student's identity safety is not undermined by an inexperienced or insensitive peer. The next two chapters will explore how learning to collaborate and developing autonomy both increase a student's sense of belonging and identity safety.

Check Yourself

When considering how you are working on teaching for understanding, check yourself with the following questions:

1. Have you shifted the cognitive load to your students? How? What more is needed to help your students take responsibility for their learning?

2. What opportunities for creativity are part of your curriculum? How can you make creativity an even greater part of your students' experience in your class?

3. How is formative assessment part of your daily lessons? What pitfalls have you found that create an unlevel playing field? How do you resolve them?

4. Do your students engage in peer assessment? What criteria do you use in forming groups? How do you build necessary conditions for a meaningful experience?

5. How do you balance the idea of learning in relation to performance? In what ways do you instill a love of learning that can lead to a lifetime value for it?

TRY IT OUT: END-OF-CHAPTER ACTIVITY

Teaching for Understanding: Trying Out an
Identity Safety Strategy

Name(s): _____

Teaching for Understanding Strategy Name/Description: _____

What did you try?

What happened?

What did you learn?

 Available for download as a full-page form at **https://resources.corwin** **.com/IdentitySafeClass6-12**

Focus on Cooperation 5

Why Focus on Cooperation Matters

In identity safety, a focus on cooperation extends beyond traditional definitions of cooperative learning activities as discrete collaborative experiences to a more holistic culture of cooperation. Students experience the value of working together and reflect on their successes and the problems encountered in a variety of settings. In identity safe classrooms, cooperation is infused throughout the day.

In his 2015 TED Talk, *Why Humans Run the World,* Yuval Harari explained that what separates humans and the rest of the animal world is our ability to cooperate in flexible ways and in very large numbers. He states that while beehives are examples of large-scale cooperation by many individuals, the roles and behaviors of individual bees are rigid. With lower primates, such as chimps, flexible cooperation only occurs in a small number of individuals and only with those whom they already know. In the case of humans, we can cooperate with strangers in a flexible manner and in large numbers. Harari also warns that collaboration is not always positive—for example, humans have cooperated on large scales to win wars and create concentration camps, and he aptly points out that chimpanzees have not.

That said, humans throughout history have survived due to both individual and collective efforts. As social beings, we are biologically wired for both. Interdependence is deeply embedded in our lives, although we may not be conscious of it. Religions from all cultures describe how we are connected and address how we should treat one another. They encourage us to "love our neighbor" and respect fellow human beings. Many studies of both humans and animals as small as mice have demonstrated an innate need for social connection (Leiberman, 2013). From the way parents naturally nurture their babies, care for their families and close friends, and support one another through hardships, our natural state is revealed as social beings expressing connection. These values can transfer to classrooms as we create environments where we take care of one another and pay attention to how each member of our classroom community feels.

Our human capacity for large- and small-scale collaboration can be fostered in the classroom and promoted together with problem-solving skills and compassion. As we described the growth mindset culture in Chapter 1: The Introduction, students can help one another learn and cooperate in an environment where mutual support becomes a way of life. In the Stanford Integrated Schools Project (SISP) research, cooperation emerged as an important component of identity safety.

Not All Students Come With the Same Experiences

Western society has emphasized rugged individualism, competition, and getting ahead as aspects of a successful life. Schools tend to promote this kind of interaction as they push students to compete. In contrast, interdependence is prevalent in many cultures where family structures exemplify this trait. Parents, siblings, grandparents, cousins, and others take care of one another and pool their resources. Many students of color come to our classrooms with family values of interdependence, which seem to be at odds with many messages that tell them they need to push ahead of others to become "number one." Educators can counter the onslaught by making space for some students to express the value of their family's interdependence, offering opportunities for other students to imbibe the value.

Taking a Deeper Look at Individualism and Interdependence in Our Lives as Educators

While students of color may have experienced interdependence in their families, together with exposure to Western views of individualism, many of their White educators have the needle pointing in the direction of individualism. And some educators of color have had to lean toward individualism to get where they are. Unpacking the ideas of interdependence versus individualism on a conscious level can help educators reconsider the messages that students are receiving through both verbal and structural experiences at school. Even as authors, we have had to spend more time on this topic than others because individualism is so deeply ingrained in us.

We are not suggesting that competition can or should be eliminated, as we discuss in Chapter 6: Classroom Autonomy. There are many benefits from developing the capacity to enter into competition. Here, we are suggesting two things: (1) Educators can work to shift the balance to include more cooperative experiences for students; and (2) students from cultures that emphasize interdependence may feel uncomfortable in an environment that only promotes competition. Adding more interdependent opportunities will increase their sense of identity safety. Finding our "personal best" can be another alternative, which has students competing with themselves to become their best version.

Identity safe environments honor individuals and help them to see themselves as part of a greater whole while learning to navigate paths that engender mutual respect and cooperation. We believe that the values of interdependence and collaboration in the context of compassion and equity have become a planetary imperative as we collaborate together and work towards equal status while seeking solutions to huge problems that affect all of us.

In this chapter, we will show simple ways to incorporate cooperation and interdependent values across the school day.

Focus on Cooperation: Making It Happen

Fostering Interdependence Through Thinking and Acting Interdependently

How do we begin to pay more attention to incorporating the practice of thinking interdependently as we help our students learn to do the same? A first step involves becoming aware of the different needs of students in the room. Some students have been taught that being a good person means sitting back to be a part of the group, blending in rather than standing out. Others have learned that standing out by speaking up is to be admired. Creating a healthy balance in addressing different student needs while also helping students stretch their boundaries and venture out from their comfort zones to become aware of each other's needs helps them develop both confidence and compassion. We can start by creating opportunities that foster and enhance collaboration. Students can learn how to arrive at consensus and navigate differences of opinion. Interdependence can be fostered through content, group work, and simply by guiding and modeling ways for students to talk together and share their thinking. Abundant ideas are available in all content areas.

For starters, biology and ecology teachers have a great opportunity to emphasize the role of interdependence in course content. Examples of interdependence in nature abound. Across history, scientists have built on each other's work. Students can experience collaboration when working together to bring out several ways to prove a hypothesis. They can also work cooperatively on building consensus for different ways to solve a problem.

In mathematics, inviting several students to share their thinking on how they solved a problem will demonstrate the many ways we can approach a situation. We can ask students to look for similarities and patterns in their thinking.

In social studies, students can address a theme in history (e.g., developing democracy, self-determination, protest movements, revolutions, land ownership) and find examples for how that theme was approached by different cultures and nations. In all these

A WHOLE SCHOOL THEATRE PERFORMANCE OF *ROMEO AND JULIET*

At Leadership Public School (LPS) High School, Hayward (California), each year every English class in the school produces and acts together in a single performance of *Romeo and Juliet*, with each class portraying a different scene. The final show is performed in an extravaganza for all students and their parents. Students are drawn into the story of forbidden love, which is both exciting and challenging for them as they work to make it flow into one coherent theatrical piece. While practicing lines, they learn about Shakespeare, analyze the text, learn how to project their voices, and experience how theatre production is very collaborative. Most of all, interdependence is fostered as this activity draws in every student in the school in a collective effort to see it work.

examples, students can express their ideas and weave them together into a whole that is more than the sum of the parts.

In English and literature courses, small groups can discuss a reading and identify key points and then work together to craft a statement that represents the consensual thinking of the whole group. Through the process of give and take, students experience the effectiveness of listening to and learning from each other as they blend their thinking.

Stephanie Frieberg (2017), an identity safety researcher at the University of Washington, shared the importance of validating students with an interdependent background. She explained that offering choices might be an unfamiliar experience for one of those students, creating discomfort. For example, an approach that validates that student's value for relationships might be to say, "I was thinking of you and picked this book I thought you might like. It seemed to match your interests. Of course, you can select a different one." For students who have grown up with interdependent values, something as basic as this simple act can help them feel valued and connected.

Building Authentic Collaboration Across the School Day

Creating a cooperative environment is built by providing continuity in experiencing positive relationships and interactions. The educator guides students by highlighting examples of ways they can help one another, including the following:

- Introducing community agreements and norms for all forms of interaction in small and large groups

- Incorporating cooperative activities into the daily curriculum, including opportunities for the class to reflect on its collective progress both academically and socially

- Encouraging the sharing of notes and bringing assignments to students who are absent

- Weaving social activities into classroom life, expressing appreciation, celebrating success and gratitude both formally and informally, and sharing treats

- Encouraging appropriate humor and laughter

- Not allowing any form of bullying or hurtful teasing to go unaddressed

As these different forms of general cooperation occur, educators can feature them, creating a metacognitive tradition in the classroom that names the different values as they appear (without going overboard, which can become annoying). Students can subsequently reflect on how they worked together and examine ways to improve.

RESEARCH: COOPERATIVE CONTAGION—SCIENTIFIC PROOF OF PAYING IT FORWARD

In a study published in the *Proceedings of the National Academy of Sciences*, researchers James Fowler and Nicholas A. Christakis (2010) created a "public goods game," which involved a simulated experience where they determined that people were likely to be more generous if they saw their peers being generous. Participants were placed in groups of four. Researchers planted a "confederate"—someone in the group secretly assigned to demonstrate generosity toward the other participants. The researchers found that each time a person would express generosity, the other three participants were generous in response. When the groups were changed and individual members mixed into new groups, the generosity was replicated by all four participants in their new groups, creating a cascade of generous behavior. This tendency carried forward into future interactions. The researchers warned that uncooperative behavior can also spread in a similar way.

Community Agreements

Community agreements are norms for respectful exchanges and can be successfully employed for all interactions, from class discussions to class meetings and cooperative groups. Educators can develop agreements together with their students by asking them to envision and write the ways they want to be treated and the way they want their classroom to be.

As part of the process for composing community agreements for respectful dialogue, educators can enlist students in conversations that will uncover elements that produce fruitful discussions with a flow of ideas (Styles, 2001). In addition to standard suggestions for treating one another with kindness and respect, it is worth including ideas that encourage openness with the intent to promote the expression of and listening to diverse perspectives, especially as it involves agreement on ways to respond in moments of conflict.

Youth are often passionate about their beliefs, and their hackles can go up when they sense opposition. They are capable of launching into a diatribe against one of their peers simply because they do not share the same beliefs. With mindful preparation and attention, these events can be prevented by teaching students to listen without interrupting, to maintain a calm voice during stressful moments, and to allow all points of view to be heard and debated without engaging in personal attacks. The tools of respectful dialogue can keep students balanced while they express their differences. The import of these skills is far-reaching and can carry them throughout their lives as they are able to supplant potential disasters with reasoned interchanges. We can literally teach students ways to respectfully disagree with one another and value multiple perspectives.

By discussing the nature of stereotypes, we can sensitize students—and often ourselves—to the harm caused by them. This includes both positive and negative stereotypes, as both project impressions upon others, often based on false assumptions. Students can learn to avoid generalizations and stereotypes, understanding the importance of speaking for oneself alone without imposing thoughts and ideas upon entire groups of people.

Students need validation for expressing feelings after they have experienced a micro-aggression or have been offended. Some schools have introduced the concept of *ouch moments* and *oops moments*. Ouch moments can be used in one of two ways: Either a person says "ouch" and describes what was said that caused them to feel slighted or hurt, or the student can simply say "ouch" to indicate discomfort without having to explain. In response, the other person, including the educator, can say "oops" to indicate they are sorry, acknowledging their regret to the offended person.

Students can learn about confidentiality and the importance of not "outing" a peer in or out of the classroom by sharing that person's personal information. Addressing these issues can prepare students for these encounters by talking at length about why it would be hurtful to spread personal information outside the safety and confidentiality of the class meeting. Students can understand how sensitive information, even when shared with goodwill, can degrade as it spreads among peers, often turning into malicious gossip. This unfairly exposes vulnerability about a student who never intended for the information to leave the class meeting.

Finally, while composing community agreements, it is useful to discuss the actual process of impulse control. The general rule "when in doubt, don't say it" is a good entry point. Guide students to understand that if they feel unsure of something they want to say, perhaps it is best to hold their tongues. Conversations of this nature can help students learn valuable communication skills, and the community agreements will prepare them for the inevitable times when conflicts occur. All norms need to be fully discussed and regularly practiced as part of whole-class experiences as well as during small groups.

SAMPLE COMMUNITY AGREEMENTS

1. We will speak for ourselves and use "I" statements, speaking exclusively from our own experiences.

2. We will actively listen and aim to understand one another's perspectives and beliefs.

3. We won't try to represent a whole group, nor will we ask others to represent an entire group.

4. We will say "ouch" when we feel hurt or uncomfortable and "oops" to show we are sorry if we hurt someone else or make them feel uncomfortable.

5. We will participate, share the floor, and refrain from interrupting. At times, we will "pass" if we do not choose to respond to a question.

6. We will value confidentiality and refrain from spreading rumors.

Designing Group Work That Fosters True Collaboration

Shortly after the Common Core State Standards were adopted, an educator at a workshop lamented, "The new standards recommend often using small cooperative groups, but that does not seem to work with my students. They play around; one student does all the work, and the others get the benefit of the grade." That was a similar complaint from my daughter, Melania, who often grumbled about group projects in high school because she ended up doing more work than her peers. While there have been many workshops on ways to implement the content of the Common Core State Standards, educators often lacked basic professional development on how to create small groups that can work effectively together. Cooperative learning can work well when it is carefully designed to avoid these pitfalls.

Elizabeth Cohen and colleagues (1994) pointed out that students with higher academic or peer group social status often dominate cooperative work. Their cooperative learning model, *complex instruction*, incorporates strategies that seek to ensure students of all academic levels contribute through open-ended curricula that requires a range of skills, rotating roles in the group, and specific teaching of collaborative skills and participation strategies. Data from several decades of research proves that cooperative instruction has many benefits when following the collaboration process described in the following section (Barron & Darling Hammond, 1996; Cohen, 1994; Slavin, 1996). This type of learning was found to benefit students of all backgrounds, races, genders, and ethnicities, all grade levels, and academic subject levels (Johnson & Johnson, 2009).

Effective Collaboration Steps

Students enter our classroom with varying degrees of experience with cooperative learning. We can begin by asking them about previous experiences with collaboration. We can proceed to teach and practice the collaboration process directly. This information will serve us to set the norms for cooperation with clear steps for the expected processes of working together.

Initially, it works to practice cooperation with content that is less challenging in order to free students to focus on their group dynamics. Eventually, more complex cooperative lessons can be added. None of this is accomplished in one session, but over time—like a well-oiled wheel—cooperative work can become very successful.

Effective cooperative activities, whether in single lessons or longer projects, include the following steps:

- Preplanning
- Forming groups carefully and determining roles to engender equal participation
- Setting and presenting clear goals and specific objectives for the activity
- Sharing norms for collaboration

- Monitoring groups to support them and resolve any problems
- Finalizing and presenting products
- Assessing individual and group accountability and grading
- Class reflection on how they worked together

In the box's description of Jah Yee's class, we describe this process in action.

CAREFUL ATTENTION TO COOPERATION THAT PROMOTES TRUE COLLABORATION

Jah Yee, a high school English/social science teacher, developed an assignment called "A Memorial Project" in respect to post-Reconstruction after the Civil War. She posed this question: "What should be remembered and studied about this time period?"

The project had multiple goals, including researching and analyzing current and past history, in addition to realizing objectives for collaboration. Students began by doing individual historical research, using primary sources and current news stories. They then formed groups to share what they learned and to organize and synthesize their content, finally arriving at a consensus on what to include and creating ways to present their work.

Another goal of the project was cooperation, as students needed to rely on one another and trust that each would complete their individual tasks for the good of the group. Jah Yee felt that was an important goal because many of her junior-year students were worrying about college applications, which placed them in a very competitive frame of mind. She noted that "our school system is already so competitive." She felt that having students experience cooperation at that time provided a healthy balance to counteract the strains and pressures acquired from expectations for them to compete with other students.

Introducing the Project and the Goals

Jah Yee introduced the project through some current news articles and essays about the controversies in removing Confederate statues in 2018 and, in some cases, replacing them with counterthemed statues. The entire class discussed the goals and objectives of the project and then generated questions and brainstormed ideas for possible projects. Finally, they moved into groups and worked in their respective teams.

Using Careful Thought in Grouping Students

Since this project dealt with issues of racism with the risk of generating controversy, Jah Yee wanted students to feel comfortable. She wondered if they might work better in same-race groups or in mixed-race groups. She decided to ask her students of color individually what would help them feel most comfortable. She also inquired about the type of product they would like to make and investigated their particular areas of interest. She learned that some students wanted same-race groups while others preferred mixed groups. Using the information to create a matrix, she formed groups based on their desires and interests. When the groups first met, she asked them to discuss ways to ensure equal participation and determine how to stay in touch if someone was absent.

Setting Norms

Jah Yee set norms for cooperation to target specific ways to ensure equal status and prevent those with higher status from dominating. In addition to expectations for sharing participation, she drew from the ideas of Cohen (1994), who recommend identifying a norm that reminds students to be sure to ask questions and probe the ideas of peers and elicit reasons for their thinking. She added an additional norm that asked students to develop a plan for equally contributing to the decision on how to present ideas at the end of the project. These norms were stated at the onset and then revisited during and after group work.

Assessing Individual Performance and Group Participation

Jah Yee based grades on three areas: individual performance, group participation, and student self-assessment. Students completed their self-assessments by gauging the success of their performance and how well they worked with their team. The class also spent some time reflecting on how the groups worked together.

End Result: From Theory to Action

Jah Yee was pleased to see that the groups turned out excellent work. As part of their research, they explored arguments in favor of removing the statues as well those proposing to maintain them. Their projects were thoughtful and imaginative. In one project, students created a spinning carousel. They incorporated cooperation in their product by requiring four people to press the buttons together to get it to move. Another group incorporated metaphor by using mirrors and water to get people to think about reflections of the past.

In addition to completing a model or product, some of the students opted to write letters to city councils and other civic organizations in towns where Confederate memorial statues still stood, stating their position about removing them. In those letters, they were tasked with including a counterargument (why statues should remain) and explaining the reasons why they disagreed with that position. One student wrote, "It is important to honor the past, but those kinds of historical artifacts are better in a museum."

Taking a Few Minutes for Student Reflection After a Cooperative Activity

Time is a critical resource in any classroom; however, incorporating reflection after an activity is an incalculable tool for supporting student retention of content and assessing collaboration skills. In a research study of problem-solving for a complex computer simulation, one small group of students reflected on how they worked together toward specific goals. Another group only had educator feedback on their group interactions.

A third group both reflected and had educator feedback. The third group's achievement and cooperation was superior to either of the first two groups (Johnson et al., 2000). Social goals can be set at the start of the group work. Then after each lesson, we can ask two simple questions: one that references academic learning ("What did you learn?") and a second that references teamwork ("How did we work together?"). The delivery method can vary; students can pen their response in a journal, speak it out loud to a partner or the whole group, or even express an opinion with a quick thumbs-up or thumbs-down.

REFLECTION TOOL: AFTER-ACTION REVIEW

by Malik Saric, Teacher
LPS High School, Richmond, California

In my class, we do presentations all year long. The topics change, but the structure stays the same: One student stands in front of the class and delivers a PowerPoint presentation. Afterward, the class performs an after-action review (AAR). This is a reflection structure used by the US military to constantly refine team performance and dynamics. Students discuss what they observe, make hypotheses about what those observations signified, celebrate what they did well, and set intentions for improvement moving forward.

In the beginning of the year, AARs are crucial to building a collaborative class culture. There was one round of presentations in my fifth period that was not going so well; students were repeatedly talking and making snarky comments while their peers presented. In the AAR, I cold-called on a couple of students to share their observations, including Alberto, a 10th-grader repeating English 1. Alberto usually keeps to himself in class and does not like to participate. However, he made a comment that changed the class for the rest of the year.

"People are talking during the presentations, and that's hella disrespectful. We should be kinder," he said. The class erupted in snaps for positive praise.

The following day, our class reflected on the next round of presentations. When I asked Brianna what she noticed, she said that there were no side conversations during the presentations. When I asked why she thought that was, she responded, "Because Alberto put us in our place yesterday."

I cannot understate the transformative effects of whole-class reflection on class culture. Students internalize the feedback that they give each other as a result of the complex social dynamics present in the classroom. It makes a world of a difference to receive feedback from your peers. At times, that feedback is even more influential than a teacher's. Giving the class tools to evaluate and correct themselves empowers them to effect their own change.

Social goals can also focus on a particular aspect of collaboration related to the structure of the lesson: "Did we all get a chance to participate?" If they determine there is room for improvement, they can check in after a new attempt and ask, "Did we do a better job at listening to each other today?" or "Did we ask questions to deepen our understanding of our peers' ideas?" These questions can be covered in a matter of minutes, yet they build the habit of reinforcing values and class norms, as well as promoting self-reflection and the desire to constantly improve. These exercises can provide a constant "read" on the temperature and mood of the classroom, helping educators cultivate awareness for the communications, relationships, and interactions between students and monitor class progress while working with students to build a strong community.

Promoting Cooperation With Class Meetings

Class meetings are a collaborative methodology that serve a variety of purposes—from curricular goals to learning about different cultures and backgrounds of the students to problem-solving. This practice, more commonly used at elementary schools, has been increasingly implemented at the secondary level. Older students are able to bring a different level of sophistication to the format while creating tremendous value for themselves. The meetings provide great opportunities for the whole class to learn and practice arriving at consensus, listening to one another and developing valuable skills for appreciating multiple perspectives. Another benefit of class meetings is to allow time for discussions of serious issues as they arise (see restorative justice circles in Chapter 12: Teacher Skill).

In science and math classes, a class meeting can be used to explore different strategies for everything from solving academic problems to resolving a behavior problem such as cheating. It can also involve getting input on improving cooperation in small groups. In English and social studies, class meetings can open discussion of social issues and current events. In any classroom, meaningful dialogue builds trust and fosters intercultural understanding and democratic interactions.

Class meetings are different from general discussions because they have formal structures. The students can come to the front of the room or sit in a circle. The meetings have norms to ensure equal participation and agreements for respectful interaction without ridicule or judgment. Some class meetings have a set schedule: The meeting begins with a greeting; then, students hold a discussion about a major area of content or theme; and finally, they conclude with time for expressing appreciations. Some educators incorporate personal sharing into the process wherein students take turns sharing something from their ethnic background or a personal story or aspect of their identity.

Before a class meeting, students can journal their intentions for it. Afterward, they can revisit the intentions, reflect on them in terms of the discussion, and write their impressions.

Educators can emphasize leadership skills and teach facilitation and ways to navigate disagreements. Students can be trained to facilitate the meetings while rotating the lead roles so that all students may enjoy the experience. Student leaders can propose the agenda and suggest discussion topics that are meaningful to them. During meetings, the educator can stay in the background and serve as a coach to ensure that the conversation follows the agenda, as well as the agreed-upon norms and timeline. Student leaders can keep an agenda moving while recognizing and redirecting hostile comments by applying these norms, sustaining respect among peers.

Quentin held a class meeting with his eighth-grade students to receive input from them on ideas for improving participation of all students in class discussions. Before the meeting, he asked students to write down their ideas and share with a partner. Students came to the class meeting ready to share many suggestions. He followed the students' recommendations. The next day, he noticed a change in group dynamics when one of the students, who usually did not speak in class, spoke up. In a domino effect, others soon followed. The new trend toward increased participation continued from there.

Infusing Social Justice Into Content

One of my most memorable high school experiences was when I worked on a team social studies project to study the impact of major increases in population. As part of the activity, we researched the topic, interviewed, and subsequently invited Paul Ehrlich, author of the *Population Bomb* (1968), to address the entire school. Then, my team and I went into all social studies classes and presented a slideshow we developed (that was the technology in the late 1960s). We then proceeded to lead a discussion about population issues. The experience stands out and was imprinted in my memory. I learned skills I employ to this day: analysis of current issues, organization and presentation of information, public speaking skills, facilitation, and teamwork. It was a first experience that led to becoming a lifelong activist and leader.

Group projects with a focus on social justice can extend the experience of classroom collaboration by learning about and applying the prosocial values in a larger context involving the community. A few simple examples include the following:

- *History*: Groups can select and study youth-led movements across history, contrasting and analyzing their strategic approaches and the effectiveness of their efforts. Studies can include examples of youth from a range of ethnic backgrounds and gender identities from the past to the present. The students create presentations while referencing multiple sources.

- *English/Social Studies*: In a class immigration research project, students can interview immigrants from their families, peers, and friends and create a presentation about the immigrant experience in the context of different social attitudes around it. They can subsequently get involved in supporting immigrants and refugees in their community.

- *Science*: Students study and contrast the impact of climate change on different island communities and nations, examine solutions, and analyze the effects of current efforts. They can get involved and take action to support community climate change efforts.

With group agreements, careful selection and monitoring of group members, rigorous standards, and meaningful social justice content, these activities can contribute richly to the student experience of identity safety.

TRYING SOMETHING DIFFERENT: INTEREST-BASED BARGAINING APPLIED IN A COOPERATIVE SOCIAL JUSTICE LESSON

In his *Edutopia* blog *PBL and Culturally Responsive Teaching*, Robert Wood (2013), an English teacher in Washington State, described several attempts to incorporate social justice content in his curriculum. Initially, he identified relevant topics based on the interests of his students (e.g., police interrogation techniques, immigration questions). They proceeded to hold debates on the content. However, although students were doing rigorous work, he discovered a problem. Using a debate format, students competed fiercely with each other, which led to tension and acrimonious interactions.

For his next unit on racism, he wanted to avoid the competitiveness and chose a different route. He again selected a problematized topic of interest to his students and described the dilemma by formulating the question "To what degree, if any, should colleges and universities in Washington State use affirmative action programs in their admissions decisions?" Once more, he assigned the students into groups, gave them roles, and asked the groups to prepare a case using various Supreme Court decisions. He provided articles, testimonies from documentary films, and assorted essays. Instead of culminating in a debate, he tried a different methodology called *interest-based negotiation*, a tool he was learning as a member of his teacher's union bargaining team. Students were asked to find areas of agreement and work through their differences by finding out what they could "live with." This led to a very different set of interactions. One student said, "I like how our goal was to consider everyone's opinions and interests in order to come to a consensus."

In his blog, he described that when discussing solutions, everyone did an excellent job of keeping an open mind and being very flexible about the proposed solutions. The structure of interest-based bargaining set up conditions for students to keep an open mind while considering a range of solutions. They also learned to compromise, which created an environment that was much more friendly and collaborative than the tone set by previous debates. He pointed out that in the real world, "all-or-nothing" attitudes often do not work well, and understanding the interests of the different positions helps people reach positive compromises.

Dilemmas and Points of Tension

Cultivating Cooperation in the Context of Competition

At one of the LPS identity safety sessions, an educator asked how to navigate the world of competition that seems to dominate high school life, even while many teachers move toward constructing more cooperative experiences for their students. As described earlier, we are not suggesting that all forms of competition be eliminated, recognizing that we are preparing students to go out into the "real world." The students will soon have to go through a rigorous competitive process, whether it is engaging in college entrance exams or applying for jobs. They will soon discover themselves at a major juncture in life. Rather than approach it as an "either/or" situation, identity safe educators see this dilemma as a "both/and." We propose considering ways to adjust the balance between competition and cooperation. Also, we can expand the different ways we acknowledge the strengths of students. We can take heed against praising only one type of strength—such as well-retained content—and instead create opportunities for students to shine in different ways.

Discussing the tensions of competition with students will allow them to share their feelings, worries, and concerns. Well-designed questions can flush up conversations that address student fears and lead to realizations that more cooperation is needed in the world-at-large. This, in turn, can advance ideas among students on ways to navigate competitive environments and lead others to more cooperative behaviors. These can be rich and often life-altering understandings for them. Thought-provoking questions posed to students can include these:

- How does it feel to win a competition? To lose?

- What does it feel like to see someone you fear win a competition? How about a friend?

- What can you say to someone who is competing with you to promote a feeling of cooperation without compromising yourself (i.e., giving up too much personal power while remaining honest and friendly)? What have you got to lose? What do you have to gain?

ACKNOWLEDGING PROGRESS

At LPS, the honor roll is used to acknowledge exemplary achievement *and* to recognize students who have demonstrated growth in content areas. This includes both those who achieve high grades as well as those students who show a gain in their GPA. Students are also recognized for exemplifying school values such as integrity and kindness.

- What matters the most to you? How can we move forward even when we do not succeed? Are there other values that matter?

- What about compassion and understanding? How does it feel to promote those values? What are the challenges and risks for promoting them? The rewards?

Your aim is to prepare students to feel confident as individuals and apply their capacity for collaborating with others while providing them with the tools to lead in sharing these values as they step out of the classroom into the world. We feel that well-planned collaborative experiences—together with friendly competitive experiences—will expand students' repertoire of social skills.

Chapter Summary

In this chapter, we explored the importance of *Focus on Cooperation* in an identity safe classroom and shared ideas for treating cooperation as a central tenet of how the classroom operates. We explored ways to promote attitudes of interdependence that validate the experiences of many students from nondominant-culture backgrounds while expanding the repertoire of skills for all students who have not previously learned to collaborate. We shared how community agreements can help students learn the norms for working together successfully. We also offered specific strategies for rigorous and authentic teamwork where all students contribute and feel included, as well as ways to use class meetings to foster cooperation skills. We suggested that content for social justice infused in group work can enhance collaboration on the classroom level while contributing to solutions for the larger community. We shared research that showed the power of social networks giving rise to generosity, also applicable in a classroom where cooperation can become the norm for interaction and effective group work. We explored the tensions involved in cultivating cooperation while also preparing students for the realities of the competitive world. Supporting collaboration skills and taking an approach that honors students from interdependent backgrounds contribute to identity safety for all students.

Check Yourself

When considering how you are working on focus on cooperation, check yourself with the following questions:

1. What are all the ways students are learning to cooperate in your classroom? Do you need to add to or change your curriculum in order to build in more interdependence?

2. How have you trained students to work in groups? How are your small groups functioning (e.g., sharing accountability and ensuring each person is contributing)?

3. Do class meetings have a place in your classroom? How often do you use them and to what purpose? What structures have you designed for them?

4. Have you examined and reflected on the words you use to embrace the values of students from more interdependent cultural backgrounds? What did you learn?

5. What place does competition have in your teaching? Have you considered all the ways you are promoting competition? Is competition safe and friendly in your classroom?

6. Do you balance the amount of competition with cooperation? What new ideas can you add to your repertoire?

TRY IT OUT: END OF CHAPTER ACTIVITIES

Enhancing Cooperation and Interdependence in Your Classroom

Types of Cooperation	What You Already Do	What You Can Add
Teaching cooperation and interdependence skills		
Cooperation in daily interactions		
Community agreements		
Growth mindset culture and interdependence in class		
Cooperative group activities		
Partner activities		
Cooperation and service in the community		
Other:		
Other:		

 Available for download as a full-page form at **https://resources.corwin .com/IdentitySafeClass6-12**

Classroom Autonomy 6

Why Classroom Autonomy Matters

Our secondary students come to us during a unique time in their lives as they move toward adulthood. They are shifting from the values, ideas, and experiences of their childhood homes. As young children, they mimicked what they saw others doing. As they grew, they learned to spread their wings and explore independence in decision-making and navigating an increasingly independent relationship from their parents.

As teens, they are faced with an array of choices about who they wish to become and how they wish to be seen. As part of their growing autonomy, they develop agency, the sense that "I am the author of my life and in control of my actions." The experience of becoming autonomous and developing agency is different for each student, based on their family background, identity, and life experiences. In identity safe classrooms, supporting students as they become more autonomous is not in contradiction with a focus on cooperation. Rather, we situate our support of *classroom autonomy* in the context of a collaborative environment where students are helping and not competing with one another.

Adolescent Brains, Agency, and Autonomy

Cognitive researchers and neuroscientists (Gallagher, 2007; Sylwester, 2008) have studied how a sense of agency develops as we come to experience more control across different aspects of our lives. Our frontal-lobe systems are important drivers of executive functioning. They serve to help us recognize and impart social awareness and regulate our actions and behavior. During adolescence, the frontal lobes are maturing in a process that advances throughout our 20s. Our frontal lobes assist us in making conscious choices based on planning, reasoning, and calculated risks. As young people mature, they gradually take charge of their own survival and destiny and are open to new opportunities while recognizing danger. They manage informed choices amidst the many options and risks.

For students, a sense of agency is enhanced as they feel their voices are heard and believe that who they are matters in the world. Progressive experiences of this nature can develop a strong sense of agency, which in turn can propel a positive academic identity (as described in Chapter 3: Listening for Student Voices). For young people, much of the process of establishing a sense of agency derives from their experiences in school, and therefore, agency and autonomy are important considerations as we orchestrate an identity safe school experience.

In the normal course of growing up (and even in adulthood), people experience stressors that cause moments of feeling totally hamstrung and out of control with events in their lives. For youth, family pressures to succeed, rejection by friends, and expectations of employers and colleges all test their sense of agency. Other experiences can undermine this sense when they feel controlled by their parents and educators to an unnecessary or extreme degree. They must grapple with contradictory feelings between loyalty and autonomy along with newly felt hormonal mood shifts.

As I was writing this, I suddenly remembered a moment of swirling emotions that may sound funny now, but was not at all funny at the time. I was 13. We had just moved to California, and all my new friends already had tickets to see the Beatles, which at the time seemed like dying and going to heaven. By the time I had moved in, tickets were sold out. The night of the concert, I felt sorry for myself and threw a little tantrum, with all the accoutrements of crying and screaming. I cannot even remember what I claimed to be upset about. In response, my father got angry and tore down all the Beatle pictures I had carefully cut out of magazines and taped on the wall in my bedroom. I was mortified. Even the small piece of a bedsheet that supposedly had belonged to Paul McCartney was destroyed. It was as if my sense of agency was ripped from me with those pictures. Can you recall a similar moment as you grew up?

Educators can play an instrumental role in escorting students through the confusion to discover their sense of agency or to assist in rebuilding it. At the secondary level, effective designs for classroom autonomy can activate an increasing independence where students learn and practice self-awareness, self-regulation of their cognitive processes, and emotional regulation of their feelings and behavior. This will blossom into confidence and maturity along with distress tolerance that can benefit them throughout their lives.

In an identity safe classroom, we can nurture the concept of agency in our students when we appropriately share some of our own challenges and life experiences. Hearing how a sense of agency has helped us take responsibility for our lives and the choices we make, as well as improve our relationships, students can connect with the confidence and trust we display in sharing our vulnerabilities. They are invited to feel the courage and apply the concept in their own lives. We can also share examples of people of all backgrounds and in different fields who have overcome great obstacles. Addressing these considerations regularly in the context of curriculum, events in the classroom, and in the school will enhance this rich inner world immeasurably.

We can also help individual students analyze their own behaviors and develop the confidence to take bold and self-affirming actions and calculated risks. Successful experiences in this capacity can develop faith in their ability to approach an array of situations that frequently emerge. Along with fostering a strong sense of agency, we model, teach, and help them develop resilience, a quality that affords them a powerful stance in the world, one that will help them overcome obstacles and manage the ups and downs in their lives.

It is also important to exercise a broad view of autonomy, recognizing that it is not synonymous with compliance. In some cases, a student who rebels may be expressing their need for autonomy rather than simply displaying oppositional behavior or a lack of impulse control. Authentic questions posed to students can help them process their behaviors and realize that they have many options. Consider saying, "I want you to live a life that *you* think is worth living. Do you feel that your actions are helping you go in a direction that is meaningful for you?" By providing quality attention and allowing students to know you as well, you can support them as they gain autonomy and agency. This serves to create motivation, confidence, and self-acceptance. In this chapter, we offer strategies for promoting autonomy and agency, leading to resiliency and to a strengthened academic mindset.

Autonomy: Making It Happen

Autonomy and the Academic Mindset

Educators can intentionally support students in developing an academic mindset. Author Zaretta Hammond (2015) defines key components of an academic mindset as such: I can succeed; my ability and competence grow with my effort; I belong in this community (not only a social community, but an intellectual one); and this work has value to me. These aspects of classroom autonomy can be developed in every subject area through the way we structure meaningful curriculum that is relevant to their lives, as well as ways that we speak to students about the growth mindset and learning from our errors. We express our high expectations while communicating to individual students that they are capable, assuring them that we will support them along the way. The sense of intellectual competence becomes internalized and absorbed into their full identities.

Many students arrive at our secondary schools with a weakened academic mindset. They have already built up a set of self-doubts, believing that they will never be able to do well in school. Some have either given up or decided that school is a waste of time. Rather than add superficial bells and whistles to motivate or trick them into participation, the identity safe educator uses culturally responsive practices that work to change these students' mindsets by building their sense of agency, demonstrating to them that they are capable. This happens when they learn to do these things:

- Set goals for themselves and monitor their progress in achieving them

- Believe in a growth mindset, understanding that with effort, they will improve as their successes breed more successes

- Develop curiosity about the world and discover interests that are meaningful to them

- Reflect on their progress toward mastery of subject content in concert with their teacher's guidance

- Develop capacities to overcome negative emotions after receiving a bad grade while maintaining the tenacity to keep working hard at school and trusting that the world is still open to them

- Focus on community assets and the strengths the students bring with them

In an identity safe classroom, students develop agency and resilience that can contribute to an academic mindset. With a sense of academic identity, students can formulate a new self-story, revealing that they are indeed smart and capable enough to experience success in school. Beyond academic benefits, students with stronger agency and resilience will be less likely to get depressed or led astray into risky choices such as drugs, alcohol, or unsafe sex.

Setting and Monitoring Goals

Goal-Setting Leads to Motivation

Researchers Edward Deci and Richard Ryan (1985) explained that when a goal is perceived as worthy and is at a level that provides an appropriate degree of challenge, people are more likely to be motivated and successful. Researcher Martin Ford (1992) created a formula for motivation that is inextricably linked to goals: *motivation = goals × emotions × personal agency beliefs* (p. 69). In Ford's theoretical framework, he posits that motivation provides the fuel that, when paired with emotions, creates the energy for the behavior. Ford considered motivation to be the combination of a person's desired outcomes together with their affective state, perceptions, and beliefs about themselves (agency).

Researcher Shane Lopez (2013) adds another significant element to goal setting: *hope*, which involves the belief that things will be better in the future together with the confidence that a person has the agency to make it happen. By incorporating hope into goal-setting, people will believe deeply that they can achieve their goals and strengthen their commitment, thus enhancing the potential for accomplishing them. Setting specific goals focuses a person's attention on what they need to do and the energy and attention necessary for bringing it to fruition. Optimism combined with a sense of agency plus a set of specific plans provides students with an experience of classroom autonomy as they set goals in identity safe classrooms.

Another caveat for setting goals concerns adaptability. For a variety of reasons, we alter our paths and need to rethink our goals. Consider Rosa's story: Throughout her childhood and in high school, she aspired to be a veterinarian. She volunteered for the local vet, caring for the animals. She had her sights set on her career and her mind made up, until the day when the vet allowed her to assist in operating on a dog. She nearly fainted at the sight of the blood and the exposed organs. That slowed her ambition quite a bit, with only a few months remaining before graduating from high school. Suddenly faced with considering a new career, she took stock of her strengths and decided to concentrate on writing, another activity that she enjoyed. She was accepted at the University of California in San Diego. Her skill allowed her to articulate her thoughts, ideas, and

SMART GOALS

SMART is an acronym invented by George Doran (1991), a consultant for the Washington Water Power Company, that has spread into mainstream use, becoming ubiquitous in corporate and educational settings. SMART goals are identified as having the following characteristics:

S = Specific: Goals need to be very concrete in order to both measure them and determine when they are achieved. Using the five *W*s of who, what, when, where, and why can serve to help with specificity.

M = Measurable: It is important to consider how the goals can be measured objectively and to ensure you have the necessary tools to do the measurements. Students need to learn what kind of evidence can be used as viable measurement tools in relation to their goals.

A = Attainable: The challenge is to set goals that are neither too low nor too high. When too low, attainment requires little effort, often engendering boredom and a sense that nothing new will be learned. Conversely, goals that are too high feel unreachable and impossible to attain, creating frustration. Goals that induce students to stretch their abilities without unreasonably challenging them work best. Although educators will often have a better sense than students for what goals are realistically achievable, we can take care not to unintentionally convey the message that we do not believe in their competence, especially when students themselves set the goals. Rather, we might suggest they set short-, medium-, and long-term goals. Forging a pathway toward realizing incremental success teaches appropriate pacing and the belief that they can eventually achieve their long-term goals. The point is that goals should motivate action, but not lead to disillusionment.

R = Relevant: Goals need to be meaningful to the students. Your challenge as an educator is to explain course goals in such a way that students find relevance. When they set their own goals, ask them to consider how the goal is personally relevant.

T = Time-Oriented: Goals need to be time sensitive with regard to what is reasonable within the time frame for the course. Setting target dates for different aspects of their goals helps students learn an important life skill.

speech to write excellent college papers, giving her impetus as a presenter. She eventually went to work for a technology company, selling their new developments to prospective buyers. And naturally, she has always enjoyed the company of a dog and a cat in her home. Like Rosa, many students will need to adjust their goals midstream when the conditions supporting them change. Helping our students think about their goals—even the big ones—with a reasonably flexible mindset prepares them for the inevitable changes that will confront them in life.

Goal-setting is a valuable life skill that can be modeled and taught in any subject area. Explaining course goals and demonstrating how the class will work to achieve them are empowering exercises to offer students. They can discuss how the course fits into the overall education they are receiving, focusing not only on school and college requirements but also how this content might help them in their lives. Whether you are an algebra, literature, or history teacher, it is worth thinking about how your content can contribute to them throughout their lives. For example, algebra sharpens critical thinking skills, logic, and abstract thinking, applicable strategies in all areas of life. The mastery of algebra can also transfer to facilitate other basic tasks more quickly, such as adjusting a recipe for the number of people eating a meal or determining complex financial decisions made in regard to bank loans and mortgages, as well as interpreting online data.

A command of a content area may lead not only to college acceptance, but to a gateway for higher-level math and science courses with greater options for future career choices. Taking the time to explore the purpose of the course, explain course goals, and task students with setting personal goals and intentions will enhance their engagement and focus. Worksheets and tools for goal-setting are readily available on the Internet with thousands of different templates.

Cultural Expressions of Autonomy

To teach and support classroom autonomy, we must take into account each student's unique background and identity. Autonomy is valued and expressed by different cultures, nationalities, and families in unique ways. Critical race theorist Tara Yosso (2005) proposes tapping the cultural wealth students bring with them to the classroom. This is diametrically opposed to and can powerfully counteract deficit thinking, where a student's background is devalued and viewed as a liability. Sources of cultural capital come from the students' parents and community members, as well as their traditions, religious rituals, language, and other cultural characteristics. In some cases, cultural capital is manifest in forms of resistance and activism that work to redress unequal conditions and strive for justice and equity.

Educators can take an essential first step toward connecting to not only the personal strengths of the student, but also to their families and communities. By placing the students' cultural assets at the center of the classroom experience and as part of the course content and design, students will be able to access the resources they need both internally and externally to meet their goals and yours. Educators can openly discuss the value of autonomy with their students, asking them to describe how they experience it within the context of their families, places of worship, and in their lives. Often, they must shift their roles and expressions as autonomous beings to a great extent, especially when the cultures between home and school are more disparate. Students can be encouraged to describe the challenges as they live in both worlds at home and school. Educators have an important role for listening and understanding first, and then working alongside students to create conditions for agency. Identity issues surrounding gender present yet another aspect of addressing autonomy.

Gender and Autonomy

Gender identity is another aspect of adolescent development where young people are discovering their identity and their perception of self in connection with gender and sexual orientation. Can you imagine what it might feel like to an LGBTQ student to move from kindergarten to 12th grade without a single reference or image reflecting any part of their lived gender experience? While many schools now have gay–straight alliances—and even LGBTQ student body presidents—gender and sexual orientation are topics that usually get sidelined to social clubs and left out of mainstream education.

Jacob Rostosky (2013) writes,

> I was 12 years old when I realized I was transgender and 14 years old when I made the most important decision of my life—to transition from female to male. I spent my childhood confused, and this confusion led to depression, which quickly spiraled out of control. As if being depressed wasn't hard enough, as soon as I arrived in middle school I began to be bullied. Not a day would go by without someone calling me names, physically harassing me, and even sending me death threats. However, I was too ashamed to tell my parents. I decided the only way out of this misery was to commit suicide. Luckily, as I was about to swallow the handful of pills, my mother walked in on me. Shocked at finding her 12-year-old daughter in this position, she broke down and cried, which allowed me to cry with her. This is when I came out to her, and we made the decision that as long as I worked on learning to love myself, I could begin my transition to male.

Unless students have the space to openly express their gender identities and sexual orientation without judgment, they cannot feel identity safe.

Gender identity involves three integral areas, which include our bodies, our identities, and the way we express ourselves to the world. It concerns what we feel internally and can involve our sexual orientation, manifest with whom we are attracted to sexually. Gender expression involves how we show up outwardly in the world, such as our clothes, and our style. Youth mature at varying rates and choose to express themselves in different ways. While some hide their feelings inside, others display the expression of their gender identities.

Schools in the United States have very different levels of acceptance for these aspects of gender autonomy for both educators and students, creating environments with vastly differing levels of openness and safety. Identity safe classrooms create safe spaces for students to express their gender identity and sexual orientation to an extent that their feelings and ideas can be shared with ease.

Identity safe educators aim to become literate about all aspects of gender identity. They learn the current terminology and the meanings of these different words, thereby increasing their understanding. It is especially important to stay tuned as terminology regarding gender identity continues to shift as people explore what it means for them, both individually and collectively. Continual communication around what teens are seeing, hearing, thinking, and feeling builds trust in the classroom and helps educators keep one ear to the ground (e.g., at the time of this writing, *genderqueer* is often used as an umbrella term for a person who does not identify with conventional gender roles). The national organization Gender Spectrum (2019) maintains an updated glossary of terms and provides an array of resources for educators and schools.

Everyone at school—staff and students—needs to become knowledgeable and aware of the sensitive ramifications surrounding gender identity and sexual orientation. Educators also need to ensure that students know they can approach any adult in the school if they are bullied or teased about their gender or sexual orientation. Most importantly, educators need to express their acceptance of teen gender identity choices. Examples of gender-inclusive practices are found in Chapter 7: Using Diversity as a Resource.

Executive Functioning: From Cacophony to a Beautifully Orchestrated Symphony

As described earlier, executive-functioning skills are housed in the frontal lobes of our brains, directing self-regulation that involves planning, working memory, and flexible thinking. It also includes knowing when to hold back and control ourselves. Our frontal lobes fulfill a role that can be compared to an orchestra conductor. The conductor directs each musician on when to start and stop playing. The conductor knows what each instrument contributes and when to bring it in, thus avoiding the cacophony that might happen if all instruments start up at once. Of course, there is no little conductor inside the brain but rather a set of neurological functions in the frontal lobes that work together to manage and coordinate their different uses. Weakened executive-functioning skills have been associated with a range of learning disabilities and mental disorders, including ADHD, Asperger's syndrome, and Tourette's syndrome. In identity safe classrooms, educators learn about the process of developing executive-functioning skills and become aware of individual students' capacities to manage and organize their thoughts, ideas, and their work. Scaffolding and support are given as needed to help students develop these skills.

Many of the brilliant minds of the world struggled with executive functions and were eventually able to overcome or deal with them and be the creators, inventors, and divergent thinkers of our societies. Sadly, many others never were able to live productive lives. Paul, a chess champion in his teens, ended up as an Uber driver and became homeless, living in his car. His nephew eventually helped him get housing after learning that he had been paying for a cell phone that had been lost for over a year. Paul never was diagnosed, but he clearly lacked executive functioning. Many great minds have been lost in the shuffle merely as a result of a lack of understanding among their families, educators, and employers, who unintentionally set up difficult roadblocks due to their ignorance of executive-functioning and self-regulation skills. Today, special educators are much quicker to identify and diagnose these issues and provide tools and strategies to help people who lack executive functioning.

WHAT DOES EXECUTIVE FUNCTIONING ENTAIL?

While researchers do not have one agreed-upon universal definition of executive functions, Eslinger (1996) describes them as a set of neurological processes that govern the following processes:

- *Metacognitive awareness*: The ability to be aware of our thoughts and evaluate our own thought processes

- *Goal-setting*: Setting goals for what you want to do, from simple day-to-day actions to larger projects like career goals

- *Planning*: Specific planning of action—in your head or written down—that includes everything from the steps needed to cook an egg to complex processes such as managing a large group project

- *Identifying strategies and moving into implementation*: The ability to select specific strategies to meet the goals and impetus to move into action to carry them out

- *Flexibility to adapt and shift plans and actions*: The ability to change the course of action when you hit a roadblock or see a better path

- *Verbal regulation*: Thinking about what you say before you speak

- *Self-control*: Inhibiting your responses and controlling your impulses both verbally and physically; stopping yourself in order to think before you react, avoiding regret later—includes anger management and consideration of the feelings of others

Executive-functioning processes have a great impact both academically and socially. The capacity to develop strong executive functioning is not only important with regard to schoolwork, but it also impacts social relationships, major life choices, and the ability to function on the job. Adults who have weak executive functioning may say and do hurtful things, engage in impulsive acts in the workplace that cause them to be fired, and make choices that ruin romantic relationships. When they lack impulse control, they might not think of the consequences of their actions and often become alienated from others who get tired of hearing their repeated hurtful remarks.

In any secondary classroom, you might witness a rainbow spectrum of frontal-lobe maturity, as well as students with executive-functioning impairments. For that reason, some are blurting out answers impulsively, while others are models of self-control. Some have organized binders with all their work bundled neatly within, while others expose a few scattered papers and—in dramatic cases—even forget to turn in the homework they had struggled to complete at home. It is easy to interpret this as not caring, but it may be much less in the control of the student than we think.

In other cases, a student who is struggling with executive-functioning issues might prefer to act as if they did not care rather than be considered stupid or lazy. Covington (2000) found that some students would prefer not to say how much effort they put into studying for a test in order to attribute their success to intelligence rather than hard work. And after repeated experiences of failure, the student might simply give up, described as *learned helplessness* (Seligman, 1975).

As educators, we can become cognizant of the lack of executive functioning as a separate issue from a student's purposeful misbehavior or lackadaisical attitude. Just as educators scaffold learning, we can also scaffold self-regulation, teaching techniques for organizing and systematic ways of approaching schoolwork. Educators can help students recognize that executive-functioning skills are separate from other aspects of intelligence. We can also find ways to support these students, helping them succeed and feel identity safe.

Having the Patience to Teach Executive-Functioning Skills That Should Have Been Learned in Elementary School

Most educators are fortunately endowed with highly developed executive-functioning skills. Good teaching requires careful goal-setting and planning across a semester and year, as well as day-to-day lesson planning, monitoring student progress in learning, and an awareness of students' needs in relation to the pressures of content coverage. Our excellent executive-functioning skills position us to develop masterful patience with our students!

Fourth grade is when educators usually teach students basic organizing and study skills, such as arranging their binders. While many high school educators feel this type of teaching is beyond their purview, it is a moral imperative to help students. At any age, students can learn basic organization. As tired as we may be of certain behaviors, we can, nevertheless, manage to weigh our words carefully and to stop the litany of chastising that the students most likely have heard throughout their educational career. "Where is your homework?" Why didn't you complete the assignment?" "You have wasted your time goofing off!"

Identity safety applies to all kinds of minds. The diversity in how our minds work has contributed greatly to advances made by humans. Helping students learn about how their own minds work and systematically learning the strategies to maximize efforts will contribute to developing a positive academic identity.

In identity safe classrooms, these strategies combine with a classroom climate that promotes acceptance of all aspects of our identities and the recognition that we all have strengths and weaknesses in different areas. In classrooms where students feel secure, educators are cognizant of the role of executive functioning and find ways to support students who lack it, while working to create a safe environment for all to flourish.

TIPS FOR HELPING STUDENTS MANAGE THEIR FRONTAL LOBES

In *Learning Outside the Lines* (Mooney & Cole, 2000), two college students with ADHD and learning disabilities share a range of strategies, speaking directly to students. They explain that these skills scaffolded their learning and helped them up through high school and college. As part of identity safety, these basic words of advice, combined with a supportive educator, can make a big difference for students.

Note-Taking Strategies

- Date and put a course title on each set of notes.

- Annotate your notes.

- Use new sheets of paper for each course with space for later additions.

- Don't try to write everything down.

- Get many pens so you always have one on hand.

- Use colored pencils, highlighters, and sticky notes to help identify important concepts.

- Organize specific notebooks for each subject area.

Templates for Class Discussions

- Limit yourself to two or three sentence comments that summarize, assert and support, or question.

- Formulate questions by asking for concrete examples or for relevance to connect to broader themes of the course.

- Think first, talk second; keep it short; offer only one or two anecdotes per class in order not to dominate.

Dilemmas and Points of Tension

Handling Failure: "This Too Shall Pass"

The theory of learned helplessness is a psychological phenomenon that fosters a repeated sense of failure. This applies to behaviors in both personal and academic realms. Educators can help their students avoid attributions like "I am a bad person" or "I am dumb." Students can experience a shift with positive and attainable attributions, such as "I can stop myself before I blow up the next time." Seligman, the researcher who identified learned helplessness, went on to research ways to transition from a negative *explanatory style* (the way we explain things to ourselves) to one of *learned optimism*. If a person perceives their repeated failures as permanent or if we extend the failure in one area to encompass all areas of our experience, we get frozen in a state of learned helplessness. Seligman suggests we take the approach that failure is a common experience and a normal part of living.

Educators can teach students to recognize that academic failures, even fights or bullying, are neither permanent nor pervasive. They can build student understanding to realize that failing a course or losing their temper once—or even repeatedly—does not permanently define their identities nor does it warrant a life of failure. Additionally, messing up in one area does not mean that they are losers in all aspects of life. It need not be a pervasive fear, paralyzing all efforts. Identity safe educators can help students learn to not define themselves by their failures but rather by reflecting on what they have done well, and they can take the opportunity to learn from their mistakes and grow (Seligman, 1990). Educators can become role models by describing their own process in confronting similar challenges.

In a series of studies (Bruehlman-Senecal & Ayduk, 2015), researchers found that when people have a "distant future" perspective and mitigate current emotional distress by adopting a longer view, they can develop the capacity to cope with life's challenges, failures, and problems. By supporting students to ask themselves, "How might I feel in a week?" they can learn to develop what is called "self-distancing." This can offer immediate removal and relief from their reactive state and create management and pacing for longer-term emotional perspectives.

As educators, we need to look at our own explanatory style and compassionately guard what we say to our students. Modeling learned optimism and highlighting these ideas will go a long way toward aiding greatly with self-regulation as well as supporting them to move from pessimistic views to optimistic ones of themselves.

Independent Student Thinking After Years of Intellectual Neglect

There are students who come to us after years of rote teaching and for whom thinking for themselves does not come easily. They may even become annoyed or bestow a blank look upon you when asked to engage in thoughtful deliberation. Students who resist independent thinking may benefit from opportunities to share stories about their lives in small groups. Responding to meaningful questions helps students draw from a personal sense of identity. Invoking popular music, art, and television shows that link to themes that matter to them can be a starting point to motivate students to express opinions and ideas. By using the arts and humanities, students are drawn into the process of forming and defending opinions, leading to other higher-order thinking skills.

Offering a menu of choices will also stimulate their thinking. Being asked to consider what they want to learn and how they want to demonstrate knowledge can spark them to find areas of particular interest.

Chapter Summary

In this chapter, we explored the importance of addressing *Classroom Autonomy* and shared strategies and approaches to forge a sense of agency leading to a strong academic identity, which are all part of creating identity safety. We offered goal-setting as a motivational tool for helping students achieve greater levels of independence and autonomy. We also approached ways to help students feel a sense of autonomy by drawing from their cultural assets and gender identity.

Some students need extra support in developing executive-functioning skills to help them achieve this autonomy. We shared strategies for strengthening executive-functioning skills and adaptability in the face of obstacles and challenges.

We addressed several points of tension in autonomy while investigating ways to help students break out of a sense of *learned helplessness* and shift toward *learned optimism*. We also tackled ways to help resistant students start the process of thinking independently. Time spent on helping students gain a sense of autonomy and agency will strengthen their confidence and capacity to navigate the complexity of challenges that will inevitably present in their lives.

Community activities, including those mentioned in previous chapters, also serve to help students develop a sense of identity and agency and discover that they can make a difference by addressing the multiplicity of problems facing their communities and the world, including poverty, climate change, xenophobia, and other threats.

Check Yourself

When considering how you are working on classroom autonomy, check yourself with the following questions:

1. In what ways do students express their needs for autonomy in your classroom? How do you honor it and help them learn to take responsibility for their learning and behavior?

2. How do you help a student identify and draw from their cultural assets and strengths?

3. How do your students set goals in the context of your content area? How do they monitor themselves to see progress toward the goals?

4. Think of a student who has trouble self-regulating. How do you manage your own reactions to the student in ways that are helpful to both of you?

5. What do you do to support students grappling with learned helplessness? How do you help students break through that barrier?

6. What opportunities do you provide for students to take a long view and explore how to make a difference in the world?

TRY IT OUT: END-OF-CHAPTER ACTIVITIES

Increasing Autonomy in Your Classroom

Autonomy	What You Already Do	What Can Be Added
Student classroom tasks		
Class input in decisions		
Individual or group project topic choices		
Individual or group choice of how to demonstrate knowledge		
Student leadership		
Student facilitation		
Goal-setting		
Formative assessment		
Self-assessment		
Peer assessment		
Student-led parent conferences		
Other:		
Other:		

 Available for download as a full-page form at **https://resources.corwin .com/IdentitySafeClass6-12**

Big Ideas:
Student-Centered Teaching

This part was guided by two Identity Safety Principles:

#5. Social and emotional safety is created by supporting students in defining their identities, refuting negative stereotypes, and countering stereotype threat, giving them a voice in the classroom, while using SEL strategies.

#6. Student learning is enhanced in diverse classrooms by teaching for understanding, creating opportunities for shared inquiry and dialogue, and offering a challenging, rigorous curriculum.

These two principles, as shared through the four component chapters, have some big ideas:

- Through listening and creating spaces for active participation, students will find their voices and discover their identities. In that way, they come to feel a sense of belonging in school.

- Being the recipient of microaggressions along with implicit biases and stereotype threats that lurk below the surface undermines a person's sense of identity safety. Identity safe educators reflect on their own biases and pay attention to others, so they are able to address all forms of bias.

- Lessons that incorporate inquiry, creativity, and content drawn from the students' lives lead to understanding. When students feel that their education is relevant and that they have a significant part to play in it, their academic identity develops.

- Formative assessment *for* learning is a way for students to monitor and guide their own progress and recognize their growth. With the support of their educators, students take charge of their learning.

- Infusing cooperation and a spirit of interdependence in classroom life develops into a growth mindset culture. These interactions reflect and validate the home experience of many students, which is especially important for students from nondominant cultures.

- Helping students achieve autonomy includes helping them learn to think for themselves. As they develop a sense of agency in their lives, those who may have already been predisposed to feeling helpless discover they are progressing and can gain new confidence.

For Further Study

- Article: "Knowledge in Action Research: Project-Based Learning Course Design" from *Edutopia*, www.edutopia.org
- TED Talk: *The Power of Believing You Can Improve* by Carol Dweck, www.ted.com
- Website: *Gender Spectrum*, www.genderspectrum.org
- Website: For Implicit Association Tests—*Project Implicit*, www.implicit.harvard.edu
- Website: *Jigsaw: How to Do It*, www.jigsaw.org/#steps
- Website: *TeachEngineering*, a free web-based digital library collection with a series of lessons geared to all grade levels, K–12, www.teachengineering.org

Cultivating Diversity as a Resource

Cultivating Diversity as a Resource addresses how to support students of all social identities and backgrounds to feel welcomed as their full selves. This support allows them to experience the beauty and value of human diversity, hold high expectations for themselves, and be challenged to use their minds. Cultivating diversity as a resource centers on embracing differences as assets rather than barriers to learning. Educators can enact language, curriculum, and pedagogy, making the commitment to cultivating diversity as a resource integral to all aspects of classroom life. Most of all, by cultivating diversity as a resource, students feel a sense of acceptance and compassion for themselves and others.

Here are short definitions of the three components that cultivate diversity as a resource in identity safe classrooms. These will be fully described in subsequent chapters:

1. *Using Diversity as a Resource* refers to activating students' curiosity and valuing the knowledge they bring into the classroom. Content and teaching that takes into account diverse cultures and perspectives can be applied to all subjects. Students learn about their ethnic histories and other aspects of their backgrounds, allowing them to explore their own identities and appreciate others. When negative stereotyping and bias arise in school, they are addressed and mitigated.

2. *High Expectations and Academic Rigor* means supporting all students in higher-level learning. When an educator

communicates and models the attitude "I believe in you," students become more inclined to hold high expectations for themselves and one another, thus learning to their fullest potential. By teaching and modeling a growth mindset and by learning to notice and disarm stereotypes and biases, educators can remove barriers to student academic identity.

3. *Challenging Curriculum* means to motivate each student by providing meaningful, purposeful learning. Curriculum is designed to excite students, encouraging them to seek increasing levels of growth. It includes innovative techniques that teach higher levels of thinking, appropriately challenging students within a broad academic range, and methods for responding to mistakes so students are not deterred and will keep trying. In challenging curriculum, educators employ pedagogy that is congruent with a range of cultural learning styles.

Together, these three chapters emphasize the way diversity can permeate a school experience, enhanced by how we communicate to students from different backgrounds that they are competent and capable of academic rigor. We can create a curriculum to inspire, motivate, and challenge them. Our intention is to demonstrate that "diversity" is not something we put on the plate along with other content areas. It is not one more thing an educator has to worry about and, as a result, quickly fix with a piece of multicultural literature or yet again an analysis of Martin Luther King Jr.'s "I Have a Dream" speech—a noble task, certainly, but it should not be the only time or one of the few times diversity is addressed in school. It is worth the effort and attention to offer regular lessons on diversity that speak to the heart of students and their experience. The rewards for educators are rich and far-reaching. When class participation, enthusiasm, and performance are on the rise, we know we are on the right track.

Countering Deficit Thinking

Deficit thinking is prevalent in the dominant culture and impacts teachers, administrators, counselors, parents, and students, consciously or unconsciously. The language of an "achievement gap" was part of a great wake-up call to address the fact that Black and Brown students regularly score below their White and Asian counterparts. Unfortunately, the hyperfocus on a "gap" also served to reproduce conscious or unconscious assumptions based on negative stereotypes. For a student of color, repeatedly hearing about this huge "gap" and the "school-to-prison pipeline" can hammer in feelings of inadequacy. The burden of deficit thinking and stereotype threat falls heavily on those facing negative and prevalent societal stereotypes. I cannot count the number of times when I was a principal that I heard parents say to their children, "I don't want you to become a statistic."

In identity safety, we ask educators to focus attention first on noticing and reflecting. To uncover deficit thinking in all of its insidiousness involves a process of sharpening our lenses for seeing and responding to it. Educators seeking to cultivate diversity as a resource take time to deconstruct their own deficit thinking when it rears its ugly head. Also, they make continuous efforts to affirm student identities as they manage the complexities of bringing together people of diverse backgrounds in the context of creating equal status.

It is important to note that diversity is not about trying to fix students. They are not broken. It is incumbent upon us to see and acknowledge them for who they are, bring out their diverse backgrounds, and offer a safe place for them to unfold and grow in their awareness of self. Cultivating diversity as a resource can enhance the classroom experience and support our students with an evergrowing sense of self and academic identity.

Using Diversity as a Resource

Why Using Diversity as a Resource Matters

Diversity makes us stronger and better—not by mixing or melting together, but by enriching our environment and bringing forth different valuable capacities. Diverse approaches, opinions, and solutions matter for learning and, therefore, for our classrooms and students. And it matters on a global basis perhaps now as much as at any other time in history. If we cultivate the ability to connect across our differences rather than fear them, humanity thrives.

Groups of people throughout recorded history have suffered in societies where hierarchies of social class and access to privilege are determined by the color of people's skin, ethnicity, religion, and gender. This history is reified today in constructs of White supremacy, misogyny, xenophobia, homophobia, and transphobia, as well as religious and other forms of intolerance. Yet, against great odds, historically people of all backgrounds have fought and continue to fight against inequities, working for civil rights and social justice.

The work of building an equitable society not only includes expressing the value of diversity but also making it a real and palpable experience for our students. Sometimes, educators fear addressing racial and other differences, worrying they will open Pandora's box and unleash controversy, unintentionally stereotype someone, or say the wrong thing. We hope that the ideas described in Chapter 7: Using Diversity as a Resource will illuminate a path to make the non-color-blind classroom a reality. It is not only because it is right and fair or helps students learn better, but it is also because it will make for a better world. The contagion from the acceptance and celebration of our diversity can enliven a school experience in surprising ways.

Reducing Prejudice Without Demanding Invisibility

In efforts to reduce prejudice in the 1940s and 1950s, social psychologist Gordon Allport (2008) proposed the *contact hypothesis*, highlighting the need for people of different backgrounds to get to know one another in the context of equal status. (We share strategies to promote equal status in Chapter 11: Positive Student Relationships).

Allport promoted developing personal relationships across differences and bringing diverse people together to work for a greater goal, such as cheering for a baseball team or teaming for projects. Allport's theories also incorporated the importance of having authorities in any given field communicate and insist on equitable treatment for all. These methods of reducing prejudice are viable today. School leaders, educators, coaches, and other personnel can all work toward these goals.

However, in subsequent years, additional research (Dovidio et al., 2008) expanded on Allport's theories. Researchers found that in mixed racial groups when cheering for a team, the Whites felt less prejudice toward people of color, but the people of color felt invisible and not fully included. The pain felt by people who experience a sense of invisibility in an assimilated environment was borne out when the US military had the "Don't ask, don't tell" system from 1994 to 2011. LGBTQ people were permitted to join the military as long as they did not let others know about their identities. The LGBTQ members of the military who were forced to hide their identities and lead a double life felt devalued and traumatized (Puglise, 2016). "Don't ask, don't tell" was finally repealed in 2011. The message behind this brand of invisibility is that discrimination is acceptable.

Many groups subject to discrimination have felt invisible when they feel that parts of their identities need to be held in secret, buried deep inside them. And for those who cannot hide the color of their skin, ironically, that same sense of invisibility occurs when they are submerged into a supposed melting pot that ignores their heritage, histories, and identities.

In this chapter, we describe strategies to ensure that student identities are affirmed, that they feel visible and counted. When students know their educators are open to varied backgrounds with a range of differences beyond race and ethnicity (e.g., special needs, religion, or mental health conditions), they can feel identity safe. We explore the crossroads of our many social identities and *intersectionality*, which involves the intersection of more than one oppressed identity. This chapter also highlights ways to include critical multicultural content, helping students learn to analyze history and current events by drawing from primary sources and counternarratives to juxtapose against the dominant narrative presented in textbooks. Inevitably, educators face conflicts and challenges as they wade into controversial waters. We share strategies for facilitating hard conversations and address the moments when we are called out or when a situation blows up. This journey is not always easy, but it is definitely worthwhile for our students and ourselves.

Using Diversity as a Resource: Making It Happen

Creating Spaces Where Students See Themselves Reflected

In a 2010 study by Good, Woodzicka, and Wingfield, researchers explored the power of images as role models in ninth- and 10th-grade textbooks. One group of girls was taught from a book that only featured images of female scientists. A second group of girls used a book with the same text but only showed images of male scientists. When both female groups were given a chemistry test, the group that viewed the book with images of female scientists performed significantly better than the group with the photos of male scientists. Boys were also included in the study, and for the group of boys that viewed texts with photos of female scientists, their performance actually declined.

Our classroom walls can become a space to give nonverbal messages in which students see people like themselves reflected, especially as contemporary or historical role models. Another simple idea is to put up photos of the students doing science experiments, solving math problems, or working in groups. Additionally, students can bring in photos of themselves with their families and valued items from their cultures. As the cited research shows, seeing themselves and people like them enhances their sense of belonging in the academic experience.

It is natural to light up when you meet someone with your birthday or who spells their name the same way you do. Yet some LGBTQ students go through their whole K–12 education without hearing validation of their sexual orientation or even the mention of an alternative to the heterosexual or cisgender identity (cisgender denotes a person whose sense of personal identity and gender corresponds with their birth sex.). As social beings, we need validation.

For decades, a slow but steady move away from focusing only on Christmas in schools concerned an effort to acknowledge Jews, Buddhists, Sikhs, and Muslims who celebrate in other ways. It was not, as some media outlets have claimed, devaluing Christianity but rather opening the doors for students from many religions to feel accepted. An activity as simple as asking students to write about their favorite family traditions, including religious holidays, can bring out a wide range of ways that families and communities celebrate them. In a safe environment, different religious traditions can be shared without confronting conflicting beliefs. Touching on the joy, connectedness, and other shared values serves as a bridge for students to honor and respect their different faiths.

In our classrooms, many ethnicities may never be highlighted in the curriculum or in classroom discussions. Students from the various Caribbean islands, Bosnia, or Pakistan may rarely hear about their countries in social studies coursework. In research projects designed to emphasize individual backgrounds, students can bring forth the history and literature or study scientists from their country. Finding points of connection is meaningful, motivating, and tides over to other areas of the curriculum (Korbey, 2013).

Creating a curriculum that draws on diversity requires integrating voices, stories, and histories, as well as learning about institutionalized inequities and the many examples of efforts to resist discrimination and establish social justice. While some multicultural content has seeped into traditional texts, it is important to help students analyze how it is presented. In addition, adding primary sources and other supplementary materials offers alternative perspectives that challenge misconceptions and assumptions.

Opening Dialogue

As educators, we have positional power in the classroom that we can leverage to engender inclusivity through dialogue. We have the opportunity to model how we use our power in a respectful way, grounded in listening, openness, and humility. Making space for authentic dialogue can be an entry point to using diversity as a resource for learning.

In her book *School Talk* (2017), Mica Pollock offers many ideas for initiating conversations that enable us to understand one another and work together in an equitable environment. She presents ways to go beyond what she calls "shallow culture talk" based on cultural stereotypes. She proposes moving past the tendency to use verbs that seek to define the behavior of entire cultures. Rather, she suggests facilitating and eliciting nuanced understanding of the different experiences of the students, recognizing that there are more variations within groups than between them. She encourages educators to have "life talks" with students and families to find out about what their lives are like, including their hopes and fears. Pollock also suggests that when educators engage in data talks, we need to look beyond numbers and scores that define kids as smart or not. We need to find the bits of information about young people that get lost when we label them. We can find alternative methods for learning about them, countering much of the erroneous information that resides in their academic files. Dialogue is an entry point to strengthen the important quality of inclusivity.

Dialogue can also follow feedback, gathered individually or through surveys. At all three LPS (Leadership Public Schools) high schools, students are invited to give anonymous feedback to educators twice yearly. From there, educators lead discussions in their classrooms, soliciting suggestions for strengthening identity safety at school.

Dialogue is extremely important after a biased-based or hate incident, whether it impacts a few students or has escalated into schoolwide controversy. In these situations, healing is enhanced by addressing and discussing what has occurred and inviting students to voice their feelings and seek solutions.

Dialogue on issues of diversity can be daunting, but ultimately, it can open spaces for students to be heard, be themselves, develop their identities, and learn to effectively engage with others who are different. Later in this chapter, we offer tools for facilitating hard conversations. It is worth noting that up-front work can lead to deeper understandings, producing a trustworthy and respectful environment.

Families and Communities: Opening Opportunities for Understanding

Schools have a tremendous opportunity to invite parents into the classroom. Parents can offer their professional skills, read from their diaries, narrate childhood experiences, and share photos. They can also bring in particular talents, including music, art, and cultural crafts, such as Guatemalan weavings or Ethiopian foods. A panel of parents can speak about their experiences of religion, bringing together Muslims, Jews, Sikhs, Buddhists,

Christians, Agnostics, and Atheists in an accepting atmosphere. Parents can share stories of their families' lives and legacies to build awareness of self and others, community spirit, and identity safety.

Homework assignments offer another option for incorporating family life in the classroom. Students can be assigned to interview family members or research their culture. Topics range from personal stories to beliefs and values, or even opinions on controversial topics. Students can explore family history and traditions in essays and stories (e.g., ask students to find out how their parents used various home remedies to cure maladies).

In some cases, students prefer not to have their parents anywhere near the school. The tension between being tied to their families and simultaneously pulling away from them may seem contradictory. This is normal teen behavior and need not dictate our approach. Their resistance does not diminish the power of family relationships, so we do not suggest shying away from involving them. The rewards for these students can manifest in strengthening the bond between themselves, their families, and their school.

Family involvement can be structured to include students as well. At LPS schools, student-led conferences take place at the end of each quarter. Students are trained to use a template and follow a routine. The template includes dialogue with parents about their course mastery, assignments, and attendance, as well as collectively reflecting on progress, next steps, and the roles each person can play. Teachers are present and add commentary.

Rosa's mom was a single parent in a school filled with two-parent families. Whenever her mother showed up for a school event, it was painfully apparent to her that her mother was alone. Her preference was to protect her mother by keeping her away from school as much as possible. When a teacher in her public speaking class tasked her with giving a speech about her mother, she poured her truth into the work. This teacher had created a safe environment for Rosa and also fostered a feeling of trust between Rosa's classmates. The result led to a compassionate response where Rosa's classmates made a point to reach out to Rosa's mom whenever they spotted her on campus. Rosa felt that her mom had become a part of her community and lost the tension she had previously felt.

At one San Francisco middle school, it took some time for counselors to convince the administration and staff that it would be beneficial to provide a space for parents to gather. The first parent center was in a hallway outside the staff lounge. Due to the success of this center, staff cleaned out a copy room to serve as a Parent Resource Center and found funding to hire parent liaisons and obtain books, computers, and furniture. They also had a small budget for coffee and refreshments and toys for the preschool siblings. Some parents became classroom volunteers and helped with events and student activities.

At another high school, parents were surveyed to identify parent education topics. As a result, the parent programs included résumé writing, employment skills, ESL, and Spanish literacy. Their monthly parent–community series included bilingual workshops on raising adolescents, positive parenting, and mental health topics.

LPS offers the College Knowledge program where parents learn about the college applications, grants, and student loans and how to find resources to assist their children in the process of selecting, applying for, and acquiring financial aid for college. LPS also works with a community agency to form parent–student dialogue groups.

At LPS in Hayward, California, the first day of professional development is a community walk. Parents and school leaders worked together to arrange presentations and dialogue with various local community groups. In the process of discovering the neighborhood on foot, the staff came to know local leaders, met and talked with parents in their community, and learned local history as well as current strengths, needs, and goals.

When including parents at school, be aware of your students' home situations. Check to see if you have students who are in foster care, are homeless, or whose parents are divorced or have died. Adjust or expand your invitation to include a family member, guardian, friend, or neighbor.

Family involvement in the classroom and school and school involvement in the community serve as powerful resources to support using diversity as a resource. Learning and development is enhanced as more voices and assets contribute to the student experience.

Exploring the Dimensions of Our Multiple Identities

In identity safe classrooms, students examine the many elements that contribute to their identities. Coming from mixed-race, national, or ethnic heritage impacts a student's sense of identity in different ways. Some have one Black and one White parent; others are Spanish-speaking African Americans who identify as both Black and Latinx. We have students who are Black and adopted into a White family and students whose parents have more than one religion. Some have two moms, two dads, or gender nonbinary parents, identifying as gender fluid or agender (without gender). Other students are raised with two religions.

Some students have been validated and encouraged by their families, developing confidence in all aspects of their identities. Other students may feel confused or pulled in multiple directions: "Who am I?" "Where do I belong?" They may have grown up hearing thoughtless or outright rude comments and questions like "What are you, anyway?" In an identity safe classroom, we work to allow students to openly discover and express their social identities and correct perceptions that have held them hostage to erroneous beliefs.

Robin had an Asian grandmother, and the rest of her antecedents were White. She is blonde and only has a hint of Asian in her appearance, so all her life she has been treated as White. Yet because of her cultural exposure to and identification with her Asian heritage, she always felt that she did not fit in and that people did not understand her ethnic identity. To those around her and to her other siblings, this was not a big issue. Yet when she and her father were interviewed and included in the book *Part Asian, 100% Hapa* (2006), it was transformative and meant a lot to her in the process of coming to accept herself. The book is a collection of photos and short bios of people with part-Asian ancestry and mixtures of other ethnicities. Author Kip Fulbeck used the Hawaiian word *hapa,* meaning "half," to make his point that nobody is half anything—our identities are complex and nuanced. As educators, when we have an open dialogue with students, we can expand our students' experiences.

Providing opportunities to explore their identities, identity safe educators are careful not to judge or define anyone's identity. They also monitor the reaction of other students and take steps to ensure everyone feels safe in the exploratory process.

Matt, humanities teacher from San Francisco, asked his students to write a counternarrative story about a part or parts of their identity. He points out that the writing prompt is specifically about writing a counternarrative, not just an essay about their culture and identity. All students have a culture and identity, but not all students confront distorted, oppressive narratives about their identities. Some of his White male students complained that they did not have much to say. He responded that perhaps they are used to experiencing their identities as the norm—their culture may be taken for granted and consequently feels invisible to them. Matt decided that even if they have less to say and feel a bit uncomfortable saying it, that in itself might be an important realization illustrating how peers of diverse backgrounds might feel uncomfortable in settings where they feel their identities are not acknowledged.

Approaching Intersectionality and Multiple Social Identities

Identity safe educators pay attention to the unique way identity manifests for each student. Each human is a unique intersection of identity and experience. *Intersectionality* is defined as

> The interconnected nature of social categorizations such as race, class, and gender, regarded as creating overlapping and interdependent systems of discrimination or disadvantage; a theoretical approach based on such a premise. (Oxford Dictionary, n.d.)

Kimberley Crenshaw (1980), intersectionality theorist, pointed out that, for example, instead of viewing racism as one problem and violence against women as another, the various oppressive circumstances can combine and more powerfully impact a person. Intersectionality is also a useful concept used to describe intragroup patterns of power, such as the treatment of women by males in their racial group or sexist or homophobic lyrics in rap songs. The theory grew out of the need to acknowledge the challenge for people who face discrimination from multiple vantage points.

Crenshaw explains that everyone experiences identities with multiple dimensions that not only intersect but also subject us to differential treatment in a world that is structured according to the dynamics of power. An understanding of the theory of intersectionality can contribute to efforts by identity safe educators to understand

SUPPORTING STUDENT INTERSECTIONALITY

After attending to the precondition of building trust (see Chapter 10: Teacher Warmth and Availability for Learning), educators can address intersectionality with students by committing to doing the following:

1. Learn about intersectionality and examine your own identity in terms of these histories—a good free resource is *Teaching Tolerance: Teaching at the Intersections* (https://www.tolerance.org/magazine/summer-2016/teaching-at-the-intersections).

2. Teach about the different kinds of oppression and discrimination and help students learn to be upstanders who speak up and stand up for themselves and others.

3. Teach students about privilege and how to recognize the different ways privilege or lack of it impacts their lives.

4. Ensure class discussions are nonjudgmental and avoid the "Oppression Olympics," where the levels of suffering of one group are compared with another to determine who has suffered more.

5. Immediately name and identify issues that touch on intersectionality when they emerge in class.

6. Keep intersectionality as part of your equity lens when considering how students are treated and treat one another.

our students' perspectives. The imbalance of power and privilege and the unequal status afforded to different aspects of identity serve as added burdens as young people develop their inner worlds. It is not enough to approach these burdens as multiple social identities, but to advance further to acknowledge and address the disparate power and privilege afforded to these identities. Through counternarratives, students gain an understanding and consider all aspects of their identities as they grow and work to make change in the world.

At identity safety workshops, we always aim to build relationships and rapport with a shared commitment to social justice across individual differences. At the conclusion of one particular session, Annette, who was both African American and gender noncon-forming, reflected to the group, saying,

> During the part of the day when we shared our racial biographies, I felt comfortable and accepted. However, when we shared about our gender identities, I felt some internal resistance. I worried that the sense of connection and safety in the room would be threatened. In my mind, I made some

assumptions—that perhaps some of my colleagues were church members and would judge me. Yet as we all shared our stories, the process of listening without judgment restored that safety. Now, I am very glad that I came today.

Intersectionality is rarely a topic included in workshops or books on diversity. It is important for identity safe educators to learn about intersectionality in order to better support students.

Breaking Out of the Gender Binary

We spoke of gender identity in Chapter 6: Classroom Autonomy, highlighting the need for educators to develop awareness and learn terminology to support student agency. Here, as part of using diversity as a resource, we explore the process of creating inclusion.

GENDER-INCLUSIVE PRACTICES

- Introduce yourself to your students with your pronouns: "Hi, my name is ____, and I use the pronouns ____.

- Post a rainbow flag or a "This is a safe space" poster to signal to students you are an ally.

- Avoid categorizing students into gender binary groups or referring to gender when addressing groups of people.

- Invite LGBTQ role models to speak to the class.

- Include information about LGBTQ people, history, and literature in the curriculum and school library. Avoid only referring to LGBTQ history during LGBTQ Pride Month (June).

- Set up opportunities for critical analysis of the portrayal of gender in the media.

- Initiate dialogue and open-ended assignments on gender topics.

- Take care not to define a student's gender identity for them or put them on the spot by asking them which pronouns they prefer.

- Learn terminology and be aware of current usage changes in different contexts. Ask individuals for guidance on how to refer to them. Ask students to optionally write their preferred pronouns on a note card and give them to you.

- Explain the power of using requested pronouns to address another person.

- Have students remind you if you ever forget to use pronouns requested by a student.

- Practice saying "they" for a person who uses that pronoun and try not to slip up.

We begin by considering how to break out of the *gender binary*, a term representing a deeply ingrained conditioning in our society—the tendency to consider that only two genders (male and female) exist. Pregnant women are immediately asked, "Are you having a boy or a girl?" While the LGBTQ rainbow flag reflects the range of identities and sexual orientations, gender binary conditioning embeds within our psyches, which can become apparent when attempting to shift into using the pronoun *they* to refer to a single person who claims a gender-fluid or transgender identity. It is particularly troublesome when, in spite of our intentions, we repeatedly slip and refer to a person as "he" or "she" when that person has requested us to use "they." Recognizing that power of the conditioning can be a first step to reverse the tendency to exclude or invisiblize people of nonbinary gender identities.

The teenage years can be crucial as adolescents become increasingly self-aware and mindful of the expressions of themselves and their peers through clothing and hairstyles, let alone their choice of pronouns. In addition, these identities may continually shift as youth question and discover new aspects of themselves. Young people can harbor strong feelings that emerge when given the opportunity to share about gender identity.

Schoolwide Gender-Inclusive Practices

Gender is an expansive area with many topics to cover, including the #MeToo movement, sexual harassment, bullying of transgender students, and the lack of equal pay for women holding the same jobs as men, which is especially evident in the unequal treatment of women of color. Schools need to provide professional development to help staff better understand issues of gender, including identity, expression, and terminology. Some educators may have strong reactions to new learning about gender as a continuum. We all need support to develop a basic literacy about the gender continuum and to examine and work through deeply ingrained beliefs and mindsets that may inadvertently exclude or even harm students holding nonbinary gender identities. It is recommended that sites assign a teacher leader as a designated go-to person on gender issues to help their colleagues.

Schools and districts are changing registration practices and other school policies, including bathroom designation policies, to become more gender inclusive. In certain areas, parents have taken strong antigay positions, and some educators understandably fear controversy. Federal law states that all students, including all gender identities, have the right to a safe and supportive school environment. Title IX prohibits sex discrimination and in 2014 was extended to include complaints of discrimination based on gender identity. In 2018, the earlier directive to permit transgender students to use bathrooms that match their gender identity was rescinded in a huge step backward after years of effort working toward the fair treatment of transgender students. However, a growing number of cities and states have moved to incorporate protections for gender-inclusive youth and have passed laws against gender-based discrimination.

EXAMINE SCHOOLWIDE GENDER PRACTICES

- Do school records allow access to specify changes to the gender marker, name, and preferred pronoun of the student?

- Does the school provide gender-neutral restroom facilities (not simply the stigmatized "nurse's" bathroom)?

- Does the school use gender-inclusive language on signage and written materials?

- Is there a protocol and training for handling sexual harassment and safe teen dating practices?

- Are staff and students educated about bullying prevention?

Gender-inclusive practices and curriculum are a significant part of an identity safe classroom. We will further address the #MeToo movement in Chapter 11.

Refuting Stereotypes and Reducing Stereotype Threat

Using diversity as a resource involves the positive process of affirming a student's identity. However, we also need to tackle the negative messaging that bombards our students through the media, biased attitudes, and discriminatory experiences. As explained in Chapter 1: The Introduction, stereotype threat research led to the concept of identity safety. The reduction of stereotype threat occurs through building a cache of positive experiences in a student's life and offering counternarratives. Stereotyping also needs to be refuted and directly confronted.

Stereotypes abound in our lives because our brains are actually wired to develop shortcuts that allow us to react quickly. When we teach students about stereotyping, we can point out that while we all do it, stereotypes need to be scrutinized in order to determine when they are invalid, unnecessary, or harmful. Even what might be considered a positive stereotype can ultimately be damaging. For example, an Asian student subjected to the stereotype that "Asians are good at math" might feel humiliated if they cannot live up to that stereotype. Here are important ways to reduce stereotyping:

1. As educators, examine our own stereotypes and biases, being and becoming as conscious as possible when we speak and act.

2. Address stereotyping with students in context, preventively, and when it emerges.

3. Offer counternarratives to deconstruct stereotypes and help students understand aspects of history that have promoted and sustained negative stereotypes about certain groups.

4. Forewarn students about stereotype threat and initiate stereotype reflection and reduction activities. Many simple activities can help students become attuned to the impact of stereotyping and increase their empathy for others.

In addition to the Stanford Integrated School Project (SISP; Steele, 2012), many studies have tested specific strategies for reducing stereotype threat. Results of these studies mirror many of the SISP findings and are incorporated into identity safe practices. Data from the research studies, briefly described here, offer additional educator moves that demonstrated effective results in reducing stereotype threat and raising academic achievement:

- *Value students' individuality.* Educators can help students highlight elements of their individual identities (Ambady et al., 2004; Gresky et al., 2005).

- *Introduce positive role models from diverse groups.* Successful diverse role models can be presented in person and in literature and serve to motivate students and contradict negative stereotypes (Marx & Roman, 2002; McIntyre et al., 2003).

- *Communicate high standards to students while conveying they have the capacity to meet the standards.* Critical feedback is given to students in the context of holding high standards and communicating to them that educators believe they can meet those standards (Cohen & Steele, 2002; Cohen et al., 2009; Yeager & Walton, 2011).

- *Teach and communicate the growth mindset.* Students can be taught that intelligence grows with effort (Aronson et al., 2002; Dweck, 2007).

- *Provide opportunities for intergroup contact and a climate of belonging.* Educators facilitate cross-group relationships (Rosenthal & Crisp, 2006) and create a climate of belonging (Walton & Cohen, 2011).

- *Teach students about stereotype threat.* Students are taught about the theory of stereotype threat (Johns et al., 2005).

- *Encourage self-affirmation* (see research described in Chapter 3: Listening for Student Voices). Students write down their values and beliefs (Cohen et al., 2009; Miyake et al., 2010).

Another approach to help students counter negative stereotypes involves inviting them to generate examples as a class and work to analyze the origins. Students will be able to deconstruct and refute stereotypes that abound in our culture. Once they develop a level of proficiency in identifying these stereotypes, they will be inclined to apply and extend their newly discovered awareness outside the classroom.

"DISSOLVING STEREOTYPES" ACTIVITY

This symbolic activity demonstrates that we all are impacted by stereotypes. Before trying it, be sure that a level of trust exists so that students feel safe enough to share vulnerabilities. Take care to ensure they take the activity seriously. Also, some students may feel emotional as they touch on pain points when examining stereotypes. Pay attention to all nuances of emotion as they engage in this process. Eliciting personal experiences from them and modeling your own can go a long way toward enhancing levels of trust in the group. Here are the steps:

- Hand out small pieces of rice paper (one inch by half-inch) and ask students to think of a stereotype that impacted their life.

- Provide water-soluble markers and ask them to write the stereotype on the rice paper.

- Instruct students to place the little papers into a small bin of water and observe the ink colors dissolving. Some students may choose to turn the paper over to hide what they wrote; most of them usually place it face up.

- Invite them to form a circle and watch the stereotypes dissolve.

- Ask them to reflect on how they felt doing the activity.

This shared metaphorical experience can be very meaningful as students realize they are not alone. The powerful process also motivates students to be kind and empathetic. The *Not In Our Town* website has a short film and lesson plan (https://www.niot.org/nios-video/dissolving-stereotypes-0).

Critical Multiculturalism: Facing Racism, Homophobia, and Bias

Critical multiculturalism is an approach that educates students about power dynamics and the history of unequal distribution of wealth and power. Educators present information with tools for analysis, affording the perspectives that lead in the direction of social justice.

At a young age—perhaps earlier than one might think—children experience structural inequalities, conscious and unconscious biased attitudes, and actual manifestations of hate. A child may hear racial slurs without understanding them, or they might pick up snippets of adult conversations or newscasts. Discriminatory experiences engrave themselves on young minds and color future perceptions.

In Chapter 1, we discussed culturally relevant teaching as a way to value and affirm different cultures and lived experiences and the role of the dominant narrative in codifying the devaluation and oppression of people of color. We also explained how the assimilation model or the color-blind classroom that aims for blanket equality does not acknowledge the experiences of inequity felt directly by students from nondominant groups. We proposed the use of counternarratives that provide an alternate view. Critical multiculturalism is a vehicle for this. The word *critical* here refers to delving deeply below the surface to a more complete and nuanced story analyzing historical and current events. Students discover what is missing from their textbooks and gain new perspectives. In any situation, there is danger in presenting only one perspective, as it can lead us to default assumptions, conclusions, and decisions that may be incomplete and create misunderstandings. With a critical approach, students view history not only through the eyes of the conquerors but also of those who were displaced and victimized. They use these tools to reflect on their own lives in the context of historical inequities and continued structural inequality. They can analyze current events, pose problems, and work to solve them.

Students from dominant groups also benefit from understanding the impact of institutionalized inequality. Males can come to understand how women are systematically exploited. White students learn about their privilege that they may have taken for granted. In this way, students can develop empathy for one another. This can translate into considering how transgender peers might feel when they are forced to use the bathroom in the nurse's office. It can lead to unified efforts to rectify unfair school policies.

The capacity to critically analyze the impact of oppression from the vantage point of unequal power relationships yields opportunities for students to reach their own conclusions. Taking this approach has valuable benefits. First, it reduces shame, self-blame, and internalized hate. Second, it helps them move from bitterness to agency; and third, it provides an avenue for positive action in seeking solutions in conjunction with educators and leaders in both school and community. Students can learn to analyze what is happening for themselves, make informed decisions, and, in many capacities, choose to become activists working for social justice.

Transforming Shame to Pride

In the prologue to *I Know Why the Caged Bird Sings*, Maya Angelou (1969) wrote about a childhood dream:

> I was really White . . . a cruel fairy stepmother, who was understandably jealous of my beauty . . . turned me into a too-big Negro girl, with nappy black hair, broad feet and a space between her teeth that would hold a number-two pencil.

With this novel, followed by decades of writing and a lifetime of speaking out, Angelou serves as an inspiring example of a person who overcame her shame.

I have personally experienced that terrible feeling of shame, growing up as a Jewish child soon after my parents escaped the Holocaust. I wondered, but was too afraid to ever ask my parents, *Why did the Nazis hate us? What is wrong with us?*

Shame is one of the terrible results of internalizing hateful and devaluing messages. These kinds of feelings are all too common for children from oppressed groups. Often, these feelings are internalized when children are too young to articulate them. By high school, some of these feelings have shifted into anger with their growing awareness of the unfairness in the world. Often, these feelings seethe with no outlet. In your classroom, you may or may not hear a student articulate such feelings aloud.

Most likely, a space where educators appreciate and value diverse backgrounds feels like a welcoming and refreshing spring to students suffering from long-term suppressed feelings. However, as identity safe educators, we can go further. While students learn about the history of the inequities, rather than including only negative and tragic stories, they also can study the many efforts for change that have been championed throughout history. Students can perceive opportunities to channel anger or shame into productive feelings. By including a focus on thinkers and activists throughout time who have struggled and continue to fight for justice and the successes they have achieved, students can avoid the sense of isolation, depression, or hopelessness that can accompany learning the sad truths of oppression.

As an author, Maya Angelou (1978) went on to capture the courage, the strength, and the power of transforming shame into pride in her writings, inspiring generations of people around the world.

CRITICAL MULTICULTURALISM ACROSS THE CURRICULUM

In the book *Critical Multiculturalism, Theory and Praxis*, editors May and Sleeter (2010) present ideas for incorporating strategies across all subject areas. They describe a process of teaching through naming invisible dominant tropes and envisioning alternative perspectives by identifying a problem, deconstructing it, and then reconstructing it with positive solutions and outcomes. The following are some suggestions for incorporating critical multiculturalism across the curriculum:

Language Arts

- Incorporate a critical multicultural perspective through literature by authors of color and nonfiction historical readings, followed by discussion and reflective writing.

- Use first-person narratives.

History/Social Studies

- Use alternative analyses of history in conjunction with traditional textbooks.

- Recognize dynamics of power in historical events.

- Use primary sources with many voices.

- Learn about protests, rebellions, and people who stood up to injustice (e.g., abolitionists, suffragettes).

- Analyze current events and issues in their own communities, seeking solutions (e.g., gentrification, sexual harassment, separation of children from their parents at the United States–Mexico border).

Math and Science

- Study the Egyptian/African origins of math.

- Study mathematicians and scientists from underrepresented groups (including women).

- Move away from the tendency to seek only one right answer, making a collective effort to understand everyone's thinking and problem-solving processes.

- Invite immigrant students to share algorithms used by their parents that may be different from the ones taught in the United States.

Ethnic Studies

- Focus on nondominant ethnic groups and student identity exploration.

- Introduce diverse histories and perspectives.

- Incorporate a wide range of literature, music, art, dance, and cultural artifacts.

- Learn about diverse leaders, scientists, artists, and inventors.

- Learn about resistance movements and social change efforts.

English Language Development (ELD) and World Languages

- Express the value of bilingualism and literacy in a second language.

- Adopt an approach that values and draws from the students' native languages.

- Help students study the sociohistorical impact of "English only" policies and efforts to promote assimilation of immigrants. Have students examine their own lives in the context of assimilationist values.

- Express the value of maintaining their culture and language while learning English (learn about code-switching in Chapter 3).

(Continued)

(Continued)

Physical Education

- Deconstruct stereotypes about body shape with unrealistic expectations that cause students, particularly girls, to develop anorexia, bulimia, and other eating disorders.

- Encourage students to question Westernized views of thin bodies as the only means of being healthy.

- Present counternarratives to stereotypes of Black athletes as "naturally talented" while demeaning their intelligence (attitudes that can result in students developing anti-intellectual attitudes).

- Break down stereotypes about male and female physical strength and also practices that serve to undermine students who do not fit traditional gender stereotypes.

Arts

- Examine art history from an anthropological perspective recognizing the role of the arts and creativity in social justice efforts throughout history.

- Study cultural meaning-making through visual art, music, dance, and theatre from different cultures. Present and support valuing a range of forms from hip hop to indigenous art forms.

- Use the arts for students to express their identities and feelings about what is happening in the world today.

Sources: Fitzpatrick, 2010; Gutstein, 2010; Kubata, 2010; Stone Hanley, 2010.

Critical Multiculturalism Leads to Positive Action

Using a critical approach, students are able to apply new awareness at school and in their lives. They can become active in movements like *Black Lives Matter, It Gets Better, Disability Rights*, and other social justice efforts. Students from nondominant backgrounds develop pride and the powerful sense that they can make social change in the world. Students from dominant backgrounds can develop or strengthen a commitment to social change and identify a role they can play in social change. Rather than feeling guilty or defensive, they will learn how people of all ethnicities joined the civil rights movement and how many Christians supported the escape of Jewish people from the Nazis. Everyone can play a role in social justice.

Each of us can develop the courage and commitment to take steps to respond to stereotyping, negative power dynamics, bullying, and hate-based bias. We can learn and be supported to call out unfair practices in the classroom and in extracurricular activities. We can question and find solutions to schoolwide practices that perpetuate inequality, such as tracking.

If we want to move toward schoolwide identity safety, we will need to critically analyze inequitable school policies. As part of this effort, we will also need to be able to talk about controversial issues, even if these become hard conversations.

STUDENT RESEARCH PROJECT LEADS TO ACTIVISM: RENAMING SCHOOLS NAMED AFTER EUGENICISTS

In Palo Alto, California, eighth-grader Kobi Johnsson (Lee, 2017), completed a researched assignment about David Starr Jordan, the man his school was named after. He discovered that not only his school, but several others in their district were named after eugenicists (people who advocate the racist belief in selective breeding of humans). Kobi was quoted saying that as a mixed-heritage person, most likely these same eugenicists would have deemed him "feeble-minded" and wanted him sterilized, highlighting that having a school with this name was contrary to the values of the Palo Alto community. Kobi and his father started a petition that turned into a community effort that resulted in renaming two schools.

A BOTTOM-UP APPROACH TO HELPING STUDENTS CRITICALLY ANALYZE THEIR WORLD

Each year, Carlee introduces a study of the "humanities" to her sixth graders, grounded in a yearlong exploration of ancient civilizations and learning about the world while actively participating in a democratic classroom community. They begin by brainstorming provocative questions: Have the problems in our world ever been dealt with in a way that actually helped? Why are there wars? Why are people so stressed? Why is there so much drama? Does violence ever stop? They then categorize questions and engage in a consensus-building activity, selecting a guiding question for the year.

The first year Carlee initiated this activity, the class explored the question, How have ancient civilizations dealt with violence? After in-depth research, using primary sources of art and music, the students created an expo project that concluded with recommendations to the adults for addressing violence in their community based entirely on evidence they had collected about what was and was not effective in the ancient world. They designed cities that included items absent from their urban neighborhoods: schools with grassy fields, outdoor spaces for families, gardens, markets where healthy food was sold,

(Continued)

(Continued)

libraries, playgrounds, and clinics/hospitals. Some grappled with the idea of police and jail and barbed-wire fences surrounding the community to prevent "bad people" from entering. An energetic debate ensued about where to put "bad people" and what makes people "bad." Students concluded that the only time violence has stopped in history was when people had everything they needed to live. That year, their achievement data improved, especially among the African American students.

ONGOING DIALOGUE AMONG STAFF

At LPS, the Solidarity Council is a diverse body of educators from all three high schools that work together to build their identity safe adult learning community. The Council initiated a series of all-staff workshops to build "understanding, will, and skill" to notice, talk about, and take action around power, privilege, and oppression—starting with race and racism. They began by creating "basic literacy" around equity and oppression, moved into building skills to notice and talk about inequities, and then worked to develop and use a shared definition of "equity consciousness" and equity principles. Over time, these practices, together with an awareness and use of shared language, are becoming a regular part of the belief system across LPS sites. A teacher commented, "Discussions around race and racism require vulnerability, courage, and hope. These important conversations are overdue, and we must be committed to them."

Talking About Race and Gender: Facilitating Hard Conversations

The Equity Lab (2019) webpage states, "The most dangerous conversation about race is the one we don't have." Yet often when discussing race, gender, and religion, strong emotions surface. These topics can evoke vulnerability, anger, blame, defensiveness, or guilt in the struggle to find common ground. When people bottle up feelings and are afraid to touch sensitive issues, simmering tensions can boil over. Some educators, especially those who have not learned how to address controversial issues or who have not received facilitation training, fear initiating the discussions. Then if a student, parent, or staff member makes an inflammatory comment or raises a touchy topic, the educator is at a loss for what to do. Some effective methods can be employed to respond to slurs in the moment, as well as time-tested tools for facilitating difficult conversations with adults or students (Miller & McCormick, 2008). As always, it is best to be proactive by setting the stage for these conversations in the context of a trusting and identity safe environment with norms for dialogue set in advance (see Chapter 3).

Responding to Inflammatory Comments

When a person blurts out a remark like "That's so gay" or "All Arabs are terrorists," it is crucial for an identity safe educator (no matter what subject they teach) to stop everything and address it. If it is not an appropriate time for a deeper conversation, you can immediately explain why the comment is unacceptable and inform students that you will address it more fully at a later time. Then, it is crucial that you follow up with a longer discussion. The identity safety of all students is impacted when one person is attacked, so responding is important for everyone. The work up front pays off in terms of student participation and interest both during these conversations and afterward as you return to your subject content.

Succinctly, you need to make it clear to all students why the comment was hurtful and unacceptable in your classroom. Following up with the students is necessary to avoid public humiliation. For the student who was targeted, assure them that you will work to make the classroom safe for them and ask them to inform you if anything further occurs after class. Check for their feelings and listen to both verbal and nonverbal cues, which are important to do in order to understand their disposition and vulnerabilities. For the student who made the remark, in addition to applying consequences in accord with school discipline policies, this becomes a teachable moment to help them learn from their mistake.

If you have restorative justice in place, hold a circle so the student(s) can repair the harm they caused. Depending on the nature of the slur, you can give them an assignment to investigate the history of it, whether it is the N-word, a study of the Muslim culture, or the swastika. Parents also need to be informed in order to understand and support your efforts. Your aim is to move them toward knowledge, understanding, and empathy and to keep all students in the class safe.

The following section holds suggested tips for facilitating hard conversations with your students. These strategies also work with parents and staff.

Tips for Facilitating Hard Conversations

Preparation

Prepare for the discussion by identifying your goals and ensuring you have sufficient knowledge of the subject. The goal of the dialogue may be to create open-ended sharing, or you may be following up on a slur or insult. At other times, you want to hold a discussion to process an incident at school or something that happened in the community or on the national level. Determine if your goal is to come to a consensus for future action or to allow students to express freely and listen to one another without needing to arrive at an agreement.

Start by reflecting on your group. Have you worked on building trust? If not, this is where you need to start. In Chapter 10, we offer ways to build trust in the classroom. In addition, consider your students' individual perspectives or concerns.

What experience have they had discussing this topic? In which possible directions could this conversation go? If you are seeking agreement, will you take a vote or seek consensus? Prepare and consider carefully the process you plan to use. Create an outline and a timed agenda with a plan for steering the discussion by formulating guiding questions.

Consider Your Role

After making your values of identity safety clear, attempt to stay neutral while allowing all viewpoints to be expressed. Inform students that if one person's viewpoint appears to insult another's, you will need to remind them of the norms to treat one another with respect, even and especially if the student who expressed the insult is unaware that the remark is offensive. In this case, it may require a longer conversation to promote understanding. Your job is to help the participants have a rich conversation and attend to ways they are reacting while being cognizant of time constraints.

Facilitating the Discussion

Set a welcoming tone by inviting everyone to join the conversation. Set norms for the dialogue or review the norms already in place in your classroom (see sample community agreements in Chapter 5: Focus on Cooperation). Applying norms helps you maintain a sense of civility as students speak their truth without intentionally or unintentionally attacking one another.

Explain the purpose and process for the dialogue. Assure them that all have a chance to express ideas (see Chapter 3 for strategies to ensure equal participation).

Keep the conversation flowing. Notice who is speaking too much and who has not spoken yet or very little. Avoid commenting after each speaker. A richer conversation flows as they speak directly to one another in accordance with the norms. Challenge participants to think deeply, express ideas without judgment, and avoid turning to you for answers to tough questions. At times, you may ask a student to clarify or you may choose to paraphrase what is said to ensure that others clearly understand differing points of view. It can also be effective to ask students to listen to another student's point of view and, before responding, play back what they heard or what they think the other person is trying to say.

Help participants look at multiple perspectives. Identify and chart the pros and cons, helping students identify commonalities. When there is disagreement, here are a few questions to ask:

- What do you hear the other person saying?
- What is at the heart of this disagreement?
- What do you think is really important to people who hold that opinion?

When attending to time constraints, you may need to wind down the conversation. In some cases, it is unlikely to reach closure, but you may ask them to summarize key points and/or articulate today's key agreements and disagreements and—if it feels like an important issue—add the caveat that you will pick up the conversation later. You can suggest they identify ways to take the next steps for future engagement. This can be done by pairing students to share or write a reflection. You can also ask, "What did you hear that made you think more deeply, or what touched you in some way?" Aim to end on an uplifting note, even if it is just to thank them for honestly approaching a hard topic.

Dilemmas and Points of Tensions

Making Space for Your Students' Full Identities Without Singling Out Any Student

Identity safe educators avoid putting students on the spot as they seek to raise awareness. Even when a teachable moment emerges, you need to consider the impact on the particular student involved. If it leads to "outing" a student and exposing a vulnerability in front of their classmates, this could be very harmful. A student should never be called upon to share sensitive topics or personal experiences (e.g., poverty, racism) without knowing if they feel comfortable doing so. Reducing shame and respecting their dignity comes first.

When the classroom is identity safe and trust is evident, often students will choose to share guarded and deeply held vulnerable feelings. Open-ended discussion that makes room for all students to share will make it safer for a student to be open about difficult experiences and understand it from multiple perspectives. Be sure all students understand that no one person can ever speak for their race, another race, or any whole group. The Dissolving Stereotypes activity described earlier is an example of how you can open a sensitive topic to everyone and, in many instances, allow a safe haven for authentic feelings to emerge.

What to Do When You Are Called Out

Many of us have had the experience of being called out by students or parents for saying something insensitive, biased, or racist. It feels terrible at the moment, but it can be a powerful learning experience. Start by remaining calm and centered. Do not take it personally, which can lead to a reactive and defensive response. If a person is upset and emotionally aroused and attacks you verbally, a defensive response could exacerbate the situation. Genuine listening at the moment can help move toward open-minded empathy.

Listen fully without interrupting and carefully consider what is being said before responding. Take note of the critique and genuinely seek to understand and learn from the underlying feeling. It is fair to ask for time to think about it and come back another day to respond. Also, you can indicate your openness for hearing the person's feelings, but remind them to speak respectfully according to the norms of the classroom. If you choose to take it offline to talk to the person privately, you also need to consider the rest of the students who have heard the comments. Find a way to come back to them and clarify how the situation was resolved in an appropriate way. This may mean acknowledging your own learning curve in the matter, which can support and motivate students and parents to reciprocate with you and each other, creating an atmosphere of shared understanding and trust to participate in difficult conversations in the future.

In some cases, you may feel the comment made about you is unfair or untrue. Remember that perception can mean reality to the person on the perceiving end, even though you never intended to be offensive. Do not dismiss the person as being touchy or oversensitive, nor conversely beat yourself up for making a mistake. You may want to reach out to a trusted colleague or your principal/supervisor for advice on following up. Try to maintain an open mind and recognize that we all have implicit and unconscious biases from swimming in the murky waters of an inequitable society. We each have the potential to make insensitive, biased, or microaggressive comments, especially in stressful situations or tense moments. As painful as it is, try to learn from what you said that was offensive. Students will respect you for acknowledging your mistakes and being accountable.

WHAT IT WAS LIKE BEING CALLED OUT RESPECTFULLY, TAKING IN THE CRITIQUE, REFLECTING, AND MAKING CHANGES

Claudia, an international presenter, shared the following experience:

> I was feeling good after a keynote at a national conference when a former superintendent came over and said, "I appreciated your keynote and took a great many ideas from it. And I know you want to be the best you can be and will be doing more of this work over the next few months, so I do want to share with you that attendees at my table found some comments you made to be classist and racist." I was taken aback, but her tone was quite calm and clear, and I wanted to live out my work on having hard conversations, so I asked for more clarification. She said, "It isn't just the specifics—which I can share with you—but it's about your mindset and your disposition and how you are coming to the work." That was challenging for me, as it wasn't detailed enough yet, but after some specifics were offered and after some reflection, and getting my ego out of the way, I really appreciated her candor.

Chapter Summary

We address identity, belonging, and diversity through all components of identity safety, yet this chapter focused on some specific aspects of *Using Diversity as a Resource* for learning. We began by explaining the value of affirming student identities—creating acceptance and belonging while confronting obstacles created by deficit thinking and negative stereotypes. In the "Making It Happen" section, we offered strategies for affirming identity, drawing from family backgrounds and experiences, and helping students examine multiple social identities and the intersectionality of oppressed identities. We specifically highlighted a gender-inclusive approach that breaks out of the mainstream view of a gender binary. From there, we proposed refuting and reducing stereotype threat with research-based methodologies and counternarratives to deconstruct the messages that lead to threat.

We returned to the topic of curriculum, explaining how a critical multicultural approach to instruction affords tools for analyzing history from multiple perspectives and reducing the sense of shame and rage a student from a nondominant culture might have internalized. Once they truly understand the historical roots, all students can feel empowered and activated to work for positive social change.

We also provided tools for facilitating the hard conversations that may result from tackling controversial topics. We concluded with two dilemmas that could result from going deeply into using diversity as a resource. First, we explored ensuring that no student feels singled out or is asked to speak for their entire race or group. Second, we closed by facing the dreaded moment when we as educators get challenged or called out for saying or doing something insensitive. Using diversity as a resource cannot be reduced to a set of steps. It can be messy work that requires careful navigation, honest reflection, and humility. Even so, it is worthy work that will develop into a classroom atmosphere that facilitates the best kind of learning and performance.

Check Yourself

When considering how you are working on using diversity as a resource, check yourself with the following questions:

1. How and with what input do you reflect, take stock of, and challenge your biases?

2. How have you drawn out experiences from your students about their families and lives in the classroom?

3. What have you taught your students about intersectionality?

4. How have you worked to make your language gender neutral, paying attention to the pronouns that students use for themselves?

5. What counternarratives have you shared that offer alternatives to dominant narratives while proffering a critical multicultural lens?

6. What have you done or plan to do to help students critically analyze stereotypes present in their textbooks and literature and ascertain what is missing?

7. How have you responded when a stereotype or slur is made in the classroom?

8. Have you held a difficult conversation? What happened, and how did you guide it in a productive direction? What might you do differently next time? Have you avoided any difficult conversations? If yes and you could go back, what would you do differently?

TRY IT OUT: END OF CHAPTER ACTIVITIES

Facilitating Hard Conversations: Reflection

1. Think of a hard conversation that you were part of as either a participant or leader. Describe it. What made it difficult? How was the tension addressed?

2. What is your experience with norms or community agreements? How have you handled it when an agreement was broken? How did that work?

3. Seek out an opportunity to try your skills using the following steps. Describe how you handled each of the aspects:
   a. How did you set a welcoming tone?
   b. What did you do to introduce the conversation explaining the purpose and ground rules?
   c. How did you use paraphrasing to assist with understanding?
   d. What did you do when students disagreed with each other?
   e. How did you summarize and conclude the discussion?
   f. What worked?
   g. What might you do differently in the future?

 Available for download as a full-page form at **https://resources.corwin .com/IdentitySafeClass6-12**

High Expectations and Academic Rigor 8

Why High Expectations and Academic Rigor Matter

Several decades of research supports the power of holding high expectations as a precursor to increased student achievement (Good, 1981). Every educator enters the classroom with a conscious or unconscious notion about what can be expected from each student in terms of both behavior and achievement. It is no surprise that students perceive and absorb the educator's attitude. When multiple educators hold similar expectations repeated over time, students come to internalize the message "I am smart and competent" or, conversely, "I am not smart or competent."

Expectations can be communicated both verbally and nonverbally. A quick look of disdain from an educator might not be missed, or the opposite, a flashing glance of encouragement, can send an affirming message! Students notice how often they are called upon or whether help is given with a tone of "I know you can do this" or, conversely, "Why don't you ever get what I am trying to teach you?" A message may be communicated in the way a student is corrected. Does the educator consider the mistake a big deal or not? Over time, the negative experiences can add up. For the student, low expectations, low grades, and low test scores can become a pattern for a self-fulfilling prophecy. That sense of low or high expectations may already be deeply embedded in the mind of a student by the time they leave elementary school.

Alfonso was one of the few Black students in his second-grade class at a private school. When he got his report card, he became upset when the teacher suggested that he read over the summer. He asked his mother to find out whether any of the other students got this message. From the teacher's point of view, this was an innocuous comment, and she had no intention to express low expectations. However, young Alfonso already had internalized a worry that he might be falling behind the other students. Clearly, even by the age of seven, he was sensitized to being judged about his performance. He did not know the meaning of the word *stereotype,* yet he was experiencing a form of stereotype threat.

These types of experiences also can result in students losing trust in their teachers, particularly true for Black and Latinx students. The challenge for secondary educators who come into contact with students who have already internalized low expectations for themselves is finding ways to flip the script and help them rewrite the internal story.

First, let's examine particular educator behaviors that have been associated with low expectations (Good & Brophy, 1980):

- Seating low-performing students farther from the educator
- Paying less attention to slower students by calling on them less and criticizing them more
- Giving more critical and less accurate or detailed public feedback to lower-achieving students
- Interrupting low-achieving students more frequently than high achievers
- Giving less-demanding work to low performers

Identity safe educators become aware of their expectations and how the sentiments are communicated to their students. They intentionally work to uproot implicit biases.

MISINTERPRETING STUDENT BEHAVIORS LOWERS EXPECTATIONS

Yearly at one middle school, several students were asked to share essays about their school experience as part of the promotion ceremony. All students were invited to submit essays, and the teachers in the English department would select the students for this honor. One particular year, the teachers told the principal that they had no appropriate candidates. At lunch one day, a Black girl, Anya, approached the principal on the school yard and showed him her essay. He was astounded at the insights and shared the essay with the two assistant principals, who agreed that this was an exceptional essay.

The principal approached the teachers to ask why this student was not selected. The teachers replied that she was loud, lacked self-control, and often interrupted in class. They felt she did not deserve to be honored as such. The principal immediately understood these attitudes as implicit bias. Anya did not fit their idea of a model student, so they did not recognize her tremendous talent. In "The Science of Verve and What It Means for Black Students" (2017), author Darla Scott writes that White middle-class norms often can clash with the cultural norms and home environments of Black students. She adds the preference for stimulation and energetic and enthusiastic verbal responses can be misinterpreted and considered disruptive. These English teachers had missed Anya's brilliance. In this case, fortunately, the principal intervened and invited Anya to share her essay at graduation.

In identity safe classrooms, educators intentionally seek to express high expectations in authentic ways. High expectations and academic rigor are combined because high standards must be paired with rigorous learning opportunities. As we discussed in Chapter 4: Teaching for Understanding, formative assessment strategies can assist a student in taking note of their progress and lead to a growing competence and confidence in their abilities. Students come to believe in and internalize high expectations while developing a positive academic mindset. High expectations, repeated over time and coupled with academic progress—even when started in middle and high school—can become a self-fulfilling prophecy.

In addition to developing a vigilance over our ingrained internal biases with an intent to change, as described in Chapter 3: Listening for Student Voices, it is important to dismantle our misconceptions about intelligence. Part of our learning curve, as we raise expectations for our students, involves deconstructing historical views of intelligence. Unfortunately, these erroneous theories are still perpetuated and as a result, some frightening beliefs are cultivated and sustained. We offer a brief overview in the next section.

Uncovering the Historical Roots: Galton, Social Darwinism, and Eugenics

Francis Galton, a cousin of Charles Darwin (Galton, 1869; Plucker, 2013), was responsible for the word *eugenics*, the mistaken notion of improving humanity through the promulgation of superior races and elimination of the supposed weaker or inferior strains. Galton wrote a series of books on the heredity of intellectual genius, which included a chapter on the comparative worth of different races that placed the "Negro" race as greatly inferior to the Europeans (Galton, 1869).

In the extreme, Adolf Hitler applied eugenics in Nazi Germany. Yet that was not the only social experiment with eugenics. Eugenics was also the basis for underlying segregation, forced sterilizations, and selective immigration policy in the United States. By the 1970s, over 60,000 sterilizations were done in 30 states that had adopted sterilization laws (Allen, 2007).

Selective immigration policies based on eugenics ended a period of open immigration with the Immigration Restriction Act of 1924; its intent was to stop "dysgenic" Italians and eastern European Jews from immigrating to the United States. Upon signing the act, President Calvin Coolidge commented, "America must remain American." The Immigration Restriction Act was not repealed until 1965 (Allen, 2007). Definitions of intelligence played a major part in the determination of which groups were "fit" to breed at the turn of the 20th century. The idea that people of some backgrounds are inferior to others was echoed in recent immigration debates.

The publication of *The Bell Curve* (Herrnstein & Murray, 1994) laid out fundamental assumptions claiming that cognitive ability is heritable. The authors acknowledged that environmental forces exist; however, they nevertheless proceeded to claim that African

American and Latinx peoples generally have lower intelligence. While the belief that the Jews, Italians, and Irish populate the ranks of the feebleminded is currently no longer in fashion, African American and Latinx people were described as "mental defectives" as recently as 2007 in a *Wall Street Journal* op-ed. In it, author Murray wrote that half of all children in the United States are below average in intelligence (para. 3). He stated that 36 percent of fourth graders have an IQ below 95.

Sadly, Murray is not considered to be an extremist nutcase, as evidenced by the fact that he received the Bradley Prize in 2016, an award given to people who exemplify the mission "to restore, strengthen and protect the principles and institutions of American exceptionalism." Murray's influence continues to be felt with proposed immigration policies that speak to supposed "merit-based" immigration.

While hopefully most educators believe a democracy needs an educated citizenry and that all children can learn, we have all been subjected to the subtle and not-so-subtle messages that contradict that belief. It is frightening to realize that Murray's and other eugenicists' beliefs continue to influence and contribute toward lowered expectations for students of color. However, after becoming aware of this history, identity safe educators can give students a very different message about intelligence and can help them actualize high expectations. Throughout this book, we have particularly highlighted Carol Dweck's (2006) theories of the growth mindset as a view, backed by research and neuroscience that is well-attuned to identity safety.

This chapter offers ways to express high expectations together with specific methods for scaffolding student learning as they engage in a rigorous curriculum. We also incorporate strategies for gradually removing the scaffolds as students achieve mastery.

High Expectations and Academic Rigor: Making It Happen

Taking a Deeper Look at the Changing Mindsets

We introduced the growth mindset in Chapter 1: The Introduction as a foundational theory that is an important consideration in identity safety. Here, we show how mindsets influence our students' views of intelligence and their expectations. The question for educators is how to convey our high expectations by making it safe for students to take risks and become willing to take on challenges in learning while believing that they are capable and can do it.

Dweck's (1999) growth mindset research showed that those who believed that their level of intelligence was fixed behaved differently from those who believed that intelligence can grow incrementally (see Chapter 1). As we examine our own language to students, there are many ways we can communicate our ideas for a growth mindset in both subtle and obvious ways; however, praise alone does not necessarily produce it. Mary Murphy (2018b) explains that many educators are taught in their preservice courses to capitalize on student strengths, and while the shift to focus our words and attention on student success may be necessary, it is not sufficient. While highlighting strengths is better than harping on deficits, the best practice may be to focus on evidence of growth, especially as it explicitly instructs the student. Pointing out successful strategies, for example, can offer students more than celebration of effort alone—it can serve to show them how and what they did to achieve their results, which they can use to build upon with other ideas. Focusing only on strengths in the form of praise may even create a lower standard, as students who are continually validated for effort or good character may believe it to be disingenuous and actually feel devalued. A focus on evidence of growth allows a student to see how they have been improving and to celebrate real progress with real examples. This also allows them to find value in the different ways of understanding information and the multiple pathways available for growth. At Leadership Public Schools (LPS) in Richmond, California, a student may be selected for the dean's list if they have either above a 3.5 grade point average or if they have gained one full grade point since the prior grading period.

While learning from history and deconstructing deeply held stereotypes and myths about intelligence, we can work on developing our own growth mindset attitudes that will translate to holding high expectations for your students.

RESEARCH ON REFRAMING STUDENT VIEWS OF INTELLIGENCE

Josh Aronson and colleagues (2002) developed a set of experiments to help students reframe their views of intelligence, based on growth mindset theories. The researchers set out to examine whether views of entity (fixed) or incremental (growth) intelligence would have an impact on Black students at Stanford University. Groups of undergraduate Black students and White students heard a lecture and saw a video about the incremental view of intelligence that included testimonials and scientific evidence of how intelligence could grow with effort. One group of study participants was assigned an elementary school-age pen pal and asked to write a motivational letter that included their new views of intelligence and the belief that through effort their intelligence would grow. Members of a second group, the control group, who were not informed about the incremental view of intelligence, were simply told to write a motivational letter.

The grades for both groups of university students were monitored over the course of the year. Researchers found that for students in the group that learned about the incremental view of intelligence, the achievement gap between White and Black college students was greatly reduced and these improvements held over time. These results suggest the value to both of adopting incremental views of intelligence (Aronson et al., 2002).

Scaffolding a Path to Rigor

Vygotsky's (1978) theory about the *zone of proximal development* is described as a state of mind that expands a student's capacity beyond what they already know and can do. One way to help students reach the "zone" is to scaffold instruction through offering a series of supports that allow them to attain knowledge and skills, thereby achieving tasks that they previously were unable to complete (Wood et al., 1976). Just as scaffolds help workers build a skyscraper, educational scaffolds allow students to rise to places that they could not reach on their own. Scaffolding can be used for any type of learning. It is the process of providing a virtual staircase of support that guides a student in the direction of learning, understanding, and ultimately successful application of learned material. Scaffolds must be carefully designed. If it becomes too easy, students will likely not put effort into comprehending, but if the steps to climb are too difficult, they can become frustrated. Scaffolding instruction is especially needed for students who speak English as a second language. Examples of scaffolding are found in the following section.

Preteach Academic and Content Vocabulary

If you have studied another language, you may know that missing the meaning of just one word can leave you totally confused. The whole gist of what is being said can be lost as our minds become distracted while trying to make sense of it all. We then stop tracking the conversation. Preteaching vocabulary is a well-researched tactic and has been shown to improve comprehension (Miller & Veatch, 2011). Academic vocabulary includes words that may not be specific to the content area but are part of academic discourse and important to know in the school context. Content vocabulary includes terminology that is specific to a particular subject (e.g., biology and algebra). When vocabulary is front-loaded in ways that are meaningful, students are more likely to absorb the new words and understand the lesson. This is particularly important for English learners in mainstreamed classes.

Puzzles, word games, visuals, graphic organizers, and activities can be used to vary the experiences. Asking students to role-play a word and having others guess the meaning can be fun and aid comprehension as well. With think/pair/share, students can explain the meaning of complex vocabulary in their own words. Frequent reminders help the students retain the new words and understand them in context. Vocabulary support can be enhanced by posting the new words on the walls. Ensuring students understand and develop a strong vocabulary builds confidence, enhancing a student's sense of belonging, thereby strengthening their academic identity.

Templates

Prompts, outlines, and templates will help a student write everything from an essay to research reports and metered poems. Templates can be used to formulate outlines and break down the required steps of a science project. Prompts with sentence starters can be quite helpful for English learners and students with learning disabilities. Ultimately, students need to think for themselves and be able to work without the templates and prompts; however, the initial provision for support can make the difference between success and failure for a student. Their successes can capture their interest for continued involvement and a commitment to work hard. Scaffolding can be explained at the outset of a lesson and reviewed again as they are being removed.

Rubrics

A well-designed rubric can guide students toward the highest level of learning by setting specific criteria for performance and communicating to students exactly what the work looks like when done well. Use of a rubric in a formative way during the learning process helps students see the path to improve their work. Rubrics can be used to score and give specific feedback on writing assignments, research or lab reports, performance tasks, cooperative science or social science projects, and virtually any task for which success criteria are clearly described.

In an LPS student video (LPS Student Interviews, 2018), Donald talks about how his teacher "puts rubrics on everything. . . . I feel like it helps because you're always in the know about what you need to have down and what you need to have learned by the end of that time. You have a certain time period to learn all of that. And she always posts it everywhere so you know."

A rubric needs to be carefully designed, using concrete descriptions that avoid subjectivity. Once developed, the educator models it, and students are taught how to use it and practice together. Students can work with peers to read each other's writing and compare it to the rubric. They also need to learn the language of constructive feedback. This includes how to make specific and helpful comments, as well as how to avoid responses that are too general, unclear, or hurtful. Then, they can they make revisions to their work and hand it in for final grading.

Modeling, Think-Alouds, and Visible Thinking

"I Do, We Do, and You Do" is a simple process of scaffolding where initially a concept is modeled to the whole group by the educator who demonstrates the lesson with "I do." Then, for "we do," the activity is done together with the class. Finally, for "you do," students are asked to do the activity themselves. In this process, each step is done long enough to ensure that all students will eventually be able to work on their own.

A "think-aloud" strategy happens when the educator or student articulates their thinking process aloud, such as when they solve a math problem or make a hypothesis in science. The class can then complete a similar process with a partner or through journaling in order to get them to think through the ideas on their own.

VISIBLE THINKING ROUTINE

To help students develop the practice of metacognitive reflection on their learning, teach them to use the following template:

1. What was my thinking process as I approached this task/problem/assignment?

2. How did it help me arrive at a conclusion/finished product?

3. Is there anything I would do differently the next time?

4. This is important to remember because____.

5. How can I apply it in future situations?

The *Visible Thinking* (2019) website (www.visiblethinkingpz.org) highlights a variety of "thinking routines," or simple protocols that assist students in approaching subjects from math and science content to the analysis of literature or historical trends. The routines offer powerful scaffolds for deeper thinking. By articulating the thinking process and revealing the tools for creating rationale, students can employ prompts and templates to facilitate an approach to higher-level thinking that students can learn to apply to other content. Specific routines for processing ideas are explicitly taught. Some examples include interpretation and justification, active reasoning and explanations, explaining how thinking has changed, and exploring diverse perspectives.

Gently Removing Scaffolds on the Road to Confidence

In an LPS identity safety workshop, educators brought up the challenge of removing scaffolds. Karen, one of the participants, said that some of her students had grown too dependent on the scaffolds, assuming they would always be there. One of her students actually told the class she feared she would be unable to operate without a scaffold. Leaving a scaffold in place too long can also become enabling and trap the student into feeling dependent on others to think and learn. Conversely, removing a scaffold too quickly can literally leave a student hanging and frustrated, unable to operate independently.

From the beginning, the goal and process of removing scaffolds can be explained to the students with the caveat that they will be able to eventually function without them. Students can reflect on the need for scaffolds and take part in determining when to release them, as well as understanding pathways and strategies for creating their own. They will eventually make their own outlines and rubrics and plan their writing without templates. They can learn to manage their time to complete assignments, just as they will need to do in college.

Moving students into the zone of proximal development underscores interdependence and helps create identity safety. Students feel a sense of belonging when they are supported by their educators, tutors, and peers, all working together toward competency. Equipped with newfound capabilities, their expectations for themselves will rise.

Dilemmas and Points of Tension

Countering the Cacophony of External Messages That Say "You Are Dumb"

I will never forget seeing a poster above the door in a high school special education class that said "Time passes, will you?" That doorway steered students to a blatant message that expressed doubt in their capacity to achieve. For some, that message echoes a continual onslaught coming from all directions. Insults about intelligence fly over social media, particularly with intentionally "stupid" sitcoms and movies with characters who repeatedly say foolish things. Shows with names like *Are You Smarter Than a Fifth Grader?* and movies like *Dumb and Dumber* rub in the societal attitudes that highlight, mock, stereotype, and internalize ideas about stupidity. *Fool, numbskull, idiot, peabrain,* and other words hammer it in. Parents can unwittingly doubt their kid's intelligence with a simple "Why won't you use your brain?" So what can you do with a student who has internalized these messages and turns them into a self-fulfilling prophecy? Often, these students have felt stupid for years.

An educator's challenge is to meet all students' needs without reproducing a hierarchy of intelligence and competence. This becomes ingrained as early as kindergarten with groups called the "Redbirds," who are the supposedly smart kids, and the "Bluebirds," who are already determined to be the "slow learners." Already in elementary school, students think they know who is "smart" and who is "dumb." By the secondary level, it is not easy to change deeply internalized beliefs stemming from sometimes very arbitrary decisions made in elementary school, but it is well worth the effort.

Here are five steps to start turning these feelings around:

1. Teach students a new way to look at intelligence by teaching the growth mindset and the triarchic theory of intelligence that highlights creative, analytic, and academic forms of intelligence (explained in Chapter 9: Challenging Curriculum). Demystify the view that intelligence is set in stone for life.

2. Share your own experiences with learning, failed attempts, and views of intelligence to show how you have grown and changed and assure them that they will, too.

3. Provide specific feedback on effective effort, progress, and work that the students did correctly ("wise feedback" will be covered in Chapter 10: Teacher Warmth and Availability for Learning).

4. Through scaffolding together with metacognitive messaging, help students experience success, which creates self-fulfilling prophecies and breeds further success.

5. Highlight and point out diverse ways of learning and knowing. Help the students discover some of their natural strengths and learn how to improve weak areas through practice.

6. Teach students to recognize and appreciate their own progress.

In addition to building trusting relationships, educators can support students to shine in unique ways and offer public validation of their varied contributions. Here is just a small sample of the many types of skills to highlight: public speaking, coming up with innovative and creative ideas, using humor, sharing from their personal experience, collaborating with others, helping peers, and showing empathy. By ascribing value to a wide range of ways to contribute and shine, students feel less competition with one another and gain a sense of the ways they can enrich classroom life.

Chapter Summary

We began this chapter about *High Expectations and Academic Rigor* with the good news that research findings support the power of expressing high expectations to influence student achievement. We then shared the sobering news that low expectations are often rooted in racially biased historical attitudes about intelligence, falsely attributing high intelligence to some groups and low intelligence to others, and that these attitudes are still prevalent today. Counternarratives are needed to help students navigate away from the negative messaging.

We then offered a set of practices to help educators express high expectations for the students, ultimately leading to the students holding high expectations for themselves. We shared scaffolding methods to help students progress into zones of proximal development. We offered specific strategies, including preteaching vocabulary, providing templates and rubrics, and modeling. We warned that when offering scaffolds, intentional plans for gradually releasing them will ensure that the students eventually can operate independently. We offered one point of tension involving the student who has already determined they are stupid, and we shared ways to help that student break out of that self-deprecating stance.

All the components of identity safety, as a holistic approach, can contribute to raising expectations. In Chapter 3, you will find think/pair/share and jigsaw, activities that foster interdependence. When we create belonging in a growth mindset culture (Chapter 1) and use student-centered teaching (Part II), while helping students become autonomous (Chapter 6), confidence grows. Chapter 9 will add more methods for providing rigorous instruction and support so students can gain the competence that demonstrates to themselves that they will reach increasingly higher levels of knowledge and achievement.

Check Yourself

1. What surprised you when reading about the historical roots of attitudes and views of intelligence? How can counternarratives help undo deeply embedded biases about intelligence? What have you tried?

2. Are your special education students given ways to contribute and shine? Are the aides who are present to support students using effective strategies to gradually release responsibility for their learning to the students? Explain.

3. What steps have you taken to undo the damage of low expectations and support individual students to change negative attitudes about their intelligence?

4. How do you communicate about growth mindset to your students? What is your attitude toward your own growth? How can mindsets be changed?

5. What scaffolds do you provide for your students, and how do you gradually remove them?

TRY IT OUT: END OF CHAPTER ACTIVITIES

Raising Expectations

First, reflect on your own experience with expectations. Do you hold high expectations for yourself? If so, who influenced and believed in you along the way? If it is hard for you to accept higher standards for yourself, what can you do in the way of self-scaffolding to buoy your own esteem?

Next, choose three students. Choose one who already holds high expectations, one who is in the middle with neither high nor low expectations, and one who does not hold high expectations. Reflect on the expectations each of these students has for themselves. Describe the three students and plan ways you will further support each of them. Try out your plans. Share what happened.

Students	Describe	How You Will Further Support This Student	What Happened
Name: (student with high expectations for self)			
Name: (student with midlevel expectations for self)			
Name: (student with low expectations for self)			

 Available for download as a full-page form at **https://resources.corwin** **.com/IdentitySafeClass6-12**

9 Challenging Curriculum

Why Challenging Curriculum Matters

In an identity safe classroom, dynamic curriculum invites students to become active players in their lives, to achieve goals and solve problems in their classroom, school, community, and world. This chapter focuses on creating a challenging curriculum in two important ways. First, offering a challenging curriculum engages students through expanding their world view and touching them in places where they care. This stimulates curiosity and wonder, bringing forth awe and amazement. Second, a challenging curriculum can motivate students to stretch themselves and take risks. This will fortify their confidence, help them grow, and value learning itself, thereby enhancing their sense of identity as lifelong learners.

When a curriculum has too many standards, content is rushed over quickly in an attempt to pump in knowledge and churn out students who scramble to pass tests. This type of education forces competition with winners and losers, conditions that ultimately dull the mind. The standardization and focus on test preparation has resulted in minimizing the focus on social studies and the arts. In contrast, Finland—one of the top scoring nations in the world—employs a completely different system (Sahlberg, 2016). It offers many individualized learning opportunities and a curriculum that values and equally distributes time to help students develop moral character, creativity, knowledge, skills, and ethics. In addition, Finland has many student-centered policies that include increasing the financial investment in education and eliminating tracking. It has only one high-stakes standardized test at the end of high school. The other assessments are decentralized and developed by the educators themselves. Finland has an equitable model that distributes resources to schools that need it most. It invests educator time in professional development and trusts its educators to develop innovative learning opportunities. We share these aspects of Finnish education to give evidence that a challenging curriculum leads to greater levels of learning and achievement.

In the SISP identity safety research, "challenge" emerged as one of the significant components. In identity safe classrooms, the content, delivery, and opportunities for student engagement with peers all come together in a stimulating environment. Creativity, curiosity, and innovation can be interwoven through inquiry, creative

CHALLENGING CURRICULUM: A FOUR-PART APPROACH

1. Create an air of intellectual excitement.

2. Offer an appropriate level of individual challenge for each student, guiding them forward into their proximal zone of development.

3. Make classrooms a safe place for thinking, offering multiple perspectives and ways of expressing ideas and feelings.

4. Differentiate instruction through personalization as you vary content, product, and process to meet student needs. (D. M. Steele & Cohn-Vargas, 2013)

writing, interesting research projects, and the arts. All content areas can draw on these methodologies as part of a challenging curriculum.

We recognize that educators are pressured and under great stress to cover content, ensure their students meet standards, and prepare them to perform well on high-stakes tests. However, we believe that much can be done in their individual classrooms to create a challenging curriculum that is increasingly more exciting and relevant without compromising the requirement to teach the standards. Offering a challenging curriculum can also keep you, as the educator, excited and motivated with vibrant lessons targeted to the needs of your particular students. Educators, working with colleagues, can make the school system more student-centered, uplifting the curriculum in transformational ways.

Challenging Curriculum: Making It Happen

Creating an Air of Intellectual Excitement: Creativity and Innovation as Part of a Challenging Curriculum

The ability to think creatively and solve problems by looking at them in new ways has led to the phenomenon of human evolution and quite possibly will be critical to our future survival. Scientists are innovators who use intuition to observe, gather, and test new data as they develop new hypotheses while building on previous discoveries. Artists also draw from intuition, building upon prior knowledge. Artists and scientists both tend to approach problems with a similar open-mindedness and curiosity. They do not fear the unknown and ask bold questions that lead them into new territory.

When creativity researcher Csikszentmihalyi (2015) studied persons endowed with inventive imaginations throughout history, he noted that most human advances were the result of creativity, intrinsic motivation, and curiosity. He also found that creativity brings purpose and meaning to human life and, consequently, helps people feel more alive. Contrary to what many people think, the quality of creativity actually arises from years of hard work within a particular domain rather than only in a sudden burst of insight.

Robert Sternberg and colleagues (Sternberg et al., 2009) developed the triarchic (three-part) theory of intelligence as follows:

1. Analytical intelligence involves being able to analyze ideas theoretically and solve problems, which is often where other definitions of intelligence end.

2. Creative intelligence is the capacity to draw on our existing knowledge and use it to deal with new situations.

3. Practical intelligence focuses on solving problems in the context of action and concrete knowledge and skills.

Sternberg et al. (2009) propose that education needs to incorporate a balance of analytical, creative, and practical skills.

For many students, creativity has all but vanished from their secondary school experience and may have been missing for a good long while. In elementary school, if they were lucky, students experienced visual art, drama, and music activities as their teachers included them in at least some of their daily experiences. Often for teens, the arts have become specialized tracks for some and completely absent for others.

Creativity can be woven into all subject areas. We may need to muster up the extra effort to help students break out of habits that have hindered creativity over the years. Students may be programmed to regurgitate what they think their educators want them to think or say. You can work with them to break these self-imposed limitations and support them in recognizing and exercising their creativity. Fostering creativity goes beyond the traditional idea of creative writing, poetry, painting, and other art forms.

Language Arts

In language arts, brainstorming sessions—where all ideas, both rational and zany, are welcome—can lead the students into a creative mindset. Responses to reading can be a source of creative thinking when students can predict what they think will happen or imagine a conversation with one of the characters. Students can write a prequel or sequel or invent a different ending to a piece of literature. Writing opens many other doors to creativity. In addition to writing fictional accounts and poems, nonfiction can also be approached creatively. Essays can include presenting innovative ideas and solutions to problems. Students can play with metaphors and similes.

Social Studies

Social studies presents many opportunities to use creative thinking as students imagine, visualize, and describe different moments in history. History comes to life through role-playing, theatre, and tableaus (doing a freeze-frame of a scene in history). They can also imagine and portray what would have happened if history took a different course, creating a science fiction story or a futuristic project based on current trends in political and social movements, scientific changes, and technology.

In both language arts and social studies, students can select how they want to demonstrate what they have learned. They can draw from art forms by inventing raps, songs, cartoons, or visual displays. Students can show what they have learned in a variety of creative products, videos, podcasts, dramatizations, comic strips, Prezis, models, puppet shows, and more.

CREATIVE BRAINSTORMING PROCESS

Brainstorming leads to an onslaught of ideas, inviting the unexpected and even what may be considered wild ideas and divergent ways of thinking. Educators present a prompt, problem, or question, and students respond. Here are some simple steps:

1. Identify the purpose and goal of the brainstorming session.

2. Set clear ground rules that elicit participation without interruption or judgment. Express the value of creative thinking and problem-solving.

3. Facilitate to ensure equitable participation.

4. Encourage all kinds of ideas offered seriously, even those that may seem far-fetched.

5. Explain that during the session, ideas will not be discussed or judged as to whether they are viable.

6. Accept and chart all ideas.

7. Do one of these next steps, depending on your goals:
   - If it is a brainstorm to get ideas for students to work on individually, they can discuss which ideas might work for them to follow up with in their work.
   - If your goal is to identify one idea for all to work on, you can use a process to rank ideas:
     ○ Participants can place sticky dots on the top-three ideas that they want to discuss further. Dots are counted. Further discussion narrows the ideas down.
     ○ Once ideas are selected, you can discuss the options, combine several, or select one and come to consensus.

8. Share the next steps on how to proceed.

Science

In science, creativity and innovation can be encouraged through developing ways to prove a hypothesis and design an experiment. Students can prepare for an inquiry or experiment by drawing a storyboard or doing a quick-write in which they explore and imagine a topic. They can record ideas or draw in journals throughout the experience to reflect, pose questions, predict answers, and test assumptions. Some science journals have a line drawn down the middle of each page. On one side, students record their observations. On the other side, they record their thoughts, questions, feelings, and concerns, all of which add to the creative mindset.

Math

In math, students can invent word problems for their peers to solve. They can draw and design graphics to demonstrate mathematical properties, invent riddles and math

PLATE TECTONICS CAN INSPIRE THE EDUCATOR AND THE STUDENTS

by Sue Boudreau
Middle School Earth Science Teacher
Orinda (California) Union School District

I used to think that geology was basically memorizing the layers of the Earth, and boring collections of rocks. Like most middle school science teachers, I'm a biologist by training and now I teach it with the integrated NGSS (Next Generation Science Standards). I'm getting more and more excited about the subject matter as I learn more, and hopefully passing that on to my classes. I dreamed up a lab to help teach the underlying big-picture concepts for both layers of the Earth and an introduction to plate tectonics. Their question: How did the Earth form?

Students began with a brief think/pair/share discussion to expose prior knowledge. Then, they did the activity, which involved putting scoops of grated candle wax, sand, and sawdust in a Mason jar. Students were taught safety procedures and wore eye protection when they added and swirled very hot water. After it cooled, they were challenged to figure out how the settling and cooling ingredients relate to the real events that geologists think led to the formation of the Earth and the tectonic plates. They also were asked to consider the differences between this experiment and what actually goes on beneath the Earth.

It went really well. Kids seemed lit up by the concepts and, of course, stirring and poking warm wax.

Note: Find more of Sue's science blogs at www.takeactionscience.wordpress.com

games, and find multiple ways to solve problems and share with one another. On a meta-level, they can explain their thinking and share different creative solutions to the same problem. The can apply a math principle to their own lives. Math journals can be used like science journals to record thinking.

Teaching as a Creative Act

Teaching itself is an act of creativity, continually bringing forth new ways of seeing and solving problems. Well-planned lessons often need to morph and change in the moment in response to student questions and insights. As we look into our students' faces, we get a steady flow of feedback. We continually adjust to ensure students understand. We watch for the spark of connection in their eyes and the "aha" in their voices as we create an air of intellectual excitement. A creative approach to life is not only interesting, motivating, and contagious for students but also for ourselves as educators.

Challenging All Students With Higher-Order Thinking

The beauty of higher-order thinking skills is that they can be easily integrated into instruction for students of all ages and academic levels and in every content area. Educational researcher Norman Webb (2015) developed the *Depths of Knowledge (DOK)* model for looking at the actual levels of thinking that form part of instruction. The four levels, or DOKs, identified by Webb include recall (facts, details, procedures), skills/concepts (applying skills, explaining how and why), strategic thinking (reasoning, planning, complex and abstract thinking), and extended thinking (complex reasoning, application to new situations and the real world). Webb suggests that the levels of thinking are not linear or hierarchical. While he says that all DOK levels form part of a rigorous academic program with higher-order thinking, we want to point out a common misnomer that students who are not achieving at grade level need to focus mainly on recall and rote learning of basic skills. This is erroneous and hampers their intellectual growth. All students, regardless of their level of achievement, can respond to activities and questions that intrigue and motivate.

Critical thinking and higher-level questioning incorporate asking students to evaluate, synthesize, analyze, summarize, and compare and contrast. Students can be taught questioning strategies for clarification and accuracy and to establish specificity, logic, significance, depth, breadth, and fairness. By tapping into their natural curiosity and wonder, you can ask them to formulate their own questions using the higher-order interrogatives. They can learn to communicate clearly and precisely as well as develop metacognitive skills as they "think about thinking" and reflect on how they came to particular conclusions.

With critical thinking strategies, students develop habits of intellectual integrity, courage, empathy, and fair-mindedness—and then are able to apply them in a range of situations, all hallmarks of identity safety. These qualities give students confidence and strengthen their academic mindset.

Socratic Questioning

Socratic questioning (Paul & Elder, 1997) is a methodology that can be used to further enhance critical thinking skills. The model is based on posing questions and responding to them with further questions. Students generate reasoned answers while being open to alternative views, learning to communicate their thoughts clearly, and listening to one another. Socratic questioning can be implemented in triads, small groups, or a fishbowl model, where a small group of students is in the center of the room surrounded by the whole class, who observes, listens, and later contributes impressions through further Socratic dialogue.

One student is selected as the Socratic questioner and is given or selects a thoughtful and probing question to initiate discussion on a particular topic. The leader encourages participants to respond. Then, subsequent participants elaborate on the contributions of their peers by paraphrasing and synthesizing ideas and clarifying ambiguities. Additional questions prompt deeper exploration, and the responses bring together differing perspectives through conscious efforts toward synthesis. The leader keeps the discussion focused and ensures fair participation. Once this structure is taught, modeled, and practiced, it becomes a way to foster higher-level thinking and creative problem-solving, benefiting students at all academic levels.

Differentiating Instruction

One of the greatest challenges for secondary educators is to simultaneously meet the needs of students at a range of academic levels in the same room during a short 40- to 50-minute lesson. While difficult, it is possible.

By "mixing it up" using a variety of differentiated instructional strategies, students can progress at their own rate and remain engaged. Lessons can be differentiated by content, process, or product (Tomlinson, 2017), offering many potential ways for all students to learn simultaneously. The strategies are not carried out in isolation but are varied in such a way that in concert they support a range of students with many differing needs.

Large groups, small groups, partners, and individualized learning are among the methods of varying the classroom structure. Each form can permit the educator to meet individual student needs and ensure all students are learning.

Differentiation is done through a variety of formats:

Individual practice: Students work individually at their own pace. The educator can circulate and focus on individual student needs.

Stations: Students rotate through stations with differing activities. The educator can remain at one station while others have activities that can be completed without educator support.

Group work: Students work with partners or in small groups, offering peer support to complete projects or activities. See Chapter 5: Focus on Cooperation for ideas on preparing students for cooperative work. Educators circulate.

Whole group: Some content can be delivered to the entire group using strategies that ensure all students are engaged and learning.

The educator varies the activities and duration based on the goals of the course and the diagnosed needs of the students. By using a flex model, an educator can have some days or blocks of time where students work groups. On other days, students can rotate through learning stations and subsequently process ideas working individually or in pairs. By varying the means of delivery, the educator is freed from constantly playing a central role as instructor, enabling individualized attention to increase the depth and rigor of learning.

Setting the Stage for Differentiation Through Assessment

Preassessment tools enable educators to determine each student's knowledge base at the start of a new topic. From there, different methods are tailored to build on individual needs. Preassessments include short quizzes or activities where students demonstrate what they already know. A KWL chart (K: what I know; W: what I want to know; L: what I learned) can be used individually or with a whole class to assess initial levels of knowledge on a topic and again at the end of a learning experience to reflect on what was learned (see *formative assessment* in Chapter 4: Teaching for Understanding).

LPS (Leadership Public Schools) uses the *Illuminate* student information system, one of many computer software systems designed to record and house student assessment data. The students are taught how to use a student portal, allowing them to monitor and reflect on their own progress and determine what are they doing effectively or find areas they need to improve.

A student explains, "In Illuminate, there are different question groups, and it tells me what specific category I need to work on. I use that information on my weakest point to work on that category."

Skill Building to Prepare for Effective Differentiation

To maximize the varied forms of learning, students need specific instruction and practice with the following skills:

- Working with a partner and learning to function as a team
- Learning to move forward at their own pace
- Setting goals
- Learning from their mistakes
- Analyzing the data on their own progress and determining next steps
- Working independently while the educator is helping other students

Grouping Strategies

Small groups can be mixed in different ways, and continually varied to include hetero-geneous groups as well as groups organized by levels of academic readiness, interest, and learning preferences. See Chapter 5 for additional considerations when forming groups.

Instructional Models for Differentiation

Graduated difficulty is a model that offers choices that can be done individually or in partners. It involves assigning all students the same thematic content but allowing them to make choices regarding the degree of difficulty based on their academic level. They can select one of three problems to explore and/or choose a piece of literature at their appropriate level of difficulty. The students are invited to make a selection based on their interests according to their own level of expertise. As the students are working on their problems, the educator focuses on the students who are having difficulty so as to scaffold the work for them. Also, the educator can challenge those who are operating on a level that is too easy for them, encouraging them to try a more difficult challenge.

Learning stations include an array of tasks, with students rotating through each one. Station tasks, based on the subject area, can include the following (Germaine-McCarthy, 2014).

- In math and science classrooms, students would approach these types of tasks:
  o Mastery task—involves solving a problem to mastery and full competency
  o Understanding task—involves presenting a problem done incorrectly and requiring students to dissect it and find out what went wrong and then solve it correctly
  o Self-expressive task—involves applying a specific math concept by having students create their own word problem related to a real-world situation they have encountered
  o Interpersonal task—involves partners or small teams working closely together to solve problems that become increasingly difficult
- In language arts and social studies classrooms, stations might have specific objectives that could include the following:
  o Researching a topic
  o Analyzing an article, essay, or piece of literature
  o Deconstructing and posing solutions to current social issues
  o Debating and contrasting different perspectives

Flipped learning (Flipped Learning Network, 2014) is a student-centered model of differentiation in which educators employ a range of strategies to create flexible instructional spaces. Digital content, including readings and videos, is assigned for study outside the classroom, allowing class time to be spent on a more rigorous analysis and application of the new information. The methods of learning outside class allow for differentiation because an educator can assign alternate materials based on needs (e.g., varied reading levels, Spanish version). In addition, students are not bound by time to complete the work. New concepts are presented from various angles, including multimedia, personalized learning tools, and other methods. In the classroom, the educator is freed up to focus on deepening the learning and meeting specific students' needs.

Careful consideration is needed to ensure this strategy increases rather than hampers equitable access. Not all students have online options at home, and some may not have adequate knowledge of English to maximize understanding the content independently. Educators need to know their students well to ensure that the learning outside the classroom is occurring and that it is appropriately scaffolded for all learners to access. LPS provides after-class structures, including lunchtime office hours and peer tutoring, that can be leveraged to support flipped learning.

Personalized learning is a model of instruction based on specific student needs. Students work with educators to set goals for individual progress and to design a personalized learning path with benchmarks that allow students themselves (as well as their educators) to monitor progress along the way. In a personalized learning model, students can make choices based on interest and what is relevant to them within specific tasks.

Blended learning is one model of personalized learning that intentionally intersperses digital learning experiences with interpersonal experiences. In many cases, this model uses adaptive computer programs to tailor instruction to the specific level of each student. During times when students are using computers or watching videos, the educator can meet with other individuals or small groups.

Blended learning has a few caveats. Educators need to ensure the digital tools are rigorous and engaging. Also, individual online experiences need to be complemented with opportunities for rich academic discourse. If students spend all their time plugged into computers, they will become too reliant on individual work, missing valuable academic social interactions.

Virtual reality is one of the array of digital tools available for blended learning. Increasingly popular and highly motivating, virtual reality allows students to enter worlds as small as a cell or atom, travel to distant places in the universe, and perform simulations. They can play educational games individually or in small or large groups. Some educators are going one step further and buying a 360-degree camera and designing their own virtual lessons.

We have presented additional differentiated strategies in Part II: Student-Centered Teaching, including the jigsaw strategy (see Chapter 3: Listening for Student Voices). For more on inquiry, see Chapter 4. All differentiated options need to be carefully managed by educators to support identity safety through rigor, increased access, and agency, as well as supporting a student's academic identity development. In identity safe classrooms, relationships and human interaction are the central mode of learning, and digital tools are added intentionally and thoughtfully at specific times to support differentiation.

Strategies to Differentiate During Whole-Group Instruction

A few simple strategies can make learning more accessible to all students in large groups:

Front-loading academic and content vocabulary is described in Chapter 8: High Expectations and Academic Rigor to ensure all students have access to key content.

Exploratory time to set the stage for new information can be an experimental or even playful space where students engage with ideas. For example, if the students are studying fractions, an educator can give students several equations with fractions and ask them to play around with them and see what they discover.

An enticing anticipatory set engages students' minds by linking prior knowledge to new knowledge, using aspects that are relevant to the content. More whole-group engagement suggestions are included in Chapter 4.

We devoted a lot of this chapter to differentiation because, when it is done well, it can be a powerful identity safe method of instruction that strengthens student voice and cooperation, promotes agency and autonomy, and actively validates student diversity. We placed it here because for educators it holds tremendous promise to provide scaffolds and supports that allow students to challenge themselves. Many additional blended and personalized learning strategies and other differentiation models used at LPS are available to all, featured on the *Learning Accelerator* (n.d.) website at www.practices. learningaccelerator.org.

Identity Safe Productive Struggle: Helping Students Find Their Own Level of Challenge

Productive struggle (the idea that there is value in struggling and persisting to overcome a hurdle) has been hailed as a way to help students develop a spirit of stick-to-itiveness. This learned habit contrasts with popular culture that promotes instant gratification. With "fast" food, "instant replay," social media, and the Internet, experiences are often truncated through rapid exposure and kept to a superficial level. Many youths in the current generation come to expect easy solutions that require little effort, which is exacerbated if they expect everything to be handed to them. Privileged students may have indeed grown up with an excess of attention and material support, and they may approach problem-solving with similar expectations. Others less fortunate may already have employed persistence in a constant struggle to survive. However, many have not yet applied the idea of endurance and continuity to their education and classroom experiences. Productive struggle, therefore, can be useful for all students when it is handled thoughtfully.

With productive struggle, students are not immediately given assistance when they do not know an answer. They are encouraged to grapple with problems rather than receive readily available solutions. With productive struggle, students learn to keep trying, think flexibly, develop both tenacity and resolve, and take time to think and consider different ways to solve a problem.

In identity safe classrooms, educators carefully consider how to implement productive struggle. Cold calling on students who do not know the answer may humiliate them. When put on the spot, their minds might go blank, causing them to actually function at a lower level than they are capable of doing. Providing a safe space for a student to think and struggle without being put on the spot will spare that student from developing a sense of learned helplessness. In identity safe productive struggle, students seek their own level of challenge and are taught about the proximal zone of development. They have already been taught a process that is less about racing to get the answer and more about the joy of doing their personal best and continuing to improve.

Using Praise Effectively to Motivate Effort

Praising students with phrases like "You really made an effort" and "I see you made progress" while pointing out evidence—as opposed to saying "You are really smart"—will shift the value of education from measuring intelligence to one of learning and growing. Carol Dweck (2006) suggests that praising intelligence promotes a fixed mindset and hinders creativity and innovation. Dweck (Bronson, 2007) created a research study in which fifth graders were given the Raven's test, a nonverbal IQ test with a set of puzzles. First, she gave students simple puzzles that all could do easily. Students from one group were praised for intelligence ("You are very smart"), and the other group members were praised for effort ("I can see you worked hard"). Then, all students were offered a second opportunity to work with a harder puzzle. Those who had been praised for effort wanted to do the harder puzzles, while those who had been praised for their intelligence opted for the easier puzzles.

Identity safe educators mete out praise intentionally. They offer praise by highlighting the specific strategies a student used on the path to solving a problem. They praise effort and perseverance and celebrate real progress.

Leveraging Mistakes as Learning Opportunities: Mistakes Can Be Our Friends

Through television commercials and social media advertisements, we are bombarded with the idea of perfection: "the perfect car," "flawless skin," and "the very best" product or experience. This kind of thinking easily triggers fear of failure and shame if we lose or do not succeed. In reality, we have the potential to learn the most from our biggest mistakes, errors, and failures. How then can we create a culture in the classroom that allows everyone to take risks and feel safe enough to make mistakes? How can we help our students learn to pick themselves up again after they fail? While educators cannot eliminate the onslaught of messaging about being perfect coming from society and often from well-meaning parents, we can start by talking with our students about the value of learning from mistakes.

In various studies, researchers demonstrated that the educators' attitudes toward mistakes impact how students react to them. They found that when educators have a positive attitude toward learning from mistakes, students do not fear making errors. In a supportive environment, students are not allowed to ridicule others for their errors. Therefore, errors do not seem so ominous but are treated as an expected part of the learning process (Goldin et al., 2007; Heimbeck et al., 2003).

Educators in identity safe classrooms intentionally begin by sharing their own vulnerabilities in ways that remind students that nobody is exempt from making mistakes. Drawing attention to missteps we have made in our daily life, sharing our reactions, and explaining how we are seeking to improve our attitudes toward mistakes serves as a catalyst to inspire our students.

We can normalize mistakes by analyzing them together, taking problems apart, and figuring out what went wrong. By doing this regularly, we can transform their fear of failure and make our classrooms into environments where mistakes are freely examined. Students develop a toolbox of strategies to use in a variety of situations.

LPS (LPS Student Interviews, 2018) videotaped students discussing growth mindset strategies and ways to approach formative assessment. According to one student, Ashley,

> [Our teacher] has us do an error analysis to help us understand the concepts better. Whatever we get wrong, he wants us to write down the right answer on a sheet of paper and then explain how we made the mistake. That way, he gets a better understanding of our thinking process and we get a better understanding of what we did wrong so we can improve on the retake.

Building student confidence also includes guiding them to handle their emotions in safe and appropriate ways and learning how to bounce back and adapt after a failure. This is where listening to student voices offers singular value, paying attention to each student's unique reaction to failure. We need to be aware of students for whom *learned helplessness* (see Chapter 4 and Chapter 6: Classroom Autonomy) is already ingrained, causing them to see each failure as further evidence that they cannot learn. We can intervene without humiliating a student who is devastated and starts shutting down. The following sections show some ways to help students deal with failure and continue to persevere without giving up.

Error Analysis in Action

Mike Fauteux, LPS's Innovator in Residence, formerly a math teacher, has developed a useful error analysis model, designed to strengthen the growth mindset of students and promote a positive attitude for turning mistakes into learning opportunities. The model has been particularly useful in math. Fauteux developed a variety of ways to normalize error analysis, removing any shame from making mistakes and showing students how much we can learn from examining our mistakes. In one model he refers to as "hero-making," Fauteux helps students who make many mistakes turn into "heroes" by scaffolding their error analysis in a humiliation-free method.

A growth-oriented attitude toward failure and mistakes is critical and can lead to realizing the simple fact that, like it or not, we all make mistakes on a regular basis throughout our lives—and it's OK because we can deal with them. We are not perfect, yet we can grow. Identity safe classrooms can be that safe haven for us to accept our humanity—complete with our vulnerabilities—and learn from our mistakes. Teaching students to feel self-compassion also adds to their ability to face failure and other difficult situations.

HERO-MAKING ERROR ANALYSIS STRATEGY: HOW TO DO IT

Preparation: Educator reviews student work and identifies common errors.

Activity:

1. Educator has students individually complete a task that often results in common errors.

2. Educator circulates to observe student work and identify students making common errors, focusing on those with anxiety over their academic identity.

3. The educator preconferences with a few, making sure they recognize and can explain the error they made.

4. Educator reviews the task and then asks students to think/pair/share about what possible errors someone might make on it to deepen their understanding.

5. Educator "randomly" calls on students (only calling on the ones the educator preconferenced with earlier), asking them to explain a common error one might make and suggest ways to avoid it.

Through "hero-making," students who often make errors gain confidence and self-esteem by participating in ways that previously were difficult and by normalizing the value of making errors.

Alternate strategies:

- Incorporate the error analysis into an exit ticket. This allows the educator to review student understandings.

- Ask students to redesign the problem so that one of the incorrect answers is now the correct one.

What to Do With a Wrong Answer

In an identity safety workshop, Ayelet, a math teacher, raised the dilemma of how to respond to a student who gives the wrong answer in the large group. She explained how she does not want to embarrass the student, yet she knows it does not help the individual or the class to have the wrong information shared without it correcting it. The group discussed ways to handle this common occurrence. They came to agree that there are ways to correct the student while taking into account the student's dignity when responding, acknowledging the student in an authentic way. You might say, "I can understand how you might have thought that way, because. . . ." Or you might clarify their thinking by adding that "logic might lead in that direction, but. . . ." If you think the student is close to catching on at that moment, you might say, "Why don't you rethink that, because. . . ."

I once observed a middle school student, Samuel, raise his hand and eagerly come up to the board to solve a math problem. Once there, he was stumped. After a few moments of awkward silence, his teacher asked, "Do you want another student to help you answer this math problem?" Samuel nodded and selected George to come to the front. George grabbed the chalk and whipped out the answer while Samuel stood by with a blank look on his face. This strategy did not appear to help him learn nor did it give him confidence. He shuffled back to his seat. An alternative might have been to direct Samuel to silently confer with George before completing the problem. He would then have received support and learned but also maintained his dignity. Preserving the integrity of the student in the process of correcting an error protects their sense of competence and models to others that this classroom is safe to express ideas.

Learning from our mistakes sets up dynamics where students feel safe to take risks and forge ahead in their work, knowing that mistakes will be corrected without damaging their confidence.

Dilemmas and Points of Tension

Reframing Our Assumptions: When You Need More Information About a Quiet Student

Students who are quiet and rarely speak up may present a daunting situation for educators who may never be sure if the student is motivated and/or challenged. Does their timidness mask the fact that they have given up on school? When students are loud, disruptive, and off task, they inevitably draw attention. However, others who are quiet and appear compliant may simply be unengaged. As well, those who are extremely shy may be paralyzed by fear and unable to express their interest.

The first step is to notice these quiet students. Approach them individually to ask questions and find out what makes each of them tick and link their interests to the particular course content. What kinds of stories do they like to either watch or read? Who is their favorite historical figure and why? What do they know about the latest technology or scientific inventions? Or invite them to tell you or write about something important to them—new information will emerge.

Take note if you spot group dynamics or peer issues that may silence a student or cause them to feel alienated from others. Address conflicts immediately (see Chapter 11: Positive Student Relationships). Personal check-ins can do wonders and encourage students to open up and share what they are feeling. Frequent check-ins allow educators to monitor student feelings without being intrusive. If they have previously shared personal stories or family issues, following up with more questions will make them realize that you were listening. Some educators open their classrooms at lunchtime for students to hang out and talk, play board games, or do simple art activities. This can really fortify confidence for students who feel socially awkward and have nowhere to go for lunch.

There is no magic formula to engage quiet students, but efforts to reach out to them will surely yield results over time.

Finding Time to Create Challenging Curriculum

One of the participants in an identity safety workshop reminded us that educators have so many demands on their time. He questioned if we were being reasonable when expecting educators to perform everything required in order to bring about identity safety. He was not the first to bring this up. We are cognizant of it and responded that identity safety is an approach that is not a checklist of strategies but rather a way to engage in the classroom with student welfare at the center. Many aspects of identity safety are not time consuming but rather are integrated within a holistic stance with which to engage students. The many ideas in the book are not a rigid set of add-ons. Identity safety strategies act as a vehicle for your content, delivering a more meaningful experience for your students and ultimately will lead to an easier and more rewarding life for you as an educator. It is not necessary to implement everything at once. You can steadily take digestible steps toward an identity safe classroom.

A good starting point is to listen to what you are saying to students, including your tone of voice and your enthusiasm as you teach. When it comes to curriculum development and content coverage, here are some tips:

- Prioritize your planning to focus on academic and social objectives. Recognize that there will always be too much to cover, but by prioritizing, you can cover the big ideas and the more necessary or useful information.

- Set goals and create timelines. Be flexible: Your best-laid plans might get waylaid.

- Reflect on the aspects of teaching that give you the most joy and bring them into your planning. Tell stories, bring in humor, and avoid feelings of drudgery.

- Invite students to participate in the process of designing and bringing in information. Instead of feeling you must be the one to know and impart information about diverse cultures, ask students to bring forward authentic experiences from their cultures and backgrounds. They can do the research and report on it to their peers. They can also help with daily tasks in the classroom, such as designing creative bulletin boards and organizing materials.

- Use formative assessment practices that give you on-the-spot feedback and limit the number of papers and reports that need to be graded.

- The Internet has a plethora of curricula, sample lessons, and blogs covering every topic imaginable that can help you save time with your planning. At the end of Part III, we share a few useful Internet resources.

- Take care of yourself. Be sure to have downtime, doing things that replenish you. Get enough rest, exercise in ways you find fun, and eat a healthy diet.

School administrators also have a responsibility to provide and maintain structures that create space and time for educators to cultivate a challenging curriculum. Here are some things administrators can do:

- Coordinate and pay attention to avoid a pileup of deadlines.

- Support teachers to partner together for planning. They can divide up and share their plans and even present content through rotations.

- Limit the number of preps given to a particular teacher.

- Create structures, including department meetings, grade-level team meetings, and/or flexible planning time for curriculum development.

- Limit the professional development content topics, avoiding the potential to overwhelm educators by asking them to absorb too many new strategies at once.

Chapter Summary

In this chapter, we presented two ways that a *Challenging Curriculum* contributes to identity safety: first, as a source of relevant and exciting learning moments and, second, as a mechanism for helping motivate students to stretch themselves to meet those high expectations, building on ideas from Chapter 8. We began by discussing ways to create an air of intellectual excitement through curriculum that is stimulating and relevant to students. We showed how to step up to challenges, where learning is seen as a process and creativity is celebrated. We then presented many ways to differentiate the curriculum so students at varying academic levels would all be engaged and challenged.

From there, we introduced strategies for helping students build their endurance muscles in the face of obstacles. We showed how students can be praised for their effort, persistence, and progress. We presented identity safe productive struggle as a stance where students are not immediately supported when they encounter a challenge but are allowed to grapple with it. We explained that these skills can be taught in an identity safe way that does not embarrass or humiliate a student.

We tackled two points of tension that are challenges for educators. First, we presented ideas for learning about and motivating quiet students. Then, we took on time, which is always a challenge as educators juggle the many tasks and pressures of teaching. We provided some tips and resources for managing time while adding challenges for students to the curriculum. Keeping students inspired goes hand in hand with helping them persist in the face of obstacles, learn from mistakes, and remain willing to grapple with difficult problems. In identity safe classrooms, a challenging curriculum engages students' hearts and minds in learning, making it safe to take risks and grow.

Check Yourself

1. What do you do to make your curriculum vibrant and meaningful?

2. How do you communicate your expectations to students? Are they rigorous and developmentally appropriate?

3. What differentiation strategies have you tried so far? How have they worked?

4. What words do you use, and what is your tone of voice when talking to the class about effort?

5. How do you praise students?

6. How do you challenge students who are struggling academically without lowering the bar? How do you motivate and support them?

7. How do you find out about and motivate the quieter students?

TRY IT OUT: END OF CHAPTER ACTIVITIES

Examining Our Approach to Learning From Mistakes and Failure and Teaching About It

1. Describe your personal experiences with handling errors you have made and with times you have failed. What have you learned from those experiences?

2. Have you incorporated productive struggle into your students' experiences? If so, describe your impressions. Try some techniques and strategies in this chapter and relate what happened. Was it different? How so?

3. Brainstorm some phrases you can say to support students to encourage them to do the following:
    a. Keep trying even when things are hard
    b. Practice over and over while incorporating improvements along the way

    c. Approach errors as learning opportunities

    d. Bounce back from failures

4. How do you help students from undermining each other's failures?

 Available for download as a full-page form at **https://resources.corwin .com/IdentitySafeClass6-12**

Big Ideas: Cultivating Diversity as a Resource

This part is guided by three Identity Safety Principles:

#1. Color-blind teaching that ignores differences is a barrier to inclusion in the classroom.

#3. Cultivating diversity as a resource for learning and expressing high expectations for students promotes learning competence and achievement.

#5. Social and emotional safety is created by supporting students in defining their identities, refuting negative stereotypes, and countering stereotype threat, giving them a voice in the classroom, and using SEL strategies.

These three principles, as shared through the three component chapters, have several big ideas:

- As a precondition for learning in identity safe classrooms, many aspects of the students' social identities are expressly valued.

- Students need to see themselves and people like them reflected in the curriculum. With authentic experiences that draw from their own backgrounds, they can safely reveal, share, and value their social identities.

- Counternarratives and critical multicultural analysis of historical inequities help students deconstruct the myths and stereotypes that can undermine their sense of competence.

- Help students expand their understanding of intelligence to incorporate the growth mindset and triarchic theories regarding intelligence. Debunk some of history's myths and erroneous theories that persist today. Help them reframe views of their own intelligence and potential.

- Open dialogue about race and gender and other aspects of identity or differences permit students of all backgrounds to learn and understand the world around them. Educators facilitate these difficult conversations in ways that students gain a respect for multiple perspectives and develop empathy.

- Setting forth high expectations for students in the context of a rigorous curriculum occurs by sharing our belief in their capacity and encouraging them to develop perseverance. The ultimate goal is to have students internalize high expectations for themselves.

- Educators can help students reframe their assumptions about learning, recognizing that their mistakes are learning opportunities and that failure is neither permanent nor pervasive. Careful use of praise to be specific and focused on effort and progress will help students access and feel a sense of accomplishment.

For Further Study

- Article: "Gender Inclusive Schools" from *Gender Spectrum*, www.genderspectrum.org

- Essay: *Mapping the Margins: Intersectionality, Identity Politics, and Violence Against Women of Color* by Kimberley Crenshaw, www.racialequitytools.org/resourcefiles/mapping-margins.pdf

- Website: *Edutopia* with blogs, videos, and strategies, www.edutopia.org

- Website: *Learning Accelerator* with resources for blended and personalized learning, www.learningaccelerator.org

- Website: *Share My Lesson* with thousands of educator-developed materials, www.sharemylesson.com

- Website: *Teaching for Change: Building for Social Justice Starting in the Classroom*, www.teachingforchange.org

- Website: *Teaching Tolerance* for anti-bias classroom resources, www.tolerance.org/classroom-resources

- Website: *Visible Thinking* for tools for fostering critical thinking, www.visiblethinkingpz.org/VisibleThinking_html_files/VisibleThinking1.html

Classroom Relationships

Brady, a Leadership Public Schools (LPS) student, said this about his relationship with his teacher:

> I'm just going to be honest—Carranza really cares about his students. I mean, other teachers also do care, but he actually worries if we're falling off, if we're not getting the subject. That's what I love about him because when he gives us respect, that tells us that he cares for us, you know? That we really matter. Us students, we're actually like, we don't want to let Mr. Carranza down, so we give him the same respect, too. (LPS Student Interviews, 2018)

Relationships of respect, trust, empathy, and integrity are the foundation of an identity safe classroom. The sense of belonging that emerges when a student feels connected, valued, and welcomed by educators and their peers can be a determining factor in keeping them engaged in school. Mrs. Kocher, my 12th-grade English teacher, always encouraged me to keep writing. It is quite possible that the fact that she wrote, "I can't wait to see you in print" in my journal is why you are getting to read this book!

We are social beings who thrive on relationships and a sense of belonging (Baumeister & Leary, 1995). Adolescent identity is extremely malleable and highly nuanced, and the need to belong intensifies. Teens can be extremely sensitive as to how they think others perceive them and may enter our classrooms with a predisposed sense of "non-belonging" (Markus, 2008). As we discussed in Chapter 1: The Introduction, stereotype threat—the "fear of confirming a negative stereotype"—and a color-blind classroom can exacerbate the sense of invisibility and not belonging. Identity safe educators develop a keen sensitivity, observing their relationships with students as well as relationships among the students.

Relationships affect a student's academic identity, which is forged out of the myriad messages they receive about their capabilities, intelligence, and effort—and all this blends with their sense of connectedness. When students feel invisible or unwelcome, they shut down, lose motivation to achieve, and possibly engage in disruptive behaviors. When a person feels they do not belong, their IQ has been known to drop (Baumeister et al., 2002) and their performance is negatively impacted (Walton & Cohen, 2007). Alienated students may attend school sporadically, feeling as if their presence will not matter anyway. It is our job to demonstrate to students that they are not invisible, that we care about what they have to say, and that we value them, all while valuing their academic progress and encouraging them to reach their potential.

The following are short definitions of the two components that make up identity safe classroom relationships. These will be fully explored in subsequent chapters.

1. *Teacher Warmth and Availability for Learning* refers to building a trusting and encouraging relationship with each student. Educators welcome and invite students to be present with their full identities. They establish close rapport through kindness and making themselves available to support rigorous learning. On a daily basis, they work to strengthen students' academic identities and sense of belonging at school and decrease the impact of stereotype threat.

2. *Positive Student Relationships* refers to helping students forge interpersonal understanding, trust, and caring among peers. Identity safe educators actively model and teach relationship and communication skills, conflict resolution, and empathy. Educators contribute to a sense of belonging by equalizing status and intentionally moving away from hierarchies that lead to exclusion. In concert with colleagues, educators examine and change policies and practices that serve to rank students and consequently divide them.

In the following two chapters, we examine aspects of promoting positive educator–student and peer-to-peer relationships in the complex setting of secondary classrooms, where educators are working with large numbers of students often in short blocks of time.

Teacher Warmth and Availability for Learning 10

Why Teacher Warmth and Availability for Learning Matters

In the SISP (Stanford Integrated Schools Project) identity safety research, teacher warmth was a separate component from teacher availability in terms of learning, with each playing a significant role for the student. In this book, we have linked the two ideas. Warmth and kindness are combined with availability, including being interested and present to support learning. Students can experience a very caring educator who does not hold them to high expectations or, conversely, an educator who holds high expectations but is cold and unapproachable. In addition, an educator can practice kindness but fail to provide scaffolds for the students to meet those high expectations. By fusing warmth and availability, we are promoting relationships that strengthen confidence and provide attention to our students, together with resources and scaffolds to help them develop a strong academic identity.

Renowned psychologist Carl Rogers (Rogers et al., 2013), who developed person-centered psychology, said that three keys to healthy relationships are unconditional positive regard, empathy, and validation. In identity safety, *positive regard* includes appreciating all aspects of the person's social identity—"I value and care about you *because of* who you are rather than *in spite* of who you are." *Empathy* is part of understanding and caring about the students' feelings and life experiences. *Validation* includes both expressing value for the student as a person and acknowledging their learning and academic growth.

Identity safe educators consider the educator–student relationship as one that links to a student's personal and academic identity. In her book *Culturally Responsive Teaching and the Brain*, Zaretta Hammond (2015) includes a chapter titled "Establishing Alliance in the Learning Partnership." She highlights the nuanced relationship particularly needed by students of color who have lost hope after going from one year to the next without receiving sufficient feedback and support. The alliance Hammond is referring to involves a process of building a supportive partnership that includes the teacher and student working together to design a pact—in other words, a commitment to specific learning goals with concrete steps. The educator's role involves supporting students as a "warm demander," a term that describes someone who conveys oneself as an ally for the student, an ally who holds and firmly communicates high expectations.

Students can immediately feel if their educator "has their back" or not. In the myriad of microinteractions that occur each day, students pick up on the fairness, friendliness, and openness of their educators. Conversely, they are also hyperaware of anger, hostility, defensiveness, or blaming. They tune in to authenticity by noticing mannerisms and discern whether actions match the words they are hearing. A warm and caring tone permeates the classroom environment as easily as a cool and detached one. We are not suggesting that you always need to be smiling. At times, there is a need to speak firmly or express discontent. However, when you do get upset, you can communicate concerns clearly and without blame. At that moment, students will take you seriously, especially if they know that you are usually warm and friendly.

Each educator has their own unique personality and style. There are many ways to be present, express care, and facilitate learning. Some of us are more comfortable with formality, while others are more casual. For those with a nurturing style, caring is often expressed verbally. It can also be shown by bringing in popular music or speaking the students' home language. For others, there are ways to express care by showing a nonjudgmental attitude with fair treatment of each student. Also, it can include intuitively knowing when to hold back and when to give students the space to destress or just to think. Students will adapt to your particular style, and they will know when you are genuine. Reflecting on different aspects of the educator–student relationship allows us to dig deeper into how we forge and strengthen our relationships with students of all backgrounds.

As the educator–student relationship is fundamental in creating identity safety, ideas for forming supportive relationships with students are spread throughout the book, affirming strategies for giving feedback. Availability for learning has been addressed in previous chapters, including many listening strategies in Chapter 3: Listening for Student Voices. In Chapter 8: High Expectations and Academic Rigor and in Chapter 9: Challenging Curriculum, we describe ways to differentiate instruction to meet each student's needs.

In this chapter, we share strategies for getting to know students, building trust, and developing rapport. We also look at the issue of finding time to support students and being present for their greater needs. We take a deep look at trauma because through the student–educator relationship, we can do many things to mitigate the impact. We address the need to find entry points to reach students whose life experiences have led to feelings of helplessness, despondency, and even despair. Some adolescents have had one or more traumatic experiences in their young lives, which can deeply impact their sense of agency and behavior. We share trauma-informed practices as well as de-escalation strategies.

Teacher Warmth and Availability for Learning: Making It Happen

Building Rapport Based on Trust

A key element of any relationship is trust. Whenever we enter into new relationships, we draw from prior experience and skills in forming trusting relationships. We can build on our students' positive past relationships and reach out to those who have not previously felt connected. When students feel their educators are concerned about their well-being and when they know about and understand their lives, they feel more connected. By finding common interests, you can forge a positive pathway to rapport with students. Belonging is strengthened through finding shared values and interests. In social psychology, researchers developed the theory of *mere belonging*, finding that people feel a connection to others by having simple things in common like a shared name or hometown. In an interesting study, researcher Greg Walton and colleagues (2012) found that students were more motivated and persistent in completing a math problem when they thought the educator shared the same birthday. Even with this minor connection, they were more positive about math and even felt the math department was more supportive.

In identity safe classrooms, educators are intentional while using discretion about what they bring forward from their personal experience. For example, an educator may share a negative experience, ensuring not to frighten or upset students (e.g., we strongly advise you never discuss a personal suicide attempt or describe a racist encounter with another member of the school staff). You can carefully express personal vulnerabilities in ways that will strengthen empathy and rapport. All the elements of building rapport with students require a sensitivity to and awareness of life from the perspective of each student.

Some of our students come to us with broken trust, having erected powerful defenses as survival skills. Some have previously had many bad experiences with White or other teachers who do not share their background. This makes for even greater hurdles to surmount in creating trust. It is not realistic to assume we can instantly break through.

The Power of a Role Model

Alex shares a time when she was a high school principal and had a student named Salvador. In his sophomore year, he was completely disengaged from school and had *F*s in all his subjects. It looked like he was heading toward dropping out. When Alex would ask Salvador how he was doing, he would sneer and reply, "Why are you asking me how I am doing?" In his junior year, he went on a field trip to a university. There, they met a professor, Dr. Rios, who had written a book sharing his personal story—his path from being a gang member to going to college and earning a PhD. For Salvador, this was a defining moment. From then on, he began trying at school. He still had his ups and downs. He would get a 4.0 on his report card, but then would have setbacks. He knew that Alex believed in him, so when he had problems, he would seek her out for a pep talk. When he crossed the stage at graduation, he gave Alex a huge hug and whispered that he had been accepted to college. Later, he admitted to her that he never thought he would get into college. Alex reflects that you need to be ready for the long game. For some kids, it takes a positive relationship and a day or even several weeks; for others, it might take all year; and then for some, it takes four long years, but there is always a chance to help a student turn things around.

However, as educators committed to identity safety, it is our responsibility to do everything in our power to reach out and connect with our students. It is also where we can reap some of the greatest rewards of teaching.

Finding Time to Connect With Each of Your 150 Students in Authentic Ways

Along with many time constraints and demands, educators have the challenge of finding ways to interact with each student, even when they have large classes for short time spans. While this is never easy, there are some ways to do it.

Knowing and Pronouncing Student Names

In one of my identity safety workshops, we discussed the significance of knowing students' names and pronouncing them correctly, and the participants shared various techniques. One teacher shared that she uses name tags for the first few weeks. Another described keeping a seating chart for each period in her lesson plan book, where she writes little notes about the students next to their names. One teacher created a name game for the first day of school and would film her students as they acted out their names. That night, she would study the video until she memorized all their names. A PE teacher asked the other workshop participants what to do when you mispronounce a name or mistake one student for another. Other participants described similar embarrassing experiences.

One teacher said, "When it happens, I immediately apologize. Then, I explain that I am working hard to learn their names. Finally, I ask the students to please correct me when I make a mistake." She smiled and added, "Believe me, they really take me up on that one."

Regularly Interacting With Each Student

In another identity safety workshop, we shared methods for interacting with each student daily. A math teacher said that he greets each student at the door with a quick friendly word, looking directly into the students' eyes to check if anything might be on their minds or disturbing them. This teacher explained that it was his job to ensure that his students are happy and ready to learn, and if not, it was his job to do something about it. A history teacher described holding brief individual check-ins during what he calls the "daily launch" to solicit questions and reflections about the coursework, showing interest in their learning. A biology teacher described taking a few minutes at the start of class to talk with the group about areas of interest that were not on the topic of the course. In that way, she learned a lot about her students, and later, she was empowered to follow up individually.

The goal of connecting with students in large classes becomes less daunting when teaching goes beyond large-group lectures and instruction becomes more decentralized and educators can circulate. Many schools have implemented block scheduling with longer periods of time, allowing for meaningful interaction and opportunities to develop relationships.

Getting to Know Students During Instruction

Building positive relationships can be woven through all learning experiences and need not be limited to nonacademic moments. Many student-centered academic activities described in Part II: Student-Centered Teaching (e.g., Socratic dialogue, jigsaw) offer opportunities to get to know students. You can pay attention to patterns of thought and feeling by listening in on small- and large-group discussions. Watch their moods and their body language as they engage with content. Notice what they bring forward as prior knowledge, how they share their opinions in class debates, and their reactions to success or failure. How do they respond when you offer feedback? Relationship building takes place during a myriad of microinteractions. Educators can take advantage of these small moments to build trust over time.

Mica Pollock (2017) described a unique approach to suspension that renowned author Gloria Ladson-Billings posted on Facebook in 2015. Ladson-Billings wrote that when she was a principal, only once did she suspend a student from school (she considered him a danger to himself and others). For all other students, suspension meant they were to spend more time with her, including eating lunch together and driving them home after school. She got to know these students, and they got to know her. Ladson-Billings emphasized that she never had repeat offenders after a "get-to-know-you" suspension.

A Unique Way to Strengthen Rapport

Amy describes a student who was sent to detention to complete math homework. Instead, she found him watching a rap video filled with guns and scantily clad women. She immediately approached him to get him back on task, and he became furious and stormed out of the room. Amy's counterintuitive solution was to make a little greeting card for him. She went online and found his favorite rap group and selected a photo, ensuring it had no guns, gang signs, or objectifying images. Inside the card, she wrote, "I know it was tough yesterday. I hope your day got better—I look forward to the next time we talk."

The next day, Amy found the boy and gave him the card. He read it and grinned, clearly a bit shocked. She asked how he was feeling about school now. He paused for a moment and then whipped out a paper, drawing a line down the middle of the page. On one side, he wrote, "What is happening that needs to change." On the other side, he wrote, "What I need to do." He proceeded to fill in the chart, including Amy in the process. In those moments, the powerful connection that reached across race, age, and experience made a difference.

How you get to know your students depends on your content area, the time in class, and your personal engagement style, but we all can make it possible to build rapport with each student.

When an educator makes the effort to meet a student on their ground and appeal to their understanding, students respond. They also notice when you pronounce their name correctly or ask after a family member who has been sick. A simple gesture has the potential to become an unforgettable moment of connection.

The Third Space: Beyond the Classroom

Kris Gutierrez (Baker, 2008), UCLA professor and researcher, describes the "third space" as places where students interact differently, places outside the typical academic environment. She recommends going to "third spaces" to deeply connect with students.

You can find time outside of class to be available to get to know students, either with office hours, lunchtime gatherings, or during extracurricular activities like sports and community events. It helps when the educators know and have been out in the community. When I was a principal, I would take new teachers on a walk around our local Fruitvale neighborhood, one of the Latinx sections of Oakland, California. I showed them the parks, churches, the Latin American Public Library, and the community center, encouraging them to go there after they started teaching to better understand and know the students in their home environment. I made sure to invite staff to the yearly Día de Los Muertos street fair and celebration that brought the whole Fruitvale community together.

Not all students require the same amount of time to connect. For some, it can mean catching their eye with a smile and a periodic friendly check-in. Others have greater needs and will take more time, for which a special meeting spot may offer more security and meaning.

 ## THE THIRD SPACE IN ACTION

When Amy worked as a counselor at a middle school, she and a colleague turned a room full of junk in the basement into an art and gathering space. They called this third space the "underground." Educators and students met there for art workshops, cultural sharing circles, and more informal opportunities to eat lunch and talk together.

At LPS (Leadership Public Schools) in Oakland, California, a Spanish teacher made his classroom into a third space when he invited students who were newcomers to the country to join him at lunch twice a week. He learned a lot more about them, and they shared how they were experiencing LPS. Subsequently, he brought these students to meet with the principal to share their perspectives, leading to some important improvements in their academic program.

Giving Wise Feedback

We have presented many ways that our words and nonverbal cues matter in identity safety. This is especially significant in the way we offer feedback. A common yet often ineffective method for giving feedback is called "sandwiching," which involves concocting a positive comment, following it with a criticism that informs the student what they did wrong, and then ending with a friendly generalized comment. Sandwiching feedback is similar to coating a bitter pill with sugar. When a student knows their work is mediocre, empty praise feels inauthentic. This is particularly true for students of color who have been subjected to negative stereotypes about their intelligence and school performance, probably on a regular basis. Unbuffered critiques could result in further alienation for students who already do not feel a sense of belonging.

In research by Claude Steele (2010), educators gave feedback to groups of Black and White students. Participants were asked to describe the impact of the feedback. One group of Black study participants received unbuffered criticism. These participants wrote that the critiques made them less motivated to improve and that they felt the educators were more biased. Another group of Black participants received criticism and suggestions along with an assurance that the educator held high standards and was confident they could meet the standards. These students stated that they were motivated to improve and felt the educators were more fair and less biased. For White participants, the differences in how the feedback was given were less significant.

Based on this research, Steele coined the term *wise feedback*. He explains that wise feedback involves a mindful response to students to ensure they do not feel judged by negative stereotypes about them or others of their background. Wise feedback is given with words and a tone indicating the educator holds high standards. Critical feedback is detailed and specific, offering concrete suggestions on how to improve. Meanwhile, the student is assured that the educator believes they have the potential to meet the high standards and that the educator will be there with tools, skills, and support to see them through the challenges. This simple shift in how we give feedback can greatly improve relationships and trust with students while motivating them to learn and improve (Yeager et al., 2013).

Mary Murphy (2018b) adds one more caveat to the process of wise feedback. She suggests that educators also incorporate acknowledgment of the student's progress during feedback. Signaling to the student ways they have improved may seem obvious to both student and educator, but often, both are more aware of how far they have yet to go, which can feel less motivating. It can be greatly beneficial to recognize how far they have come as well.

Feedback is ongoing and a necessary part of learning. How it is communicated has the tremendous potential to contribute to a student's sense of competence and identity safety.

WISE FEEDBACK: HOW TO DO IT

Giving wise feedback is expressed in your own words but can include the following points:

1. Communicate your high standards.

2. Offer suggestions for improvement, using specific language.

3. Assure students you believe they can meet the standards and will provide scaffolding to support them.

4. Point out their progress to date.

5. Give students tools to reflect on their progress for themselves as they continue to improve.

Helping Your Students (and You) Self-Regulate

In Chapter 6: Classroom Autonomy, we addressed the topic of self-regulation and executive functioning in the context of supporting a student's sense of agency. Here, our focus is on the aspects of self-regulation that have to do with helping students manage their emotions. This also applies to us as educators during difficult moments when we need to manage our own emotional reactions. Emotions rise as stress builds and tension mounts. This can happen to anyone. We get knocked off our center and do and say things that are not helpful to others. In our society, most people have not had effective self-regulation modeled for them. We include this topic in our discussion of educator–student relationships because—as part of our daily lives—we will inevitably need to manage moments of tension and high emotion while building relationships with students. Teens especially are often engaged in trying to grapple with a cache of swirling emotions, and the calm modeling of self-regulation can offer much needed relief.

In his book *Self-Reg*, author Stuart Shanker (2016) offers a process for self-regulation. These suggestions can work for both students and educators by addressing both internal and external stressors affecting our students as well as ourselves.

Before a situation escalates, take care to follow these steps:

1. *Read the signs and reframe behaviors by paying attention.* This refers to developing awareness of and maintaining vigilance for signs of stress as it builds. For students, this means learning to take a step back from their emotions when they experience agitation in any form and redirecting the energy. For educators, this involves developing awareness of student patterns of frustration—as well as their own—and applying redirection strategies.

2. *Identify the stressors and ask "why now?"* For students, internalized stressors can result from personal experiences exacerbated by overwhelming pressures to

succeed. These can manifest as a result of external sources such as parents and educators, stereotype threat, oppressive situations, poverty, or family concerns. For educators, frustration can mount with constant classroom disruptions, including rude comments directed at the teacher, and/or other external causes such as lack of sleep, personal issues, or pressures from administrators. For both, the question "Why now?" can help them to identify and focus on the triggers causing the stress cycles and find ways to avoid them.

3. *Seek ways to reduce the stressors within our control.* For students, this can include asking for help, deciding not to take a particular course at a certain time, or making personal schedule changes, such as going to bed earlier. For educators, this might include slowing down, setting priorities, eliminating unnecessary activities, curbing the tendency to take on too much, and/or making schedule changes to get more sleep or exercise. For more SEL (social and emotional learning) and stress reduction skills, see the three chapters in Part V: Caring Classroom Environments.

4. *Reflect.* For students, this involves helping them recognize when they encounter triggers in order to practice self-reflection so that they can make choices for emotional equanimity. They can learn stress-reducing mindfulness activities, such as taking a few minutes to write their feelings, identifying a safe place where they can withdraw and be by themselves, or talking with a friend (see Chapter 13: Emotional and Physical Comfort). For educators, these suggestions can also work for adults. They can practice awareness when they are overstressed. Also, it pays to find moments in an educator's day for self-reflection and schedule in that much-needed downtime for a pleasurable activity like music, exercise, or sports. Meditating, doing yoga, going for a walk, or seeking out a colleague can help reduce stress.

CONSIDER EVERY POSSIBLE ANGLE WHEN SEEKING SOLUTIONS

Ellen, a social studies teacher, had a student named Daniel who often became agitated and easily grew angry. His mother described a pattern that made sense to Ellen. When her son was hungry, his nerves became frayed and he was easily angered. His mother shared a story about Daniel when he was very hungry and stressed after soccer practice. He grew belligerent and physically attacked his sister when, as he put it, "she got in my face." That pattern rang a bell for Ellen, whose class with Daniel was right before lunch. She began keeping granola bars in her desk, and whenever she saw Daniel getting tense, she discreetly offered him a bar and told him to take a few minutes to eat it and calm himself down. Ellen also helped Daniel learn to recognize when he was getting tense. Eventually, he learned to eat a bigger breakfast and carry his own granola bars.

The support we give students to self-regulate is even more urgent with students who have experienced trauma.

Trauma

While some students have had horrific experiences and shown tremendous resilience, others are stymied by deep wounds incurred from trauma. Traumatic experiences can take many forms, such as physical or sexual abuse, violence, an acrimonious divorce, or death of a loved one. It also may result when parents have rejected their child because of the child's sexual orientation or siblings have tormented them about their learning disabilities. Sometimes, if traumatic experiences have occurred at a young age, repressed feelings emerge during adolescence. Alicia's mother died when she was eight years old. She was from a low-income family and was placed on a list to receive counseling by county mental health services. For the next seven years, her name remained on the waiting list. She never received any form of grief counseling or support. By the time she was 13, she often flew into rages, becoming extremely rebellious. Similarly, students who have been traumatized may be disruptive in class and instigate conflicts by fighting with peers or talking back to their educators. Others withdraw and shut down. The unleashing of teenage hormones and spinning emotions can add yet another challenging layer to the mix. Approaching this fragility with tender mindfulness makes sense.

Racial Trauma

In his 2013 article "Healing the Wounds of Racial Trauma," Professor Kenneth Hardy describes the wounding that results from living in our society where racial oppression manifests through a disproportionate number of people of color who experience dis-

ADVERSE CHILDHOOD EXPERIENCES STUDY

The Centers for Disease Control and Prevention (2014) and Kaiser Permanente conducted the *Adverse Childhood Experiences (ACEs) Study*, gathering data from 17,000 people about their childhood experiences in connection with their current health status. The study catalogued a set of adverse childhood experiences they called ACEs (included in those experiences were abuse, loss, neglect, etc.). The researchers then correlated the number of traumatic experiences to negative physical and mental health conditions (e.g., addiction, depression, heart disease and other chronic conditions, financial problems, and more). Researchers found that over 66 percent of the participants had experienced at least one of the adverse experiences, and more than 20 percent had three or more ACEs. They also found that the greater number of ACEs a person experienced, the greater the risk of serious negative health and well-being outcomes across their lifetime.

crimination, poverty, and a lack of access to education. He describes the following impacts of racial trauma on people of color:

- *Internalized devaluation:* In a society that privileges Whites, many people of color internalize a message that they are unworthy, disrespected, or characterized as criminals.

- *Assaulted sense of self:* This is the result of many experiences of feeling devalued and watching media coverage that continually judges and stereotypes people of color. It is especially wounding as young identities are being formed.

- *Internalized voicelessness:* This occurs when people feel incapable of defending themselves against the onslaught of negative messaging about people of their backgrounds or those who look like them. This voiceless feeling is exacerbated in color-blind environments.

Hardy also explains that racial trauma can result in what he calls the wound of rage, which is expressed as overwhelming anger and frustration, manifesting in self-destructive behaviors. He suggests that traditional methods aimed to help students can be ineffective. For example, initially forcing them to take responsibility for their behavior and be more respectful may exacerbate the negative feelings. Hardy recommends beginning by acknowledging the student's feelings. From there, he suggests openly talking about race, sharing stories, and naming the frustrations. This serves to help students realize that worrying that something is wrong with them is baseless. Rather, they can learn that this sense of devaluation stems from oppressive societal attitudes instead of something that is innate and irreversible within them, their families, or communities. He says that educators can explain that negative behaviors, while counterproductive, can be understandable for a young person seeking to gain dignity and self-respect while experiencing life's numerous trials. From there, students can be guided to take stock of their counterproductive behavior and realize that they are hurting themselves. They can seek alternate means to channel rage. Instead of being self-destructive, the student can develop a new repertoire of behaviors that will lead to both healing and positive outcomes. This is not a rapid or easy process, but by developing an awareness of the depth and roots of anger, educators—at times with the support of counselors—can help students reverse downward spirals incurred by repeated outbursts of rage.

Trauma-Informed Practice

Identity safe educators, with an understanding of trauma, mindfully attend to a student's race, culture, gender, religion, social class, and personal history. They ask themselves, What may have happened to this student? rather than What is wrong with him? By doing so, they are in a better position to support a student's path toward agency. Also, educators and counselors avoid becoming personally triggered and are able to de-escalate explosive situations. The initial pathway to engender trust begins with how students perceive we treat them.

A TEACHER WHO CARES MAKES ALL THE DIFFERENCE

Daevy, an elementary teacher in Modesto, California, described how she became a teacher in spite of the fact that she had been a disruptive student. In 10th grade, Daevy's brother was about to be deported to Cambodia, although he came to the United States from a refugee camp as a very young child and never learned the Cambodian language. That whole year, Daevy experienced many levels of worry, anger, and sadness and was very much on edge. She shares her personal "tale of two teachers," explaining that in English class, she was always cutting up, challenging the teacher, talking back, and picking fights that led to her suspension. In math class, Daevy was completely different; her behavior was less confrontational and even cooperative. She explained that— although she was not conscious of it at the time—she later realized that her behavior was based on the different treatment she received from her two teachers. In English, she felt disrespected. Her teacher was quick to judge, complained about incomplete homework, and often criticized her. Alternatively, her math teacher, who also had been her brother's teacher, would ask about the welfare of her brother and her family, and she felt safe enough to share her fears with him. Each day, he greeted her at the door, asking about her brother and her family. The math teacher cared, which was the difference. Daevy feels that her math teacher was the person who inspired her to later become a teacher.

Our brains are wired to fight, flight, or freeze in response to a threat, activating an alarm system. Additional reactions (Adamson, 2015) include to dissociate (shift attention outside the body to avoid pain), collapse (literally fall apart and lose the capacity to physically respond), and appease (behave in a way that betrays our values and beliefs to be safe).

A youth who has experienced trauma is more likely to experience threat with an overactive alarm system. The feeling of threat can be sparked by an unpredictable situation or sudden change. A student may be triggered when they feel overwhelmed and vulnerable. For example, they can react with emotions of anger, frustration, and rejection if they perceive others are confronting or excluding them. Even praise or positive attention can backfire for a traumatized student.

Trauma-informed practices are well matched to identity safe classroom strategies as follows:

- Building trusting relationships
- Teaching social and emotional skills
- Using discipline strategies that de-escalate student responses while remaining sensitive to and avoiding their triggers (see Chapter 12: Teacher Skill)
- Creating a space for students to go when they are triggered

- Providing wraparound student support services for families, including cognitive behavioral counseling, grief therapy, and other types of support

Trauma-informed educators know students and ways to preempt and avoid unnecessary confrontation. By reaching out, they can support healing and the rebuilding of their autonomy.

Trauma Literacy Sessions for Educators

Carlee Adamson (2018), an expert in trauma-informed practice, works to help educators understand trauma and generate healing in our students' lives as well as our own. She reminds us that we, also, are not immune to trauma. Many educators have faced extreme challenges in their lives. She adds that while our stress responses have helped us survive and cope with life's difficulties, they may be detrimental to our relationships. According to Adamson, in addition to building an awareness of trauma, the goal of "trauma literacy" is to do the following:

- Support students in learning to trust their own responses and self-regulate their emotions

- Learn to better respond to students who get triggered or who might trigger us

- Understand ourselves better and consider how to draw from our inner resources to interact and respond in the best way we can

- Know when to reach out to others in our school community to support us or particular students

In professional development sessions, Adamson introduces educators to the concept of trauma and guides them toward awareness of their own sensitivities that can work against their best efforts to be supportive of students. She takes educators through a process to examine their trauma histories and experientially arrive at an understanding for a wide spectrum of responses to their stressors. In the sessions, educators perform an activity where they identify their "go-to" responses and consider how these responses might trigger others, in particular our students, even though they may work to de-escalate our own stress.

Finally, Adamson (2018) encourages staff teamwork to support one another in skillfully responding to students who have experienced trauma. She reminds educators not to pity students who have experienced trauma or to consider supporting them as a "lost cause." Rather, by working with colleagues, they can find entry points, responses, and provide tools to help students manage their emotions. Many books and resources augment these suggestions and increase their understanding of trauma and self-regulation, including *The Invisible Classroom* (Olson, 2014).

One caveat for dealing with trauma involves taking care not to pathologize every student. Not all students from low-income families have experienced trauma. And some students who have experienced trauma come to us with amazing resiliency. Therefore, we must be careful on several counts: First, we must not make assumptions about our students and their families. Second, we can act in accordance with the famous adage to "not judge a person unless we have walked a mile in their shoes," which is apropos when we are seeking to understand and address the impact of trauma.

Empathetic Distress and Compassion Fatigue

Sometimes, the empathy we feel for our students can be overwhelming. Considering how much upheaval some of our students have experienced in their short lives can induce within us a measure of secondary trauma. Educators, along with counselors and social workers, at times feel a tremendous identification with their young charges, inasmuch that they become drained, imposing an emotional toll and impacting their professional and personal lives.

I recall a cathartic experience during my first year as an administrator as dean of students in East Oakland, California. A family who was squatting in an apartment without heat enrolled four children in our school. The children told us that as they huddled around gas burners on their stove, the kids would sometimes play "Heat the Fork" and would burn each other with the hot forks. We called Child Protective Services (CPS), but it opted not take action because it considered that the harm was enacted by the children and not the parents. CPS claimed that this form of parental neglect was not in its purview, which sounds strange to me as I write this many years later. We also learned that the parents sent the children to McDonald's to beg for food in the evenings. At school, each of the children behaved differently in response to these survival conditions. One, a little first grader, melted down each afternoon in a wild tantrum that we thought may have resulted from lack of sleep or—sadly—second-hand inhalation of meth. Her twin sister and her fourth-grade brother became both quiet and withdrawn, avoiding contact with others. On one occasion, the sixth-grade girl had a tantrum in which she ran through the halls screaming, punching, and tearing down bulletin boards. We had to lock down the rest of the school, keeping students confined to their classrooms to protect them, as we tried to calm her. I became obsessed with finding resources and ways to alleviate the suffering. I lay awake at night, worrying and pondering different solutions. That experience became my baptism by fire as I reached out to every community support and mental health resource that I could find. And shortly, before any of the services kicked in, the entire family disappeared and never returned to the school. I quickly realized that I could not live at that emotional pitch and be present to support the students. I needed to find ways to draw out my own resilience. My parents, who suffered tremendously when escaping Nazi Germany, were my role models. I learned to focus on what I could do, connecting with the students and their families and becoming adept at marshalling support services, but not taking it home with me in the way I had with the family in the East Oakland school. I later learned that secondary trauma that results from feelings of tremendous empathy is actually considered a work hazard (National Child Traumatic Stress Network, 2018).

Another reaction can manifest in a form of numbness known as *compassion fatigue*, a type of emotional detachment. I didn't want to fall into this trap, either. With self-care and a healthy work–home balance, I ensured that I was able to work for many years without becoming paralyzed, detached, or burned out. Identity safe teaching has inspired me to find an internal space for compassion and love for myself as well as my students.

Addressing Depression and Mental Illness

Keeping in mind the wisdom of protecting ourselves against secondary trauma and compassion fatigue, we can consider the importance of becoming knowledgeable about mental health issues, including depression, obsessive-compulsive disorder, and bipolar and eating disorders. All adolescents experience growth spurts, and the onset of hormonal changes with puberty can bring on questioning, doubts, irritability, frustration, and mood swings. However, the typical reactions to puberty can be compounded by the added stressors of childhood trauma, mental health issues, and difficult life situations.

Due to the high percentage of students in the United States with mental health disorders (Cole et al., 2009), educators need to consider how the different aspects of a student's mental health conditions can influence their behavior, in turn disrupting their education. The line between what can be considered normal development and specific mental health problems is often blurred. Yet outbursts of anger or anxiety, frequent illness, and inconsistent school attendance may signal struggles beyond a normal range, indicating trauma or mental health issues.

Some students engage in extreme behaviors, such as anorexia, cutting, delinquency, or substance abuse, while yet others manifest clinical depression or sexual deviance and, in extreme cases, take their own lives. The Centers for Disease Control and Prevention reported in 2010 that one out of every 53 US high school students (1.9 percent) made a suicide attempt that was serious enough to be treated by a doctor or a nurse (SAMHSA, 2012). During a workshop I presented to 60 high school students from diverse socio-economic and ethnic backgrounds from across the United States, I asked the group to indicate if there had been a suicide of one of their classmates. Nearly every hand in the room was raised. Suicides greatly impact the entire school community, and prevention efforts are needed.

Identity safe educators seek to be knowledgeable about adolescent mental health and trauma. They watch for signs that include a sudden drop in grades, increased absences, and physical conditions manifesting as anxiety, drowsiness, or frequent illness. Educators can reach out to students and their parents, seeking out additional counseling support. They can make programmatic accommodations to help the students during difficult periods and provide support to move forward in school. When a suicide does occur, educators need to take immediate action to support the student body and, in particular, vulnerable students in order to prevent the "copycat" effect. Efforts are needed to forestall a possible cluster of suicides that have been known to occur in a particular area in a short period of time (Gould et al., 1989).

TIPS FROM THE SAMHSA SUICIDE PREVENTION TOOLKIT

The Substance Abuse and Mental Health Services Administration (SAMHSA) offers a free Suicide Prevention Toolkit that recommends that schools implement the following:

- Protocols for helping or responding to students who are at risk of suicide

- Staff, student, and parent training

- Protocols for responding after a suicide

- Screening and health provider support and mental health counseling

One mother shared a frightening story about her daughter, Sandy. Unbeknownst to her mother, Sandy had plans to take her life. Sandy's mom noticed that her daughter was withdrawn but did not realize the extent of her distress. With an intention to execute her plan, Sandy uncharacteristically straightened up her room and departed for school earlier that day. However, she took an unplanned detour and went to find her Living Skills teacher, Mr. J. She confided her despair to him. Mr. J. was able to talk Sandy out of her plan and immediately sought help for her. Sandy's mom tells this story with tears in her eyes. Having the supportive relationship with Mr. J. saved her daughter's life.

In a trusting environment with an emphasis on belonging, identity safe educators can accomplish much to support students with mental health challenges. Schools can greatly decrease the number of suicides by taking the warning signs seriously. They can develop clear protocols, train staff, and offer mental health services.

Fostering Resilience

Developing resilience can be instrumental in overcoming the impact of trauma and emotional distress. Resilience affects and expands our capacity to recover from or adjust to difficult decisions or change. It has been studied across a range of situations, including long-term studies of people who have gone through wars, lived in concentration camps, and/or experienced devastating earthquakes or abject poverty. The researchers particularly sought to understand the characteristics of those who overcame tremendous obstacles such as these. Resilience springs from a source deep within, but researchers have discovered patterns and identified ways to foster and model it.

Bonnie Benard (1991), resilience researcher, reviewed the many long-term studies of youth who have experienced traumatic situations. She explains that those who grew into well-functioning adults were able to develop social skills—not only for coping with the situation at hand but to later prevail and lead successful lives. I witnessed this in my own family. My father fled from Nazi Germany as a 12-year-old. He lost his mother a year later and spent his teen years during the war in dire poverty, often going hungry, living in a Jewish ghetto in Shanghai, China. Yet there were some very supportive allies who helped him along the way. Although he never finished high school, he went on to continue studying and received a master's degree. He was able to become a successful adult, enjoy a good marriage and family, and complete a career as a Jewish cantor. He accomplished what Benard refers to as the capacity of "self-righting," involving the ability to transform himself.

Benard (1991) points out that resilience is not a superpower or a genetic trait. Schools can work to foster resiliency by providing protective factors through positive relationships. The protective factors, also evident in identity safe teaching practices, include acceptance of one's identity, the capacity to adapt and stay hopeful, and the formation of positive relationships with a caring adult. Educators who practice the identity safety components of listening to student voices and classroom relationships (based on trust) and who promote meaningful opportunities for classroom autonomy and cooperation can greatly contribute to developing a student's sense of resilience.

Circling Back to Educator Resilience

We spoke about educator resilience in Chapter 2: Educator Identity Safety and the Importance of Self-Awareness. Positive thinking, a spirit of compassion, and forgiveness for ourselves and others, along with self-care, are all necessary to prepare us for the long haul as we grapple with how to make a difference and become the kind of educators we seek to be. Often, the rewards do not come until years later; recently, I received a Facebook message from a former student from 20 years ago. He referred to moments in my class when he acted like "a little monster," as he phrased it, and thanked me for believing in him. Even when those thank-yous are few and far between, our resilience sustains us. As we write about each component of identity safety, we keep circling back to the single most important aspect of creating an identity safe classroom: the presence of that caring and encouraging adult in the lives of our students.

Dilemmas and Points of Tension

Loving the Student Who Has Hurt Others and Continues to Do So

Margarita, an eighth-grade science teacher, had a student named Luis who was frequently mean to her. Luis also regularly insulted and bullied his peers. He did not seem to change, despite how hard she tried to connect with him. Eventually, his disparaging comments and flippant attitude left her cold and wanting to avoid him. Finally, she, along with some of her colleagues, sat down to consider who among them enjoyed a good relationship with Luis. They realized it was Gerardo, the custodian. Gerardo was friendly, often chatting with students, and Luis was one of them. Many students liked to help Gerardo with simple tasks such as setting up chairs for an assembly. Margarita approached Luis, who gladly agreed to help with the daily lunchroom setup—Luis was amenable because he got to leave English class ten minutes before it ended. Although, missing class time was not opportune, Margarita felt it was worth it to find a way to reach through Luis's walled-up defenses.

Sometimes, mean behavior can mask deep insecurities, serving as a protective mechanism or a cover for gaps in a skill set (see Chapter 12). Yet when students engage in repeated mean behavior, it can exhaust and challenge us to our last nerve. Whatever the instigating factor, not every person is easy to love, especially the ones who appear to take pleasure in being mean. That may be why different religions have specific parables and precepts, such as the phrase "Turn the other cheek" (Christian) or Buddhist meditations for generating compassion for people in our lives who present their difficulties to us (Chodron, 2001).

As identity safe educators, the challenge of continuing to seek ways to reach these students falls to us. Sometimes, it takes many repeated efforts to awaken compassion and help break through the walls a student has built up for many years. Developing a relationship with a student who is practiced in pushing people away is not easy, but our best recommendation is to keep trying. Look for student strengths and draw from them. Avoid labeling these students (e.g., referring to them as a bully).

In identity safe classrooms, we recognize that every student is growing and changing, and we keep working to reach students who appear angry or mean. If you need inspiration, Rita Mae Pierson's (2013) TED Talk, *Every Child Needs a Champion*, can fill the bill. She points out that even if you do not like every student, you can certainly act like you do. And for those who are not easy to teach, the simple fact that they have shown up at school means they, too, deserve to be taught. She closes with the words, "Is this job tough? You betcha. Oh, God, you betcha. But it is not impossible. We can do this. We're educators. We're born to make a difference."

Dismantling "White Savior" Mentality

Marvin Pierre (2017) described how his greatest challenge as a school administrator involved dealing with the tendency of White teachers to see themselves as "saviors" who come to rescue Black and Brown students from a terrible future. This savior mentality is a trait commonly featured in movies (e.g., *Dangerous Minds, Freedom Writer*) when a White teacher or social worker saves people of color from their plight. Educators may try to "save" their students from poverty and the negative influences in their lives. Even though well-meaning, White educators in this role can unintentionally denigrate the students' backgrounds—and sometimes their entire worlds—by forging ahead with unexamined assumptions. Without appropriate training and knowledge, they may exacerbate negative stereotypes about the students' families and communities. The savior mentality can lead down a dangerous path that ultimately devalues the student and increases stereotype threat. Even efforts to create "grit" can greatly underestimate some of the obstacles students have already faced and overcome with great effort. White educators can access their desire to make a difference with students of color and work to ensure that their approach respects and honors the backgrounds and experiences of the students, their families, and communities.

When I was a school principal, the parent of an eighth grader came to me to lodge a complaint. I remember that he began speaking even before he sat down. "I was a journalist in Mexico, and I do not appreciate a teacher making disparaging comments about me or any of the other parents." This father shared that his son's teacher told the class that they needed to study hard so they wouldn't turn out like their parents, who the teacher had described as "stuck doing menial labor because they were uneducated." We spoke for a long time, and I assured the man I would follow up. The teacher claimed that his intentions were to motivate the students. As the boy's father had made patently clear, by insulting the students' parents, any positive intentions backfired, and both the student and his father felt devalued.

When we honestly look into our inner selves, we can ask if some of our attitudes are a result of implicit bias (see Chapter 3). We can intentionally work to challenge our biases and transform our attitudes. Rather than seeking to express a savior mentality, we can aim to serve as a *resource* for our students as they navigate the numerous choices for their education. We must recognize that the heavy lifting will always be done by the students and that we are there to point out possibilities, remove structural barriers, and build their confidence in the process. Pierre's suggestions for ways to counteract the savior mentality are the same criteria we suggest to create identity safety: forming authentic and caring relationships, listening to our students, understanding their stories, and expressing high expectations while providing the support needed to meet them.

Chapter Summary

Educator–student relationships are at the core of every one of the identity safety components. In *Teacher Warmth and Availability for Learning*, we focused on trust and positive rapport. We began discussing ways to build trust. We also shared ideas for getting to know our students while offering tips for finding the time to do it. We also highlighted that the way feedback is both offered and perceived can make or break a relationship. By giving wise feedback on what specifically needs to be improved, pointing out progress, and communicating our belief in our students' capacity and intelligence to succeed, we can motivate our students. We shared tools to teach self-regulation and other effective practices to help students manage their often complicated emotional reactions.

We delved into the topic of trauma, sharing statistics on the large numbers of people who have suffered adverse childhood experiences. We offered trauma-informed practices. We also described racial trauma that results from living in an unjust society where students frequently feel devalued. Educators need to be able to address all forms of trauma in order to help students overcome the negative impacts. We then addressed mental health issues, including suicide, and suggested protocols for providing educators with knowledge and effective strategies. While we discussed mental health issues in this chapter, we acknowledge that a student's mental state also impacts relationships with their peers. These relationships can be greatly impacted when anxiety, depression, or other emotional challenges are in play. The suggested self-regulation tools also apply in peer relationships. We closed this part of the chapter with a hopeful note describing the power of resilience for both students and educators.

Of the many potential educator–student dilemmas, we selected two potential challenges faced by educators to showcase: (1) Reaching into ourselves to find a way to like—even love—a student who makes our life difficult and (2) ways an educator can avoid the tendency to become a "White savior," exhibiting misguided efforts to rescue low-income students or students of color. The world of relationships is multidimensional and nuanced but well worth examining as we seek to connect with our students and facilitate learning.

Check Yourself

1. What techniques do you use to connect and get to know each of your students? What new ones can you try?

2. What kind of feedback have you been giving your students? Have you tried wise feedback? What did you notice?

3. What assumptions about your students' parents and home life might be interfering with your relationships?

4. How do you react to students who are consistently mean or hurtful to other students and/or yourself?

5. For teachers who identify as White: How do you view your role as an educator for students of color? Do your approaches demonstrate your value and respect for each student's background, including their family and community experiences?

TRY IT OUT: END-OF-CHAPTER ACTIVITIES

Wise Feedback

Consider a student and a situation where you can give wise feedback. Write a paragraph or two in your own words that aims to communicate the following ideas:

1. Communicate your high standards.

2. Offer suggestions for improvement, using specific language.

3. Assure students you believe they can meet the standards and explain how you will provide scaffolding to support them.

4. Point out their progress to date.

5. Give students tools to reflect on their progress for themselves and celebrate it as they continue to improve.

6. Offer some suggestions on what to do next.

Describe the student:

Plan what to say:

Try it out and share what happened. How did the student respond? What did you learn in the process?

 Available for download as a full-page form at **https://resources.corwin .com/IdentitySafeClass6-12**

11 Positive Student Relationships

Why Positive Student Relationships Matter

In a German study (Rohrer et al., 2018), researchers followed survey respondents for over 32 years, discovering ways that social connections are significantly linked to happiness. They learned that people who socialize on a regular basis have stronger relationships. In another longitudinal study from New Zealand, researchers followed youth into adulthood and were able to document that adolescents with positive social relationships experience higher levels of well-being, which intuitively makes perfect sense (Olsson et al., 2013). They also found that social connectedness was more predictive of future well-being than academic achievement. Promoting positive relationships among peers is paramount in creating a needed sense of belonging that supports their success in their schoolwork. High standards for the way students treat one is as important as high expectations for academic achievement.

Positive student relationships are characterized by friendly interactions, good cooperation skills, and mutual respect in and outside the classroom. Working to equalize status among peers is well worth the effort when it supports growth and confidence, contributing to a student's sense of identity safety. A classroom cannot become fully identity safe when some students feel "less than" their peers or "othered" for being different. Educators can equalize status through activities that bring out the special talents of students, highlighting many different types of value beyond the typical academic strengths—values such as friendliness, helpfulness, loyalty, artistic skills, analytic skills, leadership, humor, and more. Think of your own close friends. What are the qualities in them that you admire and want to be around? Every student has personality traits or skills they can contribute to enhance a warm environment. By highlighting a wide range of personal qualities and ascribing value to them, you can improve the status for everyone. As we have already discussed, creating learning opportunities in which every student's contribution is needed to reach a full understanding and acceptance for the entire group will create healthy interdependence.

get to know one another pays off in multiple ways. It
~~cially~~ important for students whose minds are distracted
~~n~~ additional payoff shows up in the time saved from
~~can~~ disrupt a class. A safe and happy environment

~~equalizing~~ status across gender relationships and
~~s~~ launched a greater awareness of sexual abuse
~~o~~ explore intimacy and romance, we would
young romantic relationships as we seek to
~~relationships~~ is extremely broad, so in Part V:
~~ments~~, we continue to expand on these themes of positive
relationships. We tackle conflict resolution, bullying, and restorative practices as part
of Chapter 12: Teacher Skill, and we present many aspects of strengthening SEL (social
and emotional learning) practices in Chapter 14: Attention to Prosocial Development.

Positive Student Relationships: Making Them Happen

Kindness Is Contagious: Shifting Social Norms to Create a Culture of Respect

Adolescence is a time when teens are desperately trying to fit in as they emulate their
peer's behavior. Youth acutely observe one another as they seek to ascertain what
their classmates are thinking, wearing, saying, eating, or whether they are dieting. If
their friends are getting tattoos or piercings, they often want to get some, too. If their
peers are drinking or smoking, taking drugs, staying out late, or acting mean to unpopular students, some choose to indulge as well because that is what they see as "normal"
or "cool." For that very reason, when students see their peers practicing the norms of
behavior that are positive, kindness can be contagious, too. Cooperation, helping one
another, and friendliness can spread—often much faster than its negative counterpart
because it feels so much safer.

In identity safe classrooms, educators are aware of the power of peer influences, and they
aim to make it "cool" to be respectful and kind. Allowing peers with positive attitudes
to influence the others helps flip the negative to positive. This includes embedding
conversation that fosters empathy and compassion as part of the daily curriculum. Another
significant way to spread kindness is through the intentional use of gratitude. A robust
body of research shows that expressing gratitude (King & Datu, 2018; Wood et al., 2010)
increases emotional well-being, enhances self-esteem, and strengthens relationships. Each
of these qualities helps build and sustain a healthy school culture. You can explicitly name
them among your goals as you introduce a lesson. You can include them in end-of-lesson
routines as students engage in metacognitive reflections on how they worked together.

Leadership Public Schools (LPS) has always cared deeply about creating schools where everyone feels a deep sense of belonging. LPS engages in "Family Meetings," a practice used across the network. These weekly sessions are used for student recognition as well as teaching SEL skills and grappling with school and classroom climate issues. Students and staff also regularly "shout out" to each other, highlighting positive behaviors in advisories, classes, whole-school assemblies, and faculty meetings.

When LPS Innovator in Residence Mike Fauteux was teaching ninth-grade algebra several years ago, he noticed that, while shout-outs had great value, they had certain limitations. Logistically, not everyone in his class was able to participate at one time. In addition, he explains that in terms of access, not every student feels safe calling out, in particular the shy students and English language learners. Some of the male students viewed public expressions of gratitude as a sign of weakness and showed reluctance in calling out. Fauteux also points out that, once spoken, a shout-out floats away. An amazing acknowledgment for someone, for example, presents itself then leaves the room so swiftly that little opportunity remains to absorb it. As he pondered this dilemma, he wanted to enhance their gratitude practice, making it more accessible and coherent for students and teachers. He also felt that a deeper sense of acknowledgment would help some of his algebra students—who were several years behind in math and feeling vulnerable—form supportive peer and teacher relationships. So Fauteux invented a motivating way to resolve the issue.

Fauteux approached a friend who was an engineer, and they invented a prototype for an app where students could exchange messages of gratitude with one another and their educators. Students could enter messages into the app. First, the messages were forwarded to the educator to ensure they were appropriate, and then they were passed on to the recipient. Fauteux piloted it and discovered that the students loved sending messages to one another.

Other teachers became aware of it and asked to try it with their classrooms. Eventually, they surveyed the classes who used the prototype and found that students reported feeling happier while developing stronger relationships with their peers and teachers. This, in turn, led to building a deeper sense of self in relationship with others. Fauteux witnessed such good results that he proceeded to make the app available to educators everywhere by starting a nonprofit to support the work. The app GiveThx was launched.

Equalizing Status in the Classroom

As we described earlier, adolescence is a time when young people are also sizing themselves up in comparison with others. In middle school, I often worried if I was the least popular among the popular students or the least unpopular among the others who did not fit in, a very unsafe feeling to say the least. I changed my first name from Esther to Becki in eighth grade because I thought a cooler name with a cooler spelling would help me to fit in better. It did not, however, help as much as I had hoped. I tried many other techniques as well. I even straightened my hair but stopped short of getting a nose

GIVETHX, THE APP (WWW.GIVETHX.ORG)

GiveThx emerged from LPS to become available for other schools to use in the fall of 2018. Its website describes it as a research-based curriculum and app that nurtures positive behaviors and relationships using peer-to-peer gratitude and personal reflection. Here's how it works:

Users select a person, write a digital Thx (thank-you) note, and choose a tag that best describes why they are grateful (e.g., patience, kindness, helpfulness). The tags support students in developing both a mindful and subtle practice as they learn to identify their feelings. They know that their teachers are monitoring the notes, but they appreciate the chance to express their gratitude to one other student in lieu of a public display, which feels safer. Each student has their own personal character profile that captures all the notes they have sent and received, building their confidence and self-esteem by providing the opportunity to view in totality the positive impact of their actions on the classroom community.

Educators address the concern of ensuring that all students receive expressions of gratitude by establishing routines to equalize the distribution of "thank-yous." Educators can use the app's "Social Heat Map" to identify potentially isolated students and adjust to better include them. They do this by using practices like "New Gratitude," where students are instructed to send to peers they infrequently send to, or "Gratitude Wave," where everyone sends a message to a "randomly" chosen student selected by the teacher based on the data. An example of a routine that supports everyone receiving gratitude is regularly asking students to thank collaboration partners or group mates for actions that benefited their work.

As of spring 2019, more than 3,500 students in three countries have sent over 45,000 Thx notes.

A ninth grader from Hawaii wrote on the *GiveThx* (n.d.) website, "I think that this activity would be helpful in all classes or just life in general because I have noticed over the past weeks I have done this that I feel a lot more appreciated and happy."

A seventh-grade student from Rhode Island shared that "receiving thanks from other classmates made me feel like I was welcomed in the community, and it made me feel happy."

job like my friend Heather and other Jewish girls did in those years. Luckily, the hippie movement came along when I was in tenth grade. I jumped on board, adopting the free-spirited ideas that liberated me from the yoke of traditional popularity. I stopped ironing my hair and wore it long and curly. I started writing poetry along with other hippie kids around San Francisco in the late 1960s. In other words, I exchanged one social norming group for another where I felt more accepted, and I gradually gained confidence.

Not all students have access to alternative peer groups or settings. Some have disabilities and are excluded and mocked; others question their gender identity and search for a way to belong; still others of mixed race feel they do not fit with any racial group. Some students are the only person of their racial background in an entire classroom and feel they cannot speak or act the way they do at home. Educators may feel these pressures are beyond their role or capacity to influence. However, students are looking to their educators to create a safe and welcoming space. While interrupting peer pressure can be difficult, there are many ways to counteract it. Here are ideas for equalizing status:

- Notice and address status problems (e.g., students who are left out, have no friends).

- Become aware and analyze practices that might inadvertently give some students more status than others. I always felt my seventh-grade French teacher only called on the popular kids. I may have been wrong, but that was my perception at the time. I remember getting *C*s, even though I later discovered that I like learning languages. Unfortunately, French never became one of them.

- Discuss the value of equal status with students. Have students explore their attitudes about it in writing. Ask them to share feelings and consider how they treat others.

- Teach collaboration skills that ensure that every student has a role and participates.

- Ask students to pose solutions to repair or eliminate damage caused by status hierarchies. Do this in a generic way to protect those who feel they are unpopular. They should not be named or singled out in any way.

- Provide opportunities for authentic contributions by all students. Draw out their unique qualities and acknowledge them.

- Broaden students' perceptions of intelligence and assure each one that they can make meaningful intellectual contributions.

- Promote student autonomy with peer-led activities that are rotated to enable a range of students an opportunity to assume leadership roles.

- Stay connected to students who differ from the others in some way, such as gender, race, English language learners, and those in special education. Watch how they are treated and ensure they are included in class discussions.

- Actively value and teach code-switching (see Chapter 3: Listening for Student Voices) to affirm and leverage the power of students' cultural and linguistic assets.

- "Mix the pot" by regularly changing who is in small groups to allow everyone to get to know each other.

SHIFTING SCHOOL GENDER IDENTITY NORMS AT A MIDDLE SCHOOL

Julia, a seventh grader, described how she felt at school in the short video *A Gay Straight Alliance (GSA) Creates Unity and a Culture of Acceptance* (Not In Our Town, 2019). She explains that for the vast majority of the sixth grade, she was harassed for not wearing feminine clothing. Her classmates called her names like "she-man" and "he-she." She reported the name-calling to at least four teachers, yet nothing was done. The only teacher who took any initiative moved her from one seat to another, but she could still hear the slurs across the room. Her teachers would tell her that the kids were giving her a hard time because she was different, and the advice was simply not to take it to heart. Her self-esteem and confidence diminished as hopelessness set in, and she became depressed.

Julia explains that she and her friends asked for permission to start a GSA (Genders and Sexualities Alliance) at their middle school. When the principal agreed, Julia rose to the challenge. Later in the year, the principal invited the GSA members to address the faculty. There, Julia told her story, adding that that people her age should be enabled and supported in expressing who they are. She acknowledged this as one of the most difficult things for a middle school student to do. The video revealed ways that the GSA brought students of all gender identities together to share their feelings with each other. They also sponsored awareness-building activities for the entire school. Faculty sponsor Janet Miller stated that the GSA not only changed the experience for the members, but it also changed the culture of the whole school in a single year.

- Use cooperative lessons and *complex instruction* (Cohen, 1994)—instructional strategies designed to equalize status—described in Chapter 5: Focus on Cooperation.

Consider that some activities, designed to promote kindness, may exacerbate status differences. For example, when students engage in a public appreciation activity, often the more popular students receive the majority of positive compliments. In other cases, subconsciously, educators cater to the more attractive and popular students. Look around your classroom. Imagine what it might feel like from the vantage point of each of your students, especially those who are different in some way. By growing your awareness, you can rectify practices that contribute to unequal status.

Equalizing Status Across Gender Identities

Unequal status continues to impact females, males who do not fit societal stereotypes of manhood, and people of nonbinary gender identity. In Chapter 7: Using Diversity as a Resource, we examined the critical multicultural approach that teaches students to investigate and rectify historical inequities. Students also need to critically analyze

GENDER INCLUSION: SHIFTING SCHOOL CULTURE WITH A FEW SIMPLE CHANGES

At an LPS identity safety workshop, one teacher shared that she always used to address her students as "ladies and gentlemen." One of the students pointed out that this phrase left out the students holding nonbinary gender identities. She resolved then and there to simply address the class as "students."

In that same session, the idea also arose to invite all staff members to add pronouns to their email signatures. Amy proceeded to present the idea to the LPS superintendent, who approved it. An email was sent out to the entire staff, inviting people to add a signature with their preferred pronoun at the bottom of their school emails. LPS leaders introduced the idea at a districtwide professional development session on identity safety, providing simple examples (Here is mine: Becki Cohn-Vargas—Preferred Pronouns: She/Her/Hers). Subsequently, the vast majority of staff added the signature line with their gender pronouns.

conditions for women and LGBTQ people that subjugate their status. Their portrayal in the media as well as intersectional oppression based on gender and race are significant contributing factors. Equalizing gender status needs to be part of an ongoing conversation about identity safety. As educators, we can reflect on our own messaging about gender, ensuring that we call on an equal number of students of all genders. We can examine data with faculty to establish that resources are fairly distributed and that all students have equal access to classes, clubs, sports, and campus leadership positions. We can also attend to the way students are treating one another across gender differences.

Dilemmas and Points of Tension

Responding to Contemporary Social Issues and Addressing the #MeToo Movement: A School Responsibility

Identity safe practices are holistic and include every aspect of a student's life, including romantic relationships. Identity safe educators open dialogue about safe and respectful relationships of all kinds. Many people, even those who participated in movements for women's rights, were shocked in 2017 when the #MeToo hashtag brought thousands of women, worldwide, out of the shadows to share experiences of unwanted sexual advances, sexual harassment, and rape. We cannot ignore the reality brought home by the #MeToo movement and its impact on the lives of our students. Many have already in their young lives been subjected to harassment or abuse. This underscores our role as educators to keep our students safe within and beyond the classroom doors. It also signals the need for renewed efforts to promote equitable treatment of and between males and females and other gender identities. Beyond creating a safe classroom, we are preparing tomorrow's leaders to work for a world in which people of all gender identities have equal status, feel safe, treat one another with respect, and act as upstanders when needed.

STATISTICS ON TEEN SEXUAL ABUSE FROM *TEEN HELP* WEBSITE

- Teenagers account for 51 percent of all reported sexual abuse.

- Teenagers between the ages of 16 and 19 are 3.5 times more likely than the general public to be victims of sexual abuse.

- Twenty-three percent of all sexual offenders are under the age of 18.

- Female victims of teen sexual abuse in Grades 9–12 are more likely than others to experience eating disorders, suicidal behavior, pregnancy, and risky sexual behaviors. (www.teenhelp.com; 2018)

These issues are so important that federal guidelines exist in Title IX to inform educators that addressing gender equity and responding to all forms of discrimination falls within their purview. LPS educates its leaders regarding their responsibilities with regard to Title IX, which prohibits any form of discrimination based on sex, including sexual harassment, rape, and assault. By law, schools are required to provide curriculum for sex education and healthy relationships. Some schools engage with local agencies for this effort. LPS partners with *Peer Health Exchange* (n.d.), a national organization with local branches. Health educators teach classes to ninth graders, covering healthy relationships and sexual education. However, shifting social norms about relationships cannot be fully understood during a single special class on the topic. It needs to be an integral part of the school curriculum. In-class relationships can be a model for out-of-class friendships and more intimate relationships. Here are some basic healthy relationship guidelines:

- Treat one another with mutual respect.
- Listen to each other without interrupting or overreacting.
- Recognize anger is normal, but seek to calmly express it.
- Handle disagreement without yelling, threats, intimidation, or violence.
- Do not dominate or control the other person.
- Be honest about your feelings.
- Resolve problems face-to-face.

Discuss the importance of these aspects of healthy relationships and explain that they also apply to romantic relationships. Two additional caveats are worth noting:

- Jealousy may be normal, but it is important not to let it get out of control.
- Partners must listen and respect when one of them says "no" to an unwanted advance.

Social media offers both opportunities for learning and celebration, as well as a platform for youth to mistreat one another. The dangers for a targeted student can be far-reaching when the gossip, rumors, sexting, or threats turn viral. The level of humiliation can feel intractable for them. Often, the derisive comments are indelibly embedded on the Internet platforms, with little recourse for the victim to delete them. Learning safe and respectful Internet behavior is a necessary part of promoting positive relationships. These types of conflicts online may start small and quickly accelerate. Students can learn to avoid public social media fights and refrain from posting, responding to, or liking mean comments. Students can also discuss ways to tread carefully when offering information of a personal nature. They need to know never to give out personal information. They need to know that underage sexting is illegal. It is viewed and treated as child pornography. Many schools offer Internet safety training, as well as teen dating and bullying prevention programs. Identity safe educators recognize that their role goes beyond the traditional educational programs to the fashioning of environments that incorporate ongoing dialogue and modeling. These educators are continually addressing respectful and positive peer relationships.

Chapter Summary

In an identity safe classroom, attention to student–student interactions in and outside the classroom is part of an educator's role. Maintaining an awareness of student interactions and supporting *Positive Student Relationships* among them is a dance—an art rather than a science—that includes assessing when and whether to intervene in a student exchange. Kindness can spread through positive peer role models. Expressing gratitude motivates students and enlivens them. In this chapter, we shared activities to equalize status across gender, race, and academic level, as well as other markers of social identity, with the goal to strengthen belonging and acceptance. We focused on equalizing status for students of all gender identities. Of the many dilemmas, we chose to look at the role of an educator in addressing romantic relationships and sexual abuse and assault. Student relationships do not end when they step off the school grounds. We believe it is part of an educator's role to provide, model, and teach students about safe and respectful relationships.

Check Yourself

Ask yourself some hard questions about student status and seek ways to equalize it:

1. What are some ways I work to equalize the status of all students?
2. When considering how I might inadvertently reproduce unequal status, I ask myself these questions:
   a. Do my criteria for posting student work provide opportunities for all students to share their talents? Or do I exclude students who make mistakes or did not earn a good grade?

    b. Do I praise some students above others?

    c. Do I offer inauthentic praise to some students? If so, why and to which students?

    d. Do I tend to call on certain students more or less often? Why?

3. Have I ignored it when students have been excluded? If yes, what can I change?

4. Considering how I interact with students of different gender identities, what stands out for me? If I feel any discomfort addressing gender expression, what am I doing to change?

5. How can I further educate myself about safe dating practices?

TRY IT OUT: END-OF-CHAPTER ACTIVITY

Kindness, Gratitude, Equal Status, Positive Relationships

Consider the following: kindness, gratitude, equal status, and positive relationships. Tell how you will incorporate each in your classroom.

Ways You Will Teach or Reteach It	Ways You Will Help Students Practice It
Kindness	
Gratitude	
Equal Status	
Positive Relationships	

 Available for download as a full-page form at **https://resources.corwin .com/IdentitySafeClass6-12**

Big Ideas: Classroom Relationships

This part was guided by the following Identity Safety Principle:

#2. To feel a sense of belonging and acceptance requires creating positive relationships between teacher and students and among students with equal status for different social identities.

This principle, as shared through the two component chapters, has some big ideas:

- Trust-building efforts lead to student engagement and a classroom environment that supports belonging and achievement. Trust grows when educators express care, listen and support learning, and take an interest in what matters to students.

- Educators, even with large numbers of students, can build rapport with each one by knowing and correctly pronouncing their names, greeting them daily with presence and intention, and making an effort to learn about their interests, experiences, goals, hopes, and dreams.

- Students are more likely to be open to and respond to feedback when the educators have high expectations and communicate that they believe the student can meet the expectations and will support them along the way. Helping students recognize their progress will motivate them to continue their efforts to improve.

- Trauma impacts a large number of students. By becoming knowledgeable about trauma-informed practices, educators seek to understand what a student has experienced rather than wondering what is wrong with them. Trauma-informed practices include helping students learn to self-regulate their reactions, avoid becoming triggered, and calm themselves. At times, counseling and other professional support is needed.

- Kindness spreads in an accepting climate where students see peers promoting respect and identity safety.

- Identity safe educators pay attention to equalizing student status by bringing out a range of valuable qualities from students with opportunities to contribute in different ways.

- Students benefit from explicit teaching and practicing norms and skills for positive relationships.

For Further Study

- Article: "Fostering Resiliency in Kids: Protective Factors in the Family, School, and Community" (1991) by Bonnie Benard

- Article: "Healing the Hidden Wounds of Racial Trauma" (2013) by Kenneth Hardy

- Article: "The Mentor's Dilemma: Providing Critical Feedback Across the Racial Divide" (1999) by Geoffrey Cohen, Claude Steele, and Lee Ross

- Audio: "Third Space, an Interview of Kris Gutierrez" (2008) by Betsy Baker, a *Voice of Literacy* podcast, www.voiceofliteracy.org

- Book: *Culturally Responsive Teaching and the Brain: Promoting Authentic Engagement and Rigor Among Culturally and Linguistically Diverse Students* (2015) by Zaretta Hammond

- Book: *Help Your Child Deal With Stress—and Thrive: The Transformative Power of Self-Reg* (2018) by Stuart Shanker

- Book: *School Talk: Rethinking What We Say About—and to—Students Every Day* (2017) by Micah Pollock

- Handout: *Preventing Suicide: A Toolkit for High Schools* (2012), free and downloadable from the US Department of Health and Human Services, Substance Abuse and Mental Health Services, Administration, store.samhsa.gov

Caring Classroom Environments

As a principal, I was in and out of classrooms every day. I could feel the climate of each room environment as I walked between them. The metaphor of climate to describe a classroom atmosphere is apropos. Climate addresses the temperature (hot or cold), a sunny or cloudy mood, and even the atmospheric pressure in the level of tension in a room. And the beauty of identity safety is that we, as educators, can orchestrate a warm and supportive climate as an architect of a *Caring Classroom Environment*.

When we describe identity safety as an approach, we have referred to it as a gestalt—a broader experience that is more than the sum of the parts. This part exemplifies this idea. We intentionally placed it after the previous identity safety components, as classroom environment is ideal to convey the others into a transformative whole. We have already covered the key elements of identity safety: the student-centered focus, the rigor and high expectations, and the many ways to cultivate and value diversity and foster academic identities, in addition to the careful attention imparted to student relationships. The final three components serve as a platform for classroom environment, which is the medium for bringing all these aspects together, integrating them into an intentional climate that fosters identity safety; hence, we present a view greater than any of the individual components. In this part, we investigate these last three components discovered by our Stanford Integrated Studies Project (SISP): teacher skill, emotional and physical comfort, and attention to prosocial development. They blend together with the rest of the components into an environment that promotes belonging and rigorous learning.

Here are short definitions of the three components that make up the domain of caring classroom environments. These will be fully explored in subsequent chapters.

1. *Teacher Skill* refers to establishing an orderly and purposeful classroom that facilitates student learning. Without effective instruction or in a chaotic environment, the benefits of an identity safe classroom are nullified. We use the term *teacher skill* to describe an educator's capacity to teach in a classroom where students are engaged with both agency and confidence in a flexible and instructive environment rather than a strictly controlled one. Teacher skill refers to setting clear behavioral expectations, establishing a set of procedures, and supporting students in discovering ways to manage their learning. Teacher skill also includes developing a set of routines and rituals that bring the values of the classroom to life. While teacher skill is necessary, it is not sufficient unless combined with other identity safety components. Conversely, many of the other components are not sufficient without the foundational aspect of teacher skill.

2. *Emotional and Physical Comfort* flourish in a climate where each student feels safe and connected to school and other students. Emotional and physical comfort combine to fashion a space that is warm and friendly, calm and pleasant, and neither hectic nor rushed. The emotional environment can embrace a fun and lighthearted character without sacrificing rigor. Our brains are wired to find learning fun! Every time we laugh, we get a shot of dopamine, which is an essential part of the brain's reward system. Dopamine increases our capacity to learn and remember. Every educator can create emotional and physical comfort in ways that reflect their unique personality. Some use humor while others play music to set the tone. Still others express their support through dramatic storytelling. Quiet connections, too, have their place in the ambience of learning. The physical setup and layout of furniture in the classroom can also serve to create a homelike feeling, ensuring that materials are accessible, students have room to move around, and desks are arranged in a flexible format to facilitate small and large groups as well as individual work areas.

3. *Attention to Prosocial Development* involves meeting students where they live emotionally and teaching them how to interact with one another, solve problems, and show respect and care for others. Teenagers are developing prosocial skills, and through daily discovery—and often trial and error—they learn how to treat one another. For some, rude language or snippy, sarcastic comments have become habitual. They need to consider their impact on others and learn to take the edge off their interactions. The classroom can be a

place to learn prosocial and interpersonal skills. Rather than exposing them to lectures on how to behave, the students can teach and model for one another by describing how they want to be treated.

Given the work needed to create identity safety, we suggest you take a moment to consider your deeper beliefs as you manage your classroom, especially during less pleasant interchanges or conflicts. When enacting classroom routines or responding to misbehavior, it is easy to slip into practices that maintain patterns of bias without even realizing it. Given the overrepresentation of Black and Latinx students in statistics on suspension and expulsion, we need to step back, look at the data from our school and classrooms, and ensure we match our words and actions to our antiracist stance. Here, we recommend challenging yourself to reflect on your own assumptions and beliefs about student behavior to help you uncover and address biases that may be at play without realizing it.

Finally, we wish we could say that by creating caring environments, all conflicts and tensions melt away. While we do believe that placing student interests and concerns at the center of your efforts will make your classroom a much more welcoming space, inevitably there will be problems to address. In these next three chapters, as we paint a picture of an identity safe classroom, we do not shy away from the harder moments that challenge us as educators. In truth, it is essential to meet them head-on.

12 Teacher Skill

Why Teacher Skill Matters

In the Stanford Integrated Schools Project (SISP) research, *teacher skill* refers to an educator's capacity to provide classrooms with these things:

- Well-planned lessons
- Predictable routines with moments of excitement
- Smooth transitions
- An orderly and focused atmosphere
- Clear behavioral expectations
- Effective practices to prevent and respond to conflicts and student behavior

Many aspects of teacher skill are covered in teacher preparation programs. We recognize that it takes time for a new educator to find their sea legs and their "teacher voice." These primary skills are a major focus in the first years of teaching, increasingly honed by experience. Skills and awareness that are needed to administer identity safety can sound over-the-top for new teachers struggling to absorb an abundance of other learning material; however, the approach to identity safe teaching easily subsumes and supports these positive, basic skills. It does not negate them. Educators can discover that identity safety teaching serves as a fitting context for the content of these basic skills, providing a meaningful delivery for them. Even for experienced educators, it is worth reflecting on basic teacher skills from the perspective of identity safety. We are never finished in the process of creating a safe environment for students. In identity safe classrooms, these basic skills combine with a warm, caring, and culturally sensitive environment. Student-centered practices ensure that the students feel that they matter. This is unlikely to happen when management strategies aim to control students or when students feel disrespected or fear their educators. In an identity safe classroom, the approach to behavior shifts from managing students to engaging them in self-management.

Teacher skill is all about developing our capacity as effective educators to empower students to think for themselves and take stock of their actions, trusting them to act accordingly. We have already explored many ways to do this in previous components. During your educational career, you have developed—or you will develop—a toolkit of skills for creating your classroom environment. By incorporating an identity safety lens, you can bring all your skills to task while checking yourself to ensure your management methods, relationships, and messaging to students align with the values of fostering inclusion, supporting each student's identity, and countering stereotypes and other threats.

In this chapter, we present two major aspects of identity safe teacher skill: First, we propose ways to set up a classroom for identity safety, from routines and procedures to expectations, pacing, and activities that are affirming and positive. Second, we tackle the inevitable moments of discord, offering tools for preventing and resolving conflicts. We propose using restorative practices in a growth approach that instructs rather than punishes. We present scenarios to remedy tensions and dilemmas while ensuring that students have time to process feelings after an incident. We also suggest ways to support students who repeatedly misbehave in spite of our best efforts.

Conflict is part of life, and young people inevitably have moments of tension, competition, bullying, and discord. In identity safe classrooms, students are explicitly coached and practiced in talking through, preventing, and resolving conflicts. We teach them to listen and disagree respectfully while approaching negative interactions with empathy and compassion. Guiding students to improve their communication and problem-solving skills while instilling the courage to speak up for themselves and others prepares them to deal with conflict before it occurs. We also model through our behavior and take immediate action when students exclude, tease, bully, or otherwise mistreat or disrespect a peer. Confronting bullying behaviors when students are young empowers them to avoid becoming targets. It curbs the tendencies to harass or overpower others. These skills can prevent them from becoming lifelong victims or bullies. Time spent helping students learn to communicate and resolve conflicts carries into their homes and benefits their families as well, serving to support them throughout their lives. It also eases your load as an educator, creating a more pleasant and less tense environment. Ultimately, these efforts contribute to more joyful experiences for all.

Teacher Skill: Making It Happen

Setting Up a Classroom for Identity Safety

We speak of the *science and art of teaching* as a way to acknowledge the nuanced talents required of educators (D. M. Steele & Cohn-Vargas, 2013). The *science* describes the way the educator organizes and structures each aspect of the course, setting goals and expectations and scaffolding instruction. The *art* characterizes the unique way each educator fosters creativity and innovation, adapting to student needs and responding as situations call for a change of course.

Much of the process of the art and science of teaching requires our attention in orchestrating the climate of a classroom. The educator is constantly adjusting the curriculum and dynamics of interaction to reach, challenge, and inspire students in order to bring out their best.

Meaningful Routines, Reasonable Procedures, and Clear Expectations

Routines and rituals are a way to enact and manifest values. They also create a sense of safety and security because students know what to expect. This is especially beneficial for students who come from unstable home situations. We can create simple welcoming routines to start the day or include gratitude-filled closing routines at the end of the day. As a principal, I observed many creative routines used by educators. Kang Lee started his day with a student news broadcast and brief conversation about current events. I loved to drop by and talk to the kids, hearing their opinions about the day's news. Kelly asked her students to enjoy a few minutes of mindfulness as they entered the room each morning. She dimmed the lights, and they practiced deep breathing as she led them in a guided imagery. A hushed calm would envelop the room. Amit asked students to bring in different kinds of music to play while they wrote in their journals.

Clearly delineated procedures also create a sense of rhythm and keep the classroom functioning smoothly. Midyear during my first year of teaching, I heard Harry Wong, coauthor of the book *The First Days of School* (Wong & Rosemary, 1998). When Wong spoke of the importance of teaching specific procedures, it was my epiphany. Defining specific expectations for each of my procedures became paramount in shifting my classroom after experiencing a tumultuous beginning that year. My students and I appreciated a much more even and calm springtime.

Taking the time to invite students to help determine classroom operating systems, routines, and procedures helps them feel heard and considered. They can identify which of these aspects help them feel more comfortable and engaged. They can also articulate those processes that hinder them and propose alternatives.

Teens have had time to develop strong opinions in their young lives and can easily help you answer the following questions:

- How can the room be laid out to work for both small-group and individual tasks?

- What classroom procedures work best for our class?

- What routines help express our classroom values?

- What noise levels facilitate working individually, in partners, or in groups? Do you enjoy listening to music during quiet work time? What kind of music do you like?

- What group norms and behavioral expectations will make classroom life pleasant and comfortable for you?

While students can help design their experiences, educators set the boundaries. They lay down basic expectations for acceptable behavior, using examples and nonexamples. Students love a humorous role-played demonstration of what behaviors you do not want to see.

Timing and Pacing

Educators set up schedules that balance the time required to introduce new content with time students need to work individually and in groups in order to process new ideas, practice, and apply them. They find ways to account for the fact that some students work more slowly than their peers, while others work quickly and can become restless. Knowing your students, you take care not to rush them and provoke anxiety while ensuring that those who work quickly always have focused work to do. Sometimes, provocative lessons like debates can motivate and pique student interest and motivation. Allowing the excitement to build while keeping a fever pitch at bay will support an enlivened and manageable classroom. My mother's old adage when my sisters and I grew wild and unruly with each other was to announce that "this is going to end in tears." Often, she was right. Identity safe classrooms are specifically tailored to vary the pace and activities to meet the needs of the students in the room at any given time.

Teaching Strategies

We covered many effective teaching strategies in Part II: Student-Centered Teaching. Educators listen and give students a voice, while drawing from their backgrounds and cultures. They engage their hearts and minds in instruction. When students feel a partnership with their educators and enjoy a sense of agency and independence, they will not feel the need to rebel against or resist events in the classroom.

Making Hidden Social Contracts Visible

Sometimes, students are stymied by "hidden curriculum" and unspoken social contracts. Hidden curriculum refers to certain expectations that are assumed but not stated aloud, and as a result, some students are aware of these expectations while others are not. These unattended rules can play out in many ways. For example, a kid runs into the classroom yelling and laughing and the teacher scolds him; the student immediately asks why. The hidden expectation is that the noisy entrance is inappropriate, and the student's question is viewed as disrespectful backtalk. When rules are unspoken, it often leads to unequal status or access based on whether these rules are familiar to students in the context of their home or community. In some cases, the hidden rules may even contradict a student's cultural values. As we look across the sea of faces in our classrooms, we need to question the values and expectations we hold. Are they in sync with the values the students bring with them? As we have discussed previously, we also need to question our own perspectives. Are we focused on compliance? Assimilation? How can we help every young person learn behaviors they need to be successful in the learning community and yet recognize that we are not aiming for mere robotic compliance? How can we present the options in ways that do not normalize mainstream behaviors and pathologize alternatives?

Sweating the Small Things: Determining When to Intervene

We developed an identity safe method to approach behavioral problems and to determine when and how to intervene. These ideas also serve to support trauma-informed practices. When a student acts out, the educator starts by considering their

INTERVENTION CHECKLIST

Consider the following set of questions (D. M. Steele & Cohn-Vargas, 2013) and responses to determine how to respond:

Question	Response
Was the behavior intentional?	Find out if the student is aware of the harm they caused. If so, alert the student to it and help them focus on empathy.
Was the student unaware of classroom expectations and norms for behavior?	If so, teach the expectations and explain their purpose.
Did the student lack social and emotional skills to manage their behavior?	If so, teach the needed social and communication skills, explaining their purpose and support the student's practice.
Is the student seeking attention?	If so, help the student find positive ways to gain attention.
Was the behavior caused by a lack of impulse control?	If so, help the student become aware of and monitor their behavior. Teach, reinforce, and practice techniques for self-regulating and controlling impulses. For some students, much practice is needed, and your patience will reap reward.
Was the behavior intentionally an act of anger, rebellion, or resistance?	If so, work with the student to understand the roots of the anger and the reasons for rebelling. Support student efforts to analyze the impact of their behavior on themselves and others. Guide them to come up with suggestions for effective alternative behaviors. If the behavior was an act of resistance, take time to listen and understand the reasons for it. Honor their dignity and discuss it, exploring options for an effective way to express feelings.
Have you tried all of the previous questions and still not had a change in behavior?	For extreme cases, a behavioral plan and counseling may be needed.

relationship with the student and the relationships the student has with peers. They consider the causes of the behavior and determine the responses accordingly. Identity safe educators activate a toolkit that serves to assess and address appropriate action across a range of behaviors considered within their purview. Of course, extreme behaviors need to be recognized as such, so the students can be referred to specialists to serve their needs.

For students who repeatedly misbehave in some way, identity safe educators avoid punitive measures and instead exercise consequences that teach students to monitor their own behavior. The policies of LPS and many other schools and districts ask students to deeply reflect on their behavior. Students set up behavioral plans together with their educators, counselors, or administrators. Parents are also included. Students are continually learning as they consider and adopt new ways to act and show respect to and for others. They learn to live with integrity.

Addressing Conflicts in Ways That Promote Healing and Positive Communication

Just as we seek to shift the cognitive load to students in academic learning, we can shift the accountability for managing their own behavior to them as well. In the following text, we offer several ways and processes to deal with large and small conflicts and petty misunderstandings that have the potential to blow up.

I-Messages

One way to avoid conflicts from the outset—or keep them from escalating—involves teaching students to use I-messages. After feeling slighted in some way, instead of an emotional outburst or tirade, we can support the student in sharing their feelings by using words that do not speak for the other student or cast blame upon them. Then, they can follow up by making a specific request. For example:

> If one person's music is too loud, instead of saying, "You always blast your music," which casts blame and can provoke the other person, one can say, "I feel uncomfortable when music is too loud. Could you please turn it down?" By taking responsibility for our sensitivity and by asking for a specific solution that works for us, we keep it nonthreatening.

I recall teaching my own kids about I-messages. They were teens at the time and would roll their eyes when I engaged them with an I-message, as if to say, "There you go again, Mom!" A formulaic template seemed juvenile to them, but the actual long-term effect from practicing with this template helped them to implement the spirit of it while using their own words. Communication such as this does not attack and lands very differently on the ears.

I-MESSAGE TEMPLATE (SUBJECT TO CREATIVE INTERPRETATION!)

I feel _____ when _____ happens. So could you please (make a request) _____.

Example: I feel uncomfortable when someone posts a picture of me on Facebook. Could you please take it down?

Have them practice with the template and then move to using their own words.

I-messaging can be taught in a short amount of time. However, there are some caveats to consider:

- I-messages can be too pro forma and oversimplified. Teach the concept and assist students in finding their own words to express themselves while keeping in mind the two integral elements of the messaging: taking responsibility for our feelings and asking for a specific solution.

- Some adults (parents or educators) use I-messages to manipulate and guilt-trip a young person by expressing judgments: "I felt disappointed when you got a bad grade; please work harder at school." Pay attention to how I-messages are used to avoid this pitfall. I-messages are best reserved to express our own feelings and not our perception of another's failure. In dealing with a case like this example, it can be more effective not to use an I-message, but a positive presupposition.

- Sometimes an I-message can magnify a young person's vulnerability. Support students in expressing their feelings with courage and strength. Admitting vulnerability ("It hurts my feelings") can be expressed from a place of confidence when we understand it as a normal, healthy emotion. It is useful to model it and discuss this with students.

Just as we do not define a person's identity, we do not attempt to define another person's feelings. I-messages not only dispel hurt feelings during conflicts but also can promote understandings that often create bonds between students, displacing the discord. I-messaging can be practiced between two students, in small groups, or modeled for the entire class. Students can use the format as they learn to disagree respectfully. Reminding them to practice during group work will prepare them with appropriate language during tense moments and conflicts. Opening dialogue on ways to achieve successful and satisfying communication helps students develop positive communication habits.

Recently, my adult daughter thanked me for teaching her about I-messages and other communication skills. She said that although she did not appreciate it at the time, she now feels it has really helped her get along with others, communicate, and work through problems in her life.

Conflict Resolution

If you Google *conflict resolution*, you will find many available models for all age groups from children to teens and adults. Each method includes these basic elements:

- Parties take turns listening uninterruptedly.
- Listeners paraphrase, seeking to understand the other person's perspective.
- They propose mutually beneficial solutions.
- Finally, they select one path of action that both parties agree to follow.

I worked as an elementary school principal in an urban community with a conflict resolution program that had been in place for several years before I arrived. Young students were taught to listen to one another and seek mutual solutions to problems. The students acting as conflict managers were trained and rotated duty during lunch and recess. They looked and acted so grownup holding their clipboards. Substitutes would comment on the calm and pleasant climate at the school. Even students who had not enjoyed opportunities to learn conflict resolution at a young age can begin as teens. It is never too late.

Restorative Practices

Restorative justice (RJ) is a process inspired by indigenous philosophy and practices. The criminal justice system applies it as an effective tool to help incarcerated individuals interrupt cycles of violence, actively involving them in practices to repair harm and prevent reoffending. The same process has evolved as an effective way to aid students in transforming their behavior. Educators initiate RJ circles as a community-building process to transmit positive values involving the family and community. The process has enjoyed success with students when applied to reparations for both minor and serious conflicts. When a person takes responsibility for harming another and seeks to repair the harm, they hold the key to transforming themselves into an empathetic individual.

Various models for implementing RJ are available. The RJ Sharing Circle pertains to a process that introduces and practices community values and brainstorms solutions to problems. It serves as a guide for a whole-class experience where students share a topic, listen to one another, and express feelings. Often, circles have a general theme, such as "Share a special moment in your life," "Tell us about a time when you were bullied or bullied someone," or "What does forgiveness mean to you?" At other times, a particular problem is posed that affects the class, and students explore solutions. This experience provides support for students as they articulate their feelings, get to know each other, understand different perspectives, and develop empathy. The circle can work effectively for the whole class as well as with small groups.

A Harm Circle is used to resolve conflict in which one or more parties were hurt or harmed. The success of the Harm Circle often hinges on preparing participants in

RJ QUESTIONING PROCESS

OUSD (Yusem, 2014) uses the following RJ questions to uncover root behaviors and help students become accountable:

- What happened, and what were you thinking at the time of the incident?

- What have you thought about since?

- Who has been affected by what happened, and how?

- What about this has been the hardest for you?

- What do you think needs to be done to make things as right as possible?

advance to enter with an open heart and mind. Each party describes what happened and how they felt. When RJ is used after a quarrel, all sides answer questions, not solely the party who did the harm. When presented with the disagreement in the Harm Circle, the person who initiated the conflict is asked to reflect and consider what caused the situation to escalate. Often, both parties in a conflict share some of the responsibility. They learn to take responsibility for their own behavior and seek ways to repair the harm. They make and record their agreements. Caring adults monitor the process, ensuring that the behavior does not continue (Amstutz, 2005). The goal is to provide healing via accountability and empathy.

In a 2014 study of the Oakland Unified School District (OUSD) Restorative Justice Program, researchers found that in schools with full RJ implementation, suspensions decreased, while attendance, student achievement, and graduation rates increased. Program director David Yusem (2014) described how the researchers observed a major culture shift in the district after implementing RJ on a large-scale basis. They found that both accountability and healing were meaningful for all parties in a conflict. Yusem explained that the process has become institutionalized in many schools, and students themselves often request an RJ circle to avoid a fight.

Educators need to ensure fidelity to restorative practices, allocating sufficient time, and take care not to subvert them into a means for teacher control. The process, once modeled, stays within the purview of the students, guided by adults. Also, while supporting students to accept accountability and repair harm, adults notice and provide resources to assist with the student's unmet needs. The process may not work instantly, but it can greatly diminish repeated behaviors that hurt others.

De-Escalating Conflict

In Chapter 10: Teacher Warmth and Availability for Learning, we discussed and made suggestions for addressing the challenges of trauma that can be exacerbated by adolescents with developing frontal lobes, which regulate impulse control (Sylwester, 2007). Some

TWO COMPLETELY DIFFERENT RESPONSES TO DEFIANT BEHAVIOR

Case One

In 2015, a cell phone video filmed by a student went viral (McLaughlin & Visser, 2015). It depicted a school resource officer called to a classroom because a girl was not willing to hand over her cell phone. The officer came within inches of her face while demanding the phone. When she refused and screamed back at him, he grabbed her, knocked her to the ground, and dragged her across the floor. The situation escalated rapidly and could have been avoided.

Case Two

School resource officer Moses Robinson (Not In Our Town, 2017) describes a situation that had the potential to escalate in a similar way as the viral video just described. Robinson was called to a classroom after a boy lay his head on the desk, refusing to do his classwork and leave when his teacher requested it. Robinson explains how he spoke softly in the student's ear in a voice no others could hear. He whispered, "Son, do me a favor, I want to get you out of here. Can you please get your stuff and come with me?" The student quietly got up and walked out with him. Once in the hallway, the boy crumpled to the ground and burst into tears. His best friend had been shot and killed during the night. Officer Robinson was able to walk the boy to a small conference room and listen. Later, he got additional support for the boy. Robinson explained that because the boy already had a relationship of trust and credibility with him, he knew that "Officer Moses" was not there to cause harm and opened up to him. Robinson recommends that all police officers (and others) receive training in adolescent development in order to avoid dangerous and unproductive power struggles.

students automatically respond rapidly to an emotionally charged situation, moving into action without weighing the consequences. One of my eighth graders, Yesenia, was stopped by a police officer who charged up and began yelling at her to stop when she was fighting with another girl in the street. Without stopping to think, Yesenia refused to obey the officer and launched into a string of invectives that landed her in juvenile hall. Adults, whether they are police, educators, or parents, need to consider how their response also will contribute to the difference between escalating a conflict or diffusing one.

"Willful defiance," a category that often appears on referral and suspension form checklists, has served as a common and overused excuse for suspending Black students (Adams, 2015). In schools employing "zero tolerance policies," educators often used the willful defiance designation as a broad and vague category to span everything from not turning in homework to swearing at a teacher. As part of the effort to reduce the overrepresentation of Black students for vague offenses, some California districts banned willful defiance as a reason for suspension. Subsequently, when more districts joined in, suspension rates across the state decreased. The lower suspension rates were positively correlated to improved academic achievement. In 2019, a California law was passed that expanded a ban on willful-defiance suspensions in Grades K–3 to Grades K–8 for five years (Agrawal, 2019).

Zero tolerance policies lead to dumping students out of school and usually do not remediate, contributing to the "school to prison pipeline" (Restorative Practices Working Group, 2014). Educators can work to provide alternatives to suspension. Alternatives include the introduction of positive disciplinary methods, conflict resolution strategies, and restorative practices along with social skills and counseling groups. These tools can combine with more training for educators on implicit bias (see Chapter 3: Listening for Student Voices) and trauma-informed practice, including the following de-escalation strategies. Working to shift from punitive behavioral practices to those that strengthen students' identity—while helping them take accountability for their behavior—is an important element of identity safe teacher skill.

Getting Staff on the Same Page and Speaking the Same Language

Amy explains that LPS leaders became concerned that their educators were using different language and responses to crises and emotional outbursts by students. After researching evidence-based programs, they selected *Life Space Crisis Intervention* (LSCI) for training. They brought together teams of instructional and student support staff from all three LPS high schools for training. The site teams in turn shared the strategies with their staffs, thereby strengthening and standardizing adult responses.

The teams learned to resist the temptation to immediately ask students to reflect on behavior in the midst of an outburst. The LSCI (2019) model recommends when intervening in a conflict or outburst to allow for a "drain-off" period, granting the student time to cool down while articulating feelings in an unfiltered way. Gradually, as the upset subsides, educators can assess through expression and choice of language when the student is ready to engage in a deeper analysis of the incident. Amy outlined key LSCI takeaways that serve as general guidelines:

1. When you can recognize heightened emotional states, you can develop the capacity for patience and trust that it will drain off—because it nearly always will.

2. During an explosive moment when students are in a reactive mode, asking them analytical questions will likely fail. By stepping away from power struggles and avoiding efforts to control students, they gradually cool down from an aroused state.

3. Through deep listening, you can diagnose underlying causes of the reaction (e.g. fear, anger, frustration, confusion) and respond accordingly.

4. By responding calmly and with empathy, students are more likely to reach the place where insight and action can follow.

STRATEGIES FOR DE-ESCALATION

On the *Intervention Central* website (www.interventioncentral.org), response to intervention (RTI) specialist Jim Wright (2013) draws from expert sources (Cowin et al., 2003; Fishkind, 2002; Richmond et al., 2012) to offer the following concrete suggestions for de-escalating students when they become verbally triggered, invoking the caveat that when student safety is at risk to immediately seek additional support beyond the classroom:

- Seek to redirect student behavior as opposed to forcing the student to behave according to our demands.
- Remind the student of class norms.
- Keep our voice calm and low and avoid shouting.
- Give the student a safe space; avoid "getting in the person's face" while attempting to speak privately.
- Do not get too close while a student is agitated. If possible, step away from the student to give the student a chance to cool down.
- Show open body language, such as arms and legs open (not crossed) and moving in a slower, relaxed manner.
- Paraphrase what we perceive to be the student's wants and needs with simple and short sentences. Find points of agreement and acceptable alternatives.

Avoid the following:

- Engaging in power struggles.
- Responding with defensiveness or participating in arguments.
- Catching a student's arm (even a light grasp can be perceived by a triggered person as grabbing, which can elicit a violent reaction).
- Preaching at or nagging a student.
- Cornering the student or blocking entrances.
- Forcing an apology.

Make Time for Reintegration

- Give a student sufficient time and space to calm down without interruption (about 15–20 minutes), offering an opportunity for them to seek their own ways for relaxing, recovering, and regenerating.
- Offer positive reinforcement to appropriate responses.
- Once a student is calm, schedule another time to debrief and avoid further problems.

In the event that a student becomes violent toward the educator, self, or others, seek immediate help.

Identity Safe Practices to Address Bullying

Researchers found that while 70.6 percent of teens have witnessed bullying in their schools, if someone intervenes, the bullying stops within an average of 10 seconds. This statistic holds significance because it demonstrates that—while bullying remains prevalent in schools—the potential for stopping it is great when young people are taught safe ways to intervene (Espelage et al., 2012).

On the federal *StopBullying.gov* (2018) website (www.stopbullying.gov), bullying is defined as "unwanted aggressive behavior; [with an] observed or perceived power imbalance; [including] repetition of behaviors or high likelihood of repetition." Repetition is an important element in this definition because the harm is levied over a period of time—whether it's a couple days or months or even years—and the damage for the bullied person can feel profound. There are many different types of bullying. Direct forms include verbal, physical, and cyberbullying. Spreading rumors and initiating and participating in exclusion constitute an indirect form. Often, students are bullied for being different from their peers.

Educators need to gain awareness of the many types of hurtful teasing, microaggressions, and bullying on campus. According to the National School Climate Center (Cohen & Frieberg, 2013), in working with schools across the United States, students overwhelmingly reported that they often feel unsafe, and in many cases, their educators are unaware of their feelings. This includes public and private schools in communities of all socioeconomic levels.

At one high school, Mohammed, a Muslim boy, was brought to the office for punching one of his peers. He explained to the principal that daily his friends call him a terrorist. Finally, he could not take it anymore. When the principal confronted the boy he punched, the boy admitted to the daily teasing but defended himself, claiming that Mohammed always laughed when they teased him. Mohammed agreed that yes, he did laugh because he did not know what else to do, feeling ashamed and afraid to say anything. The educators had been aware of none of this until Mohammed, pushed to his limit, had reacted.

Unfortunately, that is not an isolated incident. Muslim students are often called "terrorists" by their peers. Sikh students wearing turbans are mistaken for Muslims and are mercilessly teased, and girls wearing hijabs are frequently bullied. Also, students with many different identities are subject to harassment. LGBTQ students—and those who students perceive not to fit their ideas of "normal" gender stereotypes—are regularly targeted. Black students are called the N-word and pictured with nooses; Jewish students endure coins tossed at them and are harassed with swastika graffiti; students with disabilities and overweight students are mocked and mimicked. Identity safety can be completely undermined when students feel unsafe in school due to teasing, bullying, harassment, and bias-based attitudes.

Bullying can be greatly reduced when identity safe bullying prevention practices such as the following are active:

- Working to build understanding and empathy across a range of differences for staff and students

- Developing protocols for safe reporting and swift responding to bullying

- Training the entire staff and student body on bullying prevention and response

- Supporting students targeted by bullying to report what is happening to a trusted adult while helping them gain courage to stand up for themselves

- Helping students who bully to transform their behavior

- Teaching students to be upstanders who stand up and speak up for themselves and others

- Placing students in the lead to organize bullying prevention activities—peers inspire each other

We consider it unwise to label a student a *bully* or a *victim* because these labels can become self-fulfilling prophecies. More effective practices include increasing student supports, teaching restorative practices, providing social and emotional learning (SEL) opportunities, partnering with parents, and offering counseling for students with greater needs. For both those who bully and those who are targeted, forming trusting relationships among the students and a caring adult, combined with careful monitoring, ensures that the bullying behaviors are not repeated.

Turning Bystanders Into Upstanders

While not all students bully or become targets of bullying and harassment, nearly all students have witnessed it in some way. Some remain silent for fear of becoming targets themselves. Others cheer or even add to the taunts to impress their peers. In 2016, the *Oxford English Dictionary* ("Upstander," n.d.) added the word *upstander* in response to a national campaign launched by two New Jersey high school students (Zimmer, 2016). *Upstander* is defined as "a person who speaks or acts in support of an individual or cause, particularly someone who intervenes on behalf of a person being attacked or bullied."

Learning to be an upstander in bullying situations continues throughout students' lives. They can research upstander role models across history (e.g., Harriet Tubman rescued and led Black slaves to freedom, and Oskar Schindler saved Jews from the Nazis).

Role-playing can help students learn to speak up and prepare to respond to bullying incidents. They can practice language that is clear and forceful without being inflammatory and gain the courage to speak up when they hear harmful epithets, such as "That's so gay" or "Nobody likes you." Developing effective ways to stop the spread of vicious texts or social media posts and safely stand up for themselves or find help to avoid a fight offers the protection students need when confrontations arise.

FOUR WAYS TO BE AN UPSTANDER

Each one of these four methods can be demonstrated and practiced in the classroom:

1. *Safely intervene.* Students can learn to speak calmly and firmly to impact the person bullying and motivate them to stop. An emphasis on performing this safely will safeguard an escalation into a bigger conflict. Students learn to assess whether it is possible to intervene safely or to seek adult help.

2. *Get help by alerting a trusted adult.* Students need to know who to approach on campus to get help. A trusted adult is knowledgeable about bullying and school procedures and is committed to supporting the students.

3. *Support the target of bullying.* Students can learn to offer support by reaching out to show concern and kindness to a bullied student even after an incident. Connecting with the student through a few kind words makes a big difference.

4. *Become an activist for social justice.* In identity safe classrooms, students learn to take action and become leaders, flexing the "muscle of courage."

Some students say they do not want to be upstanders because they fear being labeled as "snitches." Educators have countered this concern with an explanation that compares the two. Snitching or tattling involves an intent to get someone in trouble, while an upstander works to keep someone from getting harmed. Upstanders can become champions for identity safety.

Dilemmas and Points of Tension

They're Doing It Again: Beyond Annoyance, Seeking Solutions Together and Recognizing Growth

Sometimes, a student repeatedly calls out, blurting out the answers and getting on our last nerves. Fellow students may also feel annoyed and probably dislike this particular kid, leading to further isolation and a lack of belonging. Students on the autism spectrum can exhibit these behaviors (for suggestions on ways to address these students, see Chapter 13: Emotional and Physical Comfort), which for them, represents a behavior beyond their control. Students with learning disabilities often manifest weak executive functioning and social skills. At other times, trauma impacts students who develop these habits from acquired defenses and insecurities.

Just as we discussed in Chapter 10, it is incumbent on us as educators to find positive qualities in each student. We can capitalize on their strengths while teaching needed skills. Here, we focus on addressing those with repeated negative misbehavior. Sometimes, a student has participated in designing the solutions and does well for a while, yet eventually the disruptions continue. Educators need to make a conscious attempt to redirect them and avoid humiliating them. We can help the student notice their improvements—we point them out, even if they are small, incremental ones. A growth mindset applies to behavior and emotional regulation as well as to academics. Ultimately, your expressions of care will be appreciated by the student and the others in the classroom. Feeling safe is contagious.

Additional social skills to support positive behaviors are offered in the two following chapters.

Knowing When It's Time to Process Feelings and When It's Time to Get Back to Work

When conflictual feelings and incidents get pushed under the rug, they fester. When students are upset, they become distracted. Their brains are not working to capacity. Whether a peer is killed in a car crash, a major fight breaks out and brings the police to campus, or a racist comment or photo appears on social media, students need to talk

BEHAVIOR PLANS WORK BEST WHEN STUDENTS CONTRIBUTE

LPS has a Districtwide Behavior Plan form. The form is filled out together with the student and includes the following items:

- Background information, including grades and report card comments about the student

- Identifying and reflecting upon specific and inappropriate behaviors without blaming others

- Analysis of behaviors that have broken agreed-upon community agreements and norms

- Identification of the student's unmet needs and other factors that may have caused the behavior

- Discussion of how others have been impacted by the misbehavior

- Identification of ways to repair harm to self and others

- Statement of fair consequences for the behavior

- Solutions that will help avoid the negative behaviors in the future

- A list of suggested ways to belong and be a part of the community

- Suggested ways team members (counselors, educators, administrators) can support the student

- Action steps for the student and specific team members on a timeline: what, who, and when

about and release their feelings. The National Center for School Crisis and Bereavement (2018) offers guidelines for students to express grief and work for healing after all major incidents (e.g., hate crimes, fights, natural disasters, suicides, and other deaths). This is also true for less serious conflicts. Taking the time to process and work through feelings is part of a student-centered approach that creates identity safety. Carving out the time to talk and share will release tension and will let you know which students need additional support or counseling. The time invested will allow students to focus once again on their work and return your classroom to a productive and safe environment.

Deciding when to get back to normal and to send students back to work can be a sensitive decision. After a suicide on the railroad tracks near one school, students posted a large paper on a wall in the quad for them to write and express their grief and offer messages of hope. School leaders supported the activity while recognizing the healing benefits, but they were also cognizant when it was time to take it down. Expressing feelings and learning to be resilient are part of the process of developing emotional regulation.

Chapter Summary

In this chapter, we examined what is known as "behavior management" and explored ways positive behaviors are enhanced through a trusting identity safe environment. We juxtaposed many of the skills an educator has learned in preservice and through experience with the identity safe approach. We particularly looked at how to set up a classroom and develop routines, procedures, pacing, and a rhythm of activity that harmonize with creating a safe place for students to thrive, a place where students of varied backgrounds feel their cultures and identities are affirmed. We shared how I-messages and conflict resolutions skills can serve as prevention strategies, as well as to diffuse and resolve conflicts. We explored restorative justice (RJ) as a model for working together with students to determine the cause of conflicts and help them repair harm. We discussed ways to prevent and address bullying and teach students to stand up for themselves and others.

We approached two dilemmas: First, we discussed handling a persistent problem when a student continually repeats disruptive and annoying behaviors. Secondly, we talked about the importance of taking time to process grief and knowing when it is the right time to move on. Creating a trusting identity safe environment will serve to prevent many conflicts. However, when conflicts do occur, responding with patience and empathy will have a cumulative benefit even if the results arrive slowly. These are all part of an educator's repertoire, which, in identity safety, we refer to as *teacher skill*.

Check Yourself

1. How do you balance the needs of an individual with the needs of the group?

2. What are your invisible rules? Which ones might serve to privilege some students over others?

3. What conflict resolutions skills have you taught your students? What could you add?

4. What is your approach to discipline? How can you work to ensure your behavioral consequences teach rather than simply punish?

5. Have you had experience with students on the autism spectrum? What have you learned, and what more can you do to support them?

6. What tend to be the reasons you send students out of class? Are Black or Latinx students sent out of your classroom more than students of other backgrounds? If so, what can you do to change this?

TRY IT OUT: END-OF-CHAPTER ACTIVITY

Student Behavior Analysis and Support

Observe one of your students who often does not follow community agreements and procedures. Describe the behaviors you observed and consider what may have been the causes. (Refer to the questions in the Intervention Checklist found on page 224).

List interventions you have tried and how have they worked.

Brainstorm three new things to try that will better meet the student's need, based on the causes of the behavior.

What were the results after trying out those strategies?

What are your next steps for supporting positive behaviors?

 Available for download as a full-page form at **https://resources.corwin .com/IdentitySafeClass6-12**

13 Emotional and Physical Comfort

Why Emotional and Physical Comfort Matters

Emotional and physical comfort addresses that gut feeling a student experiences when entering a class. What might be found in an identity safe classroom? At first impression, glance over the engaged expressions of students in the room—the educator as well. The tone is welcoming and friendly, and the pacing and rhythm of the lessons feel comfortable—attainable and fun, yet challenging. Physically, the temperature is just right. The room arrangement is conducive to collaboration, while flexible and ready at other times to facilitate independent work. The noise level is appropriate for the activity, and the lighting allows for easy reading without the stinging glare of bright lights. The gestalt of the room as a whole feels simpatico, with each individual bridging to the whole.

When I first heard that physical comfort was included in a research finding that contributed to identity safety, it surprised me. However, after consideration, I realized that our physical needs are extremely important when setting the stage for learning. Combining both physical and emotional comfort serves to create a space where students feel motivated and intellectually stimulated, and their curiosity is piqued.

Making it happen is an exercise in design on a psychological as well as physiological level. We start by highlighting the value of generating an exciting, even awesome, atmosphere for learning. We expand on earlier ideas for setting up the physical space and emotional feeling tone, or the quality of feeling in the room (e.g., a tone that evokes joy or a tone that evokes fear), to reflect the students' identities, interests, and needs for varying levels of intensity. We look at the ways to create a growth mindset culture and ensure that our words affirm rather than undermine confidence. We examine ways to make our classrooms inclusive for students with a range of differences that include students on the autism spectrum. We tackle the dilemma of fairness as we grapple with meeting a range of needs. We close by highlighting the impact of social class differences and offer ways to minimize disparities.

Emotional and Physical Comfort: Making It Happen

Putting the Awe Back in Awesome

The word *awesome* has become overused, but the concept of awe has recently gained renewed traction in schools. Awe is described as an exhilarating experience of joy and amazement that often defies words. It can be created in a myriad of ways: through shared experiences, artistic expression, a moving film or piece of literature, or field trips into nature and the outside world.

Teens often become jaded in their view of the world. Many have seen too many scenes of violence on television, if not in their personal lives. Reawakening awe can develop from the magic of a butterfly emerging from a chrysalis, the perfect beauty of a mathematical equation, or special moments of empathy. I recall the feeling of awe that enveloped me in fourth grade when looking at a snowflake on a piece of black velvet under a magnifying glass. It didn't matter that we were in our classroom on the third floor of a New York City brick school building. Miss Flynn's excitement and the thrill of taking turns to see the simple snowflake was my most memorable fourth-grade moment. I again experienced a sense of awe in my high school physics class when we were given a variety of lenses and were asked to figure out why the image in a convex lens flipped upside down. And still again in college, I felt awe when we took a field trip for my geology course, driving over the crest of the Sierras to view the spectacular Mono Craters below. The view of the lava domes and cinder cones was stunning. An identity safe classroom can be a place of awe-inspiring feelings in the context of a welcoming and aesthetic everyday environment. What do you recall about feeling a sense of awe in your school experience? How can you infuse awe in your students' lives?

Setting Up the Classroom Space for Identity Safety

The walls, seating plans, and room arrangement are all part of an intentional consideration of identity safety. In Chapter 7: Using Diversity as a Resource, we addressed the importance for students to see themselves—or people who look like them—reflected on the walls. What else would offer an interesting view on your walls? Do your displays reflect current instruction and lessons learned? Posters and references to popular culture can also deliver the message that "what you like matters to me." Some educators prepare an area with pictures of their family, hobbies, and other personal items, sharing a bit of themselves with their students and inviting students to do the same. Desk arrangements, too, can cater to comfort through adaptability, exercising flexible formats that propel into flexible attitudes for individual or group work.

Katie's classroom was equipped with a traditional desk for each student, arranged in rows for individual work. On the first day of class each year, she would instruct students to push their desks together in predetermined groups of four with masking tape on the floor to guide their move. They would then reverse the action and shift back into rows, a cycle they repeated several times, to their delight. This practice allowed students to push desks on cue throughout the school year to create collaborative or individual groups without losing valuable class time.

Creating inviting classroom decor is harder for itinerant educators who don't have their own classrooms. However, those who share a classroom can work together and come to an agreement on how the space is used, dividing the wall space and determining classroom set-up. Flexible spaces include learning centers as well as collaborative areas and quiet work areas.

QUESTIONS TO ASK YOURSELF ABOUT YOUR PHYSICAL ENVIRONMENT

When considering your classroom's physical environment, think about these issues when planning.

Regarding the Walls

Are the class values and norms as well as academic and behavioral expectations posted as easy reminders?

Do the walls reflect the content of the course and current lessons?

Have you posted helpful learning tools, such as steps for editing written work or revealing different ways students solved their math problems?

Is the work of all students, not just a chosen few, equally displayed?

Regarding the Seating

Are students seated in ways that promote collaboration?

Can the desks be rearranged to promote both independent and group work?

Regarding the Physical Setup

Is the room uncluttered and are the places to walk uncongested?

Have you brought in any furniture—a couch, a rocking chair, or cushions and rugs—to make the classroom homier?

Have the students been asked to contribute their ideas on how to set up the room?

Welcoming Youth Culture in the Classroom: Language, Music, Dance—and Why Not a Limerick?

An inner sense of curiosity and creativity is enhanced by an environment that reflects originality. Ushering in the joyful aspects of youth culture can revitalize classroom life. Poetry, music, and humor enliven the atmosphere!

Verve in a Dynamic and Challenging Curriculum

Verve is associated with vitality, liveliness, and enthusiasm. We addressed aspects of creating an air of intellectual excitement in Chapter 9: Challenging Curriculum. Here, we reiterate the power of having a stimulating environment to spark student motivation at all times. Boykin (1983) identified verve as one of the dimensions of Black culture with roots in West Africa. Verve is manifest in a preference for a high degree of physical stimulation with qualities of movement, variation, loudness, and social connection. Murrell (1999) conducted research on Black males and found that meaningful and energetic activities that were relevant to their lives both engaged and motivated them.

Meeting people and getting to know the community where your Black students live is essential for understanding and addressing the values that matter to them. Then, you are in a position to better incorporate verve. Christopher Emdin, in *For White Folks Who Teach in the Hood* (2016), describes going into the neighborhood around his urban school, visiting the Pentecostal church and the local barber shop as he sought to deeply imbibe and grasp the worlds of his students. Emdin recommends a simple process: First, build trust by discovering and frequenting places on campus where your students hang out. Then, get to know the community. Finally, share your experiences with students to juxtapose your observations with their lived reality. These actions help increase understanding of your students' identities.

Variation in the flow of the lessons can be incorporated in both the auditory experience (louder moments and quieter ones) and the timing, which involves the pace and rhythm of the activities. Music, movement, oral poetry, and call and response can each add dynamism. In addition, fast-paced games, analogies, humor, and solving mysteries are activities that incorporate novelty, all in sync with the way the brain learns and retains information.

As always, knowing your students is key. Martin, an African American educator, laughed as he shared that when he was in high school, if a teacher had asked him to do a rap, he'd have thought, "What the heck is his problem?" He added, "While a rap might have been motivating for *some* of my friends, I clearly was not one of them."

It is best not to stereotype all Black students as each possessing the same qualities; however, it is safe to say that many classrooms don't have enough activities that capitalize on verve. By mixing up the pacing of your lessons and incorporating a range of modalities, you are taking advantage of information gleaned from neuroscience. Adding

BRINGING VERVE INTO YOUR CLASSROOM

Here are just a few of the many ways to accomplish verve:

- Play different kinds of music at different times or as opening or closing songs.

- Have moments of group time where loud debate and bantering are encouraged. Contrast it with quiet moments where students work in silence.

- Offer choices and shorter blocks of learning and varying entry points.

- Incorporate dynamic storytelling, call and response, and oral poetry.

- Find a way to include dance and movement, even for a few moments, to revitalize the energy and bring life into the room.

Can you add to this list?

elements of verve into your classroom will draw out students who are active learners, like movement, and enjoy enthusiastic bantering along with a high degree of social interaction. These elements contribute, in concert, to higher retention of your content.

Humor

Laughter also lightens the mood and brings joy into the room. Humor enhances the ambience when carefully applied so as not to stereotype, insult, or embarrass anyone. Sarcasm is a form of humor that can be easily misconstrued, turning hurtful. Teaching students about appropriate humor while also addressing its value can create emotional comfort. Limericks, for example, offer a fun way to approach any topic!

> Limericks are easy to write.
>
> They pop into your head day and night.
>
> A mathematical equation
>
> Is a happy occasion
>
> When limericks turn on the light.

Ambience and Feeling Tone

The ambience of a classroom has many elements that create an overall feeling tone. Tone is defined as "the general character or attitude of a place" ("Tone," n.d.). A feeling tone is often evident as you walk in the door of a classroom. Any environment can be set up to feel attractive and evoke pleasant feelings that incorporate verve, excitement, humor, and awe.

Making a Place for Mindfulness

Jon Kabat-Zinn (2017) describes two kinds of mindfulness: (1) formal mindfulness that is practiced during some form of meditation; and (2) informal mindfulness, which is awareness practiced throughout all activities in your life, including walking, talking, and washing dishes, each performed with the intention of being in the moment. A mindfulness practice decreases stress and depression while increasing psychological health (Keng et al., 2011; Segal et al., 2010).

Mindfulness also has been found to reduce bias based on race (Lueke & Gibson, 2014). A brief intervention divided college students into two groups. One group listened to a ten-minute mindfulness meditation while the control group listened to something unrelated. During subsequent testing, those who listened to the mindfulness recording were found to be less biased than the control group in both attitudes and behaviors.

Mindfulness has developed as an umbrella term for a range of activities that promote stress reduction, calmness, and nonjudgmental self-awareness. Mindfulness activities can include a few minutes of breathing, a guided visualization, or a quiet meditation. Some

CULTURE KEEPERS: A MODEL OF PEER SUPPORT

Amy previously worked with a student wellness center at El Cerrito High School that partnered with the Niroga Project (2019) and trained a group of student leaders in dynamic mindfulness, SEL skills, and mediation. These students, known as "Culture Keepers," rotate their duty to provide one-on-one peer support during different class periods. They teach a mindfulness practice, mentor students, and mediate after a conflict. They sometimes meet their peers at the classroom door for a short "hallway walk and talk." After several minutes, the students return to class. An amazing 87 percent of surveyed students reported that the Culture Keepers made a difference in their lives by helping them focus, maintain better self-control, and help manage stress, anger, and/or anxiety.

educators start their class with a few minutes of calm breathing. Others take mindfulness breaks where students stand and stretch or observe a few minutes of silence to calm themselves. Some enjoy a mindfulness moment at the end of class, when students reflect on what they learned or think about something they are grateful for in their lives. Some schools even offer yoga or meditation classes.

Mindfulness is also good for educators! The San Francisco Unified School District has a special place in its district office for mindfulness and quiet meditation. While writing this section, I decided to take my own advice and stopped for a short yoga practice!

Watching What Comes Out of Our Mouths: Positive Presuppositions

Do any phrases stand out from your childhood memories? I can remember at four years old, a babysitter told my parents that I was as "good as gold." I basked in that light for awhile! In a less pleasant memory, as a kindergartner in New York City while walking down the hallway, I heard the vice principal's booming voice rebuking a student and threatening to wash her mouth out with soap because she'd said a bad word. Even though it wasn't addressed to me, it engraved in my mind an unforgettable memory. Years later in junior high, I also remember when a teacher scribbled in red pen, "Your writing is vague and unclear." Fortunately for me, that teacher was countered by two others. Both my English and creative writing teachers encouraged my writing, which likely saved me from abandoning my writer's pen. What messages do you remember from your childhood and teen years that have made their mark in your long-term memory? Which ones have lingered across your lifetime? Do you have more positive memories than negative ones?

We are spontaneously livestreaming words in our classrooms all day long. Unfortunately, sometimes words pop out before we have fully considered the impact. Holding an awareness of the language we use and the messages we are sending to our students will help set the tone for emotional comfort. Our words can communicate that we believe a student is capable—or conversely, our tone can contain thinly veiled exasperation. Over the course of 13 years of schooling, the cumulative effect of these comments adds up to either help or hinder a sense of one's competence.

Buried within our words, our assumptions, attitudes, and beliefs, both positive and negative messages are implied. In identity safety, we speak of positive presuppositions as an antidote to stereotype threat. If an educator says, "You better study for the test or you will fail," the assumption might be that most likely you will fail and you probably won't study either. An alternative phrase—"When you study for the test, what will you work on first?"—conveys the assumption that the student will study.

In another example, a negative assumption is hidden in the words, "You never will be ready for college if you don't turn in your homework." That message can be interpreted as saying the student rarely turns in homework and probably *will not* go to college. Another way to encourage a student to do homework is evident in the message, "This homework will give you practice for the kind of assignments you will get in college." This assumes the homework will be done and have value because the teacher is confident that the student *will* be going to college.

In the activity at the end of this chapter, you can reflect on some of your automatic responses and practice turning them into positive presuppositions. In workshops, we usually remind educators that this activity has an additional bonus. It can help improve our personal lives with our significant others, our children, and our parents!

Negative Presupposition	Positive Presupposition
You only got a few questions right on the quiz. Why didn't you review your work?	You clearly understood the concept of _____. What helped you figure out the answers that you got right?
It is not realistic to go from a C average to an honor student in one quarter.	It is great you have a goal to get on the honor roll. I know by working with a steady focus you can get there. How do you plan to start?

Source: Adapted from *Identity Safe Classrooms,: Places to Belong and Learn* (D. M. Steele & Cohn-Vargas, 2013).

Creating Identity Safe Spaces for Students on the Autism Spectrum in the Regular Classroom

One of the challenges for educators includes balancing the sometimes contradictory needs of different students. We highlighted verve, dynamism, and active learning as engendering a positive classroom atmosphere earlier in this chapter. Yet some students on the autism spectrum can easily become overstimulated from these approaches. Others have sensitivities to noise, light, and being touched. They can become agitated when there is a lot of movement around them. Some students on the autism spectrum are triggered by a disruption of their routine or experience a sensory overload when the light in the classroom is too bright or when certain perfumes or smells from the cafeteria reach their noses. A sudden announcement over the PA can jolt them. Other students on the spectrum engage in "stimming"—swinging a leg back and forth or tapping feet to release tension—yet they are unaware it is annoying others. Sometimes, they are not even aware that they are engaging in stimming behavior! The communication skills of some are weak, and they do not know how to express empathy. Without being taught social skills, students on the autism spectrum may be unaware of the impact of their behaviors. They may perseverate on a topic, repeatedly ask the same questions, or become impatient or rude without explanation to the person sitting innocently next to them. These students need extra support and practice sessions to improve their social skills. The classroom can be adjusted to consider their needs as well. Educators can learn a lot from directly engaging with their students on the autism spectrum and also from their parents.

MARSHALING ALL RESOURCES—EVEN THE DISTRICT WATERING SCHEDULE—TO SUPPORT A STUDENT

Yvonne was an elementary principal who shares her first experience with a student on the autism spectrum that involved a kindergartner named Shawn. Shawn had a fixation with running water, and he would perseverate over every running faucet. While he was mesmerized, nobody could tear him away. It appeared that he was simply being defiant. When friends invited him over, he would turn on a faucet and watch the water flow down the drain for half an hour. As you can imagine, he would often not get invited back. If the sprinklers came on at school during recess, Shawn would stand by them, fixated to the spot. If there were slugs on the grass, he would pick them up and plunk them in a bottle. No one seemed able to separate him from the slugs and water. This was the presenting problem. In class he was brilliant, reading and writing in a way that exceeded his grade level. Shawn's parents had warned the school before enrolling him that he engaged in some odd behaviors. Sometimes, he would sit in the circle with his peers and take off his sandals and pick at his toes. His mother tried to teach him to stop, but frequently he would forget. Ultimately, she resorted to ensuring that he always wore closed shoes.

(Continued)

(Continued)

Yvonne worked closely with the parents and Shawn's teachers to adapt the environment to meet his needs without attempting to change his nature. She went to the extreme of arranging with the school district to water the schoolyard on the weekends, so there would be no running water for Shawn or even wet lawns to witness during school hours. "That is what you have to do," Yvonne explained. Working closely with Shawn's parents—and also with a psychiatrist who understood autism spectrum disorder—they began a series of strategies to help Shawn:

- They prepared him verbally before he went out to recess.

- They gave him time limits, such as, "You will have five minutes to do this task and then you need to move on."

- They taught the other students about autism spectrum disorder so that they would be more understanding and empathetic.

- They assigned another student to be his partner, mentor, and coach. That helped when there was a fire drill and the loud piercing sound was terrifying to Shawn. Without a student to stay with him, he would run for cover. This practice was continued even through high school.

- Every year before the school year began, Shawn's mother would take him to school to meet his teachers and walk through the classrooms. This little bit of preparation helped him feel more comfortable when school started.

Over time, they continued the parent–school partnership to support Shawn with structures that proved successful for him. They provided a classroom environment that facilitated his emotional and physical comfort. Still, he found high school challenging as he grappled with social skills considered inappropriate for a teen. For example, Shawn had been known as an affectionate child. However, as a teen, he sometimes tried spontaneously to hug his friends. He struggled with choosing the appropriate moment for a hug or when a high five or fist bump was the better option. Eventually, he learned to first ask, "Would you like a hug?" In time, he found a small group of friends whom Yvonne describes as a bit nerdy, like him.

The good news is that for Shawn, the work paid off. He went to college and now lives a satisfying and independent life. Yvonne smiled as she asked, "Do you know what Shawn now does for a living? He stayed with his water theme. He is now a marine biologist."

Parent–educator partnerships are tremendously important to support students on the autism spectrum as they navigate their school lives. These partnerships discover and experiment with solutions that can make a big difference in creating acceptance and strong peer connections for students on the autism spectrum. In one example, Clara's mother thought that her daughter's lack of facial expressions prompted her peers to

Tips for Educators to Use With Students on the Autism Spectrum

- Review their IEP ahead of time to prepare for their academic and social needs in a classroom.

- Include notes about a student on the autism spectrum's needs in your substitute lesson plans.

- Give students with an autism spectrum disorder a short break to calm down or exercise when they are frustrated or upset without indulging them too frequently or with breaks that last too long. Identify a place they can go.

Social Skills

- Teach rules of social conduct both in advance and in the moment. This includes the positive skills of smiling, sharing, greeting, and general conversing.

- Help students practice verbalizing needs and answering questions that other students may pose for them in advance.

- Teach them about bullying and self-advocacy in the event they are mocked or bullied.

- Help them develop and practice a range of appropriate social skills, such as smiling and expressing thanks.

- Make all rules (even those that might seem obvious to others) clear and visibly accessible to students on the autism spectrum so that they may be clear on expectations.

- Work with families to ensure the student learns appropriate hygiene and dress.

Peer Interaction

Support peers in developing empathy and positive interactions with students on the autism spectrum:

- Provide opportunities for students to develop relationships of equal status and avoid patronizing or overindulging relationships.

- Pair students with partners based on shared interests.

- Help peers learn to interpret linguistic and symbolic behaviors and responses of students on the autism spectrum to enable them to understand a particular student's needs and expressions.

- Practice caution in balancing the need to provide information to support a student on the autism spectrum with the student's right to privacy.

(Continued)

(Continued)

Avoid Potential Pitfalls

A few things educators should eliminate from their repertoires:

- Using a red pen to mark errors

- Calling them out or correcting them in front of the group

draw back from her. The difference in her appearance presented an unknown element for them, translating to a scary look. Her mother taught her how to smile at the age of 12, and Clara later revealed that the simple act of smiling changed her life. The *Autism Speaks* website (www.autismspeaks.org) has a toolkit with many strategies that help create acceptance, inclusion, and academic support for students on the autism spectrum.

It can be challenging to adjust the environment to provide for one student's needs while also catering to the needs of all your students. Creating independent work stations for students on the autism spectrum in a part of the classroom that is less trafficked while providing areas for quiet time can be accomplished without stigmatizing the student. These spaces can be organized so students on the autism spectrum remain in view and can be observed while they are working.

Even when a student has an aide or additional teacher, it is important to let the student know that you, as their educator, take an active interest in their growth. They will feel your care and concern even if they cannot express their feelings. You can work with the special education team to understand their behaviors while planning and creating goal-oriented behaviors. Recognizing that each student on the autism spectrum is unique with differing needs equips us with an appropriate attitude as we approach our preparations for them. In keeping with Identity Safety Principles, include them as part of the community. Instructing and supporting their peers to practice empathy and compassion will generate an ambience for the students on the autism spectrum to feel a sense of belonging. This can also eliminate temptations to bully or tease the students. Ultimately, when the educator models high esteem and value for the dignity of their students on the autism spectrum, the strongest identity safety message for them is conveyed to all students. They are all—each and every one—valued members of the school community.

Dilemmas and Points of Tension

Promoting Fairness: What Am I . . . Chopped Liver?

A huge challenge for an educator includes both identifying and seeking to meet individual needs while balancing every student's need for fair treatment. Will other students perceive neglect while we focus our attention on special-needs students? How can we grade fairly? This characterizes the difference between equity and equality. Equality involves profering the same treatment for everyone, while equity seeks to level the playing field for those who might have greater needs than others. How can an identity safe educator achieve this balance when all the students are watching like hawks for fair treatment?

From a young age, children attend to issues of fairness, constantly assessing their chunk of attention in relation to others. An educator must walk this fine line to ensure that students feel they have been treated fairly. Unfortunately, a natural default tendency for many people drives them immediately to imagine they are being treated unfairly. Consider the world of sports. When I was visiting Nicaragua, a popular boxer lost in an upset victory. My friends in company with me echoed the fans, who were insisting that the referees were unfair! I witnessed the same attitude during the World Cup in 2018. "The referee was not fair," proclaimed my English cousin when the UK lost to Croatia. In identity safe classrooms, educators discuss fairness issues directly, openly, and honestly with the class. They express the desire to be fair while working to level the playing field for students in need. They also carefully examine and weigh each action while considering the best interests of individuals in the context of the whole group and their perceptions.

A student may challenge you by claiming that you have not been fair. Students tend to focus on two main realms for unfairness: grades and consequences. "Why did she get a better grade than me?" "When he did the exact same thing as I did, why didn't he get the same consequence?" It pays to listen with empathy to fully understand why a student might feel upset. Do your best to explain your reasoning without humiliating, insulting, or revealing private information. Not always can you satisfy everyone in this process, and ultimately, you will need to prioritize as you weigh considerations to resolve an issue. Over time, the students will come to believe you do not play favorites. They will learn to trust that your fairness stems from integrity and genuine concern for them, even if they are not presently on the winning end of the scales. Karen posted a reminder on her classroom wall: "We are equal, but different."

Minimizing the Impact of Social Class Differences and Situations

While socioeconomic status greatly influences each student's life, it is difficult for schools to redress these broad disparities through their official policies, yet we need to identify and address this aspect. Students' socioeconomic status is evident in the clothes they wear, the cars they drive or ride in, and the opportunities available to them for travel. The role of the identity safe educator includes providing access to all school-sponsored activities. As we work to equalize status among students, there are some approaches available to at least minimize the impact of socioeconomic differences.

In your classroom, you can track and eliminate activities that emphasize the disparities. I once observed a classroom where students were asked to write a short essay detailing where they went for spring break. The students in this class had huge socioeconomic differences, which became painfully evident in the essays. There were several students who traveled to Europe during their one-week break, while the few from low-income families stayed home, writing that they did not do anything. You can avoid making comments that highlight the disparities. References to new cars, new clothes, or other status symbols should also be avoided.

Many schools exacerbate socioeconomic differences by offering optional trips with high price tags for travel abroad during school vacations. Also, some offer after-school classes and schoolwide extracurricular events that are financially prohibitive for low-income students and their families. Often, low-income students miss out, even if partial scholarships are offered. When students do receive scholarships, it is important to keep the information private. Even the public solicitation of donations can create uncomfortable situations for students. One mother told me that she felt ashamed that she was unable to contribute to many fundraising campaigns. For that reason, she intentionally avoided running into the principal all year. What does your school do about international travel, expensive extracurricular activities, and major fundraisers?

Chapter Summary

By combining *Emotional and Physical Comfort* in one component, we aim to describe classrooms where educators create an emotional environment that is at once exciting and rigorous, balanced with calming experiences. From our displays on the wall to lessons that inspire awe—as well as activities drawn from youth culture—students become engaged and motivated while feeling a sense of belonging. Tools for mindfulness support students in focusing their attention and building skills to calm and soothe themselves as they self-regulate.

We ask educators to consider how simple phrases communicate to students our assumptions, attitudes, and beliefs regarding their potential. We suggested that by using "positive presuppositions," we can communicate assumptions that students will succeed.

The challenge of creating equal status while meeting a range of student needs was explored—with a particular focus on autism spectrum disorder—as an example of the value for a deeper understanding of how to create emotional and physical comfort for students with unique needs. The same process can be used to support students with a range of other differences (e.g., English Learners, gender).

Finally, the chapter ends with a deeper look at ways to tackle the dilemma of ensuring fairness in the context of varied student needs. We also explored internal conflicts generated from students with lower-socioeconomic backgrounds feeling taxed from exclusion and lost opportunity because their families lack the funds. While economic differences cannot easily be erased, we can work to avoid highlighting disparities or activities that cause those differences to become salient.

Check Yourself

1. What is the feeling tone upon entering your classroom? What is the physical and emotional temperature? What changes can you engage to enhance it?

2. What is the nature of the material posted on your walls? Is it current work? Does it represent all your students? How is the space in your room organized? What can you do to make the space more inviting and reflective of your curriculum?

3. How do you balance the needs of students on the autism spectrum who might easily become overstimulated with those of students who need enhanced movement, stimulation, and verve?

4. Are social class differences exacerbated by any practices or words spoken in your classroom or school? What can you do to minimize references to social class?

5. When thinking about the different ethnic, racial, and language backgrounds of your students, what commonalities and differences do you see in their needs for emotional and physical comfort? How are you working to ensure that those needs are being met?

6. What mindfulness activities do you engage in regularly—or are interested in engaging—with your students?

TRY IT OUT: END-OF-CHAPTER ACTIVITY

Positive Presuppositions

Change the negative phrases into positive presuppositions and add some from your own experience.

Negative Presupposition	Positive Presupposition
1. You need to take a more active role in your cooperative group.	
2. Maybe next time you can get here on time.	
3. If you want to go to college, you will need to take school more seriously.	
4. If you don't study for this test, you are at risk for not passing.	
5.	
6.	

This activity was adapted from *Identity Safe Classrooms: Places to Belong and Learn* (D. M. Steele & Cohn-Vargas, 2013).

 Available for download as a full-page form at **https://resources.corwin .com/IdentitySafeClass6-12**

14 Attention to Prosocial Development

Why Attention to Prosocial Development Matters

We have looked at many aspects of the social nature of learning, and we have now arrived at the final identity safety component, *attention to prosocial development*. This component encompasses the skills that allow students to develop into compassionate, accepting, and caring people. Students enter the classroom with a range of social skills and varying degrees of awareness. All students have learned social skills at home, in their churches, mosques, or synagogues, and at school. Attending to prosocial development includes recognizing cultural differences in social interactions and seeking to understand them before making an assumption or judgment. Educators can develop a keen eye for their students' prosocial development.

Over the last decade, social and emotional learning (SEL) has been incorporated in schools to coach students in absorbing a range of social skills to assist them in forming healthy relationships, expressing emotions, managing their reactions, and developing decision-making skills that will aid them in school and life. Attention to prosocial development encompasses SEL skills with a particular focus on preparing students for positive and caring social interactions that are conducive to learning. In identity safety, prosocial development is not treated as an add-on to the curriculum. Rather, it is a lived experience woven throughout the school day; it is an integral part of planned lessons, informal interactions, regular reflections, and teachable moments.

Attention to prosocial development will allow educators to assist students in analyzing their own interactions, weighing the options and risks of different choices, and identifying the qualities they want to develop. While supporting students as they forge their academic identities, educators can help them strengthen capacities for empathy and generosity as they grow into interdependent social beings.

CASEL (the Collaborative for Academic, Social, and Emotional Learning) has identified five competencies (CASEL, n.d.). These competencies incorporate both self-awareness and awareness of others in a social realm, managing one's emotions, and exercising the capacity to make wise decisions and enjoy positive relationships. There are many areas of overlap with identity safety and the CASEL competencies. In identity safety, the principle of self-acceptance and acceptance of others is at the heart of each of these competencies. Identity safe educators challenge themselves to uncover and address deeper assumptions and beliefs that may impede students in achieving the competencies.

In identity safety, we believe that SEL skills need to be taught and practiced, constructed on a foundation of equity literacy, taking into account student backgrounds and experience. In an unlevel playing field, some students enter our classrooms with formidable challenges, including poverty, trauma, and worries about deportation, all of which impact their behavior and serve as barriers to their educational experience. In other cases, the school has exclusionary discipline practices or the educators are operating with unexamined implicit and explicit biases. We believe that identity safe educators can ensure access to the benefits of prosocial learning by including the following:

> *Develop awareness of our attitudes and challenge our assumptions.* We ensure that we are not teaching social skills from a deficit mindset, such as assuming students have come to us without social skills. Also, we consider cultural values and avoid tasking students with relinquishing their culture to assimilate with the dominant one. We recognize that awareness of and taking action on issues of racial and other injustices are important social skills.

> *Examine and change inequitable disciplinary policies and processes.* Consider if some of the behavioral processes are fairly or unfairly applied. Use school discipline data to recognize inequitable trends.

> *Prepare educators to use trauma-informed practices.* Work on multiple levels to mitigate student challenges through wraparound services (academic support, medical care, and counseling). We need to work in tandem with others who can provide additional support for our students.

Many of the activities that promote SEL competencies have been addressed in previous component chapters. In this final component chapter, we will delve more deeply into specific aspects of prosocial development—particularly in relation to compassion—always keeping equity in mind.

Humans enter the world with a desire to belong, feel included, and be treated in ways that show that who they are matters to others. Supporting students to intentionally develop prosocial skills fosters human connectedness and strengthens their identity safety. All students are faced with ethical decisions: Do I copy someone else's work to avoid failing a course? Do I make fun of a kid just because my peers are doing it? They also face the challenge of standing up to a peer: How do I say no?

In this chapter, we expand on many SEL topics that are on the minds of educators across the United States. We begin by exploring how to hone your attention to notice the way students are treating each other and developing their prosocial skills. We discuss how a compassionate stance can be taught and expressed in the course of many mini-interac-

SEL COMPETENCIES LINKED TO IDENTITY
SAFETY COMPONENTS

In the following table, we juxtapose the SEL competencies (CASEL, 2019) with identity safety components. We also add particular inquiry questions that will help educators apply the following competencies through an identity safety lens.

SEL Competency	Identity Safety Components and Inquiry
Self-Awareness An individual demonstrates knowledge of personal strengths, challenges, cultural and linguistic assets, and aspirations.	*Components:* Classroom Autonomy, Using Diversity as a Resource, High Expectations and Academic Rigor *Inquiry:* Have you tried teaching self-talk? What activities have you done to support students' exploration of their social identities?
Social Awareness The ability to take the perspective of and empathize with others from diverse backgrounds and cultures, to understand the social and ethical norms for behavior, and to recognize family, school, and community resources and supports.	*Components:* Focus on Cooperation, Attention to Prosocial Development, Using Diversity as a Resource, Teacher Warmth and Availability for Learning, and Positive Student Relationships *Inquiry:* Social awareness can be practiced in the context of group work. How can you use reflection time after group work to embed a practice for social awareness? How can you help students learn and talk about race and social justice?
Responsible Decision-Making Individual considers the well-being of self and others when making decisions.	*Components:* Classroom Autonomy, Positive Student Relationships *Inquiry:* Decision-making impacts every aspect of academic and social learning situations. How can you treat it in a metacognitive way, helping students articulate their decision-making processes? Have you shared some of your own decision-making dilemmas?
Relationships The ability to establish and maintain healthy and rewarding relationships with diverse individuals and groups. This includes communicating, active listening, cooperating, resisting inappropriate social pressure, negotiating conflict constructively, and seeking and offering help when needed.	*Components:* Listening for Student Voices, Teaching for Understanding, Focus on Cooperation, Using Diversity as a Resource, Teacher Warmth and Availability for Learning, Positive Student Relationships *Inquiry:* Trust and communication are at the heart of identity safe practice. How can you help students reflect on their relationships? How can your equity focus help students build intergroup relationships?
Self-Management Individual demonstrates the skills to manage and express one's emotions, thoughts, impulses, and stress in constructive ways.	*Components:* Classroom Autonomy, Teacher Skill *Inquiry:* In identity safety, student agency and self-regulation are the focus of self-management. How can you use counternarratives to offset stereotypes and help all students feel some sense of control over their destinies?

tions across a school day. We bring equity and compassion together through respecting differences and valuing multiple perspectives. We consider schoolwide approaches to equity-focused prosocial development that can reinforce what is learned in classrooms. We address the impact of exclusion and the challenge of helping educators learn strategies for prosocial development that are not covered adequately if they are covered at all in their preservice programs.

Attention to Prosocial Learning: Making It Happen

Honing Your *Attention* When It Comes to Prosocial Development

Adding one more thing to your jam-packed mind may seem like the final straw, especially after yet another busy day. How do you pay attention to students' prosocial development while carrying out your many roles and responsibilities as an educator? Most likely, you already do it to some extent. The first trick involves listening to your self-talk. What goes on inside your head in the span of your daily social interactions? You can then reflect on the nature of your inner dialogue while envisioning the prosocial behaviors you are seeking to promote and develop in yourself and your students. You probably have already noted student interactions as well as the range of cultural differences that guide their behaviors. You may be aware and commend students when they exemplify caring, lending a hand, or other prosocial ways of behaving. You likely also notice moments when students need support to develop empathy and self-regulation and to interact respectfully.

Composing a mental or written note of individual students' levels of prosocial development will aid you in assessing what to highlight for the entire group. Sometimes, an entire class of students arrives in our classrooms with cooperation skills intact. In other cases, individual students stand out, needing more attention to develop those skills and work together respectfully.

Listen to how you react when you feel the entire class is misbehaving or lacking prosocial skills. The temptation to express anger and scold or lecture can wash over you, requiring vigilance at times to keep it at bay. Just as you use positive presuppositions for individual students, positive presuppositions are also beneficial for dealing with the entire class. Instead of the rebuke, "Why are you all so rude to one another?" you might declare, "Since we are working on awareness for how we are treating each other, let's find some ways to say things kindly." Or instead of announcing, "This class never puts anything away and always leaves a mess for the next class," you can share, "Let's see how fast we can clean up today to leave a bit more time for you to start on homework at the end of class."

When individual students need specific help with prosocial behavior, attempt to keep it as private as possible so as not to humiliate them, seeking to understand the causes of the behavior. Question how learning differences, trauma or toxic stress, a sense of entitlement, stressors of adolescent development, and other factors are involved. In some families, being direct is not seen as an insult. The student may feel that calling a peer "fat" is an honest appraisal—a comment they would simply brush off if delivered to them; they do not believe they have wronged anyone. Meanwhile, the one labeled *fat* feels humiliated but may laugh to mask embarrassment. Make your expectations clear to eliminate confusion and misunderstandings:

- We do not say things that could potentially hurt another person.
- We do not devalue or make fun of another student's culture.
- We do not make up and use rude nicknames with other students.

You can teach the behavioral norms expected at school while still acknowledging that their behaviors at home may be different.

As we have discussed, students who have been exposed to trauma or toxic stress may need extra support in understanding, processing, and self-regulating their feelings. These students may be experiencing hopelessness and being caught in negative self-talk loops, constructing barriers to learning. Some students who have experienced trauma may not have learned to express basic human respect and kindness in relationship to others. Sometimes, they can be downright mean. Others have developed selfish behaviors, combined with defensiveness and resentment.

No matter how badly a student needs to learn prosocial skills, we always start by learning more about their feelings and forging a trusting relationship. Take time to identify and address the specific skills to focus on and develop a rationale for why they are needed. As we described earlier, making a simple plan of action with goals and steps on a timeline will give you and the student a road map for developing these new skills. Don't attempt to teach too many skills at once.

Ultimately, attending to and addressing prosocial skills will add to creating a sense of identity safety and belonging for everyone.

ADVISORY AS A PLACE AND TIME TO WORK ON SOCIAL SKILLS

Many schools institute a form of advisory. This is a regularly scheduled time carved into a school week for secondary students that is used for advising students on academic issues, future planning, and, in many cases, social and emotional skills. Advisories can embody a specific curriculum and materials for teaching social skills. Time spent in advisory provides universal support for students and sets a standard for social interaction that will benefit them during their academic courses. Here are a few suggested practices.

Advisory Structure

- Keep the numbers of students in advisory as low as possible (15–17 students is a good number). Involve counselors and other adults to create lower group sizes.

- Consider groupings that support students in showing up as their best selves. Don't isolate students of the same ethnicity in a way that leaves them as the only student of color in their advisory group. Cluster them in a group together for mutual support.

- Try to keep the groups together as much as possible from year to year to facilitate the rapport between one another and their advisory educator.

- Meet twice a week for 30 minutes.

Advisory Topics

- Create a welcoming attitude. Advisory can serve as a safe and inclusive place where students can open up and share their worries and receive support.

- Use advisory to explore deeper topics and questions.

- Establish advisory content that is flexible and adaptable in order to deal with school issues as well as upsetting current events.

- Incorporate college prep activities such as preparing students with realistic expectations for college and mentoring them in writing college entrance essays.

Avoid Potential Pitfalls

- *Wasted time*: Ensure that the advisory sessions are relaxed but not so informal that students fall off topic and engage in random chats.

- *Advisory educators are not supported*: Establish guidance for advisors from administrators.

- *Advisory curriculum is too much like the rest of the school day*: Differentiate advisory curriculum from the regular school day by planning a special and exciting time together.

Self-Talk

Self-talk is a tool we can teach students and also fine-tune for ourselves. With self-talk, we can flip negative internal messaging to positive and encouraging thoughts. We all have stories we tell ourselves. These are the "explanatory stories" we invent to describe why things happen in our lives. Because they are invented, they are changeable. We can change entire self-deprecating or destructive stories into self-supporting and affirming ones. Self-talk can be used to develop and practice a growth mindset, counteract doubts, and prepare students with the courage to take on challenges. Many research studies have demonstrated improved performance by professional athletes who exercise self-talk (Weinberg, 2018). The studies found that positive self-talk, including motivational statements and goal-setting, are directly linked to improved performance. Self-talk can help us shift in the following ways:

Catastrophizing: "I am a terrible student and will never go to college or do anything with my life."

Can shift to a *goal-setting* message: "Every little bit of progress shows that I am committed to becoming a better student. I will get there if I keep trying."

All-or-nothing thinking: "Either I was born smart or dumb."

Can shift to a *growth mindset* message: "I grow smarter when I take on challenges."

Negating positive actions: "I only improved a little bit. I will never get there. My improvement was just due to luck."

Can shift to statements that *recognize progress*: "I have started moving forward. I will keep this up."

Statements casting blame: "This is not my fault. Why am I always being blamed?"

Can shift to *accountability*: "I will take responsibility for my part in this situation. I know that I can do better next time."

Fear statements: "I never will be able to change. I'm afraid to try."

Can shift to *courage* statements: "I know change is hard, but I will not give up trying."

Doomsday thoughts: "Things are so difficult for me. I can't take this anymore."

Can shift to *hope*: "I am in a rough patch, but it will get better!"

Students can role-play the use of self-talk and write about it in their journals.

SELF-TALK INQUIRY

Have students journal about the following:

1. Listen to the words that bounce around in your mind. What phrases might you hear inside that prompt you to doubt yourself or your capacities? Do you hear things like this?
   - I can't.
   - Not worth trying.
   - I never will succeed at this.
   - This is just the way I am.

2. Recognize that you have a choice to respond a different way. Make a decision not to let those doubts plague you. Talk to yourself with a different voice.
   - I can do this.
   - I am learning.
   - I may not be perfect, but I am making an effort.
   - I am willing to try.

Self-talk can be strengthened through a healthy dose of empathy and compassion for oneself.

Understanding and Sharing Compassion

While empathy concerns the capacity to identify with another person's feelings, compassion includes expressing care along with the motivation to help alleviate that person's suffering. Many research studies are currently being undertaken to investigate compassion (The Science of a Meaningful Life, n.d.). In one study, researchers found that when we feel compassion, our heart rate slows and the hormone oxytocin is released. Using functional magnetic resonance imaging (fMRI), the activated parts of our brains illuminate in the image. FMRIs show that during moments of compassion, the areas of our brains that harbor happiness and pleasurable feelings light up. Our brains appear to be wired to care for and nurture others. We are programmed to alleviate the suffering of our fellow human beings and to protect them from getting hurt (Keltner, 2004). However, our natural compassion-oriented tendencies can become stymied when we view people who are different from us through the lens of stereotypes and cardboard caricatures (Lavelle, 2016). Thus, our work in identity safety seeks to open hearts and minds to exercise compassion for people of all backgrounds.

Compassion can be experienced in various ways: expressing care to others, being open to receive and express gratitude and kindness, and caring for and forgiving ourselves. Cultivating compassion in our students involves helping them develop interpersonal capacities for care, empathy, and gratitude. In identity safety, compassion includes an equity focus. Students come to value their own identities while wholeheartedly accepting the identity of others.

Offering and Receiving Compassion

The best way to promote compassion is to model it, live it, and acknowledge students when they demonstrate it. Also, regularly engage students in dialogue with a metacognitive view of it. When educators express positive beliefs about human potential, a compassionate response to an incident, and share their personal journey, they transmit a caring attitude to the students. Expressing care directly to a student through a kind word when you notice they are upset and forgiving them when they have hurt you or one of their peers uplifts them to do the same.

Compassion can be cultivated by peers guiding one another, standing up for each other, and taking steps to remedy a problem at school, in the community, or in the world at large. Students can choose how they want to express compassion. They can write letters to someone in the school community who has experienced a death in the family, visit senior citizens and sing with them, or attend a city council meeting on behalf of an effort to save the local hills. Taking action on broader issues such as immigration, climate change, or homelessness empowers students to express compassion on a scale bigger than their personal lives. Service-learning projects can be integrated with specific academic curricular goals, as we discussed in Chapter 4: Teaching for Understanding.

The capacity to accept compassion from others is a desirable trait, yet it is often under-represented as we seek to become empathetic people. The act of receiving compassion is both generous and beautiful when we graciously accept it. In reality, it takes strength, courage, and humility to admit that we need help. It sometimes takes a crisis—such as the death of a loved one or getting cancer—to open us up in order to draw strength from the generosity of others. We are behaving with a greater sense of strength and integrity when we surrender to it. And it is, ironically, an act of kindness to acknowledge the giver with our sincere gratitude. If we can teach our students about receiving compassion at a young age, they can come to appreciate many of the nonmaterial gifts they have received from family, friends, and educators. They will benefit from this connection in a way that will assure them that they are not alone in the world. It is indeed a gift to know that there are others who have our best interests at heart.

Activities that foster gratitude, like the GiveThx gratitude app that we described in Chapter 11: Positive Student Relationships, can teach the value of receiving compassion. Sharing aloud what we are grateful for stimulates students to consider the many good things in their lives and fuels them with the courage to accept compassion from others, especially when they feel overwhelmed or anxious. Researchers have also found that global feelings of gratitude, defined as a general sense of appreciation for being alive, lead to feelings of well-being and optimism (Diener et al., 1985; Peterson & Seligman, 2004).

Having Compassion for Ourselves

Carrying a sense of compassion for ourselves extends to an acceptance and understanding of our mistakes and weaknesses. We can accept our mistakes, even as we are seeking to change our behaviors. This includes embracing our vulnerabilities in the context of a world that is not always fair to us. Prolonged self-blame can lead to self-hate, which can easily shift to blaming and judging others while invoking defensiveness and anger, but we can learn to disengage from it. The internal journey into the forays of our pain can be challenging and difficult, but the ah-ha rewards for understanding our behaviors and experiencing forgiveness are profoundly liberating. Self-compassion grants us the power to forgive ourselves with an awareness into the origin of our wounds and even a reflection on the pain of those who wounded us. Self-compassion and forgiveness naturally extend. The work we perform on the inside can lead us to realizations for how we may have wounded others. It makes it possible to take accountability for our actions and to change and grow.

In our classrooms, we can discuss having compassion for ourselves as part of self-reflection exercises. We can encourage our students to go easy on themselves when they fail a test or harm someone else and help them find ways to change. Reflective quick-writes can be offered in almost any class to encourage students to look back at their level of effort and consider how they can improve, sometimes by turning over a new leaf. Without the capacity to forgive ourselves and recognize our vulnerabilities, it is hard to feel our common humanity and extend compassion to others.

In discussions with Jenny, a compassion researcher friend, she expressed the caveat that we need to ensure that we do not focus on self-compassion at the expense of promoting compassion for others. She worried that on some websites, self-compassion was emphasized to the exclusion of the other forms of compassion. Having compassion for ourselves does not mean that we absolve ourselves from responsibility for others or assume a victim stance that justifies any kind of behavior. Rather, it helps us understand that we all make errors along the way, but ultimately, we have the intent to evolve into caring human beings.

Empathy Plus Compassion Is a Formula for Care

It is also important to note that research studies have shown that empathy alone without compassion does not necessarily promote prosocial behavior (e.g., Eisenberg & Miller, 1987; Hoffman, 2000). Developmentally, it is the move from an empathetic response to a compassionate one that motivates a person to take action to alleviate the suffering of others. In identity safe classrooms, educators emphasize the importance of a caring community of learners, where all forms of compassion are interwoven into the culture of collaboration and care.

Participating in National Activities: Promoting Mutual Respect and Intergroup Understanding

There are many national efforts to build awareness and compassion for others. Classroom teachers, school clubs, and the entire faculty can initiate participation in one of these events:

- *Day of Silence* (GLSEN, 2019) is a day when students choose to be silent to honor and remember the censored voices of LGBTQ people.

- *Mix It Up Day* (Teaching Tolerance, 2014) encourages students to cross social boundaries and seek out and discover new friends at lunchtime, instead of hanging with their usual buddies.

- On *World Hijab Day* (2019) at schools, female Muslim students share their personal choices for wearing a hijab and also inform peers about their religion. Non-Muslim females are invited to experience wearing a hijab for one day. The experience can bolster understanding and compassion for and from non-Muslims.

- *Holocaust Remembrance Day* (US Holocaust Memorial Museum, n.d.) marks a day to delve deeper into the history of the Holocaust and gain a better understanding for what led up to the atrocities. Participants join others to promise "never again," invoking a commitment to end genocide wherever it emerges in the world.

- *Beyond Differences* (n.d.) is an organization that promotes youth leadership with a focus on ending social isolation through student-led activities. For example, one of their schoolwide activities ensures that no student eats alone. Additional activities promote inclusive communities online and facilitate fun ways for students to get to know their classmates. All these activities work to reduce the fear of differences and reverse the isolation felt by some.

Participating in these national events and campaigns builds intercultural understanding, situating students as part of larger national and international efforts. The engagements inspire hope and the motivation to remain active. Genuine identity safe connections created between people with different customs, religions, and beliefs in these groups can open hearts and minds. Classroom activities through these events magnify and deepen the schoolwide experience. For all the campaigns just described, the efforts of one day or a week are both powerful and symbolic. They serve as a reminder that cultivating diversity and compassion needs to extend to an everyday experience for ourselves and our students.

The web addresses for these resources can be found at the end of this part.

BLACK LIVES MATTER WEEK

For the third year in a row, the Seattle School District (Black Lives Matter Week of Action, 2019) has engaged in districtwide events for Black Lives Matter Week. The week is organized by a district Ethnic Studies Work Group, a dedicated volunteer team of staff members who provided educator-developed materials for the event. Many schools and districts across the United States also participate in this yearly event that affirms Black voices (Teaching Tolerance, 2017). The week offers opportunities to experience the substantial contributions of Black Americans and learn about the conditions that have led to structural racism in order to combat them. Students need to move beyond textbooks that often boil Black history down to slavery, the Civil War, and the Civil Rights movement, leaving out inspiring developments such as the Harlem Renaissance and other significant aspects of the Black experience. Also, textbooks neglect to inform students about many of indignities suffered by Black communities, such as Jim Crow, police shootings of unarmed Black men, and the history of redlining.

Dilemmas and Points of Tension

Addressing Exclusion

Most of us have experienced being excluded or excluding someone else at some point in our lives. I recall getting together with a group of seventh-grade girls and heading up to the front door where one of our classmates, Lorraine (not her real name), lived. We knocked, and when Lorraine opened it, my friends and I laughed at her and ran away. While I still feel ashamed of this—I recognize the pain we must have inflicted—I also feel compassion for myself as a young girl who sought approval and belonging at a time when the rules for admission into an adolescent group were harsh and unforgiving. From this experience, I have acquired an intimate and compelling understanding for youth who succumb to peer pressure in search of acceptance. I realize that students who commit these acts are not evil or mean—they are simply misguided. A safe and nurturing environment can easily reverse their fears, supplanting them with compassion. That's all they want in the first place.

I had grown up hearing a story about my mother, Eva, who was born in Nazi Germany and lived there through age 16. Already by the time she was in elementary school, assemblies were hailing the superiority of Aryans. Eventually, my mother—together with the few Jewish students in the school—were excluded from the classroom. They were taken out and sent to the office during the Aryan assemblies. By her middle school years, Jewish children were no longer able to attend the school. Around the same time, my mother's best friend and neighbor, Gicka, stopped visiting her. She decided to find out why. When Eva knocked on the door and Gicka and her brothers spotted her, they slammed the door in her face. Years later and across several continents, Gicka found my mother and apologized. Eva accepted the apology, though it had been an extremely hurtful experience for her. Exclusion can be devastating, and the wounds can last a lifetime. I do not know the impact on Lorraine—I do not even remember if I apologized to her. I do remember that I felt remorse, and that has lasted to this day.

THE DESIRE FOR POPULARITY IN MIDDLE SCHOOL

For Katie, the moment when Jamie, a new student—both smart and pretty—reached out to her, she felt important simply because Jamie had chosen her as one of her first friends in the school. Jamie plied Katie with a plethora of questions: "Who is popular at school? Don't you want to be popular, too? Are your friends unpopular? Don't you want to be one of the cool kids?" To this, Katie replied yes, yes, and yes because she and her friends weren't part of the cool group. Jamie's questions opened up a vulnerable spot in her gut. Katie had felt hopelessly uncool since entering middle school. She began sitting with Jamie during lunch, ignoring her friends (per Jamie's instructions). At a school assembly, Jamie sat with Katie until several popular girls sitting in the front rows called out, "Come sit with us, Jamie! Sit here!" Without a backward glance, Jamie sprang from her seat and rushed forward to sit with her new friends. Katie found herself next to an empty seat during that assembly. Feeling dejected, she pondered Jamie's desertion and realized she had done the same thing, deserting her "real" friends. Katie felt grateful when they accepted her back into their fold after the assembly. It was an important lesson for Katie.

In *Last Boys Picked*, the authors (Edgette & Rupp, 2012) examine the experience of boys who don't participate in sports. They describe the way the American society conspires against boys who don't enjoy sports. They also point out that the common practice of team captains switching back and forth as they select members for their teams can be excruciating. I clearly recall the feeling of dread as I stood in the preselection line in my gym shorts, waiting to get picked. Edgette and Rupp suggest changing social hierarchies by raising the status for a range of social activities, from chess to robotics to drama, while moving away from the tendency to deify sports teams above all other activities. They also suggest unpacking and breaking down stereotypical gender role expectations.

Some schoolwide practices exacerbate status hierarchies and exclusion. At Palo Alto High School, located in California across the street from Stanford University, an annual practice has included printing a map in the school newspaper, highlighting where graduating seniors would be attending college. In 2019, the five co-editors made the radical decision to not publish the map. According to one co-editor, the map "helps fuel this comparison-driven culture about achieving the most elite colleges. It overshadows nontraditional post–high school plans and community college." After much debate, the student editors opted to eliminate the map.

Incoming co-editor Miranda Li added, "Sometimes, students at our school will actually use college acceptance as a metric of success, and that drives a really competitive me-against-you culture at our school" (Wick, 2019). In an effort to validate the success of some students, others are shamed by an absence of acceptance into the more esteemed universities. Indeed, they can feel devalued by their plan to attend a community college—or not attending college at all.

Identity safe educators can work to change school and district policies and practices that isolate and exclude. They can work to adjust social hierarchies by equalizing status and fostering acceptance. When we assign a value to a wider range of social activities while addressing all forms of bullying and bias, our schools will be more likely to decrease social isolation and exclusion.

Infusing Prosocial Learning for Educators Who Never Learned About SEL in College

Javier, a high school educator in one of our identity safety workshops, said that since he did not study SEL in educator preparation or beyond, he felt unprepared to incorporate prosocial learning in his classroom curriculum. He also lamented that as a Spanish teacher, he faced so many curricular demands that he lacked the time to incorporate any more into his course. Javier is not alone. Middle and high school teachers, with lots of content to squeeze into fast-moving courses, may find it overwhelming to add prosocial activities. We hope that all the examples in this book have demonstrated that prosocial learning can readily be integrated into academic lessons as part of an identity safe approach. Taking time to read and learn about adolescent development and including some of the activities we have described in this book will increase emotional comfort, warm up your classroom environment, and enhance student learning. This, in turn, can speed up productivity and, in the end, save time as students address your curriculum with more purpose and less resistance. This will create a more pleasant classroom environment for you as the educator. And if you are a Spanish teacher, you can do it in Spanish!

Chapter Summary

This chapter examines the last of the evidence-based identity safety components, *attention to prosocial development.* As we have pointed out previously, the components are not sequential but weave together into a holistic approach. Attending to prosocial development is a way to meet students where they live, supporting them without judgment. They develop more skills to treat each other with kindness and respect across their differences. We sought to show the way prosocial development and SEL are related. Rather than being a separate curricular entity, prosocial development can be woven throughout the fabric of school life, in our curriculum and all interactions, both in and outside the classroom. We also highlighted the importance of an identity safe and equity-focused approach to SEL.

We talked of ways to hone our own attention to express the nuances of prosocial development. We shared ways to foster self-compassion and to offer and receive compassion in the context of integrity and mutual respect. And then, we explained how to use prosocial learning strategies to navigate differences of opinion and perspective. We suggested ways to incorporate compassion across the school, including through participation in national prosocial campaigns.

One point of tension we highlight involves the educator's role in addressing exclusion and considering the elimination of schoolwide practices that serve to create or reinforce cliquish behavior that inevitably leads to feelings of ostracism for many students. A second dilemma is a practical one involving educators from all subject areas who have not studied SEL in their preservice courses. We suggest that they can support prosocial development by advancing their understanding and incorporating these practices in their classrooms. It is our hope that this book will help them achieve this.

Check Yourself

1. How and when do you teach prosocial skills? How have you been able to fold the skills into your lessons?

2. How do you help your students learn about and practice compassion?

3. What have you done to get up to speed on effective SEL practices? How can you consider applying an identity safety lens to these efforts?

4. How have you honed your attention to notice cliques and exclusion, along with positive prosocial interactions? What can you incorporate for those who need to develop skills?

5. Have you had training in restorative practices? If so, what tools do you use? If not, how can you glean some strategies that help students learn to repair harm?

6. How have you approached different cultural communication styles and code-switching?

TRY IT OUT: END OF CHAPTER ACTIVITIES

Teaching Students to Be Upstanders*

Reflect on your personal experiences.

- Has someone ever stood up for you?
- Have you stood up for someone else?
- Do you know of someone who stood up for another person?

Develop a plan to teach your students to be upstanders.

- How will you introduce the lesson? How will you make this safe for all students?
- How can you encourage students to share upstander experiences?
- What will you do to have students practice/role-play being an upstander?

Implement your plan.

Reflect on the impact of your lesson. What changes will you do to improve in the future?

How will you keep this learning alive in day-to-day classroom life?

*Find an example of how middle school students taught elementary students how to be upstanders in the short Not In Our Town (2013) film *Try It Out: Peer Mentoring on How to Be an Upstander* (https://www.niot.org/nios-video/try-it-out-peer-mentoring-how-be-upstander).

 Available for download as a full-page form at **https://resources.corwin .com/IdentitySafeClass6-12**

Motivating Students With Self-Talk, Change Talk, and Hope Talk

Self-Talk

Guiding Questions	What Happened When You Tried It
What themes, stories, or patterns of self-talk and explanatory stories do you hear from your students? What do you notice concerning the self-talk of teachers and other staff, parents and community, and ourselves? What are you already doing that is working to develop and support positive self-talk? What ideas, questions, concerns, and the like do we have related to self-talk?	

Change Talk

Guiding Questions	What Happened When You Tried It
How can verbal strategies like affirmations, reflections, and more be used to catalyze needed change? What ideas, questions, concerns, and the like do you have related to change talk?	

Hope-Centered Goal-Setting

Guiding Questions	What Happened When You Tried It
What role has or does goal-setting play in your life? To what degree are goal-setting habits and practices integrated into your life? Goal-setting can be a core driver of hope. In what ways do you agree and/or disagree? How can you infuse more hope in goal-setting activities? What is working well in terms of having students do goal-setting? What could be working better?	

 Available for download as a full-page form at **https://resources.corwin .com/IdentitySafeClass6-12**

Big Ideas:
Caring Environments

This part is guided by the following Identity Safety Principle:

#5. Social and emotional safety is created by supporting students in defining their identities, refuting negative stereotypes, and countering stereotype threat, giving them a voice in the classroom while using SEL strategies.

This principle, as shared through the two component chapters, has several big ideas:

- Identity safe educators set up their classrooms to be calm and well-organized with clear expectations, routines, and management methods that teach rather than punish students.

- By considering the causes of student behavior, educators can determine when and how to intervene. The response is based on ideas that will help the student grow.

- Teaching students I-messages and conflict resolution tools will help them learn from mistakes and develop important communication skills.

- Interrupting bullying, exclusion, and all forms of harassment can be enhanced by teaching students to be upstanders who speak up and stand up for themselves and others.

- Emotional and physical comfort can be created through a welcoming tone and an inviting physical space. Adding verve, creativity, and a place for mindfulness will help students feel both energized and relaxed.

- Paying attention to what we say to students creates safety—not only for the person we are speaking to, but all that are present and listening.

- Prosocial development happens all day long, not simply during SEL (social and emotional learning) lessons. Students can learn to reflect on their behavior and improve how they treat one another.

- Compassion enhances relationships, allowing students to be kind to one another, to accept kindness from others, and to forgive and feel better about themselves.

For Further Study

- Blog Posts: *The Journey Through Autism* by 17-year-old Ethan Hirschberg, www.thejourneythroughautism.com

- Book: *The Little Book of Restorative Discipline for Schools: Teaching Responsibility, Creating Caring Environments* (2005) by L. S. Amstutz

- Book: *For White Folks Who Teach in the Hood . . . and the Rest of Y'all Too: Reality Pedagogy and Urban Education* (2016) by Christopher Emdin

- Book: *Managing the Cycle of Meltdowns for Students With Autism Spectrum Disorder* (2012) by Geoff Colvin and Martin R. Sheehan

- Films and Resources: *Not In Our Town*, www.niot.org

- Organization: Life Space Crisis Intervention (2019), www.lsci.org

National Campaigns That Promote Prosocial and Social Justice Events

- Day of Silence from GLSEN, www.glsen.org/day-silence

- World Hijab Day, www.worldhijabday.com

- Black Lives Matter Week, blacklivesmatteratschool.com

- Mix It Up Day from Teaching Tolerance, www.tolerance.org

- Beyond Differences, www.beyonddifferences.org

- Holocaust Remembrance Day from the US Holocaust Memorial Museum, www.ushmm.org

Epilogue: Closing Thoughts

As we described, the SISP (Stanford Integrated Schools Project) identity safety research demonstrated that students of all backgrounds achieved at higher rates, felt more identity safe, and had a greater affinity for school in an identity safe classroom. Several people suggested to Dorothy Steele at the conclusion of her field studies that if identity safety served to benefit all students, it was not truly a "diversity" intervention aimed at students of color. However, Dorothy replied that while feeling safe in their identity is good for all students, it is particularly beneficial to those whose identities have been tarnished by conscious or inadvertent triggers and spoken or unspoken negative stereotypes about intelligence, race, gender, and other differences. Making true identity safety, belonging, and engagement a reality for *every* student takes a deep commitment, constant vigilance, and thoughtful reflection.

It is a major undertaking to topple the infrastructures that have maintained White supremacy and acts of "othering," which involves promoting patterns of separation and discrimination, conditions that have held sway for centuries. The path to identity safety is nothing less than the disruption of existing systems of inequity. It is a road that leads to the empowerment of our youth as they realize the positive impact of their complete identities and reach their potential. It is the opportunity to continue the "good fight." While the process may surface some painful moments and even serious dilemmas, it can often be a joyful journey, as we join together to make change and to break down unfair barriers to learning.

Parker Palmer (1999) captures our challenge when he says, "Good teaching cannot be reduced to technique; good teaching comes from the identity and integrity of a teacher." That is why we incorporate an exploration of our own social identities into the process of supporting our students to discover theirs. Palmer also says, "Good teachers join self, subject, and students in the fabric of life from an integral and undivided self: they manifest in their own lives and evoke in their students a 'capacity for connectedness.'" Diving into the deeper waters of our own identities and supporting our students and colleagues leads us into a powerful sense of purpose. It opens up the doors of our shared humanity and aligns us with a quest that links all cultures throughout our history. The question becomes this: How can we experience our true selves in community with other beings?

When we sincerely commit to creating identity safety, we are fulfilling the promise of education and opportunity for each and every student. We are contributing to one of the most meaningful of life's purposes—being part of the richly rewarding path that leads toward acceptance, inclusion, and social justice. Hope for realizing a vision is a driving force that keeps us relentlessly pursuing this important work. We wish you joy as you cultivate identity safety for yourself, your students, and colleagues on this lifelong journey.

References

Abrams, D. (1990). *Social identity theory*. Springer-Verlag.

Abrams, J. (2018). *Personal interview*. Leadership Public Schools.

Abrams, J. (2019). *Taking a field trip into our lives*. Personal communication.

Adams, J. M. (2015). *California suspension rates drop as willful defiance punishments decline*. EdSource. https://edsource.org/2015/california-student-suspension-rate-drops-as-willful-defiance-punishments-decline/90989

Adamson, C. (2015). *Trauma literacy: Building a pedagogy of healing* (Unpublished manuscript).

Agrawal, N. (2019). California expands ban on "willful defiance" suspensions in schools. *Los Angeles Times*. https://www.latimes.com/california/story/2019-09-10/school-suspension-willful-defiance-california

Aguilar, E. (2018). *Onward: Cultivating emotional resilience in educators*. Jossey-Bass.

Ajayi, L. (2018). *Why we need to call out casual racism ideas*. https://ideas.ted.com/why-we-need-to-call-out-casual-racism/

Allen, G. E. (2007). *Eugenics office at Cold Spring Harbor, 1910–1940: An essay in institutional history*. http://www.dnalc.org/home.html

Allport, G. W. (2008). *The nature of prejudice*. Basic Books.

Alper, C. (2018). *Embracing inquiry-based instruction*. Edutopia. www.edutopia.org/article/embracing-inquiry-based-instruction

Ambady, N., Paik, S. K., Steele, J., Owen-Smith, A., & Mitchell, J. P. (2004). Deflecting negative self-relevant stereotype activation: The effects of individuation. *Journal of Experimental Social Psychology, 40*, 401–408.

Amstutz, L. S. (2005). *The little book of restorative discipline for schools: Teaching responsibility, creating caring environments*. Good Books.

Angelou, M. (1969). *I know why the caged bird sings*. Random House.

Angelou, M. (1978). *And still I rise*. Random House.

Argyris, C. (1990). *Overcoming organizational defenses*. Simon and Schuster.

Aronson, E., & Patnoe, S. (1997). *The jigsaw classroom: Building cooperation in the classroom* (2nd ed.). Longman.

Aronson, J., Fried, C. B., & Good, C. (2002). Reducing the effects of stereotype threat on African American college students by shaping theories of intelligence. *Journal of Experimental Social Psychology, 38*, 113–125.

Baker, E. A. (2008). *Third space with Kris Gutierrez (interview)*. Voice of Literacy. http://www .voiceofliteracy.org/posts/28304

Barnes, E. W. (2017). *Parents and teachers can minimize the stress with some joint prep before school starts*. Edutopia. https://www.edutopia.org/article/helping-students-autism-transition-new-school-year-elizabeth-barnes

Barron, B., & Darling Hammond, L. (2008). *Teaching for meaningful learning: A review of research on inquiry-based and cooperative learning*. George Lucas Foundation.

Baumeister, R. F., & Leary, M. (1995). The need to belong: Desire for interpersonal attachments as a fundamental human motivation. *Psychological Bulletin, 117*, 497–529. https://doi .org/10.1037/0033-2909.117.3.497

Baumeister, R. F., Twenge, J. M., & Nuss, C. K. (2002). Effects of social exclusion on cognitive processes: Anticipated aloneness reduces intelligent thought. *Journal of Personality and Social Psychology, 83*(4), 817–827.

Benard, B. (1991). *Fostering resiliency in kids: Protective factors in the family, school, and community*. Western Center for Drug-Free Schools and Communities.

Bergoffen, D. (2018). Simone de Beauvoir. *The Stanford Encyclopedia of Philosophy*. https:// plato.stanford.edu/archives/fall2018/entries/beauvoir/

Beyond Differences. (n.d.) *Home page*. https://www.beyonddifferences.org/

Bharti, P. (2015). *Perfect integration of doctopus, Goobric and classroom for teachers*. EdTechReview. https://edtechreview.in/trends-insights/insights/1754-perfect-integration-of-doctopus-goobric-and-classroom-for-teachers

Black Lives Matter at School. (n.d.). https://blacklivesmatteratschool.com/

Boaler, J. (1997). *Equity, empowerment and different ways of knowing*. https://link.springer .com/article/10.1007/BF03217322

Boudreau, S. (2019). *Model the formation and structure of the earth. In one easy lab*. Take Action Science Projects Blog. https://takeactionscience.wordpress.com/2019/01/07/model-the-formation-and-structure-of-the-earth-in-one-easy-lab/

Boykin, A. W. (1983). The academic performance of Afro-American children. In J. T. Spence (Ed.), *Achievement and achievement motives: Psychological and sociological approach* (pp. 350–381). Freeman.

Briceño, E. (2013). *Mindsets and student agency, competency works: Learning from the cutting edge*. https://www.competencyworks.org/analysis/mindsets-and-student-agency/

Briceño, E. (2018). *Personal interview*. Leadership Public Schools.

Bronson, P. (2007). How not to talk to your kids. *New York Times Magazine*. http://nymag .com/news/features/27840/

Bruehlman-Senecal, E., & Ayduk, O. (2015). This too shall pass: Temporal distance and the regulation of emotional distress. *Journal of Personality and Social Psychology, 108*(2), 356–375. https://doi.org/10.1037/a0038324

Canning, E. A., Muenks, K., Green, D. J., & Murphy, M. C. (2019). STEM faculty who believe ability is innate have larger racial achievement gaps and inspire less student motivation in their classes. *Science Advances, 5*(2). https://doi.org/10.1126/sciadv.aau4734

CASEL. (n.d.). *Core SEL competencies.* https://casel.org/core-competencies/

CASEL. (2019). *Framework for social and emotional learning.* https://casel.org/what-is-sel/

Centers for Disease Control and Prevention. (2014). *Adverse childhood experiences (ACEs) study.* https://www.cdc.gov/violenceprevention/acestudy/index.html

Chauncey, C. (2007). An interview with Michael J. Nakkula and Eric Toshalis. *Harvard Education Letter, 23*(1).

Chodron, P. (2001). *The places that scare you: A guide to fearlessness in difficult times.* Shambhala.

Cohen, E. G. (1994). *Designing groupwork: Strategies for heterogeneous classrooms* (rev. ed.). Teachers College Press.

Cohen, E. G., Lotan, R. A., Darling-Hammond, L., & Goodlad, J. I. (2014). *Designing groupwork.* Teachers College Press.

Cohen, G. L., & Steele, C. M. (2002). A barrier of mistrust: How stereotypes affect cross-race mentoring. In J. Aronson (Ed.), *Improving academic achievement: Impact of psychological factors on education* (pp. 305–331). Academic Press.

Cohen, G. L., Garcia, J., Purdie-Vaughns, V., Apfel, N., & Brzustoski, P. (2009). Recursive processes in self-affirmation: Intervening to close the minority achievement gap. *Science, 324*, 400–403.

Cohen, G., Steele, C. M., & Ross, L. D. (1999). The mentor's dilemma: Providing critical feedback across the racial divide. *Personality and Social Psychology Bulletin, 25*, 1302–1318.

Cohen, R., & Frieberg, J. (2013). *School climate and bullying prevention.* National School Climate Center.

Cole, S., Greenwald, J., Gadd, G., Ristuccia, J., & Gregory, M. (2009). Trauma and learning policy initiative. *Massachusetts Advocates for Children & Harvard Law School.* Sixth printing. Library of Congress Control Number: 2005933604 A.

Colvin, G., & Sheehan, M. R. (2012). *Managing the cycle of meltdowns for students with autism spectrum disorder.* Corwin.

Covington, M. V. (2000). Goal theory, motivation, and school achievement: An integrative review. *Annual Review of Psychology, 23,*171.

Cowin, L., Davies, R., Estall, G., Berlin, T., Fitzgerald, M., & Hoot, S. (2003). De-escalating aggression and violence in the mental health setting. *International Journal of Mental Health Nursing, 12*, 64–73.

Crenshaw, K. (1980). *Mapping the margins: Intersectionality, identity politics, and violence against women of color.* https://www.racialequitytools.org/resourcefiles/mapping-margins.pdf

Csikszentmihalyi, M. (2015). *Creativity: The psychology of discovery and invention*. Harper Perennial Modern Classics.

Darling-Hammond, L., & Cook-Harvey, C. M. (2018). *Educating the whole child: Improving school climate to support school success*. Learning Policy Institute. https://learningpolicyinstitute .org/sites/default/files/product-files/Educating_Whole_Child_REPORT.pdf

Davies, P., Spencer, S., & Steele, C. M. (2005). Clearing the air: Identity safety moderates the effects of stereotype threat on women's leadership aspirations. *Journal of Personality and Social Psychology 88*(2), 276–287. https://doi.org/10.1037/0022-3514.88.2.276

Deci, E., & Ryan, R. M. (1985). *Intrinsic motivation and self-determination in human behavior*. Plenum Press.

Devine, P., Forscher, P. S., Austin, A. J., & Cox. W. (2012). Long-term reduction in implicit race bias: A prejudice habit-breaking intervention. *Experimental Social Psychology, 48*(6), 1267–1278.

DiAngelo, R. (2018). *White fragility: Why it's so hard for white people to talk about racism*. Beacon Press.

Diener, C. I., & Dweck, C. S. (1978). An analysis of learned helplessness: Continuous changes in performance, strategy, and achievement cognitions following failure. *Journal of Personality and Social Psychology, 36*, 451–462.

Diener, E., Emmons, R. A., Larsen, R. J., & Griffin, S. (1985). The satisfaction with life scale. *Journal of Personality Assessment, 49*, 71–75.

Doran, G. T. (1981). There's a S.M.A.R.T. way to write management's goals and objectives. *Management Review, 70*(11), 35–36.

Dovidio, J. F., Glicke, P., & Rudman, L. (2008). *On the nature of prejudice: Fifty years after Allport*. Blackwell.

Dweck, C. S. (1999). *Self-theories: Their role in motivation, personality, and development*. Psychology Press.

Dweck, C. S. (2006). *Mindset: The new psychology of success*. Random House.

Dweck, C. S. (2007). Implicit theories of intelligence predict achievement across an adolescent transition: A longitudinal study and an intervention. *Child Development, 78*, 246–263.

Dweck, C. S. (2016). *Recognizing and overcoming false growth mindset*. Edutopia. https://www .edutopia.org/blog/recognizing-overcoming-false-growth-mindset-carol-dweck

Edgette, J. S., & Rupp, B. M. (2012). *The last boys picked: Helping boys who don't play sports survive bullies and boyhood*. Penguin Group.

Edutopia. (2013). *Knowledge in action research: Project-based learning course design*. https:// www.edutopia.org/knowledge-in-action-PBL-research-course-design

Ehrlich, P. R. (1968). *The population bomb*. Buccaneer Books.

Eisenberg, N., & Miller, P. (1987). The role of empathy to prosocial and related behaviors. *Psychological Bulletin, 101*(1), 91–119.

Emdin, C. (2016). *For White folks who teach in the hood . . . and the rest of y'all too: Reality pedagogy and urban education.* Beacon Press.

Epstein, A., Fauteux, M., & Levitt, K. (2017). *6 ways to make collective feedback work in classrooms.* Education Week. https://blogs.edweek.org/edweek/next_gen_learning/2017/11/6_ways_to_make_collective_feedback_work_in_classrooms.html

Equity Lab. (2019). *Home page.* https://www.theequitylab.org/olitor

Eslinger, P. J. (1996). Conceptualizing, describing, and measuring components of executive function: A summary. In G. R. Lyon & N. Krasnegor (Eds.), *Attention memory and executive function* (pp. 367–395). P. H. Brookes.

Espelage, D., Pigott, T., & Polanin, J. (2012) A meta-analysis of school-based bullying prevention programs' effects on bystander intervention behavior. *School Psychology Review, 41*(1), 47–65.

Fass, P. (2016). *Adolescence is no longer a bridge between childhood and adulthood.* Princeton University Press.

Fishkind, A. (2002). Calming agitation with words, not drugs: 10 commandments for safety. *Current Psychiatry, 1*(4), 32–39.

Fitzpatrick, K. (2010). A critical multicultural approach to physical education: Challenging discourses of physicality and building resistant practices in schools. In C. Sleeter & S. May (Eds.), *Critical multiculturalism theory and praxis* (pp. 177–190). Routledge.

Flipped Learning Network. (2014). *The four pillars of F-L-I-P.*™ https://flippedlearning.org/wp-content/uploads/2016/07/FLIP_handout_FNL_Web.pdf

Ford, M. E. (1992). *Motivating humans: Goals, emotions, and personal agency beliefs.* SAGE.

Formative Assessment Insights. (n.d.). *Five evidence gathering routines.* https://wested.instructure.com/courses/2170523/files/108655632

Fowler, J. H., & Christakis, N. A. (2010). Cooperative behavior cascades in human social networks. *Proceedings of the National Academy of Sciences, 107*(12), 5334–5338. https://doi.org/10.1073/pnas.0913149107

Freiburg, S. (2017). *Personal communication.*

Fryberg, S. (2016). *Creating identity safe spaces: Seattle jobs initiative 2016 conference.* https://www.youtube.com/watch?v=65LT8pwD8xk

Fulbeck, K. (2006). *Part Asian, 100% Hapa.* Chronicle Books.

Gallagher, S. (2007). Moral agency, self-consciousness, and practical wisdom. *Journal of Consciousness Studies, 14*(5–6), 199–223.

Galton, F. (1869). *Hereditary genius.* Social Sciences Bookshop Ltd.

Gender Spectrum. (2019). *Home page.* https://www.genderspectrum.org/

Germain-McCarthy, Y. (2014). *Bringing the Common Core math standards to life: Exemplary practices from high schools.* Routledge.

Givethx. (2019). *Home page.* https://www.givethx.org

GiveThx. (n.d.). *Build classroom belonging.* https://www.givethx.org/

GLSEN. (2019). Day of Silence. https://www.glsen.org/day-silence

Goldin, G. A., Epstein, Y. M., & Schorr, R. Y. (2007). Affective pathways and structures in urban students' mathematical learning. In D. K. Pugalee, A. Rogerson, & A. Schinck (Eds.), *Mathematics education in a global community: Proceedings of the Ninth International Conference of the Mathematics Education Into the 21st Century Project* (pp. 260–264). Center for Mathematics, Science and Technology Education.

Good, J. J., Woodzicka, J. A., & Wingfield, L. C. (2010). The effects of gender stereotypic and counter-stereotypic textbook images on science performance. *Journal of Social Psychology 150*(2), 132–147.

Good, T., & Brophy, J. (1980). *Educational psychology: A realistic approach* (2nd ed.). Holt, Rinehart & Winston.

Good, T. L. (1981). *Teacher expectations and student perceptions: A decade of work.* ASCD.

Gorski, P. (2017). *About equity literacy, definition and abilities.* The Equity Literacy Institute. https://www.equityliteracy.org/equity-literacy

Gould, M. S., Wallenstein, S., & Davidson, L. (1989). Suicide clusters: A critical review. *Suicide and Life-Threatening Behavior, 19*, 17–27.

Gresky, D. M., Ten Eyck, L. L., Lord, C. G., & McIntyre, R. B. (2005). Effects of salient multiple identities on women's performance under mathematics stereotype threat. *Sex Roles, 53*, 703–716.

Gutiérrez, K. D., & Rogoff, B. (2003). Cultural ways of learning: Individual traits or repertoires of practice. *Educational Researcher, 32*(5), 19–25.

Gutstein, E. (2010). Critical multicultural approaches to mathematics education in urban K–12 classrooms. In C. Sleeter & S. May (Eds.), *Critical multiculturalism theory and praxis* (pp. 127–137). Routledge.

Hammond, Z. (2015). *Culturally responsive teaching and the brain: Promoting authentic engagement and rigor among culturally and linguistically diverse students.* Corwin.

Hanson, C. (2016). *Nigger vs Nigga.* Huffington Post. https://www.huffingtonpost.com/chiaku-hanson/nigger-vs-nigga_b_10602798.html

Harari, Y. (2015). *Why humans run the world.* https://ideas.ted.com/why-humans-run-the-world/

Hardy, K. (2013). Healing the hidden wounds of racial trauma. *Reclaiming Children and Youth, 22*(1), 24–28.

Hattie, J. (2012). *Visible learning for teachers: Maximizing impact on learning.* Routledge.

Heimbeck, D., Frese, M., Sonnentag, S., & Keith, N. (2003). Integrating errors into the training process: The function of error management instructions and the role of goal orientation. *Personnel Psychology, 56*, 333–362.

Heitin, L. (2015). *Should formative assessments be graded?* Education Week. https://www.edweek.org/ew/articles/2015/11/11/should-formative-assessments-be-graded.html

Hernandez-Ramos, P., & De La Paz, S. (2009). Learning history in middle school by designing multimedia in a project-based learning experience (Abstract). *Journal of Research on Technology in Education, 42*(2), 151–173.

Herrnstein, R. J., & Murray, C. (1994). *The bell curve.* The Free Press.

Hilliard, A., III. (2002). Language, culture, and assessment of African American students. In L. Delpit (Ed.), *The skin that we speak* (pp. 89–105). New York Press.

Hirschberg, E. (2019). *Journey through autism blogs*. https://www.thejourneythroughautism.com/blog/category/Autism-Blog-Posts

Hoffman, M. (2000). *Empathy*. Cambridge University Press.

Hunter, M. (1982). *Mastery teaching*. TIP Publications.

Implicit Association Tests: Project Implicit. (2011)._https://implicit.harvard.edu/implicit/education.html/

Indigenous Corporate Training, Inc. (2015). *First nation talking stick protocol*. https://www.ictinc.ca/blog/first-nation-talking-stick-protocol

Intersectionality. (n.d.). *Oxford English dictionary online*. https://en.oxforddictionaries.com/definition/intersectionality

Jigsaw Classroom. (2019). *Jigsaw in ten easy steps*. https://www.jigsaw.org/#steps

Johns, M., Schmader, T., & Martens, A. (2005). Knowing is half the battle: Teaching stereotype threat as a means of improving women's math performance. *Psychological Science, 16*, 175–179.

Johnson, D. W., & Johnson, R. T. (2009). An educational psychology success story: Social interdependence theory and cooperative learning (Abstract). *Educational Researcher, 38*(5), 365–379.

Johnson, D. W., Johnson, R. T., & Stanne, M. E. (2000). *Cooperative learning methods: A meta-analysis*. University of Minnesota Press.

Kabat-Zinn, J. (2012). *Mindfulness for beginners: Reclaiming the present moment—And your life*. Sounds True.

Keltner, D. (2004). *The compassionate instinct*. Greater Good Science Magazine. https://greatergood.berkeley.edu/article/item/the_compassionate_instinct

Keng, S. L., Smoski, M. J., & Robins, C. J. (2011). Effects of mindfulness on psychological health: A review of empirical studies. *Clinical Psychology Review, 31*(6), 1041–1056.

King, R. B., & Datu, J. A. (2018). Grateful students are motivated, engaged, and successful in school: Cross-sectional, longitudinal, and experimental evidence. *Journal of School Psychology, 70*, 105–122. https://doi.org/10.1016/j.jsp.2018.08.001

Knight, J. (2018) *An interview with Zaretta Hammond*. Instructional Coaching Group. https://www.instructionalcoaching.com/an-interview-with-zaretta-hammond/

Korbey, H. (2013). *A history in which we all see ourselves*. George Lucas Educational Foundation. https://www.edutopia.org/article/history-which-we-can-all-see-ourselves

Krashen, S. D. (1981). *Second language acquisition and second language learning*. Pergamon Press.

Kubata, R. (2010). Critical multicultural education and second/foreign language teaching. In C. Sleeter & S. May (Eds.), *Critical multiculturalism theory and praxis* (pp. 99–111). Routledge.

Ladson-Billings, G. (2002). *Dreamkeepers: Successful teachers of African American students.* Jossey-Bass.

Lavelle, B. D. (2016). *A call for more compassionate, equitable education.* Mind and Life Institute. https://www.mindandlife.org/call-compassionate-equitable-education/

Learning Accelerator. (n.d.). *Blended and personalized learning at work.* https://practices.learningaccelerator.org/learn/what-is-blended-learning

Lee, E., Menkart, D., & Okazawa-Rey, M. (Eds.). (1998). *Beyond heroes and holidays: A practical guide to K–12 anti-racist, multicultural education and staff development.* Teaching for Change.

Lee, J. (2017). Palo Alto school board set to strip schools of eugenicists' names. *Mercury News.* https://www.mercurynews.com/2017/03/16/palo-alto-school-board-set-to-rename-schools-named-after-eugenicists/

Leiberman, M. (2013). *Social: Why our brains are wired to connect.* Crown.

Levitt, M. (1960). *Freud and Dewey on the nature of man.* Philosophical Library.

Life Space Crisis Intervention. (2019). *Home page.* https://www.lsci.org/

Lindsey, D., Lindsey, R. B., & Martinez, R. S. (2007). *Culturally proficient coaching: Supporting educators to create equitable schools.* Corwin.

Lopez, S. (2013). *The science of hope: An interview with Shane Lopez.* www.takingcharge.csh.umn.edu/science-hope

LPS. (n.d.). *Mission statement.* http://www.leadps.org/

LPS. (2019). *Collective feedback guide.* https://docs.google.com/document/d/13PrB0AiE_Dl6oaBVt3oM1AxHFDfjz0jk-9tKyZjTNbU/edit

LPS Student Interviews. (2018). *Aminesh, Brady, Donald, Lucia, and Rickey.* Leadership Public Schools.

Lueke, A., & Gibson, B. (2014). Mindfulness meditation reduces implicit age and race bias: The role of reduced automaticity of responding. *Social Psychological and Personality Science, 6*(3), 284–291.

MacKenzie, T. (2016). *Bringing inquiry-based learning into your class.* Edutopia. https://www.edutopia.org/profile/trevor-mackenzie

Mann, J. (2012). *Welcoming stories: New York students share, pay it forward.* Not In Our Town. https://www.niot.org/blog/welcoming-stories-new-york-students-share-pay-it-forward

Markus, H. R. (2008). Identity matters: Ethnicity, race, and the American dream. In M. Minow, R. Shweder, & H. R. Markus (Eds.), *Just schools: Pursuing equality in societies of difference.* Russell Sage Foundation.

Marx, D. M., & Roman, J. S. (2002). Female role models: Protecting women's math test performance. *Personality and Social Psychology Bulletin, 28,* 1183–1193.

Marzano, R. J. (2008). *Classroom assessment and grading that work.* Association for Supervision and Curriculum Development.

May, S., & Sleeter, C. (2010). *Critical multiculturalism theory and praxis.* Routledge.

McIntyre, R. B., Paulson, R. M., & Lord, C. G. (2003). Alleviating women's mathematics stereotype threat through salience of group achievements. *Journal of Experimental Social Psychology, 39*, 83–90.

McLaughlin, M., & Visser, N. (2015). *Spring Valley student flung by school officer on video*. Huffington Post. https//www.huffingtonpost.com/entry/spring-valley-high-school-student-flung-by-official-in-video_us_562e9e71e4b06317990f1927

Mehrabian, A. (1972). *Nonverbal communication*. Aldine-Atherton.

Miller, A. C., & McCormick, S. (2008). *Facing racism in a diverse nation: A guide for public dialogue and problem-solving* (pp. 44–48). https://www.everyday-democracy.org/resources/facing-racism-diverse-nation#download

Miller, M., & Veatch, N. (2011). Literacy in context (LinC): Choosing instructional strategies to teach reading in content areas for students grades 5–12. Pearson.

Mitchell, R. P. (2016). *White and male and seen all over: FAS talk focuses on walls of fame and other "situational cues" that threaten identity*. Harvard Gazette. https://news.harvard.edu/gazette/story/2016/04/White-and-male-and-seen-all-over/

Miyake, A., Smith-Kost, L. E., Finkelstein, N. D., Pollock, S. J., Cohen, G. L., & Ito, T. A. (2010). Reducing the gender achievement gap in college science: A classroom study of values affirmation. *Science, 330*, 1234–1237.

Mooney, J., & Cole, D. (2000). *Learning outside the lines*. Fireside.

Moore, E., Jr. (2017). The N!gga(er) in me. In E. Moore Jr., A. Michael, & M. W. Penick-Parks (Eds.), *The guide for White women who teach Black boys*. Corwin.

Moore, E., Jr., Michael, A., & Penick-Parks, M. W. (Eds.). (2017). *The guide for White women who teach Black boys*. Corwin.

Murphy, M. (2018a). *Creating growth mindset cultures to mitigate inequalities in higher education*. College Transition Collaborative Indiana University Education. https://s3-us-west-2.amazonaws.com/csafiles2017/2018+Items/Mindset+Panel+Final.pdf

Murphy, M. (2018b). *Personal interview*.

Murray, C. (2007). Intelligence in the classroom. *Wall Street Journal* (A21, para 3).

Murrell, P. C., Jr. (1999). Responsive teaching for African American male adolescents. In V. C. Polite & J. E. Davis (Eds.), *African American males in school and society: Practices and policies for effective education* (pp. 82–96). Teachers College Press.

National Center for School Crisis and Bereavement. (2018). *Help now*. University of Southern California. https://www.schoolcrisiscenter.org/help-now/

The National Child Traumatic Stress Network. (2018). *Secondary traumatic stress*. https://www.nctsn.org/trauma-informed-care/secondary-traumatic-stress

Nieto, S. (2013). *Finding joy in teaching students of diverse backgrounds: Culturally responsive and socially just practices in US classrooms*. Heinemann.

Niroga Project. (2019). *Home page*. https://www.niroga.org/

Not In Our Town. (n.d.). *Home page*. https://www.niot.org/

Not In Our Town. (2012). *A gay–straight alliance creates unity and a culture of acceptance.* https://www.niot.org/nios-video/gay-straight-alliance-creates-unity-and-culture-acceptance-0

Not In Our Town. (2013). *Try it out: Peer mentoring on how to be an upstander.* https://www.niot.org/nios-video/try-it-out-peer-mentoring-how-be-upstander

Not In Our Town. (2017). *Moses Robinson, school guardian: A documentary by Not In Our Town and the US Department of Justice COPS Office.* https://www.niot.org/cops/moses-robinson-school-guardian

Not In Our Town. (2019). *Dissolving stereotypes.* https://www.niot.org/nios-video/dissolving-stereotypes-0

Oakland Unified School District. (2014). *Restorative justice in Oakland schools: Implementation and impacts, 2014—An effective strategy to reduce disproportionate discipline, suspensions, and improve academic outcomes.* https://www.ousd.org/cms/lib/CA01001176/Centricity/Domain/134/Exec_Summary_OUSD_RJReport_2014.pdf

Okonofua, J., & Eberhardt, J. L. (2015). Two strikes: Race and the disciplining of young students. *Psychological Science, 26*(5), 617–624. https://doi.org/10.1177/0956797615570365

Olson, K. (2014). *The invisible classroom: Relationships, neuroscience & mindfulness in school.* Norton.

Olsson, C. A., McGee, R., Nada-Raja, S., & Williams, S. (2013). A 32-year longitudinal study of child and adolescent pathways to well-being in adulthood. *Journal of Happiness Studies, 14*(3), 1069–1083. https://doi.org/10.1007/s10902-012-9369-8

Ondrasek, N., & Flook, L. (2020). *How to help all students feel safe to be themselves.* Greater Good Science Center. https://greatergood.berkeley.edu/article/item/how_to_help_all_students_feel_safe_to_be_themselves

Pacific Education Group. (n.d.). *Home page.* https://courageousconversation.com/

Paddington Teaching and Learning. (2013). *What works best? John Hattie, effect size & "visible learning."* https://paddingtonteachingandlearning.wordpress.com/2013/02/09/what-works-best-john-hattie-effect-size-visible-learning/

Palmer, P. J. (1999). *The heart of a teacher: Identity and integrity in teaching.* https://biochem.wisc.edu/sites/default/files/labs/attie/publications/Heart_of_a_Teacher.pdf

Papageorge, N., Gershenson, S., & Kang, K. M. (2018). *Teacher expectations matter.* https://doi.org/10.3386/w25255

Paul, R., & Elder, L. (1997). *Foundation for critical thinking.* http://www.criticalthinking.org/pages/socratic-teaching/606

Peer Health Exchange. (n.d.). https://www.peerhealthexchange.org/our-sites/bay-area

Peterson, C., & Seligman, M. E. (2004). *Character strengths and virtues: A handbook and classification.* Oxford University Press.

Pierre, M. (2017). Vignette: Dismantling the "White savior mentality." In E. Moore Jr., A. Michael, & M. W. Penick-Parks (Eds.), *The guide for White women who teach Black boys* (p. 32). Corwin.

Pierson, R. (2013). *Every kid needs a champion.* https://www.ted.com/talks/rita_pierson_every_kid_needs_a_champion. 0-321

Plucker, J. A. (2013). *Francis Galton.* http://www.intelltheory.com/galton.shtml

Pollock, M. (2017). *School talk: Rethinking what we say about and to students every day.* Perseus.

Porter, T. (2010). *A call to men.* https://www.ted.com/talks/tony_porter_a_call_to_men/transcript?language=en

Priest, N., Slopen, N., Woolford, S., Philip, J. T., Singer, D., Kauffman, A. D., . . . Williams, D. (2018). Stereotyping across intersections of race and age: Racial stereotyping among White adults working with children. *PLoS ONE, 13*(10), e0205614. https://doi.org/10.1371/journal.pone.0205614

Puglise, N. (2016, September 27). *Don't ask, don't tell: Military members out and proud five years after repeal.* The Guardian. https://www.theguardian.com/us-news/2016/sep/27/dont-ask-dont-tell-repeal-anniversary-us-military

Purdie-Vaughns, V., Steele, C. M., Davies, P. G., Ditlmann, R., & Crosby, J. R. (2008). Social identity contingencies: How diversity cues signal threat or safety for African Americans in mainstream institutions. *Journal of Personality and Social Psychology, 94*, 615–630.

Restorative Practices Working Group. (2014). *Restorative practices: Fostering healthy relationships & promoting positive discipline in schools—A guide for educators.* Advancement Project.

RET Program, College of Engineering. (2016). *Hands-on bone transplants: No donors needed.* Regents of the University of Colorado. https://www.teachengineering.org/activities/view/nds-1726-bone-transplants-biomedical-mimic-3d

Reynolds, M. (2018). *Interview for assessment for learning project.* Leadership Public Schools.

Richmond, J. S., Berlin, J. S., Fishkind, A. B., Holloman, G. H., Zeller, S. L., Wilson, M. P., . . . Ng, A. T. (2012). Verbal de-escalation of the agitated patient: Consensus statement of the American Association for Emergency Psychiatry Project BETA de-escalation workgroup. *Western Journal of Emergency Medicine, 13*(1), 17–25.

Rickford, J. R., & Rickford, R. J. (2000). *Spoken soul: The story of Black English.* John Wiley.

Robinson, M. L. (1985). *Princeton Blacks and the Black community: Senior thesis* (Unpublished manuscript). Department of Sociology, Princeton University, Princeton, New Jersey. https://www.politico.com/pdf/080222_MOPrincetonThesis_1-251.pdf

Rogers, C., Lyon, H. C., & Tausch, R. (2013). *On becoming an effective teacher—Person-centered teaching, psychology, philosophy.* Routledge.

Rohrer, J. M., Richter, D., Brümmer, M., Wagner, G., & Schmukle, S. C. (2018). *Successfully striving for happiness: Socially engaged pursuits predict increases in life satisfaction. Psychological Science.* http://home.uni-leipzig.de/diffdiag/pppd/wp-content/uploads/Manuscript-Pursuit-of-Happiness_final.pdf

Rosenthal, H. E. S., & Crisp, R. J. (2006). Reducing stereotype threat by blurring intergroup boundaries. *Personality and Social Psychology Bulletin, 32*, 501–511.

Rotosky, J. (2013). *Learning to love myself.* https://www.niot.org/blog/learning-love-myself-why-we-need-support-lgbtq-youth

Ruder, D. (2008, September–October). *The teen brain*. Harvard Magazine. https://harvardmagazine.com/2008/09/the-teen-brain.html

Sahlberg, P. (2016). The Finnish paradox. In F. Adamson, B. Astrand, & L. Darling-Hammond (Eds.), *Global education reform: How privatization and public investment influence education outcomes* (pp. 110–113). Routledge.

SAMHSA. (2012). *Preventing suicide: A toolkit for high schools*. https://store.samhsa.gov/product/Preventing-Suicide-A-Toolkit-for-High-Schools/SMA12-4669

The Science of a Meaningful Life. (n.d.). *Video series*. https://greatergood.berkeley.edu/

Scott, D. (2017). The science behind psychological verve and what it means for Black students. In E. Moore Jr., A. Michael, & M. W. Penick-Parks (Eds.), *The guide for White women who teach Black boys* (pp. 121–126). Corwin.

Segal, Z., Bieling, P., Young, T., & MacQueen, G. (2010). Antidepressant monotherapy vs sequential pharmacotherapy and mindfulness-based cognitive therapy, or placebo, for relapse prophylaxis in recurrent depression. *Archives of General Psychiatry, 77*(12), 1256–1264.

Seligman, M. (1975). *Helplessness: On depression, development, and death*. W. H. Freeman.

Seligman, M. (1990). *Learned optimism*. Pocket Books.

Shanker, S. (2016). *Self-reg*. Penguin Press.

Shanker, S. (2018). *Help your child deal with stress—and thrive: The transformative power of self-reg*. Yellow Kite.

Sherman, D. K., & Cohen, G. L. (2006). The psychology of self-defense: Self-affirmation theory. *Advances in Experimental Social Psychology, 38*, 183–242.

Slavin, R. (1996). *Education for all*. Swets & Zeitlinger.

Spencer, S. J., Logel, C., & Davies, P. G. (2016). Stereotype threat. *Annual Review of Psychology, 67*, 415–437.

Spencer, S. J., Steele, C. M., & Quinn, D. (1999). Stereotype threat and women's math performance. *Journal of Experimental Social Psychology, 35*, 4–28.

Steele, C. M. (1997). A threat in the air: How stereotypes shape intellectual identity and performance. *American Psychologist, 52*, 613–629.

Steele, C. M. (2010). *Whistling Vivaldi and other clues to how stereotypes affect us*. W. W. Norton & Company.

Steele, C. M. (2019, September 28). *Personal communication*.

Steele, C. M., Spencer, S. J., & Aronson, J. (1995). Stereotype threat and intellectual test performance of African Americans. *Journal of Personality and Social Psychology, 69*, 787–811.

Steele, C. M., Spencer, S. J., & Aronson, J. (2002). Contending with group image: The psychology of stereotype and social identity threat. In M. P. Zanna (Ed.), *Advances in experimental social psychology, Vol. 34* (pp. 379–440). Academic Press. https://doi.org/10.1016/S0065-2601(02)80009-0

Steele, D. M. (2012). Creating identity safe classrooms. In J. A. Banks (Ed.), *Encyclopedia of diversity in education, Vol. 1* (pp. 1125–1128). SAGE.

Steele, D. M., & Cohn-Vargas, B. (2013). *Identity safe classrooms: Places to belong and learn.* Corwin.

Sternberg, R. J., Grigorenko, E. L., & Jarvin, L. (2009). *Teaching for wisdom, intelligence, creativity, and success.* Corwin.

Stone, J., Lynch, C. I., Sjomeling, M., & Darley, J. M. (1999). Stereotype threat effects on Black and White athletic performance. *Journal of Personality and Social Psychology, 77,* 1213–1227.

Stone Hanley, M. (2010). The arts and social justice in a critical multicultural classroom. In C. Sleeter & S. May (Eds.), *Critical multiculturalism theory and praxis* (pp. 191–201). Routledge.

Stopbullying.gov. (2018). *What is bullying?* US Department of Health and Human Services. https://www.stopbullying.gov/what-is-bullying/index.html

Styles, D. (2001). *Class meetings: Building leadership, problem-solving and decision-making skills in the respectful classroom.* Pembroke.

Sue, D., Capodilupo, C., Torino, G., Bucceri, J., Holder, A. M., Nadal, K. L., & Esquilin, M. (2007). Racial microaggressions in everyday life: Implications for clinical practice. *American Psychologist, 62*(4), 271–286.

Sylwester, R. (2007). *The adolescent brain.* Corwin.

Sylwester, R. (2008). *The adolescent brain: Reaching for autonomy.* Hawker Brownlow Education.

Teaching Tolerance. (n.d.). *Classroom resources.* https://www.tolerance.org/classroom-resources

Teaching Tolerance. (2014). *Meet the Mix It Up at lunch day model schools: Get great ideas for your school's mix event.* https://www.tolerance.org/magazine/summer-2014/meet-the-mix-it-up-at-lunch-day-model-schools

Teaching Tolerance. (2016). *Teaching at the intersections.* https://www.tolerance.org/magazine/summer-2016/teaching-at-the-intersections

Teaching Tolerance. (2017). *Black lives matter week of action.* https://www.tolerance.org/magazine/black-lives-matter-week-of-action

Teaching Tolerance. (2019). *Perspectives for a diverse America.* https://www.tolerance.org/magazine/publications/perspectives-for-a-diverse-america

Teen Help. (2018). *Sexual abuse statistics.* https://www.teenhelp.com/sexual-abuse-trauma/sexual-abuse-statistics/

They. (2020). *Merriam-Webster dictionary online.* https://www.merriam-webster.com/dictionary/they

Tomlinson, C. A. (2017). *How to differentiate instruction in academically diverse classrooms* (3rd ed.). ASCD.

Tone. (n.d.). *Oxford English dictionary online.* https://www.lexico.com/en/definition/tone

Trevor Project. (2019). *Coming out as you: The spectrum.* https://www.thetrevorproject.org/about/programs-services/coming-out-as-you/the-spectrum/#sm.00016w1v7m68scz8vb41celd32e52

UCLA. (2005). *Calibrated peer review.* http://cpr.molsci.ucla.edu/

Upstander. (n.d.). *Oxford English dictionary online.* https://en.oxforddictionaries.com/definition/upstander

US Holocaust Memorial Museum. (n.d.). *International Holocaust Day of Remembrance.* https://www.ushmm.org/information/exhibitions/online-exhibitions/special-focus/international-holocaust-remembrance-day

Visible Learning. (2017, November). *250+ influences on student achievement.* https://visible-learning.org/wp-content/uploads/2018/03/VLPLUS-252-Influences-Hattie-ranking-DEC-2017.pdf

Visible Thinking. (2019). *Project zero.* http://www.visiblethinkingpz.org/VisibleThinking_html_files/03_ThinkingRoutines/03a_ThinkingRoutines.html

Vygotsky, L. (1978). Mind in society: The development of higher psychological processes. Harvard University Press.

Walton, G. M., & Cohen, G. L. (2007). A question of belonging: Race, social fit, and achievement. *Journal of Personality and Social Psychology, 92,* 82–96.

Walton, G. M., Cohen, G. L., Cwir, D., & Spencer, S. J. (2012). Mere belonging: The power of social connections. *Journal of Personality and Social Psychology, 102,* 513–532.

Webb, N. (2015). *Norman Webb describes his DOK framework.* https://video.search.yahoo.com/yhs/search?fr=yhs-pty-pty_converter&hsimp=yhs-pty_converter&hspart=pty&p=norman+webb#id=1&vid=b7310c259f2b647288e0ba6d27bcce85&action=click

Weinberg, R. (2018). Self-talk theory, research, and applications: Some personal reflections. *Sport Psychologist, 32*(1), 74–78. http://doi.org.10.1123/tsp.2017-0142

West Santa Rosa Multicultural Center. (2019). https://www.daycarecenters.us/multi-cultural-child-development-center-in-santa-rosa-ca-f3ea78faf746

WestEd. (2018). *Student agency in learning course.* https://www.wested.org

Wick, J. (2019, May 30). *Essential California: College admissions prestige and pressure at Palo Alto High School.* https://www.latimes.com/newsletters/la-me-ln-essential-california-20190530-story.html

Wong, H. K., & Rosemary, T. (1998). *The first days of school: How to be an effective teacher.* Harry K. Wong.

Woo, M. (2015). *How science is helping America tackle police racism.* Wired. http://www.wired.com/2015/01/implicit-bias-police-racism-science/

Wood, A. M., Froh, J. J., & Geraghty, A. W. (2010). Gratitude and well-being: A review and theoretical integration. *Clinical Psychology Review, 30*(7), 890–905. https://doi.org/10.1016/j.cpr.2010.03.005

Wood, D., Bruner, J., & Ross, G. (1976). The role of tutoring in problem solving. *Journal of Child Psychology and Child Psychiatry, 17,* 89–100.

Wood, R. (2013). *PBL and culturally responsive instruction.* Edutopia. https://www.edutopia.org/blog/sammamish-8-PBL-culturally-responsive-rob-wood

World Hijab Day. (2019). World Hijab Day Organization. https://www.worldhijabday.com

Wright, J. (2013). *How to: Calm an agitated student* Intervention Central. https://www
.interventioncentral.org/behavior_calm_agitated_student

Yeager, D. S., Purdie-Vaughns, V., Garcia, J., Apfel, N., Brzustoski, P., Master, A., . . . Williams,
M. E. (2013). Breaking the cycle of mistrust: Wise interventions to provide critical feedback
across the racial divide. *Journal of Experimental Psychology: General, 143*, 804–824.

Yeager, D. S., & Walton, G. M. (2011). Social-psychological interventions in education:
They're not magic. *Review of Educational Research, 81*, 267–301.

Yosso, T. J. (2005). Whose culture has capital? *Race, Ethnicity and Education, 8*(1), 69–91.

Yusem, D. (2014). *Bringing restorative justice into schools.* Not In Our Town. https://www.niot
.org/blog/bringing-restorative-justice-schools

Zambo, R., & Zambo, D. (2008). *The impact of professional development in mathematics on
teachers' individual and collective efficacy: The stigma of underperforming.* https://files.eric.ed.gov/
fulltext/EJ810663.pdf

Zimmer, B. (2016). How high-school girls won a campaign for "upstander." *Wall Street
Journal.* https://www.wsj.com/articles/how-high-school-girls-won-a-campaign-for-upstander-
1473436114

Index

AAR. *See* After-action review (AAR)
Abrams, Jennifer, 27, 85
Academic dialogue, 80 (box), 83 (box)
Academic mindset, 107–108, 165
Academic rigor. *See* High expectations and academic rigor
Academic vocabulary, 154
ACEs. *See* Adverse Childhood Experiences (ACEs) Study
Achievement gap, 122
Active participation, 51–52
Activism, 141 (box)
Adamson, Carlee, 195
Adaptability, goal-setting and, 108–109
Adolescence, 205
    brains, agency, and autonomy, 105–107
    development, identity safety in, 18–20
Adverse Childhood Experiences (ACEs) Study, 192 (box)
Advisory, 256–257
After-action review (AAR), 98 (box)
Agency
    and autonomy, 105–107
    and resilience, 108
Aguilar, Elena, 27, 86
Ajayi, Luvvie, 10, 61
Allport, Gordon, 124
Ambience of classroom, 242
Analytical intelligence, 162
Angelou, Maya, 137, 138
Anticipatory set, 52, 170
Argyris, Chris, 27
Aronson, Elliot, 48
Aronson, Josh, 8
Arts, 221
    critical multiculturalism in, 140 (box)
    finding student voices in, 54
Assimilation model, 137
Attainable goal (SMART goal), 109 (box)

Attention to prosocial development. *See* Prosocial development
Austin, A. J., 59
Autism Speaks, 248
Autism spectrum students, 244–248
Autonomy, 44, 76, 105–117
    and academic mindset, 107–108
    adolescent brains, agency, and, 105–107
    benefits of, 105–107
    cultural expressions of, 110
    defined, 44
    dilemmas and points of tension, 115–116
    executive functioning, 112–114, 113 (box)
    gender and, 111–112
    goal setting and monitoring, 108–110
    handling failure, 115–116
Awe, 238–239
Awesome, 238

The Bell Curve (Herrnstein & Murray), 151
Benard, Bonnie, 198, 199
Beyond Differences, 262
Black Lives Matter Week, 262 (box)
Blended learning, 169
Boaler, Jo, 73 (box)
Boykin, A. W., 240
Brain, 57, 59, 105–107
Brainstorming, 162, 163 (box)
Briceño, Eduardo, 77, 81
Bullying, 221, 232–234
Bystanders, 233–234

Cacophony, 56, 112–114
Called out, 145–146, 146 (box)
Canning, Elizabeth, 17
Caring classroom environment. *See* Classroom environment
CASEL. *See* Collaborative for Academic, Social, and Emotional Learning (CASEL)

Challenging curriculum. *See* Curriculum, challenging
Child Protective Services (CPS), 196
Christakis, Nicholas A., 93 (box)
Chromebook add-on Goobric, 80
Cisgender, 126
Class discussions, templates for, 115 (box)
Class meetings, 99–100
Classroom
    ambience of, 242
    autonomy. *See* Autonomy
    feeling tone of, 242
    humor in, 242
    physical environment, 240 (box)
    verve in, 240–242, 241 (box)
    youth culture in, 240–242
Classroom environment, 217–219, 268–269
    attention to prosocial development, 252–265
    emotional and physical comfort, 238–250
    teacher skill, 220–236
Classroom relationships, 181–182, 214–215
    positive student relationships, 204–212
    teacher warmth and availability for learning,
        183–202
Closure, 52
Code-switching, 63–64, 86
Cohen, Elizabeth, 95
Collaboration
    authentic, 92–94
    class meetings, 99–100
    group work and true, 95–99, 96–97 (box)
    reflection after, 97–99, 98 (box)
    social goals and, 99
    social justice content and classroom, 100–101
Collaborative for Academic, Social, and Emotional
    Learning (CASEL), 252
Collective feedback, 85–87
College Knowledge program, 129
Color-blind approach, 1–2, 4, 9–11, 137
Common Core State Standards, 95
Community agreements, 93–94, 94 (box)
Community walk, 129
Compassion, 259–261
    empathy and, 261
    fatigue, 197
    offering and receiving, 259–260
    self-compassion, 260–261
Competence, 7, 68, 69
Competition, 90, 102–103
Conflict, 221
    de-escalating, 228–230
    I-messages, 225–226, 226 (box)
    resolution, 227
    RJ, 227–228, 228 (box)
Contact hypothesis, 124

Content vocabulary, 154–156
Controlled inquiry, 70
Coolidge, Calvin, 151
Cooperation, 89–103
    authentic collaboration across school day, 92–94
    benefit of, 89–90
    with class meetings, 99–100
    community agreements, 93–94, 94 (box)
    in competition context, 102–103
    defined, 44
    dilemmas and points of tension, 102–103
    group work and true collaboration, 95–99,
        96–97 (box)
    interdependence through thinking and acting,
        91–92
    reflection, 97–99, 98 (box)
    social justice content, 100–101, 101 (box)
Cooperative learning, 95
Counternarratives, 11–12, 75, 130
    in FA, 77
    of STEM educators, 75
Covert active participation, 52
Covington, M. V., 114
Cox, W., 59
CPS. *See* Child Protective Services (CPS)
Creative intelligence, 162
Creativity, 161–165
    in language arts, 162
    in math, 164–165
    in science, 164
    in social studies, 162–163
    teaching as, 165
Crenshaw, Kimberley, 130
Critical feedback, 135, 189
Critical multiculturalism, 136–141
    across curriculum, 138–140 (box)
    defined, 136
    to positive action, 140–141
    shame to pride transformation, 137–138
Critical thinking, 165
    socratic questioning to, 166
Crowd-sourced grading (CSG), 84–85
CSG. *See* Crowd-sourced grading (CSG)
Csikszentmihalyi, M., 161
Cultivating diversity as resource, 121–122,
    179–180
    challenging curriculum, 160–177
    diversity as resource, 124–147
    high expectations and academic rigor, 149–158
Cultural capital, 110
Culturally inclusive growth mindset culture, 17
Culturally relevant teaching, 107, 137
    and equity literacy, 6–7
    and equity pedagogy, 5–6

Culturally Responsive Teaching and the Brain (Hammond), 183
Cultural proficiency, 6
Cultural relevance, 5, 6
Culture, 5
Culture Keepers, 243 (box)
Curriculum, 221–222
    class meetings, 99
    critical multiculturalism across, 138–140 (box)
    development and content coverage, 175–176
    differentiation. *See* Differentiation, curriculum
    finding student voices in, 54
    in Finland, 160
    hidden, 223
    interaction with student, 186
    interdependence across, 91–92
    learning stations task, 168
    social justice and, 110–111
Curriculum, challenging
    assumptions, reframing, 174–176
    benefits of, 160–161
    creativity and innovation as part of, 161–165
    defined, 121–122
    differentiation, 166–170
    dilemmas and points of tension, 174–176
    finding time for creating, 175–176
    four-part approach of, 161 (box)
    higher-order thinking skills, 165–166
    intellectual excitement, 161–165
    learning from mistakes, 171–174
    praising, 171
    productive struggle, 170–171
    verve in, 240–242, 241 (box)

Darwin, Charles, 151
Day of Silence, 261
Deci, Edward, 108
De-escalating conflict, 228–230
De-escalation strategies, 231 (box)
Deficit thinking, 122–123
Deliberate practice, 82
Depression, 197–198
Depths of Knowledge (DOK), 165
Devine, P., 59
Dialogue, 127
DiAngelo, Robin, 29, 30
Differentiation, curriculum, 166–170
    through assessment, 167
    blended learning model, 169
    flipped learning model, 168–169
    graduated difficulty, 168
    grouping strategies, 168
    group work, 167
    individual practice, 166

inquiry, 70–71
"jigsaw" method, 48–49, 49 (box)
learning stations, 168
models, 168–170
personalized learning model, 169
skill building for effective, 167
stations format of, 166
virtual reality, 169
whole group, 167, 170
Dilemmas and points of tension
    autonomy, 115–116
    challenging curriculum, 174–176
    cooperation, 102–103
    diversity as resource, 145–146
    emotional and physical comfort, 248–250
    high expectations and academic rigor, 157–158
    listening for student voices, 63–65
    positive student relationships, 210–212
    prosocial development, 262–265
    teacher skill, 234–236
    teacher warmth and availability for learning, 199–201
    teaching for understanding, 84–87
"Dissolving stereotypes" activity, 136 (box)
Districtwide Behavior Plan, 235 (box)
Diversity as resource, 124–147
    benefits of, 124–125
    creating spaces for students, 125–126
    critical multiculturalism, 136–141
    curriculum and, 126
    defined, 121
    dialogue, 127
    dilemmas and points of tensions, 145–146
    dimensions of multiple identities, 129–130
    families and communities, 127–133
    gender binary, 132–133
    hard conversations, 143–145
    intersectionality, 130–132, 131 (box)
    making space for students' full identities, 145–146
    race and gender, 142–145
    schoolwide gender-inclusive practices, 133–134, 134 (box)
    stereotype threat reduction, 134–135
DOK. *See* Depths of Knowledge (DOK)
Dominant culture, 5, 27
"Don't ask, don't tell" system, 125
Dopamine, 218
Doran, George, 109 (box)
Dweck, Carol, 15, 16, 152, 171
Dynamic curriculum, 160
    verve in, 240–242, 241 (box)

Edgette, J. S., 264
Educators, 4, 5, 25–27
    advisory, 257 (box)
    attention to students' prosocial development,
        255–256
    class meetings, 99–100
    culturally relevant literacy of, 6–7
    emotional resilience and optimism, 27
    equity literate, 6, 60
    fairness and, 248–249
    focus on cooperation, 89–103
    growth mindset, 17–18
    individualism and interdependence, 90
    interrogating beliefs and assumptions on
        actions, 27–29
    listening for student voices, 45–66
    low expectations behaviors of, 150
    personality and style, 184
    prosocial learning for, 264–265
    resilience, 199
    self-regulation, 190–195
    skill. See Teacher skill
    STEM, 75–76
    students on autism spectrum and, 247–248 (box)
    teaching for understanding, 68–87
    trauma literacy sessions for, 195–197
    warmth and availability. See Teacher warmth and
        availability for learning
    White fragility, 29–31
Educator-student relationship, 183–184
    interaction with each student, 186–188
    rapport and trust, 184–186
    wise feedback, 189, 190 (box)
EdWeek, 85
Elicit evidence, 80–81 (box)
Emdin, Christopher, 241
Emotional and physical comfort, 238–250
    awe, 238–239
    benefits of, 238
    classroom space set-up for identity safety, 239
    defined, 218
    dilemmas and points of tension, 248–250
    fairness, promoting, 248–249
    identity safe classrooms for students on autism
        spectrum, 244–248
    mindfulness, place for, 242–243
    positive presuppositions, 243–244
    socioeconomic differences, 249–250
    youth culture in classroom, 240–242
Emotional resilience, 27
Empathetic distress, 196
    resilience for, 198–199
Empathy, 183, 261

English language development (ELD), 139 (box)
English learners, 54–55
Entity mindset, 15, 16 (box)
Equality, 249
Equalizing status. See Status, equalizing
Equity, 249
    consciousness, 86
Equity Lab, 142
Equity literacy, 6
    culturally relevant teaching and, 6–7
Equity pedagogy, 5–6
Error analysis, 172–173, 173 (box)
Eslinger, P. J., 113 (box)
Ethnic studies, critical multiculturalism in, 139 (box)
Eugenics, 151
Exclusion, 262–264
Executive functioning, 112–114, 113 (box)
Exotic other, 10

FA. See Formative assessment (FA)
Face-to-face feedback, 86
Fairness, 248–249
False growth mindset, 16
Family Meetings, 206
Fauteux, Mike, 172
Feedback
    collective, 85–87
    critical, 135, 189
    face-to-face, 86
    growth mindset in, 86
    loop of FA, 76, 77
    peer, 81 (box), 84–87
    sandwiching, 189
    wise, 78, 189, 190 (box)
Feeling tone, 242
Field trip into ourselves, 32
Finland, curriculum in, 160
The First Days of School (Wong), 222
First Person American, 56
Fixed mindset, 15, 16 (box)
Flipped learning, 168–169
Focus on cooperation. See Cooperation
Ford, Martin, 108
Formal mindfulness, 242
Formative assessment (FA), 76–84, 151
    belief and counternarrative, 77
    digital technology and, 80
    elicit evidence, 80–81 (box)
    evidence, 80
    feedback loop, 76, 77
    grading, 82–84
    growth mindset in, 78, 172
    learning and growth mindset, 81

learning goals, 78, 79 (box)
learning zone, 77
success/growth criteria, 78
where am I going? phase, 78–79
where am I now? phase, 79–80
where to next? phase, 81–82
wise feedback and, 78
Forscher, P. S., 59
For White Folks Who Teach in the Hood (Emdin), 241
Fowler, James, 93 (box)
Free inquiry, 71
Frieberg, Stephanie, 92
Frontal lobes, 105, 112, 115 (box)
Fryberg, Stephanie, 14
Fulbeck, Kip, 130
Functional magnetic resonance imaging
    (fMRI), 259

Galton, Francis, 151
Gender
    and autonomy, 111–112
    binary, 132–133
    equalizing status across, 209–210
    identity norms, 209 (box)
    race and, 142–145
    stereotype threat by, 8
Gender-based discrimination, 133
Gender-inclusive practices, 132 (box), 210 (box)
    schoolwide, 133–134, 134 (box)
Gender Spectrum, 112
GiveThx, 206, 207 (box), 260
Goal setting, 108–110, 113 (box), 258
Gorski, Paul, 6, 45
Grading FA, 82–84
Graduated difficulty model, 168
Gratification, instant, 70, 170
Gratitude, 260
Group work instruction, 167
Growth criteria, FA, 78
Growth mindset, 15–18, 44, 89–90, 135,
    152–153
    culturally inclusive, 17
    educator, 17–18
    error analysis and, 172–173, 173 (box)
    experiment, 15–16 (box)
    in FA, 78, 172
    false, 16
    in feedback, 86
    high expectations and, 152–153
    of intelligence, 153 (box)
    learning and, 81
    self-talk to, 258
    think/pair/share method for, 48 (box)

Guided inquiry, 71
Gutierrez, Kris, 6, 188

Habits and mindsets, 86–87
Hammond, Zaretta, 11, 12, 69, 107, 183
Hanson, Chiaku, 64
Harari, Yuval, 89
Hard conversations, 143–145
Hardy, Kenneth, 191
Harm Circle, 227–228
Hero-making error analysis, 173, 173 (box)
Hidden curriculum, 223
Higher-order thinking skills, 165–166
High expectations and academic rigor, 149–158
    benefits of, 149–152
    cacophony of external messages, 157–158
    defined, 121–122
    dilemmas and points of tension, 157–158
    growth mindset and, 152–153
    scaffolding, 154–157
Hilliard, Asa, 5
Holocaust Remembrance Day, 261
Home languages and cultures value, 55–56
Homework assignments, 128
Hope, 108
Huffington Post (Hanson), 64
Human evolution, 161
Humor, 242
Hunter, Madeline, 52

Identity safe classrooms, 221–222
    for autism spectrum students, 244–248
    domains and components, 13–14 (box)
    principles of, 4–5
    space set-up for, 239
Identity safety, 1–2
    in adolescent development, 18–20
    components and SEL, 254 (box)
    educators. *See* Educators
    educator-student relationship, 183–184
    growth mindset and, 15–18
    healthy relationships in, 183
    literacy, culturally relevant, 6–7
    origins of, 7–9
    pedagogy, culturally relevant, 5–6
    principles, 41
    staff, 31–33, 32 (box)
    stereotype threat, 7–9, 12–13
    teaching, 3, 4, 14–15
    White fragility and, 30–31
I Know Why the Caged Bird Sings
    (Angelou), 137
Illuminate student information system, 167

I-messages, 225–226, 226 (box)
Immigration policies, 151
Immigration Restriction Act of 1924, 151
Implicit bias, 57–60, 57 (box), 58 (box),
       150 (box)
Incremental mindset, 15, 16 (box)
    of intelligence, 153 (box)
Individualism, 90
Individual practice instruction, 166
Inflammatory comments, 143
    N-word, 64–65
Informal mindfulness, 242
Innovation, creativity and, 161–165
Inquiry, 70–71, 254 (box)
    self-talk, 258 (box)
Instant gratification, 70, 170
Intellectual excitement, 161–165
Intellectual neglect, 116
Intelligence, 151–152
    praising, 171
    reframing student views of, 153 (box)
    triarchic theory of, 162
Interdependence, 90
    through thinking and acting, 91–92
Interest-based negotiation, 101 (box)
Interpersonal task, 168
Intersectionality, 22, 130–132, 131 (box)
Intervention Central, 231 (box)

"Jigsaw" method, 48–49, 49 (box)

Kabat-Zinn, Jon, 242
Kindness, 205–206
Krashen, Stephen, 54
KWL charts, 80 (box), 167

Ladder of inference, 27–29
Ladson-Billings, Gloria, 5, 187
Language arts
    creativity in, 162
    critical multiculturalism in, 138 (box)
    finding student voices in, 54
    learning stations task, 168
Last Boys Picked (Edgette & Rupp), 264
Learned helplessness, 69, 114, 115–116, 172
Learned optimism, 115
Learning
    blended, 169
    CASEL, 252
    flipped, 168–169
    goals, FA, 78, 79 (box)
    growth mindset and, 81
    from mistakes, 171–174

personalized, 169
prosocial, 253
SEL, 252
service, 74
stations, 168
teacher warmth and availability for, 183–202
zone, 77, 86
Learning Accelerator, 170
Learning Policy Institute (LPI), 14–15
Life Space Crisis Intervention (LSCI), 230
Lindsey, Dolores, 6
Listening for student voices. See Student voices,
       listening for
Lopez, Shane, 108
LSCI. See Life Space Crisis Intervention (LSCI)

MacKenzie, Trevor, 70, 71
Magic Hat, 26 (box)
Mainstream narratives, 11–12
Mann, Julie, 54, 56
Mastery task, 168
Mathematics
    class meeting, 99
    creativity in, 164–165
    critical multiculturalism in, 139 (box)
    interdependence in, 91
    learning stations task, 168
Measurable goal (SMART goal), 109 (box)
Mehrabian, A., 56
Memorization, 68–69
Mental illness, 197–198
Mere belonging, 185
Metacognitive awareness, 113 (box)
#MeToo movement, 210–212
Microaggressions, 26, 60–63, 61 (box)
Mindfulness, 242–243
Mindset
    academic, 107–108, 165
    creative, 162
    of emotional resilience, 27
    entity, 15, 16 (box)
    fixed, 15, 16 (box)
    growth. See Growth mindset
    habits and, 86–87
    incremental, 15, 16 (box), 153 (box)
Mindset (Dweck), 16
Mix It Up Day, 261
Modeling, 155
Moore, Eddie, 64
Motivation, goal-setting and, 108–110
Multicultural education, 5
Multiculturalism. See Critical multiculturalism
Multifaceted prejudice habit-breaking, 59

Murphy, Mary, 7, 17, 78, 152, 189
Murrell, P. C., Jr., 240

Nakkula, Michael, 19
National Center for School Crisis and Bereavement, 236
Negative presupposition, 244
Negative stereotypes, 7, 11, 75, 87, 122, 135
Neurological processes, 113 (box)
Neuroplasticity, 78
Next Generation Science Standards (NGSS), 70
NGSS. *See* Next Generation Science Standards (NGSS)
Nieto, Sonia, 6
Note-taking strategies, 115 (box)
N-word, 64–65

Oakland Unified School District (OUSD) Restorative Justice Program, 228
Obama, Michelle, 7
Onward (Aguilar), 27
Oops moments, 94
Open-ended discussion, 145
Orchestra conductor, 112
Orchestrated symphony, 112–114
Ouch moments, 94
Overt active participation, 52

Palmer, Parker, 25, 270
Parental neglect, 196
Parent-educator partnerships, 246
Parent-student dialogue groups, 129
Part Asian, 100% Hapa (Fulbeck), 129
Partnering, 47–48
PBL. *See* Project-based learning (PBL)
Peer feedback, 81 (box), 84–87
Peer Health Exchange, 211
Performance zone, 77
Personalized learning, 169
Person-centered psychology, 183
Physical education, critical multiculturalism in, 140 (box)
Pierre, Marvin, 200
Pierson, Rita Mae, 200
Pipeline to prison, 2
Plate tectonics, 164 (box)
Pollock, Mica, 127, 187
Positive presuppositions, 243–244, 255
Positive regard, 183
Positive stereotype, 134–135
Positive student relationships, 204–212
   benefits of, 204–205
   defined, 182

dilemmas and points of tension, 210–212
equalizing status, 206–210
intimate relationships, 211
kindness transmission, 205–206
#MeToo movement, 210–212
social media and, 212
Practical intelligence, 162
Praising intelligence, 171
Preassessment, 167
Prejudice, 124–125
Presuppositions, 243–244
Preteaching vocabulary, 154–156
Prior knowledge, 80 (box)
Privilege, 30 (box)
Problem-solving protocol, 51 (box)
Productive struggle, 170–171
Project-based learning (PBL), 72–73, 73 (box)
Project Implicit, 59
Prompts, 154–155
Prosocial development, 252–265
   benefits of, 252–255
   compassion, 259–261
   defined, 218–219
   dilemmas and points of tension, 262–265
   educator attention to students, 255–256
   exclusion, 262–264
   participation in national activities, 261–262
   SEL, 252, 253, 254 (box)
   self-talk, 257–259, 258 (box)
Prosocial learning, 253
Public goods game, 93 (box)

Quiet student, 174–175

Racial trauma, 192–193
Racist act, 30
Rapport, 184–186, 187 (box)
Reflection tool, 98 (box)
Relationships, 254 (box)
Relevant goal (SMART goal), 109 (box)
Repertoires of practice, 6
Resilience
   agency and, 108
   emotional of educator, 27
   RJ, 227–228, 228 (box)
   for trauma, 198–199
Resource circles, 32
Responsible decision-making, 254 (box)
Restorative justice (RJ), 227–228, 228 (box)
RJ. *See* Restorative justice (RJ)
RJ Sharing Circle, 227
Rogers, Carl, 183
Rogoff, Barbara, 6

Role model, power of, 185 (box)
Rostosky, Jacob, 111
Rubrics, 78, 155
Rupp, B. M., 264
Ryan, Richard, 108

Salience, 25
SAMHSA. *See* Substance Abuse and Mental Health Services Administration (SAMHSA)
Sandwiching feedback, 189
Sarcasm, 242
Scaffolding, 154–157
    modeling, 155
    preteach academic and content vocabulary, 156–157
    removing, 156–157
    rubrics, 78, 155
    templates, 115 (box), 128, 154–155
    think-aloud, 155
    visible thinking routines, 156, 156 (box)
School Talk (Pollock), 127
Science, 221
    class meeting, 99
    critical multiculturalism in, 139 (box)
    learning stations task, 168
    social justice and, 100
Scott, Darla, 150 (box)
Secondary trauma, 196
SEL. *See* Social and emotional learning (SEL)
Self-acceptance, 252–253
Self-affirmation, 53–54, 135
Self-assessment, 81 (box)
Self-awareness, 254 (box)
Self-compassion, 260–261
Self-control, 113 (box)
Self-distancing, 116
Self-expression, 54
Self-expressive task, 168
Self-fulfilling prophecy, 149, 151
Self-management, 254 (box)
Self-Reg (Shanker), 190
Self-regulation, 112, 114, 116, 190–195
Self-righting, 199
Self-talk, 257–259, 258 (box)
Seligman, Martin, 69, 115, 116
Service learning, 74
Sexual orientation, gender identity and, 111–112
Shallow culture talk, 127
Shame to pride transformation, 137–138
Shanker, Stuart, 190
Simone de Beauvoir, 10
SISP. *See* Stanford Integrated School Project (SISP)
SMART goals, 109 (box)
Snitching, 234

Social and emotional learning (SEL), 252, 253
    and identity safety components, 254 (box)
Social awareness, 254 (box)
Social Heat Map, 207 (box)
Social identity, 22
Social justice, 100–101, 101 (box)
Social skills, 256–257
Social studies
    class meeting, 99
    creativity in, 162–163
    critical multiculturalism in, 138 (box)
    interdependence in, 91–92
    learning stations task, 168
    social justice and, 100
Societal stereotype, 8 (box), 122
Socratic questioning, 166
Socratic Seminars, 83 (box)
Solidarity Council, 142 (box)
Sown to Grow, 80
Specific goal (SMART goal), 109 (box)
Spencer, Stephen, 8
Staff identity safety, 31–33, 32 (box)
Stanford Integrated School Project (SISP), 2, 12, 90, 135, 160, 183, 217, 220
Station instruction, 166
Status, equalizing, 204–205, 206–210
    in classroom, 206–209
    by equitable participation, 46
    across gender identities, 209–210
Steele, Claude, 7, 8, 9, 12, 189
Steele, Dorothy, 9, 12, 68
STEM classes, 75–76
Stereotype threat, 7–9, 12–13, 149
    deficit thinking and, 122
    gender, 8, 232
    golf experiment, 9 (box)
    reduction of, 9, 134–135
    research, 8–9
    societal, 8 (box)
Sterilization, 151
Sternberg, Robert, 162
Stone, Jeff, 9 (box)
StopBullying.gov, 232
Storytelling protocol, 50 (box)
Stressors, students, 190–191
Structured inquiry, 70
Structured listening protocols, 49–50, 50–51 (box)
Student(s)
    behaviors and expectations, 150 (box)
    bullying, 221, 232–234
    compassion fatigue, 197
    depression and mental illness, 197–198
    disruptive and annoying behaviors, 234–235

empathetic distress, 196
exclusion, 262–264
fairness and, 248–249
names, knowing and pronouncing, 186
racial trauma, 192–193
relationships. *See* Positive student relationships
resilience for trauma, 198–199
self-regulation, 190–195
socioeconomic status, 249–250
students on autism spectrum, 244–248
suicides, 197–198
trauma, 192
trauma-informed practice, 193–195
Student-centered teaching, 43–44, 119–120
classroom autonomy, 105–117
focus on cooperation, 89–103
listening for student voices, 45–66
teaching for understanding, 68–87
Student-led conferences, 128
Student voices, listening for, 45–66
active participation, 51–52
through cacophony, 56
code-switching, 63–64
defined, 43–44
dilemmas and points of tension, 63–65
English learners, engaging, 54–55
equitable participation, 46
home languages and cultures value, 55–56
implicit bias, 57–60, 57 (box), 58 (box)
"jigsaw" method, 48–49, 49 (box)
in language arts, 54
large-group strategies, 46
microaggressions, 60–63, 61 (box)
N-word, 64–65
through self-affirmation, 53–54
sharing Vulnerabilities, 63
small-group strategies, 46–51
structured listening protocols, 49–50, 50–51 (box)
think/pair/share method, 47–48, 48 (box)
Substance Abuse and Mental Health Services
    Administration (SAMHSA), 198 (box)
Success criteria, FA, 78
Suicide Prevention Toolkit, 198 (box)

Talking stick, 47 (box)
Tattling, 234
TeachEngineering, 71 (box)
Teacher skill, 220–236
benefits of, 220–221
bullying, identity safe practices for, 232–234
conflicts, 225–230
defined, 218, 220
dilemmas and points of tension, 234–236

hidden social contracts, 223–224
identity safe classroom, setting up, 221–222
intervention, 224–225, 225 (box)
meaningful routines, 222
primary skills, 220
reasonable procedures, 222
teaching strategies, 223
timing and pacing, 223
Teacher warmth and availability for learning, 183–202
benefits of, 183–184
defined, 182
dilemmas and points of tension, 199–201
interaction with each student, 186–188
rapport and trust, 184–186
self-regulation, 190–195
"White savior" mentality, 200–201
wise feedback, 189, 190 (box)
Teaching, 165
for understanding. *See* Understanding, teaching for
Teenage brain, 19
Teen Help, 211 (box)
Teen sexual abuse, 211 (box)
Templates, 128, 154–155
for class discussions, 115 (box)
Think-aloud, 155
Think/pair/share method, 47–48, 48 (box), 154
Third space, 188, 188 (box)
Time-oriented goal (SMART goal), 109 (box)
Title IX, 133, 211
Tone, 242
Toshalis, Eric, 19
Trauma, 192
literacy, 195–197
racial, 192–193
resilience for, 198–199
secondary, 196
Trauma-informed practice, 193–195, 224, 253
Triarchic theory of intelligence, 162
Trust, 184–186, 241

Understanding task, 168
Understanding, teaching for, 68–87
benefits of, 68–69
defined, 44
dilemmas and points of tension, 84–87
FA, 76–84
inquiry, 70–71
PBL, 72–73, 73 (box)
peer feedback, 84–87
relevance and accountability, 69–70
service learning, 74
STEM classes, 75–76
Upstanders, 233–234, 234 (box)

Validation, 183
Verve, 240–242, 241 (box)
Virtual reality, 169
Visible Thinking, 156
Visible thinking routines, 156, 156 (box)
Vygotsky, L., 154

Walton, Greg, 185
Warm demander, 183
Webb, Norman, 165
White fragility, 29–31
    identity safety and, 30–31
White Fragility (DiAngelo), 29
"White savior" mentality, 200–201
White teachers and Black students, 29 (box)
Whole Child Framework for Educational
    Practice, 14–15

Whole-group instruction, 167, 170
Willful defiance, 229
Wise feedback, 78, 189, 190 (box)
Wong, Harry, 222
Wood, Robert, 101 (box)
World Hijab Day, 261
World languages, critical multiculturalism in,
    139 (box)
Wright, Jim, 231 (box)

Yosso, Tara, 110
Youth culture in classroom,
    240–242
Yusem, David, 228

Zero tolerance policies, 229, 230
Zone of proximal development, 154, 157

Solutions YOU WANT | Experts YOU TRUST | Results YOU NEED

EVENTS

>>> **INSTITUTES**

Corwin Institutes provide large regional events where educators collaborate with peers and learn from industry experts. Prepare to be recharged and motivated!

corwin.com/institutes

ON-SITE PD

>>> **ON-SITE PROFESSIONAL LEARNING**

Corwin on-site PD is delivered through high-energy keynotes, practical workshops, and custom coaching services designed to support knowledge development and implementation.

corwin.com/pd

>>> **PROFESSIONAL DEVELOPMENT RESOURCE CENTER**

The PD Resource Center provides school and district PD facilitators with the tools and resources needed to deliver effective PD.

corwin.com/pdrc

ONLINE

>>> **ADVANCE**

Designed for K–12 teachers, Advance offers a range of online learning options that can qualify for graduate-level credit and apply toward license renewal.

corwin.com/advance

Contact a PD Advisor at (800) 831-6640 or visit www.corwin.com for more information

A SAGE Publishing Company

Helping educators make the greatest impact

CORWIN HAS ONE MISSION: to enhance education through intentional professional learning.

We build long-term relationships with our authors, educators, clients, and associations who partner with us to develop and continuously improve the best evidence-based practices that establish and support lifelong learning.